THE ADVENTURES OF ANTAR

Plate 1: Antar, dying from the poisoned arrow shot by al-Asad al-Rahīṣ, is carried in Abla's palenquin.

APPROACHES TO ARABIC LITERATURE

General Editor: Kamal Abu Deeb

No. 3

THE ADVENTURES of ANTAR

H. T. Norris

British Library Cataloguing in Publication Data

The adventures of Antar. - (Approaches to Arabic
literature; 3).
I. Norris, Harry Thirlwall II. Series
892'.7'334 PJ7702

ISBN 0-85668-161-X

Published by ARIS & PHILLIPS LTD, Warminster, Wilts, England

Printed by BIDDLES LTD, Guildford, Surrey, England

CONTENTS

LIST OF ILLUSTRATIONS

Plates 1, 8, 9 and 10 are from Devic's Les Aventures d'Antar, fils de Cheddad, *Paris, 1864, photos courtesy of the British Museum. Plate 2 is of a modern work by the artist Abū Ṣūbhi Tīnāwī of Damascus. Plates 3-7 are from the Cairo edition of Sa'īd 'Alī al-Khuṣūṣī.*

SELECTED BIBLIOGRAPHY

Arberry, A. J.	*The Seven Odes,* George Allen and Unwin, 1957.
Abbott, N.	'A ninth century fragment of the Thousand Nights', *Journal of Near Eastern Studies,* VIII, 1949, pp. 129-164.
Basset, R.	*1001 contes, récits et légendes arabes,* Paris, 1924-26.
al-Bustani, F. I.	*'Antarat al-tārīkh wa'Antarat al-usṭūra, Al-Mashriq,* Beirut, tome 28, 1930, pp. 534-40, 631-47.
Cachia, P.J.E.	'The Dramatic Monologues of al-Ma'arrī, *Journal of Arabic Literature,* Vol. 1, 1970, pp. 129-136.
Chauvin, V.	*Bibliographie des ouvrages arabes,* Liège, 1892-1922, Vol. III, Louqmane et les fabulistes, Barlaam, Antar et les romans de chevalerie.
Cheikho, L.	'Quelques légendes musulmanes anté-islamiques', *Actes* du XVe Congrès international des Orientalistes, Copenhagen, 1908.
Cherbonneau, A.	Hârith et Labna, *Journal Asiatique,* 4e série, t.5, 1845, pp. 5-38.
Crosland, J.	*The Old French Epic,* Blackwell, Oxford, 1951.
Devic, L. U.	*Les Aventures d'Antar, fils de Cheddad,* Paris, 1864.
De Perceval, C.	'La mort d'Antar' in *Journal Asiatique,* 2e série, tome 12, 1833, pp. 97-123. 'La mort de Zohaïr. Episode tiré du roman d'Antar', *ibid,* 2e série, tome 14, 1834, pp. 317-47.
Dover, C.	'The Black Knight', *Phylon,* Atlanta University Review of Race and Culture, 1954.
Gerhardt, M.	*The Art of Story Telling,* Brill, Leiden, 1963.
Ghanem, Ch.	*Antar, pièce en cinq actes,* Paris, 1910.
Goldziher, I.	'Der arabische Held 'Antar in der geographischen Nomenklatur', *Globus,* LXIV, 1893, no. 4, pp. 65-67.
Hamilton, T.	*'Antar, a Bedoueen Romance,* translated from the Arabic, London 1819/20.
Hartmann, M.	*'Antar (Romance of)* in the *Encyclopedia of Islam,* 1st edition.
Heller, B.	*'Antar (Sīrat)* in the *Encyclopedia of Islam,* revised editions.

'Der arabische 'Antar-Roman', *Ungarische Randschau, V,* 1916, pp. 83-107.
Der arabische 'Antarroman. Ein Betrag zur vergleichenden Litteraturgeschichte, Hanover, 1927.
Die Bedeutung des arabischen 'Antar-Romans für die Vergleichende Litteraturkunde, Leipzig, 1931.
'Youscha' al-Akbar et les Juifs de Kheybar dans le Roman d'Antar', *Revue des Etudes Juives,* 84, 927, 1927, pp. 301-4.

Kritzeck, J. *Anthology of Islamic Literature,* Pelican books, 1964, pp. 301-4.

Lane, E. W. *An account of the manners and customs of the Modern Egyptians,* London, 1846.

Metlizki, D. *The Matter of Araby in Medieval England,* Yale University Press, 1977.

Miquel, A. *Un conte des Mille et Une Nuits, Ajîb et Gharîb,* Flammarion, 1977.

Paret, R. *Sirat Saif b Ḏi Yazan, ein arabischer Volksroman,* Hanover, 1924.

Péres, H. 'Le roman historique dans la littérature arabe', *Annales de l'Institut d'Etudes Orientales,* XV, 1957, pp. 5-39.
'Le roman dans la littérature arabe dès origines à la fin du Moyen Age, *ibid,* XVI, 1958, pp. 5-40.

Perron, A. *Glaive des Couronnes,* Paris, 1862.

Rouger, G. *Le Roman d'Antar d'après les anciens textes arabes,* Paris, 1923.

Rückert, F. 'Auswahl von Gedichten und Gesängen aus dem arabischen Volksheldenroman Siret Antarat Ilbattal, d. i. Leben und Taten Antara's des Kämpfers', *Zeitschrift der Deutschen Morgenländischen Gesellschaft II,* pp. 188-204.

Steinbach, U. *Ḏāt al-Himma,* Freiburger Islamstudien, Band IV, Wiesbaden, 1972.

Thorbecke, H. *'Antarah, ein vorislamischer Dichter,* Leipzig, 1867.

PREFACE

This study of part of the Arabian 'epic' of 'Antara ibn Shaddād was written for several reasons. Nothing, or almost nothing, of this famous work is now to be found in an English translation. Early publications of translated and selected passages are in specialist periodicals or have long been out of print. This seemed unjust. The romance is at least the equal of parts of the One Thousand and One Nights. Translations of stories from the latter can be found on the shelves of most bookshops. One or two fragments of other Arabian romances can be read in E. W. Lane's *Manners and Customs of the Modern Egyptians.* 'Antara is nowhere represented. [1]

The complete text of the *Sīrat 'Antara* (the *Ḥijāzīya*) is of enormous length. To attempt to translate the entire text would seem impracticable. Many of its themes are repeated in different guises and are of varied merit. Its opening pages and the dramatic death of the hero can be read in English or French in books and journals which are listed in my bibliography. Although difficult to obtain they can at least be consulted. Over a period I have examined parts of the *Sīrat 'Antara* with a small group of students at the School of Oriental and African Studies. Space and content limited the selection of one part of it, a part which, condensed and analysed, seemed able to stand on its own. It had to be a narrative which was of central significance in the plot of the entire romance, and it had to illustrate stylistic and structural features of Arabic works of this genre which are popular literature in every corner of the Islamic world.

I chose Antar's adventure in 'Ethiopia', and by this I mean the 'occupied' Yemen and a large part of Africa and Spain. The choice seemed apt. Antar was half African. Besides, evidence indicated that the *Sīra* as it now reads is in many ways a product of Fatimid, Ayyubid and Mamluk Egypt and reflects a Cairene view of Africa in the later medieval period.

As I explored its content chance dictated that I should also be engaged in a study of the history and the peoples of the eastern Sahara and the Sudan. These studies were centred upon the medieval Zaghāwa, Islamic peoples in the region of Lake Chad, and on Tuareg nomad groups for whom a sacred tree was central to their beliefs. It was a surprise to discover that the further I delved into Antar's adventures, the more these seemed to correlate with African peoples who engaged my attention at that time.

Around the African exploits of the hero of ʻAbs I have arranged a series of chapters which highlight the whole plot, discuss this type of romance as a medieval literary genre, trace the evolution of the *Sīrat ʻAntara* from pre-Islamic Arabia to the Mamluk age, and which consider the relationship between 'Arab' and 'Ethiopian' in the medieval period.

I am indebted to a number of my colleagues at S.O.A.S. for their advice and help. In particular I wish to thank Professor C. Beckingham, Professor M. Boyce, Dr. J. Bynon, Dr. T. Gandjei, Dr. A. Irvine, Dr. D. J. Kamhi and Dr. M. Abdel Haleem. I am also grateful to several friends in Nigeria with whom I discussed specific details. I am grateful to John Lavers of Abdullahi Bayero College, Ahmadu Bello University of Kano, for his stimulating views. I also wish to thank Dr. G. R. Smith of the British Library for part of the text of the *Sīra,* and C. Blair, M.A., F.S.A., Keeper of the Department of Metalwork in the Victoria and Albert Museum, and my brother Malcolm, for certain details in regard to medieval armour and weapons.

I have attempted to present the exploits of Antar and his comrades against the background of Arabic Literature in general and the history of Islam in medieval Africa and Moorish Spain. Nonetheless, I hope that the narrative and some of the discussion will interest a wider public. I have adopted a 'critical transcription'. I have introduced macrons and diacritics only in the Index or where it would seem academically essential to introduce them.

The *Sīrat ʻAntara* is a work composed to entertain and to stimulate the curiosity of the listener. It is recited in instalments, and the text allows scope for extraction and improvisation. If in trying to retell the story of expeditions to the Yemen and to Africa I have explored new by-ways in literature, history and ethnology I shall have attained my objective.

H. T. Norris
Meadowford.
1978.

1. Diana Richmond has recently rewritten and arranged some of the Antar stories from the early part of the *Sīra* in her *ʻAntar and ʻAbla, a Bedouin Romance,* Quartet Books, 1978. Her book ends with the plots and counterplots among the tribes following the marriage of Antar and ʻAbla. This part of the *Sīra* may well be the oldest. I cannot agree with her, however, that Gustave Rouger devised an early death for Antar in the manner of Baldur and the Cid.

INTRODUCTION

(i) General

The Arabian romance of the bedouin hero, ‘Antara (or ‘Antar) ibn Shaddād, has the reputation of being the closest competitor to the One Thousand and One Nights in richness of content and in skill of composition. It surpasses all others in ferocity of martial narrative. The adventure of the pre-Islamic poet ‘Antara is expanded into an ‘epic’ of an African slave who by his mighty arm became ruler of the world.

The valour of this knight was once highly praised in Europe. Von Hammer-Pugstall, a Viennese Orientalist, introduced Antar to European readers in 1802. Terrick Hamilton, a servant of the East India Company and later Oriental Secretary to the British Embassy in Constantinople, published a partial translation into English in 1819 and 1820. A series of articles between 1833 and 1847 in the *Journal Asiatique* recounted episodes from Antar’s tumultuous career. In 1868 Von Hammer-Pugstall saw part of his labour published in Paris as *Les Aventures d’Antar.*

Von Hammer-Pugstall’s abridgement was published in Danish in 1871, and a Norwegian, C. A. Holmboe, compared Antar’s exploits to those of Bayard when he penned his views in 1881. However, it was above all in France that the Antar ‘vogue’ reached its peak among men of letters. Lamartine published the *‘Pensées d’Antar’* in 1849, and in his *Vie des grands hommes* he described the romance as ‘un des plus beaux chants lyriques de toutes les langues’. To him Antar was on a par with Homer, Virgil and Tasso, ‘le David moderne du désert’. Renan shared his enthusiasm, ‘Je ne sais s’il dans toute l’histoire de la civilisation un tableau plus gracieux, plus aimable, plus animé que celui de la vie arabe avant l’islamisme, telle qu’elle nous apparait dans le type admirable d’Antar’. (*Etudes d’histoire religieuse,* Paris, 1880, p. 272.) There were several partial translations into French in the latter half of the nineteenth century; that of L.-Marcel Devic in 1864 and 1878, and a successor to it by Gustave Rouger in *La Collection Piazza.*

It is perhaps not surprising that the Russian composer, Rimsky Korsakov, should have written an Oriental Symphonic Suite on this subject, his Opus 9, in 1868. It should be noted, however, that the Arabian *Sīra* was not his source. In *My Musical Life* he remarks that having indefinitely postponed the writing of his Symphony in B minor –

‘I turned to Svenkovsky’s (Baron Brambeus’s) beautiful tale Antar at Balakirev’s and Moussorgsky’s suggestion; on this subject I had planned to compose a symphony or a symphonic poem in four movements. The desert, the disillusioned Antar; the episode with the gazelle and the bird, the ruins of Palmyra; the vision of the Peri; the three joys of life – revenge, power and love – and finally Antar’s death – all of this was tempting to a composer. I set to work in mid-winter.’

In the score Rimsky Korsakov introduced Algerian folk tunes and Arab melodies he found in Khristianovich’s collection. Here he could find local colour for his composition.

In France the momentum was maintained well into the early twentieth century; it was musical, dramatic and literary. It fired a composer of promise, Gabriel Dupont who was born in Caen in 1878. He was a pupil of Widor, and he composed an opera on the subject of Antar. This was due to be produced in 1914, on August 3rd, the day on which war was declared. Owing to this event and to the death of the composer on the very same day its début did not take place until 1921. Critics spoke well of it and Gabriel Dupont was hailed as a genius. *The Musical Times* in 1921 printed a favourable review. The opera was colourful and with fine solo and choral singing, and the reviewer praised the composer for his skilful use of Arabian melodies. Yet the work was quickly forgotten.

The tragic end of Antar was staged as a drama in the Odéon in 1910, the script by the hand of a talented Syrian writer, Shukri Ghanim. Then in 1921 and in 1924 an adaption with orchestral accompaniment was performed in the Algiers Opera House. In a relatively recent survey, 1957-8, Henri Péres noted that certain Arabian stories and romances stood out from others by their substance and their form. After the One Thousand and One Nights he preferred Antar’s *Sīra* because its hero was ‘the incarnation of human frailty and knightly grandeur combined’.

Elsewhere the ‘vogue’ for the Antar romance declined. In Budapest the painstaking scholar Bernhard Heller analysed the enormous text of the romance and compared its contents with Persian epics and the sagas and legendary cycles of Nordic, Gallic and Germanic Europe. For him the impressiveness of this Arabian conception though derivative was something very real. Its richness of colour and skilfully wrought plots in verse and prose were an outstanding achievement.

In England the glamour of Antar’s exploits had several champions. Sir William Jones had decided that, ‘There is nothing graceful or sublime which cannot be found in this work.' Blunt regarded the *Sīrat 'Antara* as 'the most important of the Oriental originals on which some of our own Christian romances of the Middle Ages were founded'.

During his account of his journey to al-Madinah and Mecca Richard Burton makes passing reference to Antar whom he clearly admired.

'From ancient periods of the Arab's history we find him practising knight-errantry, the wildest form of chivalry. "The sons of Antar," says the author of the "Crescent and the Cross", "Show little of the true chivalric spirit." What thinks the reader of sentiments like these? "This valiant man," remarks Antar (who was "ever interested for the weaker sex.") "hath defended the honour of women." We read in another place, "Mercy, my lord, is the noblest quality of the noble." Again, "It is the most ignominious of deeds to take freeborn women prisoners." "Bear not malice, O Shibub," quoth the hero, "for of malice good never came." Is there no true greatness in this sentiment? – "Birth is the boast of the *fainéant*; noble is the youth who beareth every ill, who clotheth himself in mail during the noon-tide heat, and who wandereth through the outer darkness of night." And why does the "knight of knights" love Ibla? Because "she is blooming as the sun at dawn, with hair black as the midnight shades, with Paradise in her eye, her bosom an enchantment, and a form waving like the tamarisk when the soft wind blows from the hills of Nijd"? Yes! but his chest expands also with the thoughts of her "faith, purity, and affection," – it is her moral as well as her material excellence that makes her the hero's "hope, and hearing, and sight." Briefly, in Antar I discern

"a love exalted high,
By all the glow of chivalry;"

and I lament to see so many intelligent travellers misjudging the Arab after a superficial experience of a few debased Syrians or Sinaites. The true children of Antar, my Lord Lindsay, have *not* "ceased to be gentlemen."

However, Orientalists such as Lyall and Nicholson seemed less enthusiastic. The latter in his *Literary History of the Arabs* was terse in his assessment, 'Though the Romance exhibits all the anachronisms and exaggerations of popular legend, it does nevertheless portray the unchanging features of Bedouin life with admirable fidelity and picturesqueness.' Gibb in his *Arabic Literature* remarked that, 'To the European reader (or listener, as these romances are read out at breakneck speed to a coffee-house audience) the constant repetition of similar incidents gives them rather a monotonous character, but the appeal which they made to the Arab is undeniable.'

In 1954 the cause of the romance in the English-speaking world was given a new lease of life by Cedric Dover in *Phylon,* the Atlanta University Review of Race and Culture. Unfortunately the ideological motivation of his essay left no space to allude to the years of careful sifting of comparative medieval literature and folklore undertaken by Bernhard Heller and Rudi Paret on the Continent. 'Someday the rising coloured world will write its own history. Then we, too, shall have a galaxy of knights, but none will reach the stature of Antarah Ibn Shaddad al-Absi: Antar, son of Shaddad, of the tribe of Abs. The life of this Negro warrior-poet, who lived through most of the sixth century in the desert between el-Hejr and Medina, is the subject of one of the world's greatest romances – greater, it is said, than Malory's compilation from the "Frensshe books."

I am afraid I do not share, to the full, Cedric Dover's generous re-assessment. Yet I have some sympathy for his view that Antar should be viewed through 'African eyes'. Here I find his observations relevant and original. Most discussion and translation have been devoted to the early pages of the *Sīra* where the hero woos his cousin 'Abla and attains his liberty. Very little attention has been drawn to the diverse and remarkable medieval world of Africa and Europe which is unfolded on other pages.

It will simplify my task if I define my specific goals. In the main I have followed Cedric Dover's suggestions and have concentrated my research on the portions of the Antar romance which are principally concerned with the African background of the hero. I shall attempt to assess the intention of those sections of the 'epic' which disclose Antar's rediscovery of his Ethiopic or Hamitic ancestry, and other exploits in North Africa and Spain.

I will develop the argument that the definitive text of the Antar Romance, and its sister romances, is built on a common structural plan. Each romance has similarities with the legends of the exploits of the early heroes of Islam, collectively known as the *Pseudo-Maghāzī* literature. Iraq, the Yemen, Moorish Spain and Egypt may have been the first places where preliminary drafts of Antar's adventures were shaped in an unelaborated form. The *Ḥijāzīya* text of Antar which we now possess is of gargantuan dimensions. Its original was drafted between 1080 A.D. and 1400 A.D.

At certain points material could have been introduced at a later date, but the general impression is rather the opposite. It discloses much earlier material superficially re-worked, possibly about the time of the reign of the Mamluk Sultan Barqūq (1382-1398 A.D.)

The romance is by no means wholly Egyptian. Certain passages in the narrative have a content apparently derived from sundry Oriental and arguably

European sources. The text, the *aide mémoire* of the story-teller, was conceived by Asians, Copts or Franks who had read the narratives of identifiable Arab geographers, or who had met Persian, Ibāḍī Khārijite or Arab travellers, merchants and troubadours who knew Europe, Asia and the interior of Africa.

In Africa, Antar and his brethren were to lead Arabians into battle, and on the battlefield they were to rediscover their birth place and their kinsfolk. The Upper Nile, the deserts of the Fezzan and the Sudan, the silk cotton trees, acacias and baobabs near Lake Chad, the giraffes of the savannah and desert petroglyphs, and Moorish Spain are, I suggest, all to be found in the pages of the *Sīra* of Antar. The supreme kingdom in Africa is Ethiopia.

'Ethiopia' is a very different realm from the Abyssinia of today. The genuine African substance primarily indicates Nubia, the Zaghāwa kingdom of Kānem 'the land of flags and ensigns', and perhaps medieval Ghāna as well. I shall argue that the growth and expansion of Kānem from Lake Chad to the Nile and its commercial contacts with Aden, between the eleventh and fourteenth centuries may be one factor which substantially influenced this part of the Antar romance. In the *Sīra* the Sudan is 'invaded' through the Yemen and seems to be an extension of it.

The imaginary expedition is thus not without reference to historical events. This reality is partly the strong, religiously coloured, tradition in Islam of the pre-Islamic invasion of Arabia and Mecca by the Abyssinians and of expeditions by Himyarites to Abyssinia and the Sudan. It may also be a memory of the rule of the Abyssinian Mamluks, the Banū Najāḥ, in the Yemenite city of Zabīd and in the Dahlak islands during the eleventh and twelfth centuries. It may also echo news of the fall of Ghāna to the Almoravids about 1076 where a branch of the ruling dynasty in alliance with the desert Almoravids may have brought about its fall.

I shall also offer evidence to show that there are pointers to an established axis of trade and cultural contact between Kānem ('the south') and the Yemen ('the south') through Aden, Zayla', and the Sudanese port of 'Aydhāb. This port was known to Chinese vessels. This same commercial and cultural axis can be detected in another full-length martial Arabian romance which came into vogue about the same date as Antar; the exploits of Sayf ibn Dhī Yazan, a pre-Islamic Himyarite hero who liberated the Yemen from the yoke of the Abyssinians.

There are similarities and differences between the adventures of Antar and Sayf. In some ways they overlap and are complementary. There are likewise similarities between Antar and the exploits of Abū Zayd and Dhiyāb, the two heroes of the Banū Hilāl. Their battles in Arabia and North Africa, and their exploits against the Berbers disclose a similar structure to the plots of Antar and of Sayf. It can be argued that each of these elaborated romances, introduced into Africa from Asia, stem from some common pre-Islamic archetype preserved in the oral folklore and ballads of the Arabian nomads and the popular histories of Arabia.

The Koran and its heroes and anti-heroes and the folk-tales of the bedouin are suitable starting points for the exploration of the African adventures of Antar and his comrades. 'Antara ibn Shaddād may have been a pre-Islamic poet, but Antar, his medieval successor, is supposedly the champion of Islam and its Prophet. He overtly fights the Prophet's battles, as do the Imām 'Alī and the Yemenite knight, 'Amr ibn Ma'dī Karib, in the *Pseudo-Maghāzī* literature. But how sincere is his conversion? Antar dons the armour of other mighty men of the Arabs whose claim to glory was probably more justified than his own.

Antar is a dynamic figure. His *Sīra* is not only a collection of tales of adventure and love, but a challenge to the accepted norms of medieval chivalry. Some may detect in it a satire on the inherited and agreed standards of good composition and *belles lettres,* or a reaction against the stiff and lifeless form to which these had been reduced.

The *Sīra* of Antar is at times a moving work. Despite pages of ferocious combat it sets forth worthy standards of conduct towards friend and foe alike. In it the unfettered tribalism of pre-Islamic Arabia is tempered by a broad and in some ways charitable view of all humanity. The sons of Shem, Ḥām and Japheth rediscover something of their primeval brotherhood. Their unity is forged by a magic sword, the generosity and audacity of the monstrous offspring of a captive Ethiopian princess. These contradictions and juxtapositions explain much of Antar's fascination. They may also explain why Antar received the uncritical and outspoken praise of the Europeans who first read portions of the narrative or came under its undeniable spell.

'The tenth, of men from barren Occian,
Sons of the desert, a wild and godless clan;
You'll ne'er hear tell of such repulsive scamps;
Harder than iron their hide on head and flanks,
So that they scorn or harness or steel cap;
They are in battle extremely fierce and rash.'

The Song of Roland.

Translated by
Dorothy L. Sayers.

'This is a large old *seyal* tree, now dead, half lying on the ground with two thick branches sticking up in the air. On one of these, about face high, is a small patch smeared with camel fat, and on the other branch is a leather thong, cut from the skin of a camel, bound tightly round. In the crack below, where the two branches fork from the trunk are smeared the partly digested grasses . . . from the intestines of the camel.

The Arabs told us that the Guraan always slaughter a camel here before starting off on a raiding expedition and carry out these operations on the tree. It seems to be more than an ordinary *karama,* a slaughter for luck, and rather in the nature of a sacrifice to a tree spirit.'

D. Newbold and W. B. K. Shaw.

*An exploration in the
South Libyan Desert.*

(ii) Wells of receding water and Palaces raised and inverted

The raised palace and the enchanted water source.

Arabian romances owe much of their inspiration to the Koran. Often the hero or heroine in the story, or the foe who is fought and overcome, are patterned on a Koranic figure. Luqmān, the macrobite sage and king, is a figure whose varied career is particularly relevant. He began life with the status of an Ethiopian slave. He became a bedouin vagabond, and he ended his days as a king of the troglodyte peoples of 'Ād. Royal couples owe much to the example of Solomon and the Queen of Sheba. A tyrannical foe is likened to Nimrod 'the sinner' and mighty hunter, or he resembles a stubborn Pharaoh or an Amalekite giant. Images and symbols borrowed from the Koran are also to be discovered. Pillars, dark oceans, serpents and fabulous beasts are common to all Semitic religious sources. Battles in Arabian romance are sometimes patterned on reported events in the life of the Prophet. The battle of the ditch (Khandaq) in 627 A.D. and the capture of the Jewish oasis of Khaybar in 629 A.D. are prominent examples.

In the Koran symbols are subordinate to people. The personalities, like those referred to above, typify an idea. They love or hate, build or destroy or are subject to change and metamorphosis. At times they are paired or confused with the *jinn.* The germinal ideas for the story-teller may be a single image or a pair of images. An example may be found in *Sūra XXII,* verse 45 in the Koran:

> 'And how many a city have we destroyed while it yet did wrong, and it was turned over on its roofs, and (how many) a deserted well and lofty palace.'

Here there are two images, a high palace and a well. This verse presented problems to Koran commentators, particularly as to the whereabouts of the palace and the well. An inverted or condemned city was easier to locate. The fabulous 'Iram of the columns' in the desert of Aden, the architectural dream of king Shaddād, the 'Ādite, seemed to fit this context. Vanished Iram appeared elsewhere in scripture. But a lofty palace and well from which no profit could be derived from its water were so common-place as to be difficult to locate with any geographical precision in Southern Arabia.

The above verse introduces the central milieu of the Arabian tale. The Arabs were haunted by the elusive and the deserted. The story-teller's skill was aimed at presenting some version of his chosen setting or scenario at a crucial point in his narrative. He felt some need to introduce it to his listeners at climaxes, and in some form or another he used the breaking into or breaking out from this imaginary milieu as the signal for the denouement of his tale.

An upturned city, palace or human habitation and a well or water course which retreats deceptively from the approacher until vanishing point, only to fill once more as the approacher withdraws, are notions capable of symbolic, psychological or mystical interpretation. Arabian thought is concrete, its vision photographic and the mirage (*sarāb*) is an every-day event. Many a horizon in a shimmering haze conveys the impression of a water-hole or a lake which recedes, a city which floats or is upturned, or a palace raised aloft in the sky, a symbolic portrayal of treasure, death or renewal of life.

Among the best examples of this kind in Arabian legend is the enormous 'city of brass' which was sited in the remote west or the remote east. It was a formidable construction to enter, yet its spell, centred in the magnetic or carbuncle stone (*baht*) within it was irresistible. The hero who surmounted its gateless walls beheld fabulous treasure possessed by a people who were half-dead or asleep, held in a kind of suspense.

A wonderful city of this kind was the common dream of medieval Islam and Christendom. In the Troy book (1412-1420 A.D.) where King Priam rebuilds Troy there are similarities to the Arabian 'city of brass'.

> Barbykans and bolewerkys huge,
> A-fore the toun made for highe refuge,
> Yiffe nede were, erly and eke late;
> And portecolys stronge at every gate,
> That hem thar nat noon assailyng charge;
> And the lowkis thikke, brode, and large,
> Of the gatys al of yoten bras.

Or in the *Knight's Tale* Chaucer describes the Temple of Omnipotent:

Mars was erected there in steel, and burnished.
The Gateway, narrow and forbidding, furnished
A ghastly sight, and such a rushing quake
Raged from within, the portals seemed to shake.
In at the doors a northern glimmer shone
Onto the walls, for windows there were none;
Once scarce discerned a light, it was so scant.
The doors were of eternal adamant,
And vertically clenched, and clenched across
For greater strength with many an iron boss,
And every pillar to support the shrine
Weighed a full ton of iron bright and fine.

Tr. by Nevill Coghill.

This amazing city was not unknown in African epics and legends. Something akin to it is the focal point of the exploits of Sundiata, 'lion king', the founder of the kingdom of Mali in the thirteenth century. A great silk-cotton tree dominated Canco palace in Nianiba (Niani), the residence of his father, but his great enemy, Souamaoro, lived in a more fabulous structure. 'Sosso was a magnificent city. In the open plain her triple rampart with awe-inspiring towers reached into the sky. The city comprised a hundred and eighty-eight fortresses and the palace of Souamaoro loomed above the whole city like a gigantic tower. Sosso had but one gate; colossal and made of iron, the work of the sons of fire.'

Souamaoro Karte was a great sorcerer. 'His fetishes had a terrible power and it was because of them that all kings trembled before him, for he could deal a swift death to whoever he pleased. He had fortified Sosso with a triple curtain wall and in the middle of the town loomed his palace towering over the thatched huts of the villagers. He had had an immense seven-story tower built for himself and he lived on the seventh floor in the midst of his fetishes. This is why he was called The Untouchable King.' (1)

The Arabian city had no gates. The *jinn* guarded its secrets. It was fashioned from molten brass for Solomon, yet it had the same grandeur, invincibility and 'crafty bildyng and werkyng most roial' as its Occidental or African counterparts. It had much in common with Roderick's tower in Toledo, barred and bolted, and guarded by a fiery eagle, or seven-walled Kangdiz in Iran with its walls of gold, silver, steel, bronze, iron, crystal and lapis.

The city of the Arabian story-teller was a deception. Adjacent to it was a lake or water-source full of imprisoned *jinn* who guarded the city. The city and the lake were paired like the raised palace and elusive well. At no great distance could be found a cosmic and enchanted grove, growing in the city or palace or near the lake. A pattern of inter-related symbols was regularly introduced in Arabian romance: a palace-city; a water-source, well basin or lake, subject to drought and inundation; and a tree or grove of trees centred near the palace or watered by the lake.

This whole scene is a transfigured picture of ancient Ma'rib in the Yemen, the capital of Bilqīs, the legendary Queen of Sheba. To this day her alleged palace is called 'the city of brass'. Her capital was vividly portrayed by the pre-Islamic troubadour al-A'shā (Nicholson's translation):

> 'Let this warn whoever a warning will take –
> And Ma'rib withal, which the Dam fortified.
> Of marble did Himyar construct it so high,
> The water recoiled when to reach it they tried.
> It watered their acres and vineyards, and hour
> By hour, did a portion among them divide.
> So lived they in fortune, and plenty until
> Therefrom turned away by a ravaging tide.
> Then wandered their princes and noblemen through
> Mirage-shrouded deserts that baffle the guide.'

The Prophet Muhammad presented this collapse of pre-Islamic dam and dyke civilisation in Southern Arabia to the pagan Meccan community and to their Muslim successors as a 'traumatic' event. It illustrated a magnetic force which at varied periods had affected the metamorphosis of Iram or the crumbling of the Ma'rib dam.

The transfigured picture was dramatically blurred by an optical illusion of inversion or water evaporation. The picture was to be borrowed by story-tellers as the scene for the climax of their stories. The scene could be pictured once or many times. It could be shifted from one end of the world of Islam to the other. While the well or lake was retained the palace could be reconstructed in many shapes and designs.

It could be a copper tower, a ruined castle from the age of the flood or a palace in the clouds in the tree-tops, like the giant's castle in the sky at the summit of Jack's magic bean-stalk.

Solomon's palace of molten brass was located in Spain (al-Andalus) by al-Ṭabarī and other early writers. Later it was transferred to Africa beyond the sea of al-Karkar which many have identified with Chad. It was the store-house of Solomon's treasures and his books of wisdom. Its discovery was linked to the first expeditions of the Arabs into North Africa. From several of the Arab sources, however, there is much to be said for the theory that Ancient Egyptian monuments in the western desert of Egypt, or marvels of the Pharaohs on the Upper Nile, inspired the fantasy of the romancers who wished to dumbfound their listeners by the marvellous palaces they described or the well and lands discovered by the armies of Islam in their wars of expansion.

Abū Abdallāh Muḥammad ibn Abī Bakr al-Zuhrī (died circa 549/556 A.H., 1154/1161 A.D.) in his geographical work on Africa and Asia locates the magnetic palace and the well referred to in the Koran on the banks of 'the Upper Nile' (2). 'At a distance of seven days' march from Cairo on the way to Ethiopia is the derelict well and the raised palace.' He then describes how the water of the well retreats deep into the well as a stranger approaches, and how it reaches its original perimeter once that approacher withdraws. The water 'withdraws more quickly than the human eye can perceive, because God Almighty mentioned that disused and valueless well in His mighty book'.

The raised palace was a stepped pyramid to the south of the well. At its summit there were battlements. 'It has no door and none knows how it is constructed. On a slab of marble are the Syriac words, "We have built and erected. He who claims today that he possesses the like of us then let him destroy what we have built. To destroy is easier than to build. Were the people of the earth to join together to destroy anything of it they could not do so." '

Almost at once al-Zuhrī transfers the 'tale of the city of brass' (*ḥadīth madīnat al-naḥās*) to this pyramid, and the attempt to scale that city's walls as an expedition to find the treasures of the pyramid.

'Ziyād when he was governor (for Mu'āwiya ibn Abī Sufyān the Umayyad) over Egypt wished to march to this palace and to undertake its destruction. In that matter he sought the advice of Mu'āwiya who was at that time the Caliph of Damascus. He deterred him from doing that. He said to him "You cannot do it." Among the wonders of this palace is that when anyone mounts those steps, attains their summit, and he looks down on the palace and beholds what lies within it, he cries aloud and casts himself headlong into the midst of it, and he is never seen again. People offered themselves to ascend this palace. One of them went forward. His companions tied a band of hemp about him, and they held him fast and firm. When he looked down over the palace he endeavoured to cast himself into it. They held him back with the cord. He continued to be pulled into what lay hidden within the interior of the palace until he shrieked aloud and perished. None knows what lies within this palace. Everyone who has come forward to discover what is within it has perished. The first philosophers have alleged that within it are the stones known as the *baht* stones which drag a man to them from a great distance.

It was these stones which Alexander, son of Philippus collected from the country of the Zanj [East Africa], and if God wills, it will be mentioned in due course. This palace and this well are the wonders of the world. Because of this God made them proverbial in His mighty book where He said, "And (how many) a deserted well and lofty palace." '

In such a passage story-teller and geographer meet, inspired by a verse in the Koran. If palace and well are contrasted and combined in the scenario of Arabian tales, so too are the progenitor Semitic king or hero and the heroine Semitic or Cushitic queen or princess.

The Queen of Sheba and the South Arabian kings.

This royal couple are also to be found in the Koran. Solomon was master of the *jinn* while the Queen of Sheba (Bilqīs) was part human, part *jinnīya.* Palace and well or water are linked in their respective personalities. Bilqīs was a queen of Ma'rib, the centre of South Arabian fertility, while Solomon was master of Jerusalem and the builder of innumerable palaces and cities with the aid of the *jinn.* Their meeting and union took place in circumstances associated with water, whether it be a fabricated floor of glass which was swarming with fish, or by the ruse of a jar of water left by the queen's bedside when she was a guest in Solomon's palace. In most tales which involve the royal couple the supernatural character of Bilqīs is manifested by a sharp distinction drawn between black and white, this contrast portrayed in the black hair which defaced her legs and showed her hybrid origin.

According to the *Kitāb al-Tījān,* the legendary history of the kings of the Yemen, by Wahb ibn Munabbih / Ibn Hishām (3):

'He [Solomon] having mentioned that he desired to marry her, an *'ifrīt* of the *jinn* called Zawba'a said to them [the *jinn*], "I shall suffice for you in regard to Solomon." So he came to him and said, "Oh, Prophet of God, I understand that you desire to marry Bilqīs. Her mother is one of the *jinn.* No *jinnīya,* if married to human-kind has ever given birth to a son without his feet having donkey's hooves and both his legs black. He will be hard and cruel, sharp and hot in body and soul." Solomon said, "How can I behold such to be her circumstance, and this without her knowledge of my intention?" Zawba'a said to him, "Leave that to me." '

It was he who constructed a glass council chamber for Solomon. The *jinnīya* nature of Bilqīs was exorcised, spiritually by her repentance to Solomon and the divine revelation that she was free from infidelity, physically by the removal of the unsightly hair from her body.

'When Solomon decided to marry her a pious *jinnī* who used to love Solomon's pleasure, said to him, "Oh, Prophet of God, is it only her hair which you dislike?" "Yes," he replied. He said, "I will leave her with you like silver without blemish." "Act accordingly," he said. So he made a paste for her, he sent it to her, and he made a bath for her. Some scholars have said that it was the first depilatory paste made by a created being, and the first bath that a *jinnī* made. The latter fashioned two superstructures for her and various kinds of manufactured arts.'

Bilqīs – 'queen of the south', both the Yemen and Ethiopia – introduced a matriarchal break in South Arabian royalty and became symbolic of a rulership by queens in areas of Africa and southern Asia with which the Arabs became familiar. A warrior queen played an important role in Islamic romance, a role which owed much to Indian queens who went forth to fight in battle. A key figure in the switch of kingship was the father of Bilqīs who was called al-Hadhād, Sharaḥ or Sharaḥbīl. By coincidence or intention the name al-Hadhād recalls *hudhud,* the lapwing which reported to Solomon that the Queen of Sheba was a worshipper of the sun. In the account of Wahb ibn Munabbih and of most contemporaries al-Hadhād was the son of Sharaḥbīl ibn 'Amr, and his ancestors were of Himyarite stock of the seed of Qaḥṭān. He was a man of courage and resolution.

The tales of his marriage to the *jinnīya* Rawāḥa, the mother of Bilqīs, are undeniably different if a comparison is made between the account of Wahb ibn Munabbih and that of al-Ṭabarī in his history. But the account of al-Ṭabarī shows remarkable structural similarities despite the detailed differences. It more clearly reveals Persian or Indian inspiration. A direct comparison with Wahb ibn Munabbih (Ibn Hishām) casts light on the abiding retention of the frame of an Arabian tale, however much expansion and amendment may alter something of its substance (4):

Wahb ibn Munabbih (110/728 – 218/833)	*al-Ṭabarī* (d. 311/933)
Sharaḥbīl ibn 'Amr (Ruler of Qaḥṭān) al-Hadhād	Bū Sharaḥ (King of China)
Goes to al-'Āliya on a hot day while fighting 'Amr Dhū'l-Adh'ār, sees combat	Goes hunting and sees two snakes.

Negro slave (A) of *White master* (B)	*Black Snake* 1) combats *White Snake* 2).
(B) slays (A) after being refreshed by the water of al-Hadhād.	2) nearly slain by 1) but king Bu Sharaḥ sends his servants to kill 1). 2) faints but is refreshed by water and departs.
al-Hadhād meets party of *jinn.* He is offered sister of (B) Rawāḥa bint al-Sakan as wife but is told never to question her actions. Court in sluggish sleep. Al-Hadhād marries Rawāḥa.	King dreams. He sees young man who is the son of the *jinn* and who is snake 2). He offers a reward. King marries his sister but is told never to ask her the motives for her acts. If he does she will leave him.
Son (a), carried off by a dog. King keeps his peace	Son (a), *jinnīya* throws him in a fire. King weeps but keeps his peace.
Daughter (b), carried off by a dog. King keeps his peace.	Daughter (b), beautiful as sun and moon. Carried off by a dog. King keeps his peace. King goes to war. He and his Vizir Rām Rāmish are lost in a desert. The king's wife destroys all their provisions.
Son (c) King asks.	
He is told that all three were carried off to be nurtured by a dog. Son (a) is dead. Son (c) will only live as long as the father of Rawāḥa. Daughter (b) will come to live with her father.	King protests. *Jinnīya wife* says:- 1) His flour is poisoned by this Vizir. King finds it to be so. 2) Fire did not kill his son but nurtured him. 3) Dog nurtured his daughter.
Rawāḥa departs. Bilqīs reigns as queen of the Yemen until the cousin of al-Hadhād, 'Amr ibn Ya'fur ibn Ḥimyar comes of age. Al-Hadhād dies after *counselling* his nobles.	The latter, Bilqīs, returns adorned. The *Jinnīya* orders army to march to a water source and deceives the enemy who attacks. The *Jinnīya* bids farewell to her spouse telling him that his protest had broken their compact. King consoles himself with his *daughter Bilqīs* who becomes his heir to the throne. He *counsels* his nobles.

Important concepts in Arabian romance are introduced into this story of al-Hadhād, his marriage and the birth of his daughter. One is intermarriage between humans and *jinn.* Another is the royal status of women. Another is single combat between Arabian and Ethiopian, or black serpent and white. This combat of colour was to become increasingly central in the romances to be discussed.

It is noteworthy that despite the extreme brevity of this tale of al-Hadhād and his *jinnīya* wife, the personality of the king and his wife and other kindred motifs are to be to seen greatly expanded within a full-length romance, the late-medieval or post-medieval work called *Sayf al-Tījān,* 'Sword of Crowns' (5). Studying the only version of the latter it seems clear that this Sayf, whose true name is not disclosed, is an heir to the corpus of Yemenite adventure as revealed in the tale of al-Hadhād and his wife.

Sayf al-Tījān is the son of Sharaḥbīl ibn Quḍā'a ibn Nu'mān ibn Ya'rub ibn Siksik ibn Ḥimyar. Among his exploits were single combats with lions and with infidels. His mother was Ṣā'iqat al-Ḥurūb (thunderbolt of wars). Sharaḥbīl at first disowned him – a formal act in romances of this type – and he was adopted by a gazelle, then by a prince. Father and son were later reconciled. Sayf married many wives, and he ruled many kingdoms. He had several sons, one by his *jinnīya* wife with whom he lived in bliss upon an island.

Throughout the plot stress is placed on the inter-relationship between humanity and *jinn.* The romance reaches its climax in the expedition of Sa'at al-Sa'āt (hour of hours) and Liwā' al-Mulk (standard of sovereignty) both of whom were sons of Sayf al-Tījān. They enter a replica of the 'city of brass', borrowed from that tale in part if not in whole. Amidst a world of enchantments Sa'at al-Sa'āt is nearly transfixed by a talisman lance. He encounters a terrible serpent and reaches a palace wherein grows a tree laden with fruit of a taste unknown to man. Beside a spring of water he spies a black slave who is about to slay a maiden with his sword. The hero rescues the maiden.

Before he dies at the end of his adventures Sayf, like al-Hadhād, counsels his nobles and successors. The theme of the romance is that of a Yemenite dynasty established by a feat of valour, expanded by the offspring of intermarriage with female *jinn* of exceptional charm and knowledge, and led to religious victory by single combats between men of true faith and infidelity. Asian splendour is colourfully portrayed, while warriors armed with Lamṭī oryx shields add an African touch. This diffuse romance owes something to the legends of Sheba, something to the tale of the 'city of brass', and something to the Maghrib and to Persia. In it are to be found many a raised palace or subterranean water course and many a knightly encounter.

Armoured knights.

In the brief, yet expandable, tale of al-Hadhād, Wahb ibn Munabbih introduced two contrasted combatants, one black and one white. A duel to the death or to capture was a repetitive formula in Arabian romances. Frequently the combat occurred between the hero and his foe; sometimes a fateful encounter took place between the hero and one of his sons or the hero and the heroine. These single combats were occasionally mysterious, neither party knowing the identity of the other. In an extended narrative a succession of such combats was a delaying device employed by the story-teller. He used it to sustain excitement until some climax in a segment of his romance was demanded.

Also, by these combats a hero gained allies for his cause. The number of participants in the drama was increased and diversified. To obviate monotony each combat differed in the details of the weaponry carried by the opponents or in the manner of the death or capture of the vanquished. Much of the armour described was Sasanian Persian. As Professor Herzfeld wrote (6), 'In the third century A.D. chivalry and feudalism were completely developed in Iran, a thousand years earlier than in Europe. The crests identify the figures on various bas-reliefs, just as the individual crowns of the kings, compared with their coins, assign all the sculptures to their rightful owners, even in the absence of inscriptions.

Here the historical event is not condensed into one realistic and dramatic moment, as, for example, Alexander's victory over Darius III in the famous mosaic of Naples, but, contrary to the principle of Hellenistic art, is symbolized by three tournaments. These single combats never happened, but express the idea in a perfect and unmistakable way according to the naive, mythical mind of the people.'

Besides their debt to the Persians, the Arabian story-tellers borrowed much from pre-Islamic and Islamic poetry. Many of their listeners must have been ignorant of the sometimes technical catalogue which described the detail of the armour, the maker of the sword or spear or the craftsmanship of the hauberks. This mattered little, however, if the excitement and colour of the narrative was enhanced, or an atmosphere of a battle maintained or augmented.

A prototype of mounted combat may be seen in a poem by the Hudhalī poet Abū Dhu'aib Khuwaylid ibn Khālid. He was a contemporary of the Prophet Muhammad. He fought in the conquest of Egypt and of Ifrīqīya, and his most famous poem, preserved in the collection known as the *Mufaḍḍalīyāt,* is, in part, a lament for his two sons who died of the plague, possibly in 18 A.H./ 638-639 A.D. The theme of the poem is death, the death of wild asses, of an oryx attacked by hounds and of two valiant knights. Poetically the description of this battle is the least impressive, since it is mainly a description of their mounts, their armour and weapons, even so it portrays the kind of image drawn upon by the romancers to present a hero and his foe. The translation of Charles Lyall characterizes these combatants (7):

Each clad in rings of inwoven steel, King David's work,
Or the make of Tubba', the skilful weaver of coats of mail,
In his hand a lance of Dhū Yazan's store, with a point of steel
fresh furbished, shining with fiery glow like a beacon's light;
Girt round his body a flashing sword, so keen of edge
that the merest touch of its blade cuts through what meets its stroke.
Each, guileful, wrested the other's life with his deadly thrusts,
as a wanton slashes a precious mantle beyond repair.
Each man had lived in the brightest fame-year, each had won
in his world the loftiest place, if aught could keep Death away;
But the winds thereafter with sweeping skirts blot out their graves.
Time's sickle reaps in its prime the greatness himself has sown.

In his notes to these verses Lyall draws attention to the conventional ascription of mail-coats to the workmanship of King David and the Tubba's of the Yemen, likewise the naming of Yazanī or Azanī spears after Yazan, the castle of the Dhū Yazan who is identified with Sayf ibn Dhī Yazan, the liberator of the Yemen from the domination of the Abyssinians.

Early Arabian verse was plundered for epithets which were stereotyped in later romances. An example of it may be found in the Antar romance where Antar is tested by Imru'l-Qays, the foremost pre-Islamic poet, to determine whether Antar's battle ode was worthy of 'suspension' with the other pre-Islamic masterpieces in the Ka'ba at Mecca. The ode in question is a close version of the well known 'hanging ode' (*Mu'allaqa*) of 'Antara ibn Shaddād. But the test was not centred on the vocabulary which appears in this pre-Islamic ode.

Antar was examined to assess his eloquence and knowledge of epithets and synonyms and or weaponry in particular. The subjects selected were the sword, the spear, coats of mail, the horse, the she-camel, wine and snakes. Antar convinced his fellow-poet of his poetic mastery. This story manifests the talent and versatility of the romancers themselves, their range of vocabulary, their ability to enrich the presentation of their tales and to avoid monotony in their descriptions of similar engagements.

Many famous Arab poets used weaponry and armour as an excuse to excel in metaphor and imaginative description. This topic formed the subject matter of the *Dir'īyāt* (poems about hauberks) by the blind poet Abū'l- 'Alā' al-Ma'arrī (973-1057 A.D.). This is a collection of poems of varied metre and length all of them descriptive of armour and weapons and of those who wore them. The poems abound in epithets wherein a suit of armour is compared to honey or to water glistening in a pool, to the sloughed skins of snakes, or to objects which indicate high antiquity. Eight of these poems are descriptive pieces, five are on hauberks, one on an armed encounter, one on a bent spear and one on women warriors who wore armour in battle. King David's prized hauberks were particularly in demand. The desire to possess them led to bitter competition between the pre-Islamic Lakhmid rulers of Iraq. Hauberks were said to have 'locusts eyes', a term which appears often in the *Sīrat 'Antara.* These eyes indicate the nails (*al-fatīr*) used in the riveting of the hauberks. When the links were worn the nails protruded, hence the poet's image. One verse challenges a wearer to eat a prized suit of mail, likening its nails to locusts' eyes in a period of great dearth and famine. In a famine the bedouin eat locusts in order to survive.

Throughout Arabian romances like Antar and Sayf, the weaponry is basically the same as was used and worn from the days of the early Caliphs. The Arabian cavalry is dressed in long coats of mail and the helmets are made of iron. The weapons carried are lances, broad-swords, and battle axes with sundry shaped shields as the chief defence. The swords are certainly straight and double-edged with a fuller in the centre of the blade. The blades have cross-hilts and curved cuillons and are similar in shape to medieval Western weapons.

The contest between Arabian and Ethiopian.

Second only to the decay of the Ma'rib dam as the supremely traumatic event in Arabian history is the long period of Abyssinian domination culminating in the alleged attack on Mecca by the army of Abraha and his elephant. It can be argued that the latter event was of greater significance than the former. It was to feature in some form in popular tales, in verse, in the life of the Prophet and in the late romances where the aftermath of the Abyssinian occupation is presented as a war for Islam and Arabism which is carried into the heart of the African continent.

Shiqq, one of the pre-Islamic soothsayers, alludes to the Abyssinian invasions of the sixth century A.D. (8):

> By the men of the plains I swear
> The blacks on your land shall bear
> Pluck your little ones from your care
> Ruling from Abyan to Najrān, everywhere.

The memory of these disasters left such a mark on the Arab imagination that the Ethiopians were commonly equated with the supreme enemies of Islam in Africa, despite the welcome and shelter given to Muhammad's early followers by the Negus. A distinction was drawn between Abraha, the enemy of God's house, and Aṣḥuma/Aṣkhuma the Negus who was granted the reward of Paradise because of the assistance he had given to Islam in its infancy.

Hence combats between warriors, black and white, were to symbolize either ideological and religious conflict or ethnic and religious accord. This depended whether the motive of the story had a relationship with Abraha and the liberation of the Yemen, or with the Negus and the many cultural and commercial links between the Arabs and the Ethiopians. The conflict in age and circumstance demanded some kind of resolution.

Two epics in particular were to explore and exploit this dilemma in their content, the *Sīrat 'Antara* which is the object of my study and the *Sīrat Sayf ibn Dhī Yazan* which is likely to have been the earlier of the two to be elaborated. As will be shown there is some inter-relationship between these two romances. Something will also be said about other epics which are about the Yemen. They are alluded to in the *Sīrat 'Antara.*

The 'saga' of Sayf ibn Dhī Yazan and the triumph of the Himyarites.

The date when the *Sīrat 'Antara* was finally composed into a comprehensive and structured romance is a matter which can be argued from the internal evidence of its text. The sundry exploits of Sayf ibn Dhī Yazan in the form of a romance are better documented. Sayf appears in many Arab histories. A 'romance' version seems to have existed in the tenth century A.D. Ibn al-Nadīm, who died in Baghdad in 988 A.D., in his 'catalogue and index' (*Fihrist*) of Arabic literature does not mention Antar at all, although he lists a large number of popular tales, particularly those which involve pairs of lovers. Some of these were poets, some human and some *jinn.* Antar and 'Abla are nowhere to be found among them. Yet Ibn al-Nadīm specifically mentions Sayf ibn Dhī Yazan. He includes a work by Hishām al-Kalbī (d. 821 A.D.) called *Kitāb al-Yaman wa 'Amr Sayf* (9). It seems reasonable to conclude that the latter is a central figure in the contents of this work.

Al-Ṭabarī who lived in the same century as Ibn al-Nadīm devotes two chapters of his chronicle (10) to the story of the exploits of the family of Dhū Yazan, more particularly Sayf or Ma'dī Karib. The latter delivered the Yemen from the Ethiopian Masrūq with the aid of an army of Persian archers and vagabonds from the court of Chosroes Anushirwān. The chief of the archers was Wahriz, the devoted ally of Sayf, who, although half-blind, aimed his mighty bow at the head of Masrūq, the half-brother of Sayf and king of the Ethiopians. Sayf ruled supreme in Ghumdān palace in Ṣan'ā' served by Abyssinian slaves and lancers. His sway extended deep into Arabia. He gave gifts to 'Abd al-Muṭṭalib, the grandfather of the Prophet Muhammad, and to the princes of the Quraysh who came from Mecca to congratulate him on his success. Sayf kept a loyal bodyguard of Abyssinian descendants of his former enemies, but one day, while he was hunting, they treacherously murdered him.

The exciting story of Sayf's liberation of his people and his complex relationship with the Abyssinians who were both kinsmen and foemen was perhaps the foremost 'epic' of the Islamic East in the tenth century, although it is now thought that its inspiration was Persian rather than Arab and it more properly belongs to Persian literature.

This first written 'epic' of Sayf seems to be earlier than the Antar Romance. The post-Mamluk written version of Sayf's adventures, however, is later than the *Sīrat 'Antara* (11). The existing recension of the adventures of Sayf owes some of its ideas to the Antar Romance which had been finalized by the fifteenth century. Several of the names of characters who appear in the post-Mamluk Sayf have been borrowed from the Antar Romance or from an unknown source which was common to them both.

Professor Henri Péres summarizes the finalized romance of Sayf ibn Dhī Yazan as follows (12):

'The hero is a prince of the Yemen, son of a slave mother who leaves him in the desert when he has just been born. A gazelle cares for him, feeds him and rears him. When he is a man he recruits an army and achieves fame by his adventures and extraordinary exploits. The basis is historical; it is linked to the expulsion of the Abyssinians from southern Arabia where they had ruled since Dhū Nuwās. Tradition tells that Sayf ibn Dhī Yazan went to seek aid at the Byzantine court, then from the Persian king Chosroes. Thanks to the assistance of the latter, Sayf drives out the Abyssinians, and he is proclaimed king by the Persians. The victory over the Abyssinians must have taken place about 570 A.D., the approximate year of the birth of the Prophet Muhammad.

Here is the history. The legend has embellished these facts and has sought to make Sayf ibn Dhi Yazan the champion of the Muslim Arabs of the Yemen against the pagan Abyssinian negroes. One perceives the anachronism. During the course of his numerous journeys in the land of men and *jinn* he propagates the religion of Islam by force of arms, often aided by the *jinn* who are submissive to him. As Muhammad had not preached the new religion his name is replaced in the confession of the faith by that of Abraham (Ibrāhīm), the Friend of God (Khalīl Allāh). Profane history overloaded by facts outside the subject occupy an enormous part. There is talk of the foundation of towns, of localities and well-known edifices; of the arrival of the Nile in Egypt, one is told of journeys and adventures in which Sayf participates, his sons, his giants, his *jinn,* and naturally the love stories in which Sayf is the hero. Furthermore magic and enchantments occupy a large part; there is often the involvement of those skilled in geomancy, of dangerous magicians who constitute the greatest obstacle to the propagation of Islam and of whose powers there is no question although inferior to that of Muslim thaumaturges. The belief in *jinn* is likewise extraordinarily developed, grouped in terrible and formidable squadrons, they fight for or against Islam.

As a whole, the impression persists that the *Sīra* or romance of Sayf ibn Dhī Yazan is a work which has sprung forth from the heart of the people, composed by it and for it; the juxtaposition of tendencies which are pure Islam and of true paganism which cannot be squared with Muslim principles appears to be the clearest proof of it; on the other hand, the place which superstitious beliefs and marvels occupy seem surely to indicate that the basic elements have been borrowed on African soil, more especially in Egypt. The Romance of Sayf ibn Dhī Yazan reflects a very faithful image of the popular Muslim soul of the lower valley of the Nile at the close of the Middle Ages and so constitutes a partial but valuable source for Islamic history in its widest sense.'

The final recension of the *Sīra* of Sayf ibn Dhī Yazan is certainly late. Professor Smith (13) argues that since much of the plot concentrates on Sayf's relations with the Ethiopian king Sayfa Ar'ad who lived in the fourteenth century A.D. it would seem unlikely that the definitive romance would have been written in the life-time of this king. It is more likely to have been composed when the Ottoman authorities were in direct conflict with the rulers of Ethiopia. However, we shall see that lineal descent from Sayf was of some consequence in Africa at least as early as the thirteenth century A.D. It is reasonable to assume therefore that elaborated versions of the short and early 'epic' to be found in al-Ṭabarī, Sayfite fragments in the *Sīra* of the Prophet by Ibn Isḥāq (d. 768 A.D.) and Ibn Hishām (d. 833 A.D.) and in the *Kitāb al-Tījān* by Wahb ibn Munabbih (d. 732 A.D.) must have been current or in the process of expansion at the time when the sister romance of Antar evolved from oral tales into a final textual form. Despite its ethnic conflict, there are in the definitive *Sīrat Sayf* several references to marital alliances with African princesses. There are three Sayfs in the plot; one of them, Sayf ibn Asad, has a lineage beyond Ḥimyar to Kūsh ibn Ḥām, the African brother of Shem.

As in the *Sīrat 'Antara* an important theme is the common ancestry of the warring Arabians and the Ethiopians. Their unity is lost in the remote past. This past is brought to light as the hero's battles with his enemies are described. The contest between black and white, human and *jinn* is transcended and explained. Contradiction is resolved as each sees the other reflected in some aspect of the personality of the hero of the 'epic'.

Before leaving the ancient Yemen mention may be made of two personalities who, although they do not figure prominently in the *Sīrat 'Antara,* seem to have strayed into its plot from that particular quarter of Arabia. The first of these is a pre-Islamic warrior called King Riyāsh. He captured the mother of Antar in the Sudan and brought her to Arabia. The second character is named Wajh al-Ghūl, 'the ogre's face'. He is an ally of the Ethiopians of the Yemen and he meets his death at the hands of Antar during one of the combats which fill the narrative. It is likely that Wajh al-Ghūl has become confused with Ra's al-Ghūl, a pagan king of the Yemen who was slain by 'Alī, son-in-law of the Prophet, in late medieval legendary tales.

King Riyāsh is a variant of the pre-Islamic king of the Himyarite Yemen called al-Ḥārith al-Rā'ishī. Arabic literature has several references to this character. Al-Ma'arrī in his *Epistles* (14) alludes to him. He probably derived his information from Ibn Qutayba (d. 889 A.D.):

'Now the chroniclers mention no king of the sons of Ḥimyar until fifteen generations had passed, who wasted whole ages over their sovereignty, without making forays into other people's territory, living and dying. Until at last there arose al-Ḥarith called al-Rā'ish, who made raids upon the surrounding enemies, and clad himself in an honourable robe of fine deeds. He was called al-Rā'ish (the featherer) because he took captive whole families, and made much booty. Whereby he 'feathered' the inhabitants of Yemen, this being in his early time; then one of God's messengers summoned him, and his kingdom became like a deceptive mirage. Then in the time of al-Rā'ish perished Lokmān, he of the vultures, after drinking the last dregs of life; for indeed God has chosen for Himself perpetuity, and has decreed that there shall be no escape.'

Nashwān ibn Sa'īd al-Ḥimyarī (15) quotes one of this king's alleged verses. He gives al-Ḥārith the title of Najāshī or Negus as though he were an ancient Abyssinian king. Al-Khazrajī, in his history of the Rasūlid dynasty of the Yemen (16), alludes to Ḥārith as a warrior king, a poet and a soothsayer. He is portrayed as an enemy of the sons of Ḥām. He is a foreteller of the coming of the Prophet, the Tihāmite, whose age would succeed that of the Abyssinian domination of the Yemen. From these few references it is clear that Harith or King Riyāsh was a hero of some repute in early Yemenite romance, and that his name was known to Muslim historians in general.

Heroes of the Banū Hilāl and the meteoroidal well of life and death.

The *Sīrat Banī Hilāl* is another major Arabian 'epic' of the later Middle Ages. At first sight it would seem to differ markedly from the romances of

Antar and Sayf. All three are rooted in pre-Islamic society and in the tales of the 'wars of the Arabs' (*Ayyām al-'Arab*), but the exploits of the Banū Hilāl seem to have little relation to any central conflict between Arab and Ethiopian, or the reconciliation of this conflict in the person of the principal hero.

Closer acquaintance discloses similarities which are not at first apparent. The *Taghrība* or *Raḥīl* of the Banū Hilāl is about Africa. It is centred in Tunisia and Algeria, and much of its plot is built upon a conflict between Arab and Hamitic Berber, their intermarriage and similarity of social customs. The earliest events in the epic of the Banū Hilāl are in pre-Islamic Arabia. In Arabia the oral traditions of the bedouin in the Hilālī homelands offer parallels to the exploits of Antar and Sayf. The Hilālī heroes Abū Zayd and Dhiyāb ibn Ghānim perform feats similar to those of the hero of 'Abs and the hero of Qaḥṭān.

In a study of correlation and mutual borrowing the very late and embellished versions of the Hilālī saga may be excluded. These late versions draw upon shared exotic material so that the Hilālī heroes are confused with Yemenite kings. They seek for the 'treasure of the Tubba's' and engage in exploits of a similar nature. Such feats are decadent elaboration, added at a time when the *Siyar* of Antar and Sayf, the tales of the Mamluk Sultan Baybars, the heroes of *Pseudo-Maghāzī* literature and the exploits of the Imām 'Alī against Rās al-Ghūl were already in circulation. The earliest tales are often to be found in oral traditions.

The latter are to be found all over the Arabian peninsula and in parts of North Africa. Among the Ruwāla bedouin the tales of Antar have been superceded, if they were ever widely known. According to Musil the popular hero and heroine are Abū Zayd al-Hilālī and 'Alja 'who used to dwell in manors high'. It is the Hilālīs who are supposed to have owned the ruined towns, to have lived in manors or raised palaces, the crumbling walls of which rise high above the horizon on the borders of the desert. Musil remarks that 'Abū Zayd is the hero of the Antar tales' (17). Such tales are not only found in the north by also in the south. Some of the tales of the Arabic and Mahri-speaking groups bordering the 'Empty Quarter' of Arabia have been collected by Bertram Thomas and H. St. John Philby. Their stories were particularly centred in the Wadi Markha and Wadi Jardan.

The 'castle' of Abū Zayd al-Hilālī is identified with the Maihar sandstone peak. His castle matches the mansion of Dhū Yazan in the Yemenites' 'epics'. Philby copied several drawings on the adjacent rocks, and it seems clear that 'Abū Zayd' was regarded as a supreme progenitor, and that his Herculean deeds were centred around 'a battle royal between human beings and large snakes'. This battle is retained in the most elaborated versions of the Hilālī romances.

It was to be the prelude to the foundation of states by the progenitor and the triumph of the Banū Hilāl. In this achievement Abū Zayd was to be paired by his half-brother Dhiyāb, for he, Abū Zayd, more correctly Barakāt 'the black', had married Buthayna, the sister of Dhiyāb ibn Ghānim.

As in the romances of Antar and Sayf, the youthful Abū Zayd was estranged from his true father. He was brought up by Amīr Fāḍil Zahlānī who had adopted him when he offered shelter and protection to his mother. Abū Zayd grew up to be a hero, and in a combat he rediscovered his father Amīr Rizq in the land of Sharbat, the name of which recalls al-Sharabba, the home-lands of 'Abs and their rocky citadel which figures prominently in Antar's exploits.

Some Tunisian stories introduce the Sharif of Mecca, who is a figure of importance in Hilālī tales from the days of Ibn Khaldūn, the fourteenth century historian (18), as a distant ancestor in the Hilālī succession. The Sharif sought the aid of the Hilālīs against the people of Damascus and Amīr Rizq was sent with thirty knights of the Banū Ghānim. As a reward for his exploits the Sharif married his daughter, Amīra Khaḍrā, to Amīr Rizq. The couple was blessed with a daughter called Shīḥa but after her birth his wife became barren. In her despair she gave a bowl of couscous to the birds, and she beseeched the Almighty to favour her with a son. The first bird which alighted upon the bowl was a black crow (*ghurāb*). This bird is symbolic of the black slave who becomes a warrior in all Arabian tales. She asked for a son with the qualities of this bird and who 'when he stabs with the sword will cause much blood to flow'. God favoured her with a son, a son as black as night, but endowed with the nature of a white or 'free-man'. When the birth was reported to Amīr Rizq he banished the Sharif's daughter, accompanied only by her slaves and her kinsfolk. There are marked similarities between the stories of the birth of the 'two crows', Abū Zayd and Antar.

Among the Hilālīs, as in all the Arabian tribal epics, the hero is a member of a band of courageous kinsmen. There was much debate as to who was the mightiest; Zaydān the supreme thruster with the spear, Dhiyāb the steadfast maintainer of the ranks in battle, or Abū Zayd (Barakāt) who 'like the hawk of Ethiopia hovering above the bustard' found adventure in the desert, trod the wastelands and destroyed the tribal camps 'with only the owl to tell their tale'. The roles of this trio were interchangeable as is clear from one of the Hilālī tales collected by Bertram Thomas (19). Noteworthy is the feature of the castle, or raised palace, and a great well, Bīr Jawfa (Asma') in Wadi Markha. The palace or manor high and the well of life and death are central to Hilālī tales.

Dhiyāb, although noble in birth, had the features of a black slave. One day he found himself in captivity with Bū Zayd and Barayga. His captors deemed him a useless simpleton in their task of building the fortress of Zanayti (Zanāti in the North African context). He was told to look after the herds of cows (the cattle on the Maihar engravings?) but he neglected them. He was entrusted with the care of asses and the collection of firewood. He cut two sticks and sharpened them. He thrust them through the backs of a pair of donkeys to provide a frame to carry his firewood. His masters were pleased with the load but angry at the subsequent death of their asses. Deeming Dhiyāb to be an imbecile they told him to watch the captured camels of the Banū Hilāl. They grew fatter, and Dhiyāb won the favour of his masters. Each time he watered the camels he selected a more distant water-hole. He acted without arousing the suspicion of his masters. Then one day he made good his escape, and he returned to the camp of the Banū Hilāl with the camels.

The Banū Hilāl planned to rescue Bū Zayd and Burayqa. The tribe came to a pool into which flowed three valleys. The Banū Hilāl decided to leave their women and sixty horsemen to protect them, while the rest of their warriors continued to march to the fortress of Zanayti. On the following day they changed their plans, and they left Dhiyāb as the sole guardian. He promised to protect their women and animals with his life.

That night Dhiyāb discovered that one of the *jinn* had speared the best of his camels and had carried it away. The act was repeated on the following night. The camp was filled with fear on the third night. Only the wife of Dhiyāb had seen the *jinnī* but she was too full of fear to tell him. However, when threatened by Dhiyāb she informed him about the appearance and nature of the *jinnī*.

Dhiyāb pursued the latter to a well which had been hollowed by a meteorite or a falling star. Its mouth was strewn with camel-bones. Dhiyāb was mounted on his horse, and he faced the *jinnī* at the well 'for its body was as much outside the well as within it'. Dhiyāb cut the *jinnī* in half with his mighty sword. One half stood within the well and the other lay fallen without. The upper half of the *jinnī* challenged Dhiyāb to strike a second blow, but Dhiyāb did not fall into the trap, since he knew that whereas one blow will kill a *jinnī*, two blows will surely bring two *jinns* to life.

There is considerable variation in this episode. Some versions make Abū Zayd the hero. Having killed the *jinnī*, the serpent or the dragon, he inherits a kingdom. Certain other accounts involve a combined plan by three of the Hilālī heroes to slaughter the monster. A contest to leap highest against a castle wall in order to touch the monster's severed head was a subsequent test to determine the winner. Abū Zayd was seen to be champion who had truely slain the monster serpent – *jinnī*. By reason of his coup de grâce he merited the reward.

In all the accounts remoteness in the context of wells suggests safety and escape while proximity to, or entry into a single well implies danger, death and the curse of the supernatural. Another such well is to be found in Tunisian stories (20). Abū Zayd and Yaḥyā, his nephew, escape from captivity in Tunis but when they reach the well of Naqwa, Yaḥyā is bitten at the bottom of the well which he enters to fetch water for his uncle and their camels. He dies in accordance with fate, for Mar'ī, seer of the Banū Hilāl, had foretold, 'As for Yaḥyā he will die in the well of Naqwa where a hungry serpent has lain in wait for him for seven whole years.'

A number of episodes revolve around the wells of Bīr Jawfa, or Naqwa or others in the wanderings of the Banū Hilāl. Linked to this well is the recurrent entry or exit from a fortress. The latter is either in Arabia, or, in Maghribi stories, the city of Tunis, the capital of King Khalīfa al-Zanāti, who symbolizes bedouin Berber heroism, or of al-'Allam who typifies sedentary or nomad Berber tenacity. Among the Banū Hilāl, the fortress of Zanayti in Arabia and the palace of al-'Azīza Ṣafīra in the heart of the city of Tunis are symbolic of a raised palace around which, or within which, are fought battles which involve the principal characters in the Hilālī epic. Tunis and its surroundings are a centre of fertility, like Ma'rib and Ghumdān in the south of Arabia, while the conflict between Arabian and Abyssinian is transformed into a struggle between Arabian and Berber Amazighen of Tozeur.

Among the bedouin of the 'Empty Quarter', al-'Allam seems to pair 'Alan the slave of Rīsha (21), 'the slave of Zanayti'. He was an enemy of the Hilālīs who could only be challenged by Abū Zayd or Dhiyāb. The former had sworn an oath which debarred him from combat with 'Alan, while the latter had already lost sons and relatives in combats with this slave champion of Zanayti. 'Alan 'was mounted on a horse the like of which was never seen before nor since'. His strategem was to unseat his adversary by means of a long chain that had a hook attached. He launched it skilfully to catch in the chain-armour of his opponent, whom 'Alan would drag from the saddle and slay.

Only Dhiyāb could face this 'slave of the chain'. Dhiyāb took three garments and boiled them so that they were reduced to pulp, and he donned these instead of chain-mail. Then he filled the ears of his mare with mud so that it should not hear the terrible neigh of 'Alan's horse. The field of combat lay before the fort of Zanayti and was fronted by a deep moat which 'Alan, after he had slaughtered his foe, had to jump over in order to enter the fortress.

The two warriors charged, and 'Alan's horse neighed. Dhiyāb turned his mare back upon the Banū Hilāl and retreated to draw his enemy from the fortress. 'Alan pursued Dhiyāb and hurled his chain and hook. It caught in the outer mantle but did not unseat him and only tore a piece of his outer garment. 'Alan tried again and tore Dhiyāb's second garment, then a third time but with no better success. 'Alan retired pursued by Dhiyāb. The latter's horse, deaf to the neigh of 'Alan's steed, leapt the moat immediately, and so Dhiyāb and 'Alan met face to face at the entrance to the fortress of Zanayti.

'Alan was covered in a suit of chain-armour, so that only his eyes were visible. He turned his head to see where Dhiyāb might be. The latter launched his spear. It penetrated 'Alan's eye, passed through his head and buried itself to a half of its length in the wall of the fortress. 'Alan, as he lay dying, asked his slayer to disclose his name. When Dhiyāb told him, 'Alan knew that a prophecy regarding his death had been fulfilled.

A post-medieval example, which shows how prototype heroes such as Abū Zayd and Antar are fused is to be found in the oral traditions which are told in the Sahara about the Awlād Dulaym. The latter are Banū Ma'qil, who claim a Yemenite origin, and they are brethren of the Banū Maghfar ibn Uday ibn Ma'qil through Dulaym ibn Uday ibn Ma'qil. However, the social standing of the Banū Dulaym is deemed to be different, even inferior, to their brethren among the Banū Uday. The reason for this is that the mother of the Banū Uday was a noble woman of the Banū Hilāl, whereas the mother of the Banū Dulaym was a dark skinned, shortish woman, called Dulayma who was a servant of Uday, the common eponym of all these tribes.

Uday married Dulayma in secret, and she gave birth to a son who was unbecoming in his features like his mother. Popular gossip reported that 'Dulayma has given birth to Dulaym.' He grew into manhood and was disowned by his father, Uday, who was afraid of the jealousy of his Hilālī wife. Dulaym was a courageous and famous young warrior.

One day the whole tribe departed but their Hilālī mother remained behind with her sons. Dulaym was with them. When she was adjusting her palenquin an enemy attacked them. Her sons and guards forsook her, all save Dulaym who delivered her from captivity. His act of gallantry earned him the acknowledgement of paternity by his father, Uday.

This account has all the hallmarks of the birth of the hero as seen in the legends of the Arabian peninsula, and it comes as no surprise that Orientalists – René Basset among them – believed that a direct borrowing from the *Sīrat 'Antara* was the source of this tradition which had presumably come into existence because this particular branch of the Maʻqil appears to have been set apart from the rest on account of its origins.

However, if the story is closely analysed it can be seen that the folktales of the birth of Abū Zayd al-Hilālī, or of ʻAntara al-ʻAbsī, or of several other heroes of ancient Arabia could equally have inspired such a story. Structurally, its theme must reflect a very common state of affairs in bedouin societies, and its apparent universality explains the facility of interchange between the galaxy of heroes of Arabian romance when these biographies and exploits were expanded by the popular romancers.

All the heroes discussed, Sayf ibn Dhī Yazan, Antar ibn Shaddād, Abū Zayd or Dhiyāb of the Banū Hilāl, and Sayf al-Tījān seem to pursue a career of adventure which offers a number of similar exploits. Part of this career has a pre-Islamic character, while the *dénouement,* as found in the definitive recensions of these romances, has a chronological association with the conquests of Islam. This radically alters the primitive dimensions of the romance. All these collections of early tales have evolved over a long period of time, spanning the Jāhilīya and the wars of Islam, with details added as late as the period of the Crusades and even later.

Similarities and contrasts between *'Owners of mansions high':*			
Hilālī heroes	*Antar*	*Sayf ibn Dhī Yazan*	*Sayf al-Tījān*
(Abū Zayd/Dhiyāb	(Abū'l-Fawāris)	(Maʻdī Karib)	(al-Hadhād?)
Hero of Banū Hilāl offspring of Arab prince and daughter of Sharif	Hero of Banū ʻAbs offspring of Arab prince and relative of Negus	Himyarite hero offspring of Yemen-ite king and mother compelled to marry Abraha of Ethiopia	Himyarite hero offspring of Yemenite king and of princess 'thunderbolt of wars'
Black son of giant strength	Black son of giant strength	Believes the Ethio-pian Abraha to be his father	Son will be a sun whose rays burn black
Disowned by father, befriended	Disowned by father, shares life with brother, runs with gazelles	Tended by gazelles Seeks the aid of Chosroes of Persia.	Tended by gazelle and reared by foster father.

Woo in the manner of famous lovers, e.g. Jamīl-Buthayna and Qays-Lubnā			
Abū Zayd- 'Alja Dhiyāb-Jāziya	Antar- 'Abla (marries others)	Sayf-Shāma (marries others)	Sayf-Fāḍiḥat al-Jamāl (marries others)
Giant sword Shahbān, horse Shahbā.	Magic sword Ḍāmī Horse al-Abjar (big belly)	Sayf = sword	Sayf = sword
Conquers Maghrib and defeats the Berbers	Master of the world and defeats the Negus	Frees the Yemen from the Negus and wars in Ethiopia	Founds states and spreads Islam to east and west
a)Dies at the hand of Dhiyāb from hidden pin of iron or mace b)Dies from the front by an iron weapon	a)Dies of old age in dust storm b)Dies shot by an arrow of hidden shooter.	Dies of old age Abyssinian slaves stab him to death	Dies of old age

The magic sword, the well of death, the well of receding water and the inverted palace.

Having highlighted certain predictable recurrences to be found in major Arabian romances, it remains to suggest a link between raised or inverted palaces, wells of death or illusion, and the plots of these romances. Is it possible to find common sources or prototypes which explain a hidden unity? What are the symbolic objects which are shared by all these tales? Destiny – pre-Islamic *dahr,* or a decree of Allah – is too vague a theme to link them together.

Arab romancers are prone to unite and concentrate diffuse forces of fate. They depict an irresistible magnetism, an ultimate triumph or death, in a magical meteorite (sometimes called the *baht* stone), the presence or absence of which distinguishes objects or localities which are holy, bewitched or impenetrable from those which are safe or neutral. It is only a prophylactic that the power of the meteorite or carbuncle or some other magical force is mastered or defused. In the Old French Epic, the Sultan of Cairo's fleet had vessels which were brightly lit by 'unnumbered lanterns and carbuncles ablaze'.

According to al-Zuhrī, the *baht* loadstone was quarried by Alexander. Borrowings from Syriac or Arabic versions of Pseudo-Callisthenes, the Romance of Alexander, inspired the magic armoury of the medieval Arabian knight. The *baht* loadstone controlled the magneticism of the raised palace and the ebb and flow of water in an adjacent well, lake or sea. Al-Zuhrī also records that Alexander's employment of the power and reflection of an iron mirror destroyed a one-eyed monster in a well near Hamadhān. Where was the mine or source of the *baht* stone? According to al-Zuhrī it was in Africa, somewhere in the region of Ethiopia (22).

'Between the country of Nubia and that of the Zanj are the mountains of Ardakān. In them is the stone from which are made the flasks wherein is collected "the ape's poison" to which we have referred. Between these mountains and the land of Nubia are the idols which were mentioned by al-Mas'ūdī in his *Kitāb al-tanbīh wal-ishrāf* as being the constructions of King al-Jabbār (the tyrant giant).

Al-Mas'ūdī mentioned that in this place are the stones known as the *baht* stones which were brought by Alexander, son of Philippus. They are stones which when a man looks at them he is dumbstruck. He cannot speak, and he is dragged towards them at a great distance. Alexander brought them after he had consulted Aristotle in that matter. It is said that from them he built 'the raised palace' which has been mentioned.'

The hero, in this case the Oriental Alexander, is shown to be the possessor, hence master, of the *baht* stone. With it he built his power-house, the raised palace and its adjacent well of magnetic ebb and flow. In Arabian epic romances the hero will become master of a talisman by some prophylactic. Having mastered it he will be assured of the attainment of his goal. But the hero has other exceptional powers. We have seen that Abū Zayd or Dhiyāb slew the denizen of the well of death because of his supernatural strength. This strength was given by the *jinn* as a favour or a reward, through marriage with a *jinnīya,* or because the physical peculiarities and the humours of the hero were a prophylactic against the evil powers of his opponents.

A recurrent feature is the magic sword made from a meteorite. Here Arabian and Western romance share common ground. In the *Chanson de Roland* the renowned sword of Turpin called Almace (probably derived from the Arabic *al-mās,* the diamond) is an example. Sometimes heroes had more than one sword. The giant Loquifer had Isdose, Recuite and Dolerose, and Sir Ferumbras possessed Bautisme, Plourance and Garbain. Most famous of all swords was Durendal, the sword of Roland which was sheathed in a serpent-skin scabbard.

The sword was studded with diamonds, rubies and other precious stones. It was said to have been made by Munificans, one of three brothers who forged nine famous swords which included the swords of Ferumbras.

The principal sword of Antar was as renowned in the East as Durendal of Roland, Cortain of Ogier, and La Tizona and La Colada of the Cid were renowned in the West. Antar's meteoric sword, Ḍāmī, could cut an enemy in twain.

Antar describes his sword, likening it to a star : 'I have a sword whose brilliancy flashes like lightening, and when my hand wields it, it sparkles like the shooting stars.' (Translation by Terrick Hamilton, John Murray, 1820, Vol. IV, p. 145.)

There is a persistent sword theme or motif which runs through the whole of the *Sīrāt 'Antara* as it does in all the cycles of Western *Chansons de geste.* The sword of Antar's son, Ghaḍbān, aided by enchantments, achieved feats of wonder outside the talisman castle of Madīnat 'Umān when the Banū 'Abs were in peril from the evil and magic of Sahm al-Nizāl. Sayf ibn Dhī Yazan has the Arabic word for 'sword' in his name. His family were famous for their collection of weapons and implements of war. Abū Zayd al-Hilālī was also the possessor of a giant magic sword. It was called Shahmān. A blow from it severed two mounted camels and sundred them into four halves (23).

The authors of the French Epic depict the 'gods' of the Saracens as armed with such weapons. Apollin was armed with a club and upon his head was a carbuncle, the radiance of which could be seen for seven leagues in all directions. The gold statue of Muhammad held a sword with which he struck a Christian. The image of Muhammad at Cadiz was filled with a legion of devils; elsewhere, it was mounted upon an elephant, or the portrait of Muhammad was depicted on a shield which had a carbuncle set in the buckle.

Perhaps the two most famous swords known to the Arabs were the sword of the Caliph 'Alī, Dhū'l-Faqār, and the sword of the Yemenite hero knight, 'Amr ibn Ma'dī Karib al-Zubaydī, who appears as the ally of 'Alī in the *Pseudo-Maghāzī* literature, more particularly the tale of Ra's al-Ghūl. His knightly ventures and swordsmanship gave him the title of the most invincible of the Arabs, his sword the cherished possession of the Caliphs. It would not be an exaggeration to suggest that medieval Arabian romance gives the prize of swordsmanship to 'Amr ibn Ma'dī Karib.

‘Amr had extolled his weaponry and skill in verse :

I gathered to meet the chances of Time
a hauberk flowing, a swift strong steed,
Stout and hardy, a grooved blade that cleaves
helmets and coats of mail in twain,
And a straight spear shaft that quivers.
I poise it, aiming it straight and true.

(C. J. Lyall’s translation.)

Nashwān ibn Sa‘īd al-Ḥimyarī has this to say of ‘Amr’s fabulous sword (24), ‘Every knight of the Arabs was called ‘the knight of so and so’ save for ‘Amr who was called ‘the knight of the Arabs’. He captured many knights including ‘Antar of ‘Abs. The sword of ‘Amr was known as al-Ṣamṣāmah. Its cutting edge was sharp and hard. It had been given to him by ‘Alqamah ibn Dhī Qayfān, one of the Himyarite kings. It dated from the age of the ‘Ādites, and it could rend helm and body asunder. One day Sa‘d ibn Abī Waqqāṣ passed by ‘Amr, and the latter gave it to him. The sword was handed down in the Muslim armies until it was purchased by the Abbasid Caliph al-Mahdī. (775-785 A.D.).’ The poets were lavish in their praise of its qualities. But the Caliph ordered that the sword should be tempered with water, and as a result of this treatment it was blunted. Its fame remained. Called Ṣamṣāmah, it became a synonym for the sword of quality (*firind*).

Magic may also be found in other weapons. It may be a point of steel of Dhū Yazan’s store ‘fresh furbished, shining with fiery glow like a beacon’s light’; the beacon suggesting the fire beacons erected by the heroic kings who sought the *baht* stone, the carbuncle stone of Tervegant in *Chansons de geste.* Essential to any epic is that the personality of the hero, who emulates the feats of Alexander, is integrated through his weapon into the major combats at the centre of the climax of the romances, the investment or capture of a city, well, tower, sacred tree, talismanic fetish or power source of the supernatural. The might and stature of the hero expands in relation to the number of foes he slays or the allies he gains on his way to his goal. He absorbs the strength of his slain enemies as he absorbs the strength of his allies. At the same time he absorbs the power of talismanic recepticles, and he makes their power his own.

The theme of the enchanted structure and enchanted key, seal or sword of the hero owes much to two episodes which are told in the Oriental versions of Pseudo-Callisthenes (25). Prayer to the Prophet for aid in the thick of battle is answered by the bestowal of superhuman powers or invincible weapons. In Pseudo-Callisthenes they were given to Alexander by his counsellor Aristotle. The weapons were magic figures, and a talisman, to aid in entering cities, fortified palaces and towers situated on high mountains; 'whensoever thou art before a fort which is difficult for thee, hold up this talisman towards the eastern side of that city or against that fortress, and it shall cause its gates to open before thee, and its people shall obey thy commands.' Such a talisman is used in the *Pseudo-Maghāzī* literature. It is bestowed by Gabriel or the Prophet Muhammad upon the Imām 'Alī and his army of knights. The third talisman located hidden water sources, while the fourth protected against exhaustion and fatigue.

The four amulets were four stones, the first a seal in a ring, the second a prophylactic against rain and cold, the third a deflector of weapons, and the fourth a spiritual shield which preserved Alexander's men from immorality. The hero also had in his possession a secured box of wax figures which represented enemies and which, by sympathetic magic gave him power to neutralize and reverse the evil of his enemies.

Talismans of this kind were legion in the literature of Western *Chansons de geste.* In the romance of Sir Ferumbras, Florepas, the daughter of the Saracen prince Balan possessed a girdle which was a talisman against hunger. As Balan and his men were suffering from hunger he sent a wily thief to steal his daughter's girdle from her chamber. He opened her door with the aid of another talisman which also charmed to sleep the Christian knights who were concealed in her chamber.

Every Arabian hero likewise had in his armoury one or other of such weapons, charms, talismans, rings, swords or access to Prophetic power, even though, by a fiction in the story, the hero's lifetime predated the revelation of the Prophet. Since the latter is a crucial figure in times of crisis it is safe to assume that popular accounts of the wars of the Prophet and his Companions were already in wide circulation before elaborated tales such as Antar and Sayf captured the popular imagination.

The enchanted structure, which figures so frequently in the plots is a variation in some shape, form or mutation of the citadel of adamant, store-house of the loadstone, the *baht* carbuncle or magnetic metal which was combined with brass, iron and lead. The *jinn* who were masters of it were also masters of fire or some process of manufacture associated with metal, usually the fabrication of swords, spears, impenetrable mail or other weaponry (26). These *jinn* are akin to the legendary smiths who fabricated the swords in the Old French epics.

Innumerable are the forms of the romances which disclose the combat between the magic weapon of the hero and the force of the seat of sorcery, blocking his path, hindering but never thwarting him from the attainment of his goal. This allegory is rephrased by the story-teller and frequently reduced to a fantasy prefaced by a mystery in the circumstances of the birth of the hero. As each obstacle is cleared away on the route of his onward march, so an obstacle is removed in the discovery of the mystery of his birth and his true origin and lineage. Hence, the conflict without is also a conflict within. The discovery of the uttermost parts of the earth is at the same time the self-discovery of the hero.

ARABIAN ROMANCE SEGMENT STRUCTURES.*

Sayf	*Antar*	*Abū Zayd*
	Emergence of hero	
NORTH-WEST**		NORTH-EAST
Qayṣar of Byzantium. (subordinate chiefs)		Chosroes of Persia (subordinate chiefs)
	Problem of status in tribe or kingdom	
	Rises to fame with help of kinsmen, *jinn* or helpers.	
	Combats enemies	
	Delay mechanism in	
White versus Black	Romance	Human versus *Jinn.*
	Entry — Entry	
	CENTRAL EDIFICE OR TALISMAN	
	Exit — Exit	
	Resolution.	
SOUTH-WEST		SOUTH-EAST
Negus in Ethiopia (subord-inate chiefs)	*Triumphal return*	Rulers of India (subordinate chiefs)
	Marred by death of relation foreshadowing the hero's death.	

* As distinct from the 'frame story' which characterizes The One Thousand and One Nights and which is discussed in Chapter 2

** Arabic authors vary as to the four or more nations to whom these rulers relate. Al-Jāḥiẓ (d.869 A.D.) lists them as the Arabs, Persians, Indians and Byzantines while the 7th century al-Kalbī affirms these as the Himyarites, the Negus, Chosroe's son and Caesar's son.

Notes

1. See D. T. Niane, *Sundiata: an epic of old Mali,* Longman, 1965 pp. 38, 65.
2. al-Zuhrī, *Kitāb al-Ja'rafiyya,* (ed. by Muhammad Hadj-Sadok), Bulletin d'Etudes Orientales, XXI, (1968), Sections 78, 80, of the Arabic text.
3. *Kitāb al-Tījān,* (Hyderabad, 1367 A.H.), pp. 136 ff.
4. For this and other references in al-Ṭabarī, see *Chronique de Tabari,* tr. by M. H. Zotenburg, 4 vols., Paris 1867-1874. H.A.R. Gibb qualifies this Persian abridgement as giving a very imperfect idea of the Arabic original, but it is adequate for the outline of the tales of the city of adamant (pp. 45-50), the wars of Sayf ibn Dhī Yazan (pp. 203-219) and the birth of Bilqīs (pp. 443-448).
5. *Kitāb al-Tījān, ibid,* pp. 134-137, and *Glaive des Couronnes,* translated by M. le Dr. Perron, Paris, 1862, more particularly pp. 275-307. It is these tales which seem to have a closer resemblance to Svenkovski's *Antar* where the latter rescues a gazelle which is none other than Gul-Nazar, Queen of Palmyra. Antar is offered three rewards; revenge, power and love.
6. Ernest E. Herzefeld, *Archaeological History of Iran,* The Schweich Lectures of the British Academy, 1934, O.U.P., 1935, pp. 78, 79. Persian parallels to the Arabian epics under discussion are to be found on pp. 64-66 of this work.
7. Sir Charles Lyall, *Translations of the Mufaḍḍalīyāt,* Oxford, 1918, pp. 358-359.
8. A. Guillaume, *The Life of Muhammad,* O.U.P., 1955, pp. 5, 6.
9. See Bayard Dodge, *The Fihrist,* Columbia University Press, 1970, p. 208.
10. *op. cit.,* pp. 203-219.
11. Rudi Paret, *Sīrat Saif ibn Dhī Yazan,* Hanover, 1924, pp. 28, 29, 76, 77, 96, 99, 102, 103, 110, 111, *passim.*
12. Henri Péres, "le roman dans la littérature arabe dès origines à la fin du Moyen Age", *Annales de l'Institut d'Etudes Orientales XXI,* 1958, pp. 28-30.
13. In an unpublished paper submitted to the Bornu Seminar of Departments of History, Ahmadu Bello University in December 1972 by Abdullahi Smith, the paper entitled *The Legend of the Sefuwa,* p. 48.
14. See *The Letters of Abū'l- 'Alā'* translated by D. S. Margoliouth, Oxford, 1898, pp. 108-9.
15. Nashwān ibn Sa'īd, *Shamsu'l- 'Ulūm* (Extracts) by Azimuddin Ahmad, E. J. W. Gibb Memorial Series, Vol. XXIV, p. 60.
16. J. W. Redhouse's translation of al-Khazraj's *The Pearl Strings,* Leyden, 1906, Vol.1, pp. 46-48.
17. Alois Musil, *The Manners and Customs of the Rwala Bedouins,* New York, 1928, pp. 12, 13, 291, 292. The Banū Ḥassān of the Mauritanian Hodh claim descent from the Awlād al-Nāṣir, a branch of the Uday ibn Hassān, part Yemenite Ma'qil, part Hilālī with their chief eponym a certain 'Antara who lived in the fifteenth and sixteenth centuries.
18. See *Kitāb al-'Ibar,* Dār al-Kitāb al-Lubnānī, 1959, Part 6, p. 39.
19. Bertram Thomas, *Arabia Felix,* Jonathan Cape, Readers' Union Ltd.), 1938, pp. 208, 211, 213, 219, 220, 277-281. A simple calque for this story of Abū Zayd and his comrades is to be found in the Ḥassānīya (Mauritanian) Arabic story of the man and his seven rings (cf. R. Pierret, *Etude du Dialecte Maure,* Paris, 1948, pp. 230-233). The interest of this version is that the bare plot of the Hilālī story is preserved, more particularly the encounter with a multi-headed serpent, the rescue of a princess and a test to find the deserving suitor; yet no mention is made of the hero's name. He is

simply called 'the father, or possessor, of seven rings'. At no point is there the least hint that a parallel with the Hilālī story exists. I find it far harder to accept a Moorish bedouin tale derived from the *Hilālīya,* yet shorn of its well known hero, than to accept its alternative, namely, that in this calque may be seen a variant of a very archaic bedouin story which at a later date formed the ground of the elaborated *Hilālīya.*

20. 'Abd al-Raḥmān Guiga, *Min aqāṣīṣ Banī Hilāl.* Stories from the romance of the Banu Hilal in Tunisian dialect and Classical Arabic; introduced by al-Ṭāhir Guiga, Tunis, 1968. See in particular pp. 120-131. This same well is identified with Kusugu well in Daura in Hausaland. Bayajida / Abuyazidu is simply Abū Zayd who is the progenitor of the Emirates of Northern Nigeria. The well now has a bronze plaque which reads, 'This is the well at which, according to ancient legend, Bayajida, son of the King of Baghdad, slew the fetish snake known as Sarki and afterwards married the reigning Queen of Daura.'

21. Bertram Thomas, *ibid,* pp. 290-292. The battle which follows seems to be part fancy, part factual description of types of weaponry and armour which were known in the medieval period. The survival of such details in a remote part of the 'Empty Quarter' is interesting. Mail which all but covers the body and face can be seen on armed figures on the west front of Wells Cathedral. It can also be seen in a photo of chain-mail which survived among Khevsul tribesmen in Georgia in the Caucasus. See W. E. D. Allen, *A History of the Georgian People,* London, 1932, plate facing page 203. In the *tārīkh-i-Hind wa Sind* which describes the Arab conquest of Sind the Arab horseman were 'so covered with coats of mail that they appeared to be as it were, drowned in iron'. Crescent-shaped face-mail in Medieval Spain is to be seen in Ada Bruhn De Hoffmeyer, *Arms and Armour in Spain,* Instituto de Estudios Sobre Armas Antiguas, Madrid, 1972, figs. 88 and 110, pp. 133 and 177.

22. al-Zuhrī, *op. cit.,* sections 137, 322 and 323 of the Arabic text.

23. Bertram Thomas, *ibid,* p. 213.

24. *Shamsu'l- 'Ulūm, op. cit.,* pp. 62, 63, 91.

25. See E. A. Wallis Budge, *The History of Alexander the Great,* London, 1896, pp. 389-391 and 458-464.

26. This principally 'cosmological' or thaumaturgic view of the nature of weapons and weaponry and their metallurgy - typical of the Fatimid, Ayyubid and Mamluk ages - cannot be disassociated from the ancient scientific or pseudo-scientific theories which were believed and practised at the same time.

In the treaty on arms and armaments composed by the Alexandrian Armenian, Murḍā ibn 'Alī ibn Murḍā al-Ṭarsūsī, for Saladin the author maintains that the qualities of swords were associated with the source of their metallic substance and with the curious methods of their manufacture.

The basic substances of the metals came from mines of varied quality and purity. These mines were in the Maghrib, Spain, Byzantine Asia, India and China. The metal of the first two of these localities was among the most inferior. Steel (*fūlādh*) of varied type was the best. One type was so cast, tempered and manufactured as to 'magnetize' the iron substance, while other methods were aimed at fragmenting and eliminating foreign particles. The true *fūlādh* at the moment of its manufacture was treated with drugs to increase the dryness and to purify it of all base matter. Detailed instructions are provided as to these methods of fabrication and the drugs used at the moment of tempering the steel. All this would determine the cutting sharpness of the finished weapon dependent upon the iron, whether it be *narm-āhān* (soft iron), *shāburqān* (hard iron) or *slimānī.*

See Claude Cahen 'Un traité d'Armurie composé pour Saladin, *Bulletin d'Etudes Orientales,* tome XI, 1945-1946, pp. 106-108, Arabic text; pp. 127-129, French translation.

For an examination of the manufacture of the Arabian sword, reference is drawn to De Hammer Pugstall's article 'Sur les lames des Orientaux', *Journal Asiatique,* t. iii, January 1854, pp. 66-93. In the treatise of Ya'qūb ibn Isḥāq al-Kindī (circa 801-

870 A.D.) there is a wide examination of the varied manufacture of blades and their terminology. Some relate to swords made from two types of iron found in mines (*shāburqāni / sayraqāni,* and *narm-āhaniya / birmāhiniya*) from which is composed a third, *al-murakkab.* Steel (*al-fūlādh*) is differently classed and subdivided, and among the most famous swords were those of the Yemen, forged from the steel of Ceylon or Transozania. Other blades were made in Egypt, Khurasan, Basra, Kufa (the blade called *al-biḍ*) and Damascus. Yemenite swords were broad with a decorated handle in the form of a horseshoe and double-serpent, and among the most famous type of all as the grooved *al-Ṣamṣām* blade. Frankish swords were broad at the base and narrower towards the tip 'in the manner of the ancient blades of the Yemen'. The sword, al-Ṣamṣāmah, of 'Amr ibn Ma'dī Karib (see page 33) can be identified in these types, and it seems clear that a prolonged investigation of sword typology and Arabian hero might shed considerable light on the original provenance of some of these tales.

It is not impossible that certain schools which manufactured types of swords and other military equipment had some say in the stories which told of the adventures of the knights who used them, hence heroes with the name of Sayf may ultimately relate to a special kind of blade. It seems doubtful, however, whether surviving documentation enables this to be proved, since the subject is overlaid with fable and magic. A very full text of al-Kindī's manual, *Al-Suyūf wa ajnāsuhā* has been edited by A. Rahman Zaky in the *Bulletin of the Faculty of Arts,* University of Cairo, Vol. 14, part II, Dec. 1952, pp. 1-36, (Arabic text).

The occult side of the Arabian hero's personality, his sword and his amazing horse are to be observed in the inter-relation between medieval star names, swords and a mighty hero (*jabbār*) who is one of two brothers and one of three royal children. *Jabbār* and *Sayf* (sword) are found combined in the name Algarsayf which is associated with the group of stars (*al-sayf*) in the constellation of Orion (*al-jabbār*). The association of these ideas with the writings of Chaucer, particularly in 'The Squire's Tale', is fully discussed in Dorothee Metlitzki's, *The Matter of Araby in Medieval England,* Yale, 1977, pp. 78-88.

COMMENTARY

Plate 2: Antar in armour on his steed Abjar, portrayed by the famous modern artist Abū Ṣūbhi Tīnāwī of Damascus.

CHAPTER 1 : THE MANUFACTURE OF THE BLACK KNIGHT

In recent years specialists in Arabic speaking countries have begun to explore their heritage of popular romance. This is particularly true of Egypt and Tunisia. In the latter, Tahar Cheriaa of the Tunisian Ministry of Culture and Information has systematically examined the themes from North African oral tradition. Foremost among these are the romances of the heroes of the Banū Hilāl and the exploits of 'Antara ibn Shaddād (1).

The *Hilālīya* is both oral and written. It is presented as an anonymous work of art. In it are combined free prose passages and passages in rhymed prose and in verse, particularly at climaxes of dramatic tension. Both forms of the *Hilālīya* reveal a parallel pursuit of narrative threads and a cross polination and symbiosis between the literary (*al-khāṣṣa*) and the oral (*al- 'āmma*).

'Oral tradition draws upon classical literature for its themes, references and philosophical and aesthetic values and even models itself on its style, pursuing formal mimetism to the ill-defined limits of a certain naive pedantry where story-telling and song approximate more closely to an intermediary area (of 'low grade' literature or trumped up 'super' folklore) than to the authentic oral tradition stemming from and nourished by the live springs of the true and vigorous popular imagination.' . . . 'The greatest enthusiasts for the epic chronicles of Antarah and the Hilalians are to be found in the North African hinterland, among the villages of the Egyptian Said, the Tunisian interior and the Algerian tablelands, or among the nomads of the Saharan borderlands, that is, the Berber and Moorish nomads of southern Algeria and Morocco. By contrast, the tales of the *Thousand and One Nights* are still more popular in the working-class districts of the big cities and, in particular, the coastal towns.'

With the passing of time the oral tradition has become increasingly dependent on a written text. 'There are probably no story-tellers now living who are capable of rendering from memory any complete version of the great epic chronicles such as the *Antarahya* and the *Hilalya,* or the legendary tales of the *Thousand and One Nights.* This folk art is thus at a more advanced stage on the path to final extinction.'

The Hilali stories still told by the bedouin approximate to 'ballads'. One can conjecture a linking of such 'ballads' into something structural in a grand → 43 those of the Sultan al-Ẓāhir Baybars (3). The *Sīrat Abū Zayd* was of little merit as a 'literary composition'. The verse was unmeasured 'though it is the opinion of some of the learned in Cairo that it was originally conformed to the prescribed measures of poetry.' The *shā'ir,* or reciter, memorized the text and accompanied his recitation with a mono-chord viol. As for the tale of the Sultan Baybars, Lane remarks that 'the work is written in the most vulgar style of modern Egyptian Arabic; but as it was intended for the vulgar, it is likely that copyists may have altered and modernized the language, which was evidently never classical in style nor in age.'

The "Anâtireh" were different. They were much less numerous. The reciters read Antar's exploits from the book, they chanted the poetry, but read the prose in the popular manner unaccompanied by the *rabāb.* 'As the poetry in this work is very imperfectly understood by the vulgar, those who listen to it are mostly persons of some education.' These same "Anâtireh" also recited from the *Pseudo-Maghāzī* literature, *Sayf ibn Dhī Yazan* and the *One Thousand and One Nights.* There would seem to be a link between these works which set them aside from other recited tales.

Lane observes, 'When El-Asma'ee (or, as he is vulgarly called El-Asmo'ee) composed, or compiled, the history of 'Antar, that work (they say) became extremely popular, and created so great an enthusiasm on the subjects of the adventures of Arab warriors, that a diligent search was made for all tales of the same kind; and from these was compiled the Seeret al-Mugáhideen or Delhemeh, by some author now unknown, who, as he could not equal the author of 'Antar in eloquence, determined to surpass him in the length of his narratives; and 'Antar being generally in forty-five volumes, he made his book fifty-five.'

If the texts of Antar are examined they can be approximately dated by stylistic features. The final recensions can be assigned to an epoch not later than 1400 A.D. Some evidence also points to a progressive evolution of the composition of the *Sīrat 'Antara* in courtly circles between 1080 and 1350 A.D. The exploits of Antar are relatively rare among the oral tales of the modern bedouin, whereas Abū Zayd and his comrades dominate their repertoire. There is nothing haphazard in the style, language or content of the *Sīrat 'Antara.* The plot of the romance is clearly laid out, the mind behind it is that of an artist or artists steeped in the literature of the Abbasid age. They were experts in weaponry and in geographical literature and were acquainted with the Persian chroniclers and their epics.

'Antara ibn Shaddād is a fusion of personalities. Those personalities are the product of the bookish rather than the bard. He is in goodly part a manner (2). Accompanied often by a *rabāb* or viol, the bedouin story-teller *(rāwī)* improvises a tale of ruse or amatory adventure. Even so, on the basis of numerous and widely spaced European examples it has been argued by some that a ballad will always remain a ballad, not an epic, however long its segments or fragments. Some Spanish 'romances' are younger than the literary *'cantares de gesta'*. Those ballads which dealt with the destruction of Spain by the Moors and King Roderick's death in 711 A.D. were based on a prose text, the *Crónica Sarracina* of 1430 A.D. This, and certain French epics, show the same characteristic, the evolution of epic ballads from chronicles and like literary source material.

Another feature frequently found is contemporaneous co-existence of ballads and 'oral traditions' and written versions which do not entirely correspond. For example, a page from the Codex Emiliense 39 attests the existence, at or shortly before the date of the *Chanson de Roland* (soon after the First Crusade) of a Roland legend, analogous to, though independent of the *Chanson.*

The acknowledged link which exists between the Byzantine *Digenis Akritas* and an Arabian sister epos to that of Antar, known as *Dhāt al-Himma,* indicates that an oral, as opposed to a written literary tradition each wholly dissimilar, is untenable. In the *Ṣubḥ al-A'shā* of al-Qalqashandī, the author makes it clear that before his lifetime (circa 1412 A.D.) the ardour of the warlike Banū Kilāb in raiding the Byzantines had led to their composition of *Dhū 'l-Himma* (*Dhāt al-Himma*) and *al-Baṭṭāl.* In this epic the Banū Kilāb were the subject of 'remarkable tales and brilliant and heroic deeds'. Some written and formalized work was described, not an improvised or semi-aleatory form of corpus orally transmitted, even less a cycle in the repertoire of 'coffee-house' entertainers. One can assume a good deal of give and take between oral tales and standardized plots based on written texts. Each recension would jettison personalities and replace them by others, as is known from the example of the 'Poem of the Cid' of 1140 A.D. which differed markedly in participant and legendary material by the fourteenth century when it was rearranged. The *Sīrat 'Antara,* like *Dhāt al-Himma,* is without doubt in a category of literary genre which knows no formal separation between the oral and the written. Evidence for textual borrowings is beyond dispute.

There is little that is dialectical, colloquial or distinctly oral in its Arabic style. Concessions to strict grammar rules, and the adoption of a concordance frowned upon by the erudite are certainly found; but these are few in comparison with lexicographical borrowings, the quantity of verse which follows standard rules of Classical Arabic prosody and themes and details which stem directly from geographical texts or masterpieces of Abbasid *adab* or belles-lettres.

E. W. Lane's observations on the "Anâtireh" are significant. For him this class of reciters was distinct from the reciters of the tales of the Banū Hilāl or

THE 'MANUFACTURE' OF 'ANTAR, 'THE FATHER OF KNIGHTS'

Prototypes of 'Adnānī and Yamanī bedouin hero
(Abū Zayd: 'Antara: 'Amr ibn Ma'dī Karib: Khufāf ibn 'Umayr: Rabī'a ibn Muqaddam)

Exploits of 'Antar mentioned in Muslim and Christian dialogues circa 800 A.D.

"Antar Abū'l-Fawāris?"

'Antara ibn Shaddād al-'Absī Abū 'l-Mughallis

9th Century
(1) Ibn al-Kalbī
(2) *al-Aṣma'ī*
(3) *Abū 'Ubayda*
(4) Ibn Qutayba
(5) Ibn al-Sikkīt

10th Century
(6) al-Anbārī
(7) Abu'l-Faraj al-Iṣfahānī (d.967)

'Antara, a 'crow' who gained his freedom and birthright. Composer of Mu'allaqa, married his cousin 'Abla and died in old age.

(A)	(B)	(C)
Shot by arrow of Wizr ibn Jābir of Ṭayy' (1) (3)	in a hot wind (3)	Shot by a scout of Ṭayy' when he fell from horse

(8) Ibn al-Nadīm (d 988) does not refer to a written Antar/'Abla romance.
(9) The Yemenite al-Hamdānī (945) describes 'Antara and 'Abla in battle with Yemenites. His steed is Abjar and he is the hero of 'Abs.
(10) In Spain the verses of 'Antara are popular in courtly circles for their martial spirit.

Fatimid Egypt
(Cosmopolitan court).
Circa 975 - 996
Yūsuf ibn Ismā'īl?
(*First draft of Sīra*?)

11th Century

Recensions of Abu Mu'ayyad ibn al-Mujallī ibn al-Ṣā'igh al-Jazarī al-Antarī (circa 1150) and reports by Samaw'al ibn Yaḥyā al-Maghribī (circa 1160)

12th Century
(Fusion with death (of Rabī'a Ibn Muqaddam?))

Nashwān ibn Sa'īd al-Ḥimyarī (d 1177) opts for (A) as the accepted death for 'Antar.

13th/14th Century
Ḥijāzīya/Shāmīya (Sīrat 'Antara)

Datable by reference to Crusades, military equipment, Mamlūk Dīwans and to Ayyūbid and Mamlūk terms.
Borrowings from 14th century *Pseudo-Maghāzī* literatures.

‘manufactured hero’, and his credentials often appear to fit him better for life in a Camelot or a Córdoba than in the tents of Arabia.

In Byzantium he gazes with simple bedouin eyes at the statue made of him, his horse, his brother and his son, fashioned as a token of esteem by the ruler of the Christian East. He wishes at first to destroy it, but he is finally dissuaded by soft words and dazzling riches. This statue is, in a sense, symbolic of his *Sīra.*

The Dual Antar, ‘Antara and Antar.

Antar is two heroes in one person. How one hero became the other is a story with many missing chapters. Documentary evidence is scanty. A few clues exist to establish a chronological evolution of the ‘text’. The latter is suitable for adaption in recitation. It is a recitative interspersed with poetic ‘arias’. It is a *sui generis* of medieval romance in Arabic literature. A non-Arabist, Mia Gerhardt, has analysed and disclosed this *genre* most convincingly (4).

The early Abbasid ‘Antara ibn Shaddād.

A number of *rāwīs* or reciters appear by name in the *Sīrat ‘Antara.* They include Abū Ḥāzim, Najd ibn Hishām and two famous grammarians of Basra, Abū ‘Ubayda and al-Aṣma‘ī. For some time it was thought the latter (who died 213 A.H. / 830 A.D.) had some say in the elaboration of the *Sīra.* It is plausible that the grammarian al-Aṣma‘ī knew of popular tales about ‘Antara, the poet, tales which at some later stage were incorporated into sections of the *Sīra.* Nabia Abbott is prepared to support his credentials further in so far as the *One Thousand and One Nights* is concerned (5). ‘In view of the Oriental Institute’s manuscript confirming the existence of a “Thousand Nights” in Aṣma‘ī’s own day it does not seem impossible that this famed and prolific scholar made reference to the collection in some of his works still unknown to us.’

The *Sīra* of Antar in fact opens with a didactic quotation of al-Aṣma‘ī, ‘As for the reason for the composition of this remarkable *Sīra* and strange and unique tale, it is because I have observed that the people indulge to excess in the fabrication of spurious narratives and reports. They have become pre-occupied by slander, calumny and defamation; hence I desired to assemble together these true tales and reports and by means of them distract people from evil companionship and association. The blessing and peace be upon the Prophet, the lord of the noble creation.’

We now know that at least one ‘pseudo al-Aṣma‘ī’ existed to whom important books were attributed. Among such books were the *Nihāyat al-’arab fī akhbār al-Furs wal-'Arab* and other collections of history and romance. Al-Aṣma'ī in the ***Sīrat 'Antara*** is not the Basran grammarian at all but a ghostly double. Cedric Dover has argued that the true al-Aṣma'ī might have written the ***Sīra*** for the Caliph al-Ma'mūn, who was a mulatto like Antar himself. But that the true Aṣma'ī had any real say in fashioning the extant and evolved form of the ***Sīra*** is untenable. A glance at the existing text shows much that is alien to the ninth century.

Furthermore the final page of the *Ḥijāzīya* unmasks the late date of its partial composition and the artificial al-Aṣma'ī who allegedly composed it. 'The author said . . . the *Ḥijāzīya* is attributed to Abd al-Malik ibn Qarīb al-Aṣma'ī – may God be pleased with him. Its composition was completed on the blessed Friday at the end of Jumādā II in the year 473 A.D. / 1080 A.D., in the days of the Commander of the Faithful, Hārūn al-Rashīd al-'Abbāsī [*sic*]. Its composition was guided by my wish to hear its discourse, its prose and its verse. I gathered together what papers I possessed about those things which I had heard of the *Sīra* of the famous 'Antara ibn Shaddād. To this I added what I beheld with my eyes, and I neatly arranged the rhymes without any adding or deletion of the same and I chose the choicest of Arabic expressions.

I have related this *Ḥijāzīya Sīra* quoting the firm reports which are on the authority of Ḥamza, Abū Ṭālib, 'Amr ibn Ma'dī Karib al-Zubaydī, Ḥātim Ṭayy', Imru'l-Qays, al-Kindī, Hānī ibn Mas'ūd, Hāzim al-Makkī, 'Ubayda, 'Amr ibn Wadd al-'Āmirī, Durayd ibn al-Ṣimma and 'Āmir ibn al-Ṭufayl.

After Antara's death his deeds and exploits circulated on the tongues of the Arabs. I began to write down that which I saw and heard. I did so on leaves and sheets of paper, whether poems or deeds. Regarding that which I neither saw nor heard, it was the arranging and systematic presentation of the rhymes. God knows best that which is true and it is to Him that we return.'

Grammarians who were contemporaries of al-Aṣma'ī or who lived a little later have information to give on 'Antara whom they knew as a poet. Ibn Qutayba (d. 889 A.D.) quotes the lineage of 'Antara as 'Antara ibn 'Amr ibn Shaddād ibn 'Amr ibn Qurād. Ibn al-Kalbī (d. 821/2 A.D.) reported that Shaddād was 'Antara's grandfather, not his father, and that another tradition maintained that Shaddād was his paternal uncle under whose protection he grew up; when 'Antara became a man his father claimed him as his own son. He was the son of a slave-woman Zabība. He had slave brothers by the same mother. 'Antara's freedom was granted as recompense. When the Banū 'Abs, his tribe, pursued raiders, who had robbed them of their herds, the father of 'Antara offered him liberty if he charged the enemy. At first 'Antara refused, claiming that all a slave could do was to milk camels and bind their udders. Yet he obeyed his father and recovered the spoil. 'Antara was one of the 'three crows' – three slaves of valour. The other two were Khufāf ibn 'Umayr al-Sharīdī of the Banū Sulaym and al-Sulayk ibn 'Amr al-Sa'dī. 'Antara fought in the war of Dāḥis and Ghabrā' (6) which was on account of a race-horse. This war allegedly lasted for forty years. Ibn Qutayba briefly refers to 'Antara's death. The hero was then an old man. He died in a violent desert storm on his way to claim a camel from a man of Ghaṭafān. It is the only version of 'Antara's death mentioned by Ibn Qutayba, who quotes the grammarian Ibn 'Ubayda as his source.

Another portrait is presented by al-Anbārī (d. 916 A.D.) in his commentary to 'Antara's ode. But there is little or nothing to show that the framework of an 'epic' was well known or even in existence. The biographical details of the poet's life are contradictory and sketchy. If tales about 'Antara were well-known, al-Anbārī considered that they formed no part of the background he needed to give his readers about the poet of the ode.

The agnomen (*kunya*) of 'Antara was Abū'l-Mughallis (the traveller in the darkness). He was the son of Mu'āwiya ibn Shaddād ibn Qurād, to quote Ibn al-Sikkīt (d. 858 A.D.) in regard to 'Antara's lineage. Abū Ja'far Aḥmad ibn 'Ubayd, however, reported his lineage as 'Antara (the bluebottle?) ibn Shaddād ibn Mu'āwiya ibn Qurād, one of the Banū Makhzūm ibn 'Awdh ibn Ghālib.

A verse of 'Antara allegedly states:
'Among them was my father Shaddād, noblest father,
while my mother stems from Ḥām.
They are my maternal uncles.'

'Antara's father was from 'Abs. The praise of this tribe opens the *Sīrat 'Antara.* The Banū 'Abs were one of the Jamarat al-'Arab (fire-brands of the Arabs). They were named 'the knights of fate'.

The mother of 'Antara was an 'Ethiopian' woman called Zabība. Nothing is said of her original status before her capture. 'Antara had brothers who were also slaves. He was among the most courageous and the most liberal in giving away his possessions.

Fifty years later than al-Anbārī, in the Book of Songs by Abū'l-Faraj al-Iṣfahānī (d. 967 A.D.) the biography of 'Antara provides a wider coverage of the events of his life and the circumstances of his death. As late as the middle of the tenth century there was still much confusion as to his true lineage. He was nicknamed *al-falḥā'* – the split (lower)-lipped; his mother was Zabība, an

'Ethiopian' woman of unknown origin.

Abū'l-Faraj al-Iṣfahānī delved deep into earlier traditions which amplified the background of the hero of 'Abs. The tale of the raid to recover stolen camels – attributed to Ibn al-Kalbī – is retold, but considerably expanded from other sources. 'Abs had raided Ṭayy' and had captured their herds. When they wished to divide their booty they said to 'Antara, 'We shall not give you a share like our own. You are a slave.' As they were discussing the matter Ṭayy' attacked. 'Antara left them and said, 'Watch out for the enemy they are upon you.' Ṭayy' recovered their camels. 'Antara's father said to him, 'Charge, 'Antara!' He replied, 'Can a slave charge in battle?' His father said, 'Charge and be free. You shall be a slave no longer.' He recognized him as his son. 'Antara was proud of his mixed blood and claimed that it was from his mother that he derived his power to smite with the sword.

'Antara protected 'Abs when they were attacked by Tamīm. His tribe was ruled by Qays ibn Zuhayr, 'Antara's feats displeased him, and when Qays returned from the battle, he exclaimed, 'Only the son of the negress guarded the people.' 'Antara, annoyed, satirized Qays who was renowned for his gluttony; 'Antara could march all night without shelter, food and water.

'Antara's valour was praised by the Prophet. Ibn 'Ā' isha had said that when the verses which referred to the abstemious 'Antara were recited to him the Prophet replied that the only *badawī* he had wanted to meet was 'Antara ibn Shaddād.

'Antara's brothers receive little mention. Ibn al- 'Arabī and Abū 'Ubayda report that 'Antara wanted his people to acknowledge his brothers like himself. He said to the brother he loved the most, Hanbal, who corresponds to Shaybūb in the *Sīra,* 'Give your colt milk to drink, then pass me by at supper-time. When I say to you, "Why is your colt thin and skinny," smite its stomach with the sword as though you are showing them that you are angry at my remark.' Ḥanbal acted as his brother had commanded, and he passed by the company. 'Antara said, 'Oh, Ḥanbal, what ails your colt? It is skinny. Is there milk in its stomach?' His brother smote the belly of his colt with a sword, and the milk was revealed.

According to al-Ḥaytham ibn 'Adiyy, 'Antara was asked, 'Are you the most courageous and doughtiest of Arabs?' 'No,' he replied, 'Then how has it come about that you enjoy this reputation?' He said, 'I advanced boldly when I thought it a sound and resolute decision, and I avoided combat when I deemed it the correct course to take. I enter nowhere unless I see a way of escape from it. I make for the weak and the cowardly and deal him a fearful blow. The courageous loses heart because of this, so then I set upon him next and kill him.'

According to 'Umar ibn Shābbah, the Caliph 'Umar ibn al-Khaṭṭāb said to al-Ḥuṭay'a, 'How did you fight in battle?' He replied, 'We were a thousand resolute knights.' 'How can that be?' 'Qays ibn Zuhayr was among us. He was resolute. We did not disobey him. Our knight was 'Antara. We attacked when he did so and refrained when he did so. Among us was al-Rabī' ibn Ziyād who was of sound sense, and we sought his advice and did not oppose him. We had amongst us 'Urwa ibn Ward, and we used to follow the example of his verse. We were as I have described to you.' 'Umar said, 'You have truly spoken.'

These and similar accounts were the type of stories circulating in the early Abbasid era. The heroism of 'Antara was openly acknowledged, and heroic material was not lacking. The Ethiopian slave had gained his freedom. 'Abla his beloved was a vague and shadowy cousin. But there were gaps in his biography which had to be filled before 'Antara could become a truly 'epic' hero according to a convention. The most important of these was his death. There was wide disagreement on this matter.

According to these earliest tales, the death of 'Antara was a heroic one, if heroism is judged by the common concepts of the hard, rugged standards of bedouin society. Death in old age when the hero had lost his ability to smite was both tragic and heroic. Heroic likewise was death in a raging sand-storm or at the hands of a youthful foeman whose nimbler tactics served to illustrate the inevitability of the impotence of old age, the pitiable limitations of the senile, and the inescapable hand of fate.

According to Ibn al-Kalbī and Abū 'Ubayda, 'Antara was over eighty years old when he raided the Banū Nabhān of Ṭayy'. Wizr ibn Jābir al-Nabhānī, who lay in wait for him, shot him in the back with an arrow. 'Antara, sorely wounded, returned to his people where he died. According to Ibn al-Kalbī, the man who slew him was nicknamed al-Asad al-Rahīṣ (the lion crippled in the foot). Abū 'Ubayda also reported this tale and added that Ṭayy' claimed to have slain 'Antara.

Elsewhere the death of the hero came about for wholly different reasons. Al-Shaybānī maintained that 'Antara raided Ṭayy', and 'Abs were defeated. 'Antara fell from his horse. Due to his old age he was unable to remount. He crawled into a thicket. A scout of Ṭayy' saw him and came up to him. Fearful lest 'Antara should take him captive he shot and killed him. Another report, attributed to Abū 'Ubayda, was that 'Antara was old and his infirmity prevented him from participating in this raid. A man of Ghaṭafān owed him a camel, and 'Antara went forth to claim it. A hot summer wind blew up while he was travelling between Sharj and Naẓīra. He was torn to pieces by the wind.

All the evidence suggests a different sort of hero in the making. In order to compose his life of adventure more material was needed, especially a death which would form the finale of his adventures.

Another necessity was some kind of literary framework of composition. The format which was finally selected was that of the aretalogical composition, a narrative technique which was akin to that of the apocryphal acts of the Apostles. A number of independent acts of the heroic or saintly personality, whose life forms the subject of the story, were grouped together in a chain. The relation to the central figure is the sole link between the various episodes which were simply put side by side with little attempt to be truly dramatic. Episodes could be added or omitted with little detriment to the composition as a whole. The death of the hero, which assumed a key importance in the balance of the composition, put an end to the story. With the exception of atypical tales, such as *'Ajīb and Gharīb,* this format sharply distinguishes the *Sīrat 'Antara* from the *One Thousand and One Nights.*

'Antara ibn Shaddād in Syria, the Yemen, Egypt and Spain.

As the tenth century drew to its close there were other sources and other parts of the Islamic world where events and literary developments were shaping the 'Antara story into something more comprehensive and more obviously a romance.

It would seem from the Epistles *(rasā'il)* of al-Ma'arrī (976-1057 A.D.) (7) that the exploits of 'Antara, his competitors and the other 'crows' were familiar to the lettered, who took a delight in retelling their adventures. In Epistle (or letters), no. XXX, al-Ma'arrī wrote as follows:

'Likewise the heroes and champions of the Arabs have not been spared by the shafts and darts of fortune. What happened to 'Utaibah son of Al-Ḥārith, brother of Yarbū', albeit he had a great following in the field? Fate sent against him Dhu'āb son of Rubayyi'ah at Khaww, who brought upon him a day of mischief. Bisṭām son of Ḳais made a raid to keep off famine; and he was slain by 'Āsim son of Khalīfah. 'Amr son of Ma'dī Kariba was slain at Nahāwend; he died a martyr indeed, and it was as though he had not perished. 'Antarah son of 'Abs met his doom at the hands of Asad Al-Rahīṣ. Al-Sulaik son of Sulakah was slain by the Banū Ḥanīfah. It is idle to repine or to be angry with fate! 'Āmir son of Ṭufail died of scab, and Zaid of the horses died of fever; only 'Āmir was taken unbelieving, whereas Zaid came on a visit to the Prophet, and swore allegiance to him like a firm confessor. Khālid son of Ja'far was slain by Ibn Ẓālim in the protection of Al-Nu'mān, so wonderful are time's vicissitudes. How many a brave champion is gone, who fought so well with his opponent! And this is no exhaustive list of those that are gone, but merely a selection.'

It is of interest that al-Ma'arrī alludes elsewhere in his Epistles to the blackness of 'Antara and his colleagues among the 'crows'. In another work of his *Siqṭ al-Zand,* which is a lengthy *dīwān* of verse, he has several references to the Zaghāwa, the Africans whose name and repute were most familiar to him. Seven slave girls of the Zaghāwa are likened to seven nights and seven slaves of the Byzantines to seven days. In Ode no. 62 in this collection he introduces crows as the bearers of evil tidings, more especially the break-up of Arabian tribes. None of God's warners had been sent from the peoples of black Africa, and in one verse al-Ma'arrī selects the Zaghāwa as the representatives of the peoples of the Sudan whom he likens to crows. It is indeed remarkable how so many of the seminal ideas of the *Sīrat 'Antara* seem to be foreshadowed in al-Ma'arrī's writings.

Another region where 'Antara was popular was the Yemen. Although 'Antara was allegedly a 'northern' Arab of 'Adnān, he was also greatly admired in the Yemen. The Yemen was the scene for several of his adventures. The greatest hero of the Yemen was 'Amr ibn Ma'dī Karib whose fame was enhanced by his appearance in written tales which recounted the exploits and miracles of the Imām 'Ali. According to the *Book of Songs,* 'Amr ibn Ma'dī Karib used to say, 'I paid no heed to those knights of the Arabs I met as long as I was not confronted by the two noble ones and the two base.' By the first two he meant 'Āmir ibn al-Tufayl and 'Utayba ibn al-Ḥārith ibn al-Shihāb, and by the two 'base' slaves, 'Antara and al-Sulayk ibn Sulaka.

Of greater interest is the appearance of an adventure of 'Antara ibn Shaddād in the tenth book of the *Iklīl,* that masterpiece of al-Hamdānī who was a geographer, poet, grammarian, genealogist and historian. He died in the prison of Ṣan'ā' in 945 A.D. How did 'Antara (or Antar) appear in Yemenite eyes? It is almost a casual reference where the knight of Hamdān Abū Thumāma, Yazīd ibn Thumāma al-Aṣamm is introduced (8).

'It is related that 'Abla (beloved) of 'Antar al-'Absī said to him, "Oh, Abū'l-Mughallis, do you still aim to encounter any knight of the Arabs? To test him is this an aim you seek?" He said, "Yes, Yazīd ibn Thumāma ibn al-Asfa'." While they were mentioning his name, lo, horsemen approached, so he sent a horseman to bring him news of them. The horseman asked them, "Who are you? Who has these cavalry?" They said, "They belong to Yazīd ibn al-Asfa'." The horseman returned and informed 'Antar. 'Abla said to him, "Methinks what you so desired has come about!" So he went to his horse reciting the following verses [in *rajaz* metre]:

> "Oh, companion, tighten the girth of al-Abjar
> When destruction draws nigh I am not one to
> feel ill at ease."

So he mounted, together with those who were with him in the camel party of Banū 'Abs. Yazīd stabbed 'Antar in his hand, and he lost hold of his spear. 'Antar attacked him and grabbed him by the neck. Both men fell, and Yazīd was on his chest. The Banū 'Abs turned and fled.

He let him go and said, "Away with you, we were on our way to meet others." When 'Antar left, 'Abla said to him, "What did you think of Yazīd?" She said it as if she was reviling him, so he said:

> "For sure, 'Abla, the people turned their backs
> And the chiefs of the noble met me.
> I met the most noble of them, but my
> hand lost its grip on my spear.
> The combat brought it down
> (var. My spear failed me, and the sword missed its aim.)
> And it was thrown down, and I repelled him.
> Promptly I act like the haughty sword." (?)

Yazīd once said:

> "Oh, thou reproacher. Wealth which is novel and rare
> I far prefer to wealth which I have inherited.
> Oh, thou reproacher. Only the bearing of the sword
> belt wasted away my youth and gave ulcers to my shoulders."

He also said:

> "Ask Murād, he who knows among them will tell you
> that we give spears a first draught, then a second.
> We extinguish the flame of war when men of battle
> ignite it, at times, and we too, ignite it." '

This brief engagement indicates how sundry episodes about Antar were already in a form which could be exploited in the pages of a full length *Sīra.* Yet even in this passage, although a knight supreme among knights, Antar was not invulnerable, nor were the Banū 'Abs depicted in a favourable light. Antar – not 'Antara here – was still Abū'l-Mughallis, not Abū'l-Fawāris, 'father of knights'. His sword *Ḍāmī* received little attention and appears to have missed its aim. 'Abla on the other hand is a forceful personality. She chides Antar. His horse al-Abjar is mentioned by name. Antar boasts of his skill in being able to unseat the well-armed knight by hand, a feat alluded to in his ode. The style and content of the passage is, indeed, in many ways nearer to that of his *Mu'allaqa* or 'golden ode' than that of the canonical *Sīra.* This fragment would appear to typify transitional material. The rhymed prose (*saj'*) broken by passages of verse is already foreshadowed, as is a quite free, semi-dialogue type of narrative. Towards the end of the tenth century the use of rhymed prose was almost an obession in both courtly and popular literature (9).

An episode in Antar's exploits in the Yemen, transitional in date, is to be found in a poem in all editions of his *dīwān.* It is allegedly *his* composition, but is surely post-Islamic, and it introduces several important characters who appear in the *Sīra.* It seems likely that the poem embodies elements of a story, oral or written, which was current at the time of its composition.

Antar had heard of the capture of his sons Ghaḍūb (usually spelt Ghaṣūb in the *Sīra,* suggestive of a textual inspiration through a copyist's error) and Maysara, together with a friend of theirs of the Banū 'Abs named 'Urwa ibn al-Ward. They were imprisoned in Ḥiṣn al- 'Uqāb (the fortress of the eagle) which was located in the Yemen. Antar went forth with the intention of rescuing them, and he recited the following poem (*Khafīf* in metre):

The fire of grief at the absence of 'Abla in the homelands,
and the remoteness of my sons has burnt my soul
My head is old, its hair is now white after having
colour like the blackness of jet.
I recalled 'Abla on the day she came to be me farewell.
Anxiety and love's extasy were clearly manifest.
She wept due to her fear of being distant, and her
tears revealed ardent passion and sleeplessness.
I said, 'Restrain your weeping. My heart has melted in
sorrow and my passion waxes hotter.'
Woe to this time, how it has shot me with arrows
which have struck the depths of my heart.
But I am like the sword, when it is freshly burnished
it excels in generosity in the blows of battle.
The vicissitudes of time have taught me roughly and
have guided me firmly on the path of wisdom.

I have encountered heroes in every war, and I have defeated
men in every valley bottom.
I left the knights smitten and felled with a jab of
a spear-head like the tops of giant water-skins.
And by the thrust of a sword which I have cherished
and surely guarded from the time of Shaddād, [my father?]
a sword of great age, fashioned in the days of 'Ād.
I conquered the kings in both the east and west and I
destroyed courageous equals in the day of rout.
I have little patience on account of the separation from
Ghaḍūb, for he was aforetime my aid and my support.
Likewise were 'Urwa and Maysara, the guardian of our
hallowed territory when the steeds are spurred in
fierce engagement.
Surely and quickly I shall release them from their
captivity, out of the hands of enemies and the envious.

One or two of the features of the above poem display an affinity with the episode which is recounted by al-Hamdānī in his *Iklīl.* Among these features are the intimate relationship between Antar and 'Abla, the hero's prized sword of high antiquity, wars fought with kings of the east and the west – a Yemenite boast in their early romances – and a campaign in the heart of the Yemen. This finds no mention at all in the short biographies of the earlier grammarians.

On the other hand Ḥiṣn al- 'Uqāb appears twice in the *Sīrat 'Antara.* One such *ḥiṣn* is located in 'Umān, while the other is central to Antar's expedition to the Yemen and into Africa. In both cases there is a tale of imprisonment and rescue in the romance, a breaking into a fortress, a capture of it, and a breaking out of it. An example of capture will be seen later in the romance where Ghaṣūb and Maysara fall into the hands of al- 'Abd Zinjīr, the champion of the Negus of 'Ethiopia'.

One tradition maintains that the composition of a full-length *Sīrat 'Antara* began as a courtly pastime in Egypt at the end of the tenth century. The evidence is weak. It is almost wholly based on an assertion in the anonymous Beirut edition of the text, but also on the views of Caussin de Perceval and of Brockelmann (10). The composer of this romance was a certain Yūsuf ibn Ismā'īl who lived in Cairo during the reign of the Fatimid Caliph, Abū Mansūr al- 'Azīz Billāh (975-996 A.D.). The latter was a ruler of fabulous wealth. He erected a two million *dīnār* palace in Cairo to house his Abbasid rivals. He was tolerant towards Christians. His Christian *vizir,* 'Īsā ibn Nasṭūr, and his Russian wife, sister of the Melkite Patriarchs of Alexandria and Jerusalem could have favoured his eclectic tastes.

The Caliph imported many Turkish and Negro troops and had his own Berber bodyguard. It can be suggested that this might have favoured the dissemination of a romance which depicted its hero as a warrior who was mixed in race and universal in appeal.

Yūsuf ibn Ismā'īl was allegedly a connoiseur of Arabian tales. Whenever some scandal in the court occurred which aroused undesirable popular interest, much to the chagrin of the Caliph, he told Yūsuf to publish material to distract the common people. Yūsuf undertook to write an 'epic' and to distribute it in order to preserve the Caliph's privacy. So keen was he to arouse pleasure and delight that he divided the book into parts, some seven-two, and he made it a rule that at the end of each part he would leave the discourse incomplete to hold the listener or reader in suspense.

This tradition is not to be summarily dismissed. The Egyptian geographer al-Muhallabī (d. 990 A.D.) dedicated a composition to the Fatimid Caliph al- 'Azīz. In that book called *al- 'Azīzī,* he included detailed descriptions of exotic lands in Africa. He described the western Sudan and the region towards Chad where were sited Mānān and Tarazki, the two towns of the Zaghāwa. The limits of these Zaghāwa reached as far as the Nuba, the Upper Nile and the Fezzān, and their proximity would have been of major interest to the Fatimid court. An Afro-Arab hero at this time would not have been inappropriate. Furthermore, we know that a certain 'Abdullāh ibn Sālim al-Aswānī wrote a history of Nubia and the Beja for the same Caliph, al- 'Azīz. In his work he recounted tales of strange peoples and animals which were told him by Simon the king of 'Alwa in the heart of Nubia. The Copts at this time had an influence in the administration. As will be seen, there are Coptic passages to parts of the Antar romance, more especially where Patriarchs and governors, some with Coptic or Greek names, are introduced in the text.

A principal objection, however, to the existence of a popular romance among the populous of Egypt at this time is linguistic. While Arabic was known at court, among the bedouin and among a substantial Arabic-speaking minority who were cultured and well educated, it is unlikely that Arabic was the spoken language for all Egyptians without distinction much before the eleventh century A.D. Hence, this hypothetical Fatimid version of the *Sīrat 'Antara* could only have been appreciated by a lettered few. The distraction of the populace from unwelcome interest in courtly intrigue seems to be a story with slender substance to support it.

Even if we dismiss as speculative the contribution of Yūsuf ibn Ismā'īl to the evolution of the *Sīrat 'Antara,* the tradition of its courtly inspiration is not without interest. It is important to note that Ibn al-Nadīm (d. 987/8 A.D.) in his *Fihrist* did not refer to 'Antara or to 'Abla. Despite this, we now know from the *Iklīl,* that in the tenth century Yemen 'Antara ibn Shaddād was regarded as a major hero among Arabian knights.

In Spain, too, 'Antara and his martial valour aroused interest. His exploits were sometimes deemed seditious and inspiring revolt. They stirred emotional sentiment and latent nationalism among peoples who were already composing romances like the so-called 'leyenda de Izrāq, rey de Guadalajara'. The Muslim Spanish historian Ibn al-Qūṭīya (the son of the Gothic princess), who died in 367A.H. / 997 A.D., the author of The History of the Conquest of Spain (*Ta'rīkh Iftitāḥ al-Andalus*) introduces the story of Irzāq – a more correct reading than Izrāq – into his narrative. In it one is able to see the style and pattern of these budding romances.

'We shall return to the final episode in the tale of Mūsā ibn Mūsā [lord of Aragon and Zaragoza]. He assembled [an army] and came to Irzāq ibn Mint, the lord of the valley of stones and its marches. He was of long-standing submission and obedience to the Caliphs [of Córdoba] and was one of the handsomest of men. When Mūsā entered the field against him and Irzaq moved towards him to do him battle, Mūsā spoke to him, saying, "Oh, Irzāq, I have not gone forth to fight you. I have only come to wed you to my daughter. I have a beautiful daughter. She has grown up to be the most beautiful maiden in Al-Andalus. My sole wish is that only the most handsome youth in Al-Andalus should be her husband and you are that man." Irzāq consented, and the marriage was contracted. Mūsā ibn Mūsā returned to his marches and sent Irzāq his wife.

When the news reached Muḥammad [Umayyad *Amīr* of Córdoba (852-86)] he was much disturbed. He knew that he could lose the nearer marches as he had already lost the further ones. He sent a trusty representative to Irzāq to test his obedience and to assess the import of his act. He sent away the representative and said, "Whether he [variant. 'I', as if Irzāq was speaking] is to be trusted or is disobedient will be made apparent."

When Irzāq had cooled his passion through his wife, he set out among a small group of men who were his followers. He did not march along a well-used road, and the eye of none who knew him fell upon him until he stopped at the 'Gate of the Gardens' [in Córdoba]. A tumult broke out in the palace, and the slaves hastened to the *Amīr* Muḥammad announcing the news to him. He ordered that Irzāq should be brought into his presence. He chided him for having married into the house of his enemy. Irzāq told him how this affair had come about. Then he said, "It will do you no harm that your supporter is wedded to the daughter of your enemy. If by this marriage I can make him disposed to [prefer your] obedience, then I will do so. However, if I fail then count me among the number of those who will fight him to render homage to you as we have done." The *Amīr* invited him to be his boon companion for a number of days, then he gave him gifts, clothed him in raiment and sent him away.

When news of that reached the ears of Mūsā ibn Mūsā he assembled an army against Irzāq and besieged him in the valley of stones. Irzāq was sleeping in the castle which overlooked the river of the valley of stones and his head was resting in the lap of his wife. The people of the valley of stones had gone their various ways in order to attend to their vines and their gardens. Mūsā ibn Mūsā and those who were with him charged upon them. He cast them into the valley. The maid [the wife of Irzāq] was delighted by the deeds of her father. She awoke Irzāq and said to him, "Behold that lion and his deeds." He said to her, "Methinks you boast of your father's deeds to my detriment. Is he more courageous than I am, or is he without honour?"

Then Irzāq took his hauberk and threw it over him. He sallied forth and caught up with Mūsā. Now Irzāq was one of the doughtiest and most skilful in handling a lance and he smote him with a single piercing thrust. Mūsā felt its impact and he withdrew, but he died before he reached the city of Tudela.'

In that tenth century 'Antara ibn Shaddād and his verses were greatly admired by the Córdoban princes of Spain. This is made clear in an anecdote of Ibn al-Qūṭīya :

'We shall return to the tales of Umayya ibn 'Īsā ibn Shuhayd. Among his experiences was that he found himself at the abode of the hostages, a building adjacent to Bāb al-Qanṭara. He heard the hostages of the Banū Qasī [princes of Aragon] reciting the verses of 'Antara ibn Shaddād. He said to one of his aides, "Bring me the teacher." When he was accommodated in the city and the teacher came to him, he said to him, "Were it not for the excuse that you are an ignorant fellow I would have taught you a sharp lesson. You attend to devils who have sorely afflicted the Caliphs and you ask these devils to recite poetry which will increase their understanding of knightly courage. Stop doing it! Only have them recite the bacchic verses of al-Ḥasan ibn Hāni' [Abū Nuwās] and poems of this genre, poems which tell of sport and frivolous jest.' (11)

The later Abbasid 'Antar ibn Shaddad.

The twelfth century is apparently the period when sundry *'Antarīya* tales and snippets, some oral and popular, others literary and courtly, were written down in a grand format. Earlier material was sifted and some of it like that in the *Iklīl* rejected.

It was at this time that the name of a collector, compiler and writer of a *Sīrat 'Antara* is recorded. He was Abū Mu'ayyad Muḥammad ibn al-Mujallī (var. al-Mujallā) ibn al-Ṣā'igh al-Jazarī. He was a doctor and wrote a letter to Ḥujjat al-Dīn Marwān, *vizir* of the Atabeg 'Imād al-Dīn Zangī (d. 1146 A.D.) (12).

This would date his composition of a *Sīra* in Syria, Iraq or Egypt during the period of the Crusades. Muḥammad ibn al-Mujallī ibn al-Ṣā'igh was known as 'al-'Antarī' because in his early days he used to transcribe the stories of 'Antar al- 'Absī. There is no evidence, as A. J. Arberry observes (13), to credit this doctor with the composition of the canonical *Ḥijāzīya Sīra* as we now know it.

Written collections of exploits were already extant. There were other *littérateurs* interested in the same pastime. A converted Jew, Samouel ibn Yehouda ibn Aboun informs us that when he was young he avidly absorbed lengthy Arabian stories and tales. Among them were the adventures of Antar. Samouel was converted to Islam in 1163 A.D. and called himself Samaw'al ibn Yaḥyā al-Maghribī. His youth was contemporaneous with the literary activities of Muḥammad al-'Antari.

One important factor determined the fully-fledged composition of the *Sīra*. This was the introduction of a more conventional climax for its ending. Thereafter it had an aretalogical shape and showed its aged hero to be a majestic figure. The *Sīra* does not possess the character of a 'frame story', common in Oriental literature. A good example is the *One Thousand and One Nights*. Here there are tales within a tale, the vignette of Sheharazade's nightly ordeal of an imminent execution, and the postponement of her sentence by recounting a tale. Sheharazade knits that work of varied date and contrasted substance into a unified composition (14).

The *Sīra* of Antar required three primary divisions before it could be indefinitely expanded by the introduction of new Märchen material or numerous passages in verse. It needed a satisfactory opening, a central section of varied exploits and a crowning and heroic conclusion. If the earliest Arab sources, the Book of Songs included, are examined it can be seen that only the first of these, and parts of the second, were fixed. All were agreed that Antar was half-Ethiopian, son of a slave woman. All were agreed that his father, or grandfather or a paternal relation was named Shaddād. All were agreed that he attained his liberty in battle, and that he became the champion of the Banū 'Abs, fighting with success against Ṭayy' and Tamīm. Disagreement was wide over the hero's death. Was he senile, a non-combatant, shot by a scout or by al-Asad al-Rahīṣ, or was he blasted to death by a summer tempest? Some device was needed whereby the stirring character of the hero at the end of the *Sīra* could balance the promise of his gallantry and the acknowledgement of his nobility by his grateful father.

By the date of Nashwān ibn Sa'īd al-Ḥimyarī (d. 1177 A.D.) it seems clear that the version of Ibn al-Kalbī, which makes the archer, al-Asad al-Rahīṣ of Ṭayy', the slayer of Antar, had established itself as the preferred version of the hero's death (15). At a date perhaps prior to 1100 A.D. an idea had occurred to the compilers of the *Sīra* whereby the story of a senile hero shot by an arrow could be shorn of an unconvincing finale. One idea was to make Wizr ibn Jābir, al-Asad al-Rahīṣ, an inveterate foe of Antar, captured by him again and again, then released. In despair of ever making him his friend Antar blinded him. Wizr learnt to shoot arrows at birds and gazelles guided by their sounds. Antar was struck, almost by accident, by one of Wizr's poisoned arrows. Wizr died believing he had missed his opponent. So an element of chance or fate, which casts no discredit on Antar's invincible heroism, signalled the finale of the epic.

The death of Muslim heroes by poisoned or inescapable arrows were reported by Spanish Arabic and Maghribi writers as early as the eleventh century. There was then a vogue for such a martyrdom. From al-Bakrī (d. 1068 A.D.) onwards there are reports of the tragic death of a champion at the hands of infidels armed with bows and arrows. As there were references to super-human bowmen in pre-Islamic and Persian literature, for example Wahriz in the *Sīrat Sayf,* these stories passed into popular folk-tales wherever Islam spread.

Another idea was to depict Antar, the deceased hero, as a lifeless warrior on his horse like the Cid. Leaning on his spear he deterred the enemy by the terror and size of his person. His people found safety in their rocky retreat of al-Sharabba. The enemy plucked up courage to disturb his steed, al-Abjar. Antar fell to the ground and al-Abjar ran away. It could serve no other master. Here there seems to be a deliberate borrowing of another hero's tragic end. Charles Lyall was among the first to scorn it (16). That hero was Rabī'a ibn Muqaddam of the Banū Firās. In the *Sīrat 'Antara,* Rabī'a and Antar are engaged in a combat. The sword of one breaks in two, and his opponent gives him another. The two are reconciled and become brothers-in-law.

The early Abbasid grammarians record that once while Rabī'a was escorting a party of women he caught sight of the enemy in the distance. He told them to ride on quickly while he would wait behind. They would meet at the Gazelle Pass or 'Usfān. The women would at least reach safety. Rabī'a went out to meet the men of Sulaym, and he appeared from the trees. They attacked him.

Rabī'a was a skilful archer, and he slew many with his arrows. Then he followed his womenfolk pursued by the enemy. He used up all his arrows, and he fought with the spear and the sword until he was speared by Nubaysha ibn Ḥabīb. The latter cried out that Rabī'a had been slain, but Rabī'a refuted him.

Though wounded, he galloped until he reached his women-folk at the Gazelle Pass. He cried out to his mother to give him a drink. She refused his request saying that he would die on the spot, and that her sisters would be captured. He told her to bind his wound, and she did so with her veil. He returned to his opponents. He sat on his steed and barred the road. When he was about to die he leaned upon his spear, and he remained fixed like a statue in the twilight. Sulaym saw him, they dared not attack him. They waited, assuming him to be alive. Then Nubaysha saw Rabī'a's head drop onto his neck, and he ordered a man of Khuzā'a to shoot an arrow at his mare. Rabī'a fell forward on his face. His foes were afraid to follow the women any further. By this time they had reached safety. Rabī'a was buried where he lay at the head of the Gazelle Pass, and over him they built a cairn of black stones.

Lyall concludes, 'Notwithstanding the distinct assertion of the old traditions that no other man was known among the Arabs who died as did Rabī'a, the author of the late and apocryphal "Adventures of Antar" (which is largely made up of stories stolen from others, their rightful owners) has not scrupled to appropriate this heroic death for 'Antarah of 'Abs. The real 'Antarah died in extreme old age in quite another way than that of "the boy with the long locks" as one of the accounts call Rabī'a.'

The beginning and end of the canonical *Sīra* had been established. Within its frame a romancer could slot the segments of each part of the narrative. Each segment is influenced by the tripartite division of the pre-Islamic ode, the erotic prelude (*nasīb*), the march (*raḥīl*) and an ending of praise (*madīḥ*) and heroic triumph. Each segment is a microcosm of the macrocosm of the complete *Sīra*. The latter describes the exploits of the hero in at least four geographical quarters, each ruled by supreme monarchy, Qayṣar and Byzantium, Kisrā and al-Madā'in (Ctesiphon), rulers of al-Hind wal-Sind centred in a vague region along the coast of the Indian Ocean (Madīnat 'Umān and the adjacent islands of Qamar) and the Negus in 'Ethiopia'. Under each of these supreme rulers is a series of lesser rulers who need to be defeated or won as allies before confrontation with one of the rulers of the quarters of the world. This idea is Persian. It is combined with the tales of Islamic conquest found in the *Pseudo-Maghāzī* literature.

The Persians were familiar with an artistic scheme in which the kings of the Earth paid homage to Chosroes on his throne. Yāqūt referred to a composition of this kind at Qarmīsīn (Kirmanshah) in its *dukkān* where Faghfūr (Baghbūr) Emperor of China, Khāqān, King of the Turks, Dāhir, King of Sind and Qayṣar, the Byzantine Emperor are convoked by Kisrā Aparwīz. Some concept of this kind was clearly applied to the overall structure of the *Sīrat 'Antara.* As the story unfolded so the hero assumed or won the pomp and status of a Sasanian King of Kings.

The symbolic seat of kingship had within it something of the mystery of 'the raised palace' or a centre of magic power. In the Sasanian court there are artificial birds made of metal which sing in various tunes by means of bells and organ pipes. They resemble the automata in Adamant castle or the 'city of brass'. The city of Madīnat 'Umān is controlled by a sorceress Sahm al-Nizāl (the arrow of battle) who from within its walls casts magic spells which induce psychedelic fantasies in her foe, leading them to destruction or producing a cloud over the city rendering it invisible to the besiegers. Some of these additions must have come late into the *Sīra.*

Bernhard Heller has argued a far narrower setting for Antar's original adventures. They would have taken place in Arabia, Iraq, Syria and Persia. If the cautious deductions of André Miquel about a ninth or tenth century composition for the calque of the romance of *'Ajīb and Gharīb* are eventually proved correct, then one might be tempted to include an excursion into Ethiopia (the land of the Ogre in *'Ajīb and Gharīb*) as well. (17) But this is an assumption which has yet to be proved. The logic of these romances indeed favours the introduction of such lands as Spain, Byzantium, 'Greater Rome' and the kingdoms of the Franks as later additions. At the moment, however, there is no evidence to prove this conclusively.

It is probable that the climax-structures in the various segments of the *Sīra* predate the Ayyubids and early Mamluks (twelfth to fourteenth centuries). At the same time there is a detectable 'Crusader' influence, post-dating the First Crusade. Ayyubid Egypt and Syria, or the Mamluk period, were particularly relevant for the completed and edited text of the *Sīra* in its definitive form.

If the climax of each segment required a city, a palace, a castle or a magic source, so the lead up to this climax required allies and foes whose battles, escapades and amatory adventures enabled the story-teller to prolong the narrative. The earliest exploits of Antar had a handful of characters. Several of these were known to Ibn al-Kalbī, Abū 'Ubayda, and al-Ma'arrī, including the 'three crows'. The final list is immense including famous Jāhilīya knights like 'Amr ibn Ma'dī Karib al-Zubaydī and al-Muhalhil ibn al-Nabhān. The heroines include 'Abla, the daughter of Mālik ibn Qurād, Antar's beloved; al-Mutajarrida, sister of Qays, the wife of King al-Nu'mān, and Kabsha and Rayḥāna, the sisters of 'Amr ibn Ma'dī Karib. There is a comprehensive coverage of Yemenite as well as North Arabian names.

The text of the *Sīra* indicates Antar's principal foes in combat, and it is noteworthy that 'Amr ibn Ma'dī Karib is not to be deemed amongst them. Perhaps he was held in too great respect. His 'historical' defeat of 'Antara, as recorded by the poets, was possibly too well-known to maintain the fictions which the *Sīra* constantly disguised.

Who then were Antar's principal competitors? The answer is attributed to al-Aṣma'ī, 'Bisṭām (ibn Qays, the king of the Banū Shaybān) was one of the nine renowned knights. I asked about the famous Arab lineages until I knew all their knights and heroes, and I had a full knowledge of the knights of the Jāhilīya and what courage and tribal zeal they possessed. They were nine in number. Six were free men, noble in lineage. Three were sons of slave women. But they possessed a power and capability which exceeded all normal limits. The first of the six who were held in esteem and were of noble honour and birth was prince Bisṭām. The second was 'Āmir ibn al-Ṭufayl. The third was 'Abd Hayyāf, and the fourth 'the green king'. The fifth was 'Utba ('Utayba) ibn al-Shihāb al-Yarbū'ī, and the sixth was Sabī' ibn al-Ḥāris. It is said that instead of the latter (the honour is due to) 'Amr ibn al-Ward al-'Āmirī. As for the three slaves, the first of them was 'Antara ibn Shaddād who surpassed and led the people of his time (18).

His mother was an Ethiopian woman as has already been mentioned in this *Sīra*. The Negus was her nephew. Her name was Shamāma. Those who took her captive from her people named her Zabība. Her lineage stemmed from Ḥām. It is recalled that the lineage of 'Antara stemmed from Shem, son of Noah, peace be upon him. 'Antara was not of base lineage. In fact his father was one of the lords of 'Adnān. He was Shaddād ibn Rawāḥa ibn Sarāḥa ibn Khuzā'a ibn Tihāma ibn Baghīḍ ibn Qays ibn 'Abs ibn Ghaylān ('Aylān) ibn Arfahān ibn Nizār ibn Ma'add ibn 'Adnān ibn Mudar ibn Kināna ibn Arqash ibn Ghuwayy ibn Zafwān ibn Irtiḥdār ibn Samārīb ibn Shalḥā ibn Yūnus, son of Shem, the son of Noah, peace be upon him. This is the lineage of 'Antara, the courageous hero among knights.

As for the second of the slaves he was Sulayk ibn [al-] Sulaka. As for the third he was Khufāf ibn Nadba [his negress mother]. These are the famous nine from the age of the Jāhilīya, famous for courageous and tribal heroism, except that 'Antara surpassed them all because they one and all fought him, and he discomforted all of them. It was he whom the Prophet mentioned when the people reminded him of 'Antara's courage. He said, "Yes, the Banū 'Adnān had a noble knight. Had he lived and come to me, by him I would have directed the lands of the Muslims and have guided them aright." '

Several names have subsequently been added to the heroes of the Jāhilīya who are known in the earliest collections of verse. Among them are 'Abd Hayyāf and 'the green king' (*al-Akhḍar*). Coloured kings figure in several Islamic romances. 'The red' (*al-Aḥmar*) is a king of the *jinn* in *'Ajīb and Gharīb.* 'Abd Hayyaf and 'the green king' appear in the part of the *Sīra* where Antar and his company war in southern Arabia against Yemenites, Ethiopians and the rulers of India and Sind. 'Abd Hayyāf was the son of an Amazon queen of Sind who worshipped an idol called Hayyāf.

The name of this idol or deity could conceivably be a corrupted Indian or Asian name at present unidentifiable. As it stands, letter for letter, it could have been derived from *hayf* which was a dry, hot or cold, wind which blew from the Yemen. It was and is well known to bedouin nomads and lettered alike in the whole Arabian peninsula. It is a hated wind because it dries up green herbage and makes cattle and flocks thirsty. A connection between a menacing wind from the very region occupied and invaded by 'Abd Hayyāf is a tempting hypothesis. Antar could be a symbol of the forces which countered or averted this dessicating wind. His heroic person like the Ruwāla wolf (which combats two winds, the *shimālī* and the *hayf*) could have become linked to early Arabian metereological ideas and fables.

'Abd Hayyāf planned to overthrow the Persian Emperor, Kisrā Anushirwān, He carried three maces, two of gold and one of Chinese iron, and each of these weighed two hundred pounds. He bore a shield of elephant hide. There seems little doubt that this description of him entered the *Sīra* from Persian or Indian sources. It is clear too from his great battle with Antar, illustrated in the following diagram. The scenario is Asiatic and exotic, the skill of the plot in introducing suspense and variety is apparent. Yet there is also a naivety of structure which is not dissimilar to genuinely Arabian bedouin tales exemplified in the adventures of Abū Zayd and Dhiyāb among the Banū Hilāl.

'ANTAR VERSUS 'ABD HAYYĀF.

Scene – A jungle thicket.

'Abd Hayyāf enters the thicket to hunt gazelles and wild beasts.	meets (unknown to each other)	X (un-named) (Who holds a lion in his right hand and a lioness in his left)

The two men agree to eat the
lion. 'Abd Hayyāf lights the
fire, X skins the lion.
Both eat.

Beast appears. It is a serpent or dragon
with a head like a camel. Tail 30 cubits.
Fire comes from its eyes and jaws, and
there is tissue between its claws.

X attacks the beast after praying for aid to the Almighty and to the Prophet Muhammad. He severs the head of the beast and casts it before 'Abd Hayyāf.

'Abd Hayyāf asks X his name. X asks 'Abd Hayyāf his name. X discloses himself to be 'Antar ibn Shaddād. They recognize each other as deadly enemies.

End of scene.
'Abd Hayyāf and 'Antar fight until it is almost total darkness. Each makes use of a giant tree which can shelter one thousand knights as a position for defense. The boughs of the tree are hacked to pieces by their swords. 'Abd Hayyāf grows weary and suggests that they renew their combat on horseback on the battle field. 'Antar agrees.

Exit combatants.

Other foes and allies of Antar's are to be found among warriors who were either Crusaders or Franks. The passage where many of these Franks are conveniently listed occurs in the ninety-fifth part of the *Sīra*:

'After a few days had passed Caesar [Emperor of Byzantium] received a letter from his sister's son, Balqam who was the lord of Greater Rome. He opened it, read it and knew its purport. The reason for that was one of the Frankish kings called Buhamanẓ ibn Mawrān (var. Mawzān and Marwān) – who was the brother of al-Khīlajān, who was slain by 'Antar, and the brother of Sūbart and Nūbart and Kūbart. Antar had slain al-Khīlajān, as we have explained at the beginning of the *Sīra,* when he besieged Madā'in of Chosroes and had slain his brothers Sūbart and Nūbart and after that made peace with Caesar. Al-Khīlajān had a brother called Buhmand who was young. When he grew up he became a knight unmatched and as a colocynth bitter to the taste. He was the king of the town of Ifranjīya and the fortress of Kafranjīya. He rode among one hundred thousand knights.'

I shall allude to this in some detail in my concluding chapter. There are incidental descriptions of Christian ritual, weaponry, heraldry and knightly society including kinds of tournaments and jousts. No reference occurs anywhere to fire-arms. They would certainly have found their way into the text if it had been written down as late as 1500 A.D.

Whatever the terminal date of the composition there is undoubtedly much Crusading fervour in the *Sīrat 'Antara.* It is detectable also in near-contemporary Arabic works such as the *Kitāb al-I'tibār* of Usāma ibn Munqidh. The memoirs of this Syrian warrior, hunter, gentleman, poet and man of letters vividly compare and contrast the beliefs, customs and ideals of the Muslims and the Franks between 1095 and 1188 A.D. It is not surprising that 'Antara ibn Shaddād, the poet, should be extolled in Usāma's work in a passage where an engagement with lances is described. Amazed by the skill of the combatants, the reporter and Usāma were inspired to quote the hero-poet of 'Abs in a poem which began :

> 'I am a man of whom one part belongs to the noble
> lineage of 'Abs,
> But the other part I protect with my own sword . . . '

The feats of 'the father of knights' were not far from the minds of Muslim warriors at this time.

Jewish sources are used to furnish material for Antar's attack upon the oasis of Khaybar in Arabia. The latter episode (in the eighteenth volume) also involves Antar's Banu Quda'a and part-African wife, Ghamra bint Fā'iz, and immediately precedes Antar's exploits in 'Ethiopia'. The sack of Khaybar is inspired by the Prophet's alleged conquest and dispersion of its people as described in the *Sīra* of the Prophet by Ibn Isḥāq (d. 768 A.D.) and Ibn Hishām (d. 833 A.D.). But other sources (some Khazar?) have been employed to portray the Jewish background to the expedition. In a noteworthy piece of research by Bernhard Heller, supplemented and to some extent criticized by Rudi Paret (19), the eclecticism of the *Sīrat 'Antara* is shown, particularly through the detailed correlation which can be found in the plot of the story and in the borrowing of names and Jewish customs.

There are allusions to Jewish doctors, a soporiphic 'plant of lethargy' (*waraq al-subāt*) of Indian origin, Byzantine control of Khaybar, and a secret underground tunnel through a cave or water course which connected the outside of Khaybar with the floor of the principal synagogue. This story bears no resemblance to the early Arabic accounts of the Prophet's capture of Khaybar. It superficially recalls the romances of the siege of Arles, held by the Saracens, who were supplied with victuals through a tunnel. In the *Roman d'Arles* Charlemagne diverts this tunnel which passed beneath the chapel of Saint-Pierre des Aliscamps. He captured the city with a great slaughter. There is also reference to an underground passage to a 'synagogue', filled with statues of Tervagent, Appolon and Jupiter, in the epic of Fierabras. The French barons were led deep into the castle-palace of Balan, the Saracen, by his treacherous daughter Floripas who was in love with a French knight. Love, treacherous princesses, secret entrances and exits are common to both Western and Eastern romances.

In the *Sirat 'Antara,* Khaybar, after many assaults suffers the fate of 'inverted' 'Ād and Thamūd and their raised palaces. The whole city is set ablaze.

Antar meets adventure with and fights the chief of the Jews of Khaybar, Jabbār ibn Sahr, a doughty warrior who falls in love with 'Abla, Antar's wife, and kills Shaddād, the father of Antar. Jabbār comes to Mecca at the time when Antar hangs his ode in triumph inside the Ka'ba. He announces the imminent return of Yūsha' al-Akbar, 'Joshua the Great', who will come forth upon a white ass from beyond the distant valley of Sambation. The Messiah would renew the law of Moses and triumph over all other creeds. The personality of Yūsha' al-Akbar seems to have been inspired principally by the first verse of Chapter 3 of the Book of Zechariah: 'And he shewed me Joshua the high priest (al-Akbar) standing before the angel of the Lord, and Satan standing at his right hand to resist him.' (20)

Romancer and story-teller

The text of the *Sīra,* despite stylistic variation and occasional concessions to vulgar taste, is remarkably consistent in its lay-out and presentation. It is composed throughout in an elaborate rhymed prose (*saj'*) which brings together phrases of varied length. This rhyme is limited to a vocabulary which largely consists of proper names, repeated epithets or varied pause. Some of these epithets and names are borrowed from the vocabulary of poems in the *Dīwān* of 'Antara ibn Shaddād. Because of the enormous length of the full text there is a good deal of repetition and some monotony. Nevertheless, the regular insertion of true poems of varied metre, occasionally strophic (*zajal*) (21), and unexpected twists in the plot somehow succeed in maintaining the momentum and fascination of the narrative. The latter is a libretto which requires the human voice to make its dramatic effect. When recited this risk of monotony is much reduced. The expressive voice of the 'poet' or 'bard' (*shā'ir*) does much to rouse the excitement which is often harder to sense in the written text.

The adaption and rephrasing of the text is a pastime and entertainment common to both urban and rural communities in the Islamic world. Some reference has already been made to the observations of E. W. Lane. Caussin de Perceval who was also writing in the early nineteenth century observed that examples of the *Sīrat 'Antara* were rare in Egypt and that more could be found in Syria. He noted the fact that almost all the copies in Europe had been taken from Aleppo and Damascus, but he doubted though whether the *Shāmīya,* or short Syrian version, was the earliest recension. His examination of manuscripts indicated that versions in Iraq and the Hijaz could be earlier. Despite his research no conclusive evidence favoured one country more than another as a sole venue for compilers or editors. The quantity of borrowed Indo-Persian material favoured Iraq. Against this must be set the fact that the two 'editors' in tradition, Yūsuf ibn Ismā'il and Muḥammad ibn al-Mujallī ibn al-Ṣā'igh, lived in Egypt or Syria, nor could tales from the Yemen or Spain be excluded from consideration.

Antar eventually achieved great popularity in Morocco, in Egypt, Syria and all over the Islamic world. Episodes were and are depicted in poster art and were borrowed for every kind of entertainment. But much of the complete text could never have been used or recited. It was extremely long and fashion favoured highlights. Some parts of it are almost esoteric, and their frequent allusions to medieval topics and literary sources would bore or baffle all save the most sophisticated audiences unless the reciter furnished a commentary. None-theless, Cedric Dover in his article in *Phylon* quotes the first-hand account of his friend Claude McKay :

> 'One of the big surprises of my living in North Africa was the discovery that even the illiterate Moor is acquainted with the history and poetry of Antar. Often in the Arab cafes, when I was especially enthralled by the phrasing of a song, I was informed that it was an Antari. When I was first introduced as a poet there was not a suspicion of surprise among the natives. Instead, I was surprised by their flattering remarks, "A poet! *Mezziane Mezziane!* Our greatest poet, Antar, was a Negro." '

The famous Egyptian scholar Taha Husayn makes passing reference to the *Sīrat 'Antara* in his autobiographical *Al-Ayyām* ('the days'). He recalls his child-hood memories :

'His father and a group of his friends used to be more than partial to story-telling. When they prayed the *'aṣr* prayer in the late afternoon they gathered around one of them who would recite aloud tales of the raids and of the conquest by the heroes of Islam, and stories of 'Antara and of the Mamlūk Sulṭān Baybars, similarly stories of the prophets and mystic ascetics and saints and holy-men and books of sermons and the practise of the Prophet.'

Taha Husayn notes that at the hour of the *'ishā'* prayer, in the late evening, the *shā'ir* or 'bard' would sing to them tales from the romance of the Banū Hilāl and the Zenāta. This small detail is interesting since it appears to differentiate between the more textual and less musical presentation of 'Antara, the *Maghāzī* works, and similar tales among his rural community. It would seem to confirm Lane's observations on the relaxation of 'Classical' style in the *Sīrat Banī Hilāl,* its less formalised composition and the scope for its presentation in a sung recitative.

Fu'ād Ifram al-Bustānī remarks (22), 'In the main the epic [of Antar] is written in an easy style in rhymed prose. In it there is much allusion to early episodes of the Arabs and their wars, their proverbs and their poems. It has attracted a goodly portion of pleasure, admiration and diffusion in both East and West. Arabic speakers in Syria, Egypt and Morocco used to, or still do, enjoy their night life in their coffee houses and in their homes in order to hear story-tellers and reciters who narrate the exploits of their beloved hero.

Some indication of their passion for this is contained within an account told by Iskandar Agha Abacarius. He said, "I heard about a man from the people of Ḥimṣ [Syria] who every night used to attend the circle of a story-teller, and he heard a section of the Antar 'saga'. One night he stayed on late in his shop until after sunset, and he attended the circle without taking his supper. During that night the topic was the war between Antar and Chosroes [Kisrā]. The story-teller recited to the point where Antar was taken captive among the Persians. They imprisoned him and put chains on his feet. There he terminated the recitation, and the people broke up and dispersed. The man was very upset. He was disturbed and distressed. He went home sad and dejected. His wife offered him food but he kicked the table. The dishes broke in pieces, and their contents spilled over the furniture. He abused his wife in a rude manner, and she answered him back, cross and sharp. So he struck her roughly and left the house.

He went around the markets uncertain in his mind and at a loss to know what to do. Eventually he realized what was the matter. He made his way to the house of the story-teller and found him asleep. He woke him up and said to him, 'You have put the man fettered in prison, yet you have gone to bed with peace of mind! I beg of you, complete this episode for me until you bring him out of prison. I cannot sleep nor is life sweet as long as this condition remains. Reckon how much money you collect from the crowd each night. I will give it to you here and now.' So the story-teller took the book and read to him the rest of the episode until Antar came out of the prison. He said to him, 'May God cool your eyes and rest your mind. Now my heart is contented and my anxieties are at an end. Take these dirhams and keep the change.' Then he returned home glad and happy. He asked his wife for food. He apologised to her saying that the story-teller had put fetters on Antar's foot. She had brought him food to eat, but how could he taste food while Antar was imprisoned and fettered. Then he said, 'Now I have just been to the house of the story-teller, and he read me the rest of the story until he brought him forth from prison. God be praised, my heart is now content. Please, bring me what food you have, and please, forgive me for my exceedingly rude behaviour.' " '

The early 'Antara of the *dīwāns* and the *Iklīl* of Hamdānī has still much of the pre-Islamic bedouin warrior in his character. He is a child of bedouin tales and ballads, some oral, others written down at an early date. 'Abla remains his beloved, the mistress of his dreams. But the later Antar of the *Ḥijāzīya* seems at times to distort this bedouin hero. In the romancer's view of ideal womanhood 'Abla recedes within the heart of the narrative. She is idealized in verse but in the prose she is sometimes cruel and vindictive. She gives way to other Amazon companions, like Ghamra, who fights alongside her spouse and their valiant sons. The Arabian pedigree of Antar is not his sole birthright. His African blood is accepted as of equal importance as his Arabian ancestry. At times he is titanic 'client' (*mawlā*), the challenger and destroyer of accepted ethnic divisions. He establishes exotic kings upon their thrones, and he unseats them. He wears their crowns and rules their subjects. Like his pre-Islamic predecessor he is a carouser, and he may on occasion be the boon-companion of an infidel. By his sword the client is given power, the wealth of the rich is distributed among the plebians. Everywhere he goes, an ever-wandering hero, he heralds social revolution. He turns the medieval world upside down in his restless obsession to shape or shatter the powers which dictated the lives of men.

The *Sīra* of Antar is sometimes profane, sometimes religious, sometimes nostalgic, philosophical perhaps. Antar prepares for the triumph of the Prophet whom he is supposed to pre-date. He still remains the champion of pagan 'Abs, but he reaps the triumphs which Islam was to achieve in the future. At one moment he has a Frank as his friend, at another he preaches a sermon on the unity of God and the prophethood of His Messenger. Is this really something of a satire, skilfully concealed, the desire to surprise and shock uppermost in the narrative? For it is clear that unlike heroes such as Sayf, or Gharīb in the *One Thousand and One Nights,* the Islamic message is only intermittent in the *Sīra.*

How could an illiterate half-Ethiopian, of whom a classical statue was cast in Byzantium, be deemed an ideal Muslim who was the harbinger of the Prophet to come or a true Arab hero? Antar defeats the Yemenites by wielding their borrowed swords and wearing their mantles. Is 'Antara ibn Shaddād reborn as the Yemenite 'two-horned' ruler, Shaddād ibn 'Ād, builder of columned Iram, in the flesh of an African slave? He mocks the lettered fraternity when he hangs his ode in the Ka'ba. His poetic skill is not the reason for his triumph. His rivals are cowed by the fear of his sword. The ʻĀdite armour which he penetrates is so thick, so monstrous and grotesque that conventional poetry cannot compete in the portrayal of its pomp and pageantry. Aided by the puck-like, half-savage, Wodehouse figure of his brother Shaybūb he enters castles and loots their treasuries. No wonder some of the lettered frowned on him, denigrated the romance and eschewed the exposition of his adventures.

Notes

1. Tahar Cheriaa, 'Selection and formulation of themes from oral tradition (in Egypt, Libya, Tunisia, Algeria and Morocco)' in U.N.E.S.C.O., *African Oral Tradition,* Documentary dossier no. 3, pp. 35, 44, 62-69.
2. *The Journal of Arabic Literature,* Vol. IV, pp. 18-47.
3. See E. W. Lane, *Manners and Customs of the Modern Egyptians,* Everyman's Library, J. M. Dent and Co., pp. 397-431.
4. Mia I. Gerhardt, *The Art of Story Telling,* E. J. Brill, Leiden, 1963, pp. 9-64.
5. Nabia Abbott, A Ninth Century Fragment of the "Thousand Nights". New Light on the Early History of the Arabian Nights, *Journal of Near Eastern Studies,* Vol. VIII, July 1949, No. 3, pp. 157-161.
6. See Charles James Lyall, *Translations of Ancient Arabian Poetry,* Columbia University Press, 1930, pp. 115-117.
7. See *The Letters of Abū'l-'Alā',* tr. by D. S. Margoliouth, Oxford, 1898, pp. 120-121; and *Shurūḥ Siqṭ al-Zand,* Cairo, 1948, pp. 259, 360, 1332, 1333, 1335.
8. *al- 'Āshir min al-Iklīl.* Edited with notes by Muḥibb al-Dīn al-Khaṭīb. 1948, pp. 168-170.
9. H. A. R. Gibb, *Arabic Literature, an introduction,* Oxford, 1963, p. 89.
10. See A. J. Arberry, *The Seven Odes,* London, 1957, pp. 168-160; and F. I. al-Bustani, *'Antarat al-tārīkh wa 'Antarat al- usṭūra, al-Mashriq,* Beirut, Vol. 28 (1930), pp. 631-647; see in particular p. 638.
11. Henri Péres, *La Poésie Andalouse, en Arabe Classique au XI siècle,* Paris, 1953, pp. 33-34. Both these passages in Ibn al-Qūṭīya are to be found in *Colección de Obras Arabigas,* tr. by Don Julian Ribera, Vol. 2, Madrid, 1926.
12. al-Bustānī, *op. cit.,* p. 638.
13. A. J. Arberry, *op. cit.,* pp. 168-169.
14. See Mia Gerhardt, *op. cit.,* pp. 395-416.
15. Nashwān Ibn Sa'īd, *Shamsu l- 'Ulūm,* edited by Azimuddin Ahmad E. J. W. Gibb Memorial XXIV, 1916, p. 42. See note 6. It would appear that al-Ma'arrī favoured this version of Antar's death.
16. See Lyall, *op. cit.,* pp. 55-58. Lyall acidly disapproves of this plagiarism; on the other hand French Orientalists at that time saw it as a stroke of genius, or an excusable transference known elsewhere in chansons de geste. They reserved their criticism for other character deformations. For example, A. Coussin de Perceval in the *Journal Asiatique,* Série III, tome V, Paris, 1838, p. 144.
17. See Bernhard Heller, *Die Bedeutung des Arabischen Antar- Romans für die vergleichende Litteraturkunde,* Leipzig, 1931, pp. 3, 27, 28, 90-92, 100-101, and *'Antar (Sīrah)* in the Encyclopedia of Islam. See also André Miquel, *Un Conte des Mille et Une Nuits, Ajīb et Gharīb,* Flammarion, 1877, pp. 24-243.
18. See note 6. Sulayk ibn al-Sulaka appears in Lyall, *op. cit.,* pp. 59-60. 'Āmir ibn al-Ṭufayl is mentioned in *Shams al-'Ulūm, op. cit.,* note 15. He was defeated by 'Amr ibn Ma'dī Karib. Bisṭām ibn Qays was a Christian chief of Shaybān who lived in the seventh century A.D.

    A sinister trio of 'crows' or 'ravens' is to be observed in European literature of chivalry and in folklore. The image appears to date back to medieval times, if not earlier, and can be found in the following verses of a traditional English folk-song, The Three Ravens,

There were three ravens sat on a tree,
down a down hey down hey down,
and they were black as they might be,
with a down.
Then one of them said to his make
'where shall we our breakfast take?'
with a down derry derry derry down down.

Down in yonder greene field,
down a down hey down hey down,
there lies a knight slain under his shield,
with a down.
His hounds they lie down at his feet,
so well they can their master keep,
with a down derry derry derry down down.

In this song the body of the dead knight is preserved from the three ravens by hawks and by a fallow doe which carries him to a lake and buries him there before she herself dies.

19. cf. *Revue des Etudes Juives*, no. 84, 1927, pp. 113-7; no. 85, 1928, pp. 56-62.
20. I am grateful to my colleague Dr. D. J. Kamhi for drawing my attention to this.
21. See p. 137f.
22. See al-Bustānī, *op. cit.*, pp. 639-640. The Sudanese scholar, Ḍirār Ṣāliḥ Dirār, in his book *Hal kāna 'Antara sūdāniyan*, Khartoum, 1976, vividly describes his first encounter with the hero of 'Abs on page 5 :

'My acquaintance with 'Antar goes back to the days of my childhood on the day we used to vie in joyous pride that we were like 'Antara in the force of our courage and horsemanship. We used to adopt palm leaves as our mounts – and what marvellous steeds they were – and pieces of wood served as our swords. It was not long afterwards that I met this knight face to face for the first time in those pictures which were nailed on the walls of barbers' shops, cafes and restaurants. We used to see them when we were on our way to the Koranic school or on our way home. Many were the times I used to stop and ponder on that knight as he shed blood and slaughtered his enemies and my enemies. Behind him was 'Abla upon her palenquin and her she-camel surveying the situation with her eyes open wide in admiration and pride at my friend 'Antara. She was wholly unconcerned about me and totally disregarded my very existence.'

CHAPTER 2 : THE ETHIOPIANS

Africa in the *Sīrat 'Antara* is a blackcloth to a drama. The intention of the reciter is to excite and to entertain. If the first compilers had to take liberties to achieve dramatic effect then they happily distorted geographical or historical reality. The African continent is the homeland of Antar's maternal relations, and it is the place where he rediscovers them while he is engaged in recovering lands stolen from Ghamra, one of his wives.

Ethiopia, as it is presented, seems to be contrary to what one might expect. Far from being a land of Christianity, its ruler the Negus having scriptuaries as his subjects, Ethiopia is a land of paganism and worship of fire; the majority of its lesser rulers, who hold parts of the Yemen and 'Umān within their grip, are barbarous in their habits or ugly in their looks.

No sea divides Ethiopia from the Hijaz and the Yemen. If the story-teller knew of the Red Sea's existence then its presence of absence was irrelevant to his *Sīra.* Africa embraces Egypt, Libya and Spain. The oases (*wāḥāt*) of the Libyan desert of Egypt are apparently transformed into islands – in water, not in sand – while the whole of Upper Egypt, Nubia and the Maghrib are ruled neither by Muslims nor Arabs but by Christian Franks, Copts and Greeks. The king of Qayrawān, for example, is called Mardūs, a name which is close to that of the Saracen king, Moradas, who figures in the Charlemagne romance of *Sir Ferumbras.* Such distortion seems deliberate. It is not simply attributable to literary license allowed in romances of this type.

Ethiopia in the *Sīrat 'Antara* is not confined to Abyssinia. It includes countries known to Persian travellers and merchants who journeyed with cotton and other items of trade from the Red Sea coasts or the Fezzān to Ghāna. Something is also owed to one or two well known geographers who can be identified. East Africa (*Bilād al-Zanj*) and even India may furnish certain details but of greater importance are the lands around Lake Chad (*Bilād Kānem*). The Ethiopians in the *Sīrat 'Antara* are primarily the peoples of Wadai, the Zaghāwa, the Takrūrīs, the Berbers and the Beja.

The name of the Negus, the supreme ruler of Ethiopia, can only be explained by conjecture. The spelling in the *Sīrat 'Antara* does not suggest any of the rulers who were contemporary with the Prophet, rulers prior to his birth, or rulers who reigned after the rise of Islam. Mystery surrounds his capital. Al-Ya'qūbī (d. 891 A.D.), for example, calls the principal city of the Negus, Ka'bar, or a name similar to it. Al-Ya'qūbī also reports that the kingdom of the Negus had important towns, one or two of them on the coast. Only one real town is mentioned in the *Sīrat 'Antara,* and it is not ruled by the Negus. Villages are vaguely mentioned, but a Persian word familiar in post-Ayyubid Egypt *rasātīq,* is used to describe them. The Koranic Negus was a Christian. Nowhere is this mentioned. It is especially surprising since Oriental Christians, including the Byzantine ruler, Frankish knights and Crusaders figure notably. In fact, Abyssinians feature only once or twice. At the commencement of Antar's African expedition his army marches south into the Yemen combatting Sudanese occupiers – presumably Abyssinians – as they advance. The second instance occurs in a wholly different passage in the text where Antar is fighting in the region of 'Umān apparently under Abyssinian and Indian occupation. One Ethiopian foe is named Shimrākh ibn Fallāq al-Amkhākh ('date palm panicle' son of 'the splitter of brains'), a fictitious name. On the other hand the Abyssinian ruler, Yaksūm ibn Abraha, who is also introduced, was a historical figure of royal lineage. He is mentioned in the *Sīra* of the Prophet and in other early writings including the *Sīrat Sayf.* In the *Sīrat 'Antara* he is involved in conflicts with kings and queens from India and from Sind.

Antar's Negus, as will be seen, is not a ruler of Christian Abyssinia at all. He is conceived of as a monarch in a vast Hamitic or Cushitic empire in Africa and the Yemen. He is the supreme king of all *al-Ḥabasha.* The latter was a wide and vague term. To the medieval Arabs it might include the whole of Africa south of Egypt and the Maghrib, and possibly southern India as well.

The Ethiopia of the Arabs.

Early Arab accounts speak of Jerma in the Fezzān as the capital of the Negus. As late as al-Zuhrī (d. 1154/1161 A.D.) Ethiopia had wide limits. To the west it was the Great Nile, its lakes and branches towards the Atlantic. To the east it was the Red Sea, to the south the region of the Equator. In the north it embraced the extremity of the country of Kawkaw (Gao?) to the beginning of the land of Aswan in Egypt. 'In this zone among the towns of 'Ḥabasha' is the city of Kawkaw which is the capital of Ḥabasha. Towards it the caravans of Egypt and Ouargla make their way. Few caravans go there from Sijilmāsa. This city is on an island isolated in the midst of the Nile which surrounds it on every side. One can only enter it by travelling by boat.' (1)

A similar description of 'Ḥabasha' may be found in Benjamin of Tudela who died about 1173 A.D. Describing Jewish caravan commerce across the

Sahara via Zawīla in the Fezzān, but also 'in the territory of Ghāna' he proceeds to recount the dangers of the desert crossing and the survivors who returned with gold and precious stones. The territory was on the edge of Kūsh which was called by the name of 'al-Ḥabash'.

In the *Sīrat 'Antara,* Ethiopia is a region of gold and commerce to the south and west of Egypt. It bordered the Red Sea, the Fezzān, Lake Chad, Lake Fitri, the Bahr al-Ghazal and the Niger. If this is the second homeland of the hero, who then were his relations? They were sons of Ḥām. Antar's mother Zabība was a princess of Ḥām. Among the writers of the eighth century Wahb ibn Munabbih discussed Ḥām's descendants. He says that they formed the Sudan and a certain number of them settled in the Maghrib. Among these were the sons of Kūsh and Kan'ān. They included the Nūba, Zanj, Fuzān or Qar'ān (Guraan or southern Tubu), Zaghāwa, Ḥabasha, Copts and Berbers. Al-Mas'ūdī (d. 956/957 A.D.) expands this list. The descendants of Kūsh, son of Kan'ān, crossed the Nile. One group, the Nuba Beja and Zanj went south and east, the other marched to the west. The latter included the Zaghāwa, Kānem, Markah, Kawkaw, Ghāna, Damādim, Qumāṭī (Qumāṭn/Garamantes?) and Qarma (Jerma in the Fezzān?). 'Each of the latter, like the other Ethiopian groups had a king and royal residence.'

The impression persists that of the Sudanese, familiar to the Arabs, the Beja, Zaghāwa, the Fezzānis and certain peoples from Kanem and Chad remained among the best known. Beyond Libya the Ibāḍite Muslim merchant communities exported Sudanese slaves via Kawār and Zawīla to Egypt and the East. These slaves included Zaghāwa, Maruwīyūn (Tubu?) and peoples who were adjacent to the Sudan.

The slaves in question attained notoriety during the Khārijite Zanj revolt in the lower Tigris of Iraq during the ninth century. The slaves were employed in the saltpetre mines and in clearing the salt flats, and they appear to have been from a variety of African peoples. Among their leaders was Sālim al-Zaghāwī, and a prominent group of them were the Furātīya / Gor'ān(?), Fuzānīya (?), Qarmātīyūn (from Jerma?), and Nubians. They were distinguished from the rest because they could speak Arabic. Their settlements illustrate an Arab contact with their African homelands from at least the eighth century. This is supported by documentary evidence. Mālik ibn Anas, the jurist, was asked about the Fezzānis 'who are a race of Ethiopians'. It was his view that they should not be fought before they were invited to embrace Islam.

In the ninth century little was generally known about the ethnology of the southern Fezzān and the area of Lake Chad to the south. Ibn Khurradādhbih

(d. circa 885 A.D.) and al-Ya'qūbī (d. 891 A.D.) offer a few items of information The ruler of the lands which bordered Idrisid Morocco to the south was a certain Zāghī ibn Zāghī (or Rā'ī ibn Rā'ī) who was probably Zaghāwa having a kingdom in Kānem under a ruler called Ka-Karah (possibly Koā-kurā "a great man" in Kanuri). There were other Zaghāwa kings but they had not towns nor did they build palaces. They were semi-nomadic or lived in huts of reeds. But, in the tenth century, reports from Persian travellers tell of Egyptian merchants passing through these lands carrying salt, glass and lead to exchange for gold or stolen children for sale as eunuchs in Egypt. According to the anonymous Ḥudūd al- 'Ālam, King Rā'ī ibn Rā'ī (Zāghī ibn Zāghī) spread the report that he drank only three cups of wine every three days. What was essentially a primitive Sahelian society was sophistically coloured by Persian taste and imagination.

Kingdoms of Chad, Ghana and the Nile.

Oriental fantasies about Africa are at their most exotic in the reports of al-Hasan ibn 'Amr al-Sīrāfī (d. 961/971 A.D.) a trader from the major port of Sīrāf in southern Persia, who is quoted in the *Ṭabā'i' al-Ḥayawān* by Sharaf al-Zamān Ṭāhir Marvazī (1046-1120 A.D.). According to al-Sīrāfī he saw with his own eyes enormous trees which grew in Kānem. Two of them could shelter thirty thousand horsemen. Their king dwelt on the summit of these trees. To reach his cloud-covered palace one was obliged to ascend to a height of one thousand steps. On these trees they had wooden dwellings. These were not only the palaces of kings. There, too, dwelt his servants, his wives and his court of ten thousand persons. In Kānem the cotton-trees grew high enough for a man to repose in its branches. Men were tall, and their bodies were in proportion to the height of these trees. The kingdoms in the trees were among the wonders of the world.

The legendary trees of Kānem are referred to and can be identified in the text of the *Sīrat 'Antara.* Material from the following Arabic passage in Marvazī is borrowed in the romance (2). It appears not only in Antar's march to Ethiopia but also in the combats in 'Umān with 'Abd Hayyāf.

وحكى حمزة بن الحسن الاصفهاني عن الحسن بن عمرو
السيرافي انه ذكر انه رأى ببلاد السودان اشجارًا
عظيمة ورأى ببلد يقال له كانم شجرتين (شجرتين)
تظلّان ثلاثين الف فارس وملكهم يسكن على
ذروتهما والى مجلس الملك من قرار الارض الف
مرقاة وفوق الشجرتين (الشجرتين) مجالس

معمولة من الخشب وهناك من خدم الملك ونسائه
وحاشيته زهاء عشرة آلاف انسان ويقال ان
نبت القطن عندكم يصير شجرة يصعد عليها الرجل
فتناسبت ابدانهم واشجارهم . . . . .

Another 'geographer' whose writings would appear to be known to the compilers of the *Sīra* was al-Mas'ūdī, whose 'Golden Meadows' (*Murūj al-dhahab*) and 'The Reports of the Age' (*Akhbār al-zamān*) are sources for suitable material. In the first work there are references to Karkar (Chad and Kānem) and also to Ghāna since within its borders were the tracts of silent trade and dumb barter where gold dust was exchanged for merchandise, and the gold was minted into *dīnārs* at Sijilmāsa in Morocco (3). Near Karkar were the Damdam cannibals who were ruled by a king. In their land was a fortress wherein was stored the image of a woman. It was venerated, and many went to it on pilgrimage. Amidst all these lands flowed the Nile near Kawkaw, Ghāna, the Zaghāwa and Kānem. Dumb barter and a semi-divine princess and her fortress are found in the *Sīrat 'Antara.*

In the second work of al-Mas'ūdī (4) there is a comprehensive history of the sons of Ḥām. Some lived in Syria, others in Africa. Among them were Amalekite giants, the Pharaohs, the Sudan and seventy races in the Maghrib. Some of the Sudan still wore skins, others skirts of grass. Some wore horns of beasts. They had a white mouse (?) which they ate and named or considered heavenly *manna.* Their kings married up to ten wives. The king could spend the night with two. If they were to his satisfaction he retained them, if not he divorced them and married again. Periods of drought afflicted the Sudan. To obtain rain they gathered bones and heaped them up and then set them alight. They would dance around the bones with their hands raised in supplication. Then the rain would fall. At weddings they smeared their faces with a substance like ink. Then they seated the bride-groom on a mound, and the spectators also sat on a mound. They placed his bride before him, and they made a tent of reeds and covered it with grass. They stayed by her for three days and drank much millet wine. After that they left, and the husband took his wife and went with her to his dwelling. They wore copper bracelets and the women ear-rings. Only the king wore red-dyed imported *Kardāwinīya*(5) garments. These people had a mighty tree for which they held a festival once a year when they assembled beneath it. They played and danced around it until its leaves dropped. From these leaves they obtained *baraka* – blessing or supernatural power. They adorned the women with copper bangles and with shells for their hair.

Here, too, there are similarities with the Africa of the *Sīrat 'Antara,* although the latter is greatly expanded. Either the details of al-Mas'ūdī have been elaborated, or the weavers of the romance have tapped alternative but similar sources. This will be further discussed in my final chapter.

From the above it is apparent that there is common ground between the *Sīra* and certain reports of tenth and eleventh century Muslim geographers. There is the possibility of Kānem, Ghāna, Nubia, or all three of these, being the setting for Ethiopia in the tale.

Kānem has pride of place. There is the specific reference to its palaces in the trees. According to the Egyptian al-Muhallabī (d. 990 A.D.), whose missing geographical work is buried amidst the pages of Abū'l-Fidā' (d. 1321 A.D.), the area of Chad was dominated by the Zaghāwa. The region they roamed was wide in its horizons. It was deemed to border Nubia and Upper Egypt. The Zaghāwa dwelt in huts but two 'towns', Mānān (Mātān) and Tarazki, form a pair. They seem to match the two royal trees of al-Sīrāfī, giant trees which are more like mountains of the Tibesti massif than any arboreal vegetation known to man. The Zaghāwa adored their king as a god. His food was secretly carried to him. If by chance a passer-by caught a glimpse of the camel which carried the royal dish, this innocent beholder was killed on the spot. With his boon-companions the king drank a toast of sorgho sweetened with honey. He wore trousers of light wool, and he covered his left shoulder with a single piece of Sūsī silk or with silk of many colours. His authority was absolute, he enslaved whom he wished, and he owned herds of sheep, oxen, camels and horses. His subjects grew millet, kidney-beans and corn. They were naked or semi-naked. The king ordered their deaths and granted them sickness or health. Royal power with the help of the nomads extended far into the Sahara, to Bilma to al-Qaṣaba and into the Fezzān.

Certain characteristic features of life and society among the Zaghāwa extended right across the pagan belt of the Sudan. If Ibn Ḥawqal (d. 988 A.D.) is correct the people of Ghāna, Kūgha and elsewhere burnt their dead, and if the latter were nobles their slaves were cremated with them.

Today archaeology is gradually revealing the remarkable medieval sites around the Niger Buckle. These disclose a state or states wherein the Mossi practised inhumation in sepulchral 'pyramids' and the Gurma planned and outlined veritable towns. Sites of this kind abound in the region of Ayoru on the Niger banks and at Shatt and elsewhere in the Dallol Bosso. The Songhay-Zarma recount many legends about those who built or inhabited these sites, both giants and dwarfs. They tell of white kings who reigned over a negroid people. Their king was a Pharaoh (Pharaniani) who was aided by a giant servant called Youhouzou who rode a steed which only ate the *borgu* grass. Other giants were Asaaba (*Ṣaḥāba* Companions of the Prophet). Three of them were brothers who wore sandals which were three yards in length. Each brother could dine on a giraffe as his daily meal. In Songhai-Zerma cosmogony room was found for a race of titans or *jinn* who ruled the sky and the river. Among them was a black captive, yet 'master of the soil' called *gandji bi,* under the Berber *gandji koare. Gandji bi* was the son of *Zubuda bala* who lived in a cavern or a secret locality in the land of the Gurma.

By the eleventh century a slightly different portrayal of 'Ethiopian' life emerges. It is one which offers some firm evidence to suggest that commercial links with the Ibāḍī merchants of the Maghrib and with Persian and other traders of the Islamic East had led to a more profound infusion of Muslim ideas into the region of Chad and into the major kingdoms to the west of it. Some *modus vivendi* seems to have been established between Islamic and pagan societies. They existed side by side or shared common economic and commercial activities.

Al Bakrī (d. 1068 A.D.) draws attention to this (6). He reports a story of the conversion of a rich king of Malal in Mali, later known by his Persian name, al-Muslimānī. During a drought he sought the aid of a Muslim Ibāḍī merchant of Zawīla, Shaykh 'Alī ibn Yakhlaf, who told the king that if he was converted to the true faith God's mercy would be bestowed on him much to the envy of his foes. The king agreed, performed the ablutions and donned a cotton garment. On the eve of Friday the king and the merchant went to a hillock. They prayed for much of the night. At day-break God bestowed a heavy rain, and the river flooded. The king had all the fetishes broken into pieces, and he drove out the sorcerers. His son was also converted, and many other members of the court. But his subjects clung to their pagan ways. They said, 'We are your servants, do not change our religion.' The king forbade any infidel entry to the royal town.

In Ghāna the division of the city was even more marked. One town was Muslim and the other pagan. The court was pagan with a distinct ritual, and the ruler had twenty thousand men of whom forty thousand were archers. Al-Bakrī describes the pagan rituals in great detail. Amid the royal town there were huts, great trees and leafy vegetation. In that locality dwelt the sorcerers and the priests. It was here that the fetishes were kept, and the kings were buried. The groves were guarded and secluded, and the royal prisons were located there. The king's interpreters were Muslims, so too the treasurer and most of his ministers. Among those who followed of the king only the king himself and his heir, his sister's son, could wear sewn garments.

Their pagan religion was described *al-Majūsīya* (the adoration of fire), though fetishes were the principal objects of reverence. When a king died they erected an immense cone of wood (*sāj* – teak?) over his sepulchre. The body was carried upon a stretcher covered with carpets and cushions. Near the deceased were buried his ornaments, his weapons, his eating utensils and vessels of food and drink. When the door of the sepulchre was closed, mats and cloth covering were laid upon the dome. A crowd gathered. They covered the tomb with earth, and in time it resembled a tumulus. Around it they dug a ditch. A single passage-way was left to reach the tomb. It was their custom to offer sacrifices, libations and fermented drinks to their dead.

Gold was abundant. The king charged a *dīnār* of gold on each ass laden with salt which entered his country, and two *dīnārs* on the export of the same. For each load of copper he imposed five *mithqāl* and ten for other merchandise. The best local gold came from Ghiyāru which was situated at a distance of eighteen days's journey from the capital.

All around the capital there were bushes with long stems, *tawrza,* (Calotropis procera) which bore a fruit covered in a kind of white wool used for the making of clothes and material resistant to fire. Al-Bakrī repeats al-Mas'ūdī's report of the Damdam cannibals who were ruled by a king who was lord over other kings. In his territory was that extraordinary fortress upon which stood an idol in the form of a woman who was adored and venerated.

The glory of pagan Ghāna passed after 1076 A.D. It vanished due to reasons still not clear but in some way linked to the rise of the Almoravids in the Sahara. The later Islamic Ghāna was also an exotic kingdom for the Arabs. It had standards and ensigns, processions of elephants and giraffes, and a fleet of fishing boats. It was ruled by an Islamic *sharīf,* an alleged descendant of Ḥasan, the son of the Caliph 'Alī. He possessed a picket of gold for his prized steed.

In Kānem, too, there was a blending of Muslim and pagan traditions. In the thirteenth century Ibn Khallikān (d. 1274 A.D.) records the name of at least one Muslim scholar, Abū Ishāq Ibrāhīm Ya'qūb al-Kānimī. The people of Kānem were paternal cousins of the people of al-Takrūr, despite their ignorance of genealogies. Kānem had a town of some size, though Ghāna remained the capital of the Sudan, then termed al-Takrūr. All the negroes were descended from the sons of Kūsh ibn Ḥām ibn Nūḥ. These Sudanese warriors had fought well for Islam. They had shown their worth at al-Zallāqa in Spain in 1086 A.D. in the army of the Almoravid ruler of Morocco Yūsuf ibn Tāshfīn. They had been armed with Lamṭī shields, Indian swords and (Yazanī?) spears of beech-wood (*zān*?)

Ibn Sa'īd al-Gharnāṭī (d. 1286 A.D.) reveals a comprehensive if distorted view of Kānem and Chad. The kingdom flourished among brutish cannibals, and there were several settlements sited around the lake. Among the most important was Jaja where there were peacocks, parrots, guinea fowl, spotted sheep shorter than young asses and many giraffes. To the east of Jaja at one corner of the lake was sited the Maghzā, the arsenal or naval base, of the Sultan of Kānem. To the south of Jaja lay Jimi, Kānem's capital. It was the seat of its ruler, the warrior in the *jihād,* who claimed to be a descendant of the Yemenite hero, Sayf ibn Dhī Yazan. The old pagan capital was Mātān. By this date Kānem was nominally an Islamic state like Kawār and the Fezzān. At Nayy there was a pleasure garden which bordered the 'Nile'. In it there grew exotic fruits including pomegranates and peaches. Both Berbers and Zaghāwa were under the authority of Kānem which may have reached as far as Darfur in the Sudan.

This royal landscape seems very different from the tree-kingdom of Marvazī, yet there is some recollection of the latter in the writings of al-Dimashqī (d. 1327 A.D.). Kawkaw (Gao), he wrote, stands on a river which rises in Lake Chad. On its banks were sown corn and other crops. There the cotton tree grew into a giant tree (7). Five men were needed to carry one tree, in the shade of which ten men could repose. But this cotton tree was a dwarf compared with the giant palaces described by the Persian merchants several centuries before.

Al- 'Umarī (d. 1342/1349 A.D.) borrows much of his material from Ibn Sa'īd and al-Dimashqī. Kānem, he said, ruled to the Egyptian border, its forces wore the Saharan muffler (*lithām*). The king of Kānem was poor yet proud. 'His head touches the remotest points of the sky and the heavens.' Hidden from mortal gaze he only appeared publicly at the great feasts. During the rest of the year he spoke to none save behind a curtain or a veil. 'He gazed on the stars, seeking their light to guide his feeble intelligence.'

Commerce in Kānem was conducted in the *dandi* cloth which they wore, also cowri shells, glass beads, copper and fragments of iron.

Kānem was a land of lights and fires, a description which owed something to the reports of the Kānem scholar and poet Abū Isḥāq Ibrāhīm al-Kānemī, 'There appear in the land of Kānem and in its neighbourhood before those who march at night, objects which resemble a sparkling fire. If one goes to meet them, these jack o'lanterns go far away, if one runs after them one cannot reach them but they remain in front. If one decides to throw a stone at them and hits them, they pour forth a shower of sparks' (8). A land of lights and fires figures prominently in the *Sīrat 'Antara.*

By repute the first to establish Islam in Kānem was al-Hādī al- 'Uthmānī who claimed descent from the Caliph 'Uthmān ibn 'Affān. Then after him the power passed to the sons of Sayf ibn Dhī Yazan and the Himyarites. Among the greatest of the kings was Dunama Dibbalemi ibn Salma who was ruler of Kānem in the middle of the thirteenth century. He fought the *jihād,* and he tightened his control of the Saharan routes into the Fezzān. In 1257 A.D. he sent a giraffe with a rich present to the Hafsid ruler of Tunis, al-Mustanṣir. He delegated power to his sons. He probably laid the foundations of a 'feudal system.' He established Islamic public offices, and he broke open the sacred *mune,* talisman of royal authority and its sacred symbol (9). In his day the Muslim law school was that of Malik ibn Anas. The Kānemis were devout in their observance having established a *madrasa* in Cairo which became a hostel or a hospice for all the pilgrims of Kanem who visited the East. The hospice was founded in 1242 A.D. by pilgrims who paid money to the Qāḍī 'Ilm al-Dīn Ibn Rashīq who built the *Madrasa* and taught there.

In their homeland they had left behind a dynasty of monarchs who ruled five kings or kingdoms. The kings claimed to be emigrant sons of Sayf ibn Dhī Yazan. They had once been nomads. Of Zaghāwa or mixed Zaghāwa and Berber blood they were centred on Jimi. Their rule reached the borders of Egypt, the Fezzān and up to Kaka within the limits of Bornu. About the year 1300 A.D. the king of Kanem was named al-Ḥājj Ibrāhīm Nikale. His claim to descent from Sayf is reported by al-Maqrīzī (d. 1442 A.D.), who also reports his pilgrimage to the holy places.

As the Arab world and its story-tellers delved into the archives of the geographers, heard tales from traders, pilgrims or students in the courts of the *Madrasa* of Ibn Rashīq, so the lands of 'Ethiopia' in their romances emerged as a geographical entity. It seems unlikely that one region monopolized their fertiale imagination. The pomp, gold and mystery of Ghāna, the pageantry of Mansa Musa, the pilgrim king of Mali, his stay in Cairo and gifts of giraffes, pagan rites and Islamic pageantry, one and all provided ideal material with which to weave a tale, an epic in which Antar could display his prowess and discover his African origins. However, amid the marvels of Takrūr, Ghāna, Mali and Abyssinia one is still left with the impression that Kānem and Nubia are the very heart of 'Ethiopia' in the *Sīrat 'Antara.*

Kānem was a land of giant trees and monarchs who dwelt in these trees. Its deserts bordered a lake or sea or river, and it was a major source of Egypt's Nile. Close to it were cannibals who adored a deified queen. Within its borders lived a semi-deified king hidden from men's eyes but whose lineage seemed to attach him to the pre-Islamic rulers of Antar's Arabia. Kānem was a land of fires, sparks and will o' the whisps. It was one of the cross-roads of Africa, a highway for merchants and for cloth. It ruled deep into the interior, and its royal house of Zaghāwa may once have come forth from the lunar peaks of Tibesti. They were shepherd kings who gazed into stars and lived in castles hidden in the clouds. King Janṭāyil, one of Antar's major foes, was king of the Zarwāt and the Murāwāt. Both allude to the Zaghāwa.

However, part of Antar's African expedition seems to enter other desert regions of Africa. There is, for example, a certain king spelt al-Dahmār, sometimes al-Damhār, the lord of the Fortress of Dīnār. The first part of his name could come from an Arabic root – *adham/dahmā'/ duhm.* This root denotes a deep black, brown or green. It could hardly be the proper name of an indigenous ruler but like 'the red, blue or green king' it might convey a certain concept to the audience who were listening to the romance. If Africa inspired the name then perhaps the Berber root in *amghar* or *maqqar* or *maï âgré* in Tubu indicating chief, elder master or 'great one' lies at the heart of Damhār, should this be the correct reading. *Dīnār* might be connected with the Zaghāwa word *diner* (var. *dingār*) which denotes the kettle drum of royalty and authority. Thus one might construct the concept of *'Maï agré* (Tubu) lord of the fortress of the *diner',* 'master lord of the citadel of the drum of his authority' which could be in a rocky mountainous terrain or seat of his power. In Beja and Nuba *dungāra* is a word which denotes 'gold'.

Several towns between Ghāna, Kānem and Egypt and the Maghrib were commercial centres where *dīnārs* were minted or stored in treasuries. Sijilmāsa under the Almoravids was the centre for the minting of gold. The Ibāḍī merchants of Libya, who lived in the southern Saharan city of Tadamakkat, sent hundreds of *dīnārs* annually to their northern relatives (10).

There is a second fortress or palace in the clouds in the *Sīrat 'Antara.* It seems to be different from that described among the Kānem trees. It is a ruin inhabited by the *jinn* and is the treasure house of Dāhiya, a *jinnīya* who appears to be identifiable with the Kāhina, the Berber queen of the Algerian Aures to whom were attributed acts of sorcery at the time of the Arab invasion of North Africa. Her descendant in the *Sīrat 'Antara* is al-Khāṭif, an enemy of Antar and his allies.

Here again there is difficulty in identifying the inspiration of this passage although there are several castles which seem to fit the description of the ruin 'from the days of Noah'. Bornu is said by the Arabs to be 'the land of Noah' (*barr Nūḥ*), because it is reported that the ark landed on the desert rock of Hajar Tious in the vicinity of Chad. There is no shortage of rocky, wind-blown 'castles' in the terrain to the north-east of the lake. It is equally probable that elements in the romance are conceived of as much further to the north at this point. Dāhiya and the Kāhina may be the same. According to al-Bakrī the oasis of Ghadames in Libya had subterranean prisons of the Kāhina, queen of Ifrīqīya.

Al-Idrīsī (d. 1166 A.D.) locates the abode of the 'cunning woman' or 'the misfortune' – both meanings are possible – by the banks of the Nile in Upper

Egypt near Zamākhir and Akhmīm. 'Overlooking its banks of buildings and gardens is the mountain of al-Ṭaylamūn which obstructs the course of the Nile so that its waters require force and pressure in flow to surmount the obstacle. The people of Zamākhir say that Dāhiya, the sorceress, formerly lived on the summit of this mountain in a castle of which only a few traces remained. By pronouncing certain spells she prevented boats from passing beneath the mountain despite the force of the Nile current.' This folk-tale of Upper Egypt is one likely source for the appearance of Dāhiya, the Kāhina, in the *Sīrat 'Antara.*

Tales may also have come to the ears of the story-tellers from North Africa. Legends of the Kāhina in the Aures mountains were long remembered. An extensive passage in the *Kitāb al-Istibṣār* (11), an anonymous work composed about 1192 A.D., is concerned with Tahert, an Ibāḍī Khārijite centre in Algeria in the tenth century, and with the desert areas adjacent to it. The author makes several allusions to cloud-covered citadels and fortresses of the *jinn,* and these bear some resemblance to tales which are to be found in the *Sīra.*

'The town of Tahert is very cold, with much cloud and much snow. Ibn Ḥammād said in a description of it, "How hard is the cold and its pervasiveness, and how agreeable and rare is it to see the sun in Tahert. It appears from the cloud (*ghamām*) whenever it does so, as though it is diffused and scattered from beneath. We rejoice to see the sun, when it shines forth, like the joy of the Jew and the Christian when the Sabbath comes." It is said that a man from the people of Tahert went on pilgrimage, and he saw the sun blazing in Mecca. He said to it when it had burnt him, "Burn as much as you like, for, by God, you are weak and contemptible in Tahert."

Near this town is the fortress of the Hawwāra. It is an inaccessible fortress in a fertile mountain. In the latter are gardens and fruits and trees and fields and grapes. Beneath it is an even ground, some four miles long cut by the Sīrāt river, and it waters most of its land. That terrain is named Sīrāt, after the name of the river. The river of Sīrāt is famous, and it reaches the sea at the town of Azwāwā. It is an ancient Byzantine town. The terrain of Sīrāt is inhabited by many Berber tribes, the Matghāra and other tribes of the Zanāta. The Zanāta branch forth into many tribes. Their country is wide. From the side of Ifrīqiya (Tunisia) they are intermingled and mixed with the Banū Zughba of the bedouin of the Banū Hilāl ibn 'Āmir.

To the west is the country of the Massūfa who are many tribes of the Ṣanhāja who dwell in that desert and do not settle permanently in any town. They live solely on milk and meat. They are many in number. In the deserts of their country is a huge mountain called Qalqal. It is very fertile and has springs and rivers. In it are many traces of habitations and fortified houses and wide villages unfrequented and where no human resides. It is said that the *jinn* emptied those habitations and towns. In those deserts at night may be seen fires of the *jinn.* Their singing and their sound of music is heard. Very often they snatch away (*yakhtaṭifūna*) human beings and carry them off with them. Sometimes the human escapes from them and returns to his people, and he reports what he has seen among them. This is commonly known. It is said that they substitute the offspring of human beings. For that reason the people of Ifrīqīya say, "Oh, replaced one,"(*yā mabdūl*). We have already mentioned the secret of that,'

Another locality in Northern Africa or in the southern part of Greece (Greater Rūm) or Italy is referred to as 'the islands' in the *Sīrat 'Antara.* They vary from 'the island of camphor' and 'the island of crystal' to 'the islands or island of the oases' (*wāḥāt*). These islands are ruled by Frankish or Byzantine governors or kings and have relics of Alexander.

'The island of the oases' was ruled by King Shamrūṭ but is captured by Antar's mulatto son al-Jufrān who arrives in the Hijaz following the death of his father. After the capture of this 'island' he gives away many camels and much wealth. He visits its citadels accompanied by Maryam his mother. One passage in the romance (in the ninety-seventh part of the *Sīra*) seems to draw upon the tale of Roderick's opening of the tower of Toledo and the account of the visit of Alexander to the shrine of Ammon in the western Egyptian oasis of Siwa for its material.

The passage read, 'Al-Jufrān visited the palace of Alexander one day. He went around it beholding its wonders. He was accompanied by his chamberlains, his people and his deputies. He had adopted as his *vizir* a man noted for his wisdom and his eminence in 'the island of the oases'. Al-Jufrān examined that palace from every side, and he pondered the beauty of its building. Whenever he passed by a place he asked the *vizir* about it, and the latter would answer him. Thus they continued until they reached the cupola of locks once visited by Antar, his father. The latter had alone been able to open it. Within it he found the horse which was the lord of the *jinn.* He rescued it from fetters and chains, and in return it helped him avenge the death of his son, Ghaḍbān, who had lost his life fighting the *jinn.*

When al-Jufrān reached that place he ordered that it should be opened in all haste. They cast aside its locks and opened it up. Al-Jufrān entered and beheld the portrait of a being riding on the back of a black ram. He was perplexed by what he saw. He asked the *vizir* about it, and the latter told him its story and significance. Then they found a closet wherein stood a mighty coffer. They opened the coffer, and inside it they found a silken garment. On that garment there was a plaque of gold, and upon it were designs and inscriptions so bright and dazzling that they almost burst into flame.

The *vizir* read it and said, "This city will be conquered by the hand of a horseman whose portrait most closely resembles this. These sayings are reported by the ancients."

Then the *vizir* explained to King al-Jufrān which events had happened to Antar in that place.'

The *Kitab al-Istibṣār* (12) describes oasis 'islands' to the west of the Nile. They were inhabited by Berber Luwāta tribes and Copts. Dākhila, Khārija and Ṣabrū (Taizerbo) were on routes to Cyrenaica, the Fezzān and Kānem and were by repute the sites of cities of copper and lost groves. Their fantastic buildings figure prominently in Arabian books of marvels. As early as al-Mas'ūdī (13) the dwellers claimed to have Arabian connections. He records that in 942/3 A.D. the master of these oases, commander of horsemen and cameleers was a certain 'Abd al-Malik ibn Marwān whose name suggested an Umayyad Arab, though al-Mas'ūdī indicates a Luwāta Berber.

It is possible that the romancers in no way indicated locations which approximated to Mediterranean islands, known to the medieval Islamic geographers. It would be highly speculative to see in Shamrūṭ a corruption of Shabrū - the spelling given by al-Idrīsī of the oasis of Ṣabrū (Taizerbo) or 'the island of camphor' (*jazīrat kāfūr*) as a reference to Kufra oasis. An explanation as to how these oases (*wāḥāt*) became 'islands' may be found in the *Kitāb al-Istibṣār* (14) where it is said that between the *Wāḥ* – the outer oases of Egypt – and the *Jarīd* – the oases of southern Tunisia – there was a region of broad sand-dunes wherein were localities called the 'islands' (*al-jazā'ir*). They were full of springs and date groves and empty of dwellers save for the *jinn.*

By contrast the cities of Barqa, Tunis, Qayrawān and other localities on the North African coast are specifically named in the *Sīrat 'Antara.* As in Egypt and Nubia, whose Nilotic towns are also listed by name, the rulers are principally Greeks, Byzantines and Copts.

Antar's royal relations and enemies among the sons of Ham.

A number of Arabian and African names appear in the pages of the *Sīra.* Many of the names are epithets and, as far as can be judged, cannot be equated with historical characters or with others known in oral or written literature. Among such names are Badr al-Tamām (full moon), Lawn al-Ẓalām (the colour of darkness), princess 'U'jūbat al-Anām (the wonder of mankind), or King Hammām/Humām(Heller calls him Hammām) who is the king of the misty or cloudy citadel and sacred tree of The Land of Flags and Ensigns. His Fortress of the Clouds may allude to a poetic source for his name in a verse of the pre-Islamic poet Imru'l-Qays:

أَصَدَّ نَشَاصَ ذِي القَرْنَيْنِ حَتَّى   تَوَلَّى عَارِضُ المَلِكِ الهُمَامِ

In this verse the poet Imru'l-Qays praises al-Mu'allā, one of the Banū Tamīm. The latter had protected the poet from King al-Mundhir ibn Mā' al-Samā' who boasted of the title 'the two-horned'. Al-Mu'allā had successfully repulsed the king's forces which the poet likened to a heaped-up cloudy barrier in the sky. So the poet said in the verse above:

> He repulsed the rising cloud of 'the two-horned'
> until the heaped cloud which formed a barrier in
> the sky, the might of the heroic king (*al-malik*
> *al-humām*), turned its back and fled.

Some intermediary figure between this monarch and the king in the *Sīrat 'Antara* is to be found in the undatable legendary *Maghāzī* literature where the Caliph 'Ali leads an expedition into the Yemen in order to reduce the sky-blue castle of a king called Humām who is the ruler of 60,000 Yemenites. Here and elsewhere in the *Maghāzī* literature there are names also to be found in the *Sīra,* names such as Khaṭṭāf, Ghaḍbān, Habbār and Ḥārith.

King Ghawwār is another important African king. Ghawwār implies a person who is bold and deep in penetration, but the king who is named in this instance may be related by name to an African ruler either heard of by report or discovered in books. In medieval Nubia *ouro* was the title of a king.Examples west of Egypt abound like Kā-Karah, the king of Kānem in al-Ya'qūbī (d. 891 A.D.), or Kawari, Kure Gana, Kure Kura, Yama Kuri (Gao), Kwōre (gey Ra), or *kire* (king) among the Zaghāwa. The name of the oasis of Kawār (Khuwwār) on the commercial route which led from Egypt to the Sudan via the southern Fezzān is a possible source, so too is al-Ghawr in the Tihāma, adjacent to the Yemen. It might refer to Lake Chad which is called Kawarī by Ibn Sa'īd (d. 1286 A.D.). Karkar is an African name in many Arabic records, and it seems to relate in some way to these names.

Dhāt al-Anwār, the Mistress of Fires, who became a queen and introduced fire worship into 'Ethiopia' bears a resemblance to the tenth century Queen

Juditta of Samen in Abyssinia. She was also known as Esther and Flame of Fire. She allegedly seized the kingdom of Aksum, massacred the royal princes, made herself Queen of Abyssinia and tried to overthrow Christianity.

A major mystery in the *Sīrat 'Antara* concerns the identity of the Ethiopian Negus and his chief warrior, supreme foe of Antar, called al- 'Abd Zinjīr (the slave 'chain') or the slave 'the Zanjīr / Zinjīr *dīnār'.* He is a ruler's champion like 'Allam or 'Alan (Ilem among the Shuwa Arabs of Chad), the warrior with a chain who fights with Dhiyāb ibn Ghānim in the legends of the Banū Hilāl. Al- 'Abd Zinjīr is a monster from water and plain. He rides a steed of the ocean or the Nile, and he is armed with a leather or round skin-shield like the Moorish *targa* or bucklers carried by the Berbers or by the Bouddouma on the islands of Chad. According to the Bouddouma (16) their lake is ruled by a genie, who, in the form of a giant serpent, dwells in its depths.

The easiest and most obvious African explanation for such a name is to consider Zinjīr as a corrupt or variant form of Zanjī or Zinjī. This denotes a negro either of the region of the Niger or Lake Chad, or more often one of the peoples who lived on the east coast of Africa. They were exported as slaves to Iraq, to Sind and elsewhere. The text of the *Sīra* refers to Habbār, who was the son of al- 'Abd Zinjīr. Habbār was the son of 'the black' *(al-Aswad)* which conveys the same idea of 'negro' as Zanji or Zinjī, so by extention Zinjīr.

Habbār ibn al-Aswad was a historical figure. He was at first celebrated for his opposition to the Prophet Muhammad. But later he became a convert to Islam, and in the second century of the Hijra his descendants (who claimed to be Nizārī, 'Northern Arabs') settled and later came to rule the Arab citadel of al-Mansūra in Sind where they boasted of an army of eighty mail covered war elephants. According to Yāqūt, quoting al-Muhallabī (al-Manṣūra in his *Mu'jam al-Buldān*), 'Its people are Muslims, and their king a Qurashī of whom it is said that he is a descendant of Habbār ibn al-Aswad. He conquered it. His ancestors inherited the kingship in it. However, the *Khuṭba* is said in the name of the Abbasid Caliph.'

There remains another African alternative. Al- 'Abd Zinjīr (العبد زنجير) could be a written distortion of a divinity of the Beja of the Sudan, noted by al-Ya 'qūbī, the geographer. The Beja were ruled by a number of kings according to this writer. In their kingdom of Baqlīn they worshipped a divinity called al-Zabahīr (ا زبحير) which may be derived from the Ethiopic *ǝgzi' abǝḥer.* Al- 'Abd Zinjīr could be a garbled version of a hypothetical *'Abd Zabḥīr* from *'Abd (ig) zabhīr,* 'servant of God', in Ethiopic *gäbrä* (= *'Abd*) *ǝgzi' abǝher.* According to Dr. A. Irvine this last was a fairly common name in Christian

Ethiopia where *ǝgzi' abǝḥer* was the standard name of God, though probably of pagan origin, meaning 'Lord of the Earth'. One might be tempted to see in *'Abd* (عبد) a mis-writing of *ghbr* (غبر) which might in its turn represent the Ethiopic *gäbrä,* though phonologically there are weighty objections.

The father of al- 'Abd Zinjīr was named al- 'Abd Barāq, Burāq, maybe Bilāq. He lived on an island in a river or sea, and he was a threat to the king of 'Ethiopia' who only managed to restrain him by surrounding his island retreat. In the *Sīra* of Sayf ibn Dhī Yazan, Barāq and Barq al-Burūq ('flash of flashes') are common names for the *jinn,* while Bulaq is the son of Sayf and his negress wife Takrūr. A link here with popular tales of Egypt and the Nile seems apparent.

There is a possibility that Barāq / Burāq is a warrior ruler of Bilāq to whom reference is made by al-Idrīsī (17). The locality of his exploits is called Tājūwa, Djado to the north-east of Chad, the territory of which was adjacent to Nubia. The ruler of Bilāq marched to the town of Samina (Samiya, Simiat or Samta) to the east of El-Fasher in Darfur and ruined it. Bilāq was located between two branches of the Nile – Burāq's island retreat ? – near 'Alwa, one of the Christian kingdoms of Nubia, and its *Amīr* may have carried out the raid in the name of the supreme king of the Nubians. Bilāq was a meeting place for merchants from Nubia, Abyssinia and Egypt. As we have seen Christian 'Alwa was a source for 'Africana' in Arabic literature of the Fatimid period.

Could the name of the Negus – Manklā or Mankalā[n] (منكلا) in the *Sīrat 'Antara* likewise be Nubian or Beja? Perhaps the name was a copyist's misreading of Haykalan (هيكلا), the sanctuary wherein the medieval Christian kings of Nubia celebrated the liturgy? The geographer al-Fazārī (eighth century A.D.) states that the Najāshī was the king of the Nūba. Since Antar's mother, Zabība, was allegedly a relation of the Negus this could suggest that the hero of 'Abs was part Nubian or Beja in birth. The hypothesis is attractive. There are identifiable references elsewhere in the *Sīra* to the Nubians and the Beja. What is certain is that this name does not fit an Abyssinian ruler who was well known. The names of 'the Negus' before or about the time of the Prophet can be excluded. Menelik or Menyelik requires a metathesis; Amlak, a divine name which interchanges with *ǝgzi abǝḥer,* also requires a metathesis. If one accepts Antar's *Sīra,* word for word, that 'Mankalā(n) believed in the Prophet and sent gifts to him,' then the varied names of that Negus can be discounted. Seven of the eight variants reported by Jalāl al-Dīn al-Suyūṭī (d. 1505 A.D.) are recognisable differences of pronunciation or spelling of the name al-Aṣḥam ibn Abjar (the latter by coincidence the name of Antar's horse) mentioned by Ibn Isḥāq, while the eighth, quoted on the authority of al-Zarkashī and Muqātil appears as Makḥūl ibn Ṣa'sa'ah. The names in the Abyssinian King Lists

(600 – 970 A.D.) which are closest to Mankalā are 'Akla, 'Akālā (Wedem) or 'Ikelā, but next to nothing is known of these kings, and there is no special reason why they should have come to the ear of an Islamic romancer.

In my concluding chapter I will argue that there are several channels whereby 'the Negus' could have been introduced as the supreme ruler of Africa at a climax in the Antar romance. The sources of the story-teller are diverse and his geographical horizons are immense. I will argue that there are possible Frankish sources for his name. However, if the limit of discussion be confined to Africa near the sources of the Nile there is something to be said for seeking Mankalā(n) somewhere within the whole narrative of Antar's exploits in the African continent.

I shall show that the names of the kings of the Nubians and the Beja who engage in a great battle in Upper Egypt against Antar and his allies were derived from rulers of Nobadia and Muqurra in the Northern Sudan. These kings, Maksūḥ (Makshūḥ) and Ghaliq ('Aliq or 'Aflaq) were allies of the Greeks in Upper Egypt and aided them to resist the southward march of the Arab armies under Khālid ibn al-Walīd about 641 A.D. African troops mounted on elephants participated in the battle. In these royal names there is a link between the *Sīrat 'Antara* and historical records.

There was, however, a third king mentioned in these records, and he receives no mention anywhere in the Antar romance. That king was *al-Kaikalag,* the lord of Aswan, whose authority extended to Aden and the salt sea, the country of the Nubians, the Beja and the whole of the Sudan. The Nubians of Faras (Pakhoras – Bakharas) near the second cataract of the Nile claimed descent from Kikalañ or Kikelai 'father of a hundred, grandfather of a thousand,' who lived in a citadel. This name is thought to be derived from Caecilianus. It is identical with *al-Kaikalag* in the Arabic sources. Kikelañ was the son of Niokel (Nokl) in Nubian oral traditions.

If it is possible that Kikelan or Ñokel was corrupted by the romancers into Mankalā(n), then it is not impossible though far less likely, that Pakhoras, also spelt Bū Kharas, likewise Faras, in some way relates to Abū'l-Fawāris 'the father of knights', Antar himself, whose ties of kinship with the supreme king of the Sudan or 'Ethiopia' is the theme at the heart of the text of the *Sīra* (18).

Notes

1. See Joseph M. Cuoq, *Recueil des Sources Arabes concernant l'Afrique Occidentale du VIII[e] au XVI[e] siecle.* Editions du Centre National de la Recherche Scientifique, Paris, 1975, pp. 117-118 for 'greater Ethiopia' in al- Zuhri, and p. 171 for the subsequent reference to Benjamin of Tudela.
2. See *Sharaf al-Zamān Ṭāhir Marvazī on China, the Turks and India,* translated and edited by V. Minorsky, the Royal Asiatic Society, 1942, pp. 53-56 and pp. 156-158, and his Arabic text p. 42. Also Cuoq, *ibid,* p. 111. For a possible factual explanation of part of this, see Gustave Nachtigal, *Sahara et Soudan,* Paris, 1881, pp. 405 and 408. The village of Taraka which he describes was grouped around an impressive isolated rock the sheer face of which was some twenty-five metres high. One could see enormous ladders of palm trunks which gave access to the narrow plateau which served as a place of refuge.

    Sir Rennell Rodd in a journey to Elakkos and Termit, which are situated to the north-west of Chad, a locality frequented by the Tubu, Tuareg and Kanuri, remarks, 'When we first entered the dunes there was a thick white mist on all the land and the green trees and white sand looked very mysterious and beautiful in the early dawn.' *People of the Veil,* London, 1926, p. 447. The existence of these mists near Lake Chad and the presence of cotton trees could create the fable of trees in the midst of the cloud.

    My personal view is that, particularly in the light of references to 'Antara in al-Ma'arrī's works, Zaghāwa country or the region near the Sudan border is the original setting for Antar's fictitious African expedition. What is truly descriptive in it reflects an eye witness's view of that region. See for example, and by way of comparison, Marie-Jose Tubiana and Joseph Tubiana, *The Zaghawa from an Ecological Perspective,* Rotterdam, 1977, pp. 34-36.

    It might be noted that Marvazi was living when the *Ḥijāzīya* was allegedly composed about 1080 A.D.
3. All these matters are discussed in P. F. de Moraes Farias 'Silent Trade: Myth and Historical Evidence, *History in Africa,* (African Studies Association U.S.A.), Vol. i, 1974, pp. 9-24.
4. al-Mas'ūdī, *Akhbār al-Zamān,* ed. by al-Sāwī, Cairo, 1938, pp. 64 ff. See page 233. The Arabic passage in question reads as follows:

ومن ولد سودان بن كنعان أمم منهم الاشبان والزنج وأجناس كثيرة
تناسلت بالمغرب نحو سبعين جنسا ، وهم مختلفون فى افعالهم ، ولهم ملوك .

ومنهم اجناس يلبسون الجلود وهم عراة ، ومنهم من يتزر بالحشيش ، ومنهم
قوم يعملون لرؤوسهم قرونا من عظام الدواب ؛ وعندهم فأر أبيض يأكلونه
ويسمونه منّ السماء

ويتزوج الواحد منهم عشر نسوة يبيت كل ليلة عند اثنين منهم ، فان جامعهن على ما يحب وإلا طلقهن الملك بعد ثالثة

وربما أجدبوا ، فاذا ارادوا أن يستسقوا جمعوا عظاما فكوموها كالتل ، ثم أضرموها بالنار ، وداروا حولها ورفعوا ايديهم إلى السماء ، وتكلموا بكلام فينزل المطر ويسقوا

فاذا اعرس احدهم لطخوا وجهه بشيء يشبه الحبر ، ثم اجلسوه على تل ، وجلسوا على تل ، واجلسوا المرأة بين يديه وجعلوا قصبا مثل القبة ، وستروها بشيء من الحشيش ، واقاموا حولها ثلاثة ايام يشربون نبيذ الذرة ، ويلعبون ثم ينصرفون ويأخذ الزوج امرأته ويسير بها الى موضع سكناه

ويلبسون حلق النحاس فى ايديهم وآذان نسائهم ، ويحمل اليهم الكرداونية التى تصبغ بالحمرة يلبسونها ولا يلبسها منهم إلا الملك

ولهم شجرة عظيمة يعملون لها عيدا فى كل سنة يجتمعون عندها ، ويلعبون حولها حتى يسقط عليهم ورقها فيتبركون به ويزينون المرأة بحلق النحاس والودع فى شعرها

ومن والد سودان الكركر وبهم سميت المملكة ، التي هى اعظم ممالك السودان واجلها قدرا ، وكل ملك لهم يعطى ملك الكركر حق الطاعة ، وتنسب الى الكركر ممالك كثيرة

ومملكة غانة وملكها ايضا عظيم الشأن ، ويتصل ببلاد معادن الذهب وبها منهم امم عظيمة ، ولهم خط لا يجاوزه من صدر اليهم فاذا وصلوا الى ذلك الخط جعلوا الأمتعة والأكسية عليه وانصرفوا ، فيأتون اولئك السودان ، ومعهم الذهب فيتركونه عند الأمتعة وينصرفون ، ويأتى اصحاب الأمتعة فأن ارضاهم

وإلا عادوا ورجعوا فيعود السودان ، فيزيدونهم حتى تتم المبايعة كما يفعل
التجار الذين يبتاعون القرنفل من أهله سواء [بسواء] ، وربما رجع التجار بعد زوالهم
مختفين فوضعوا النيران فى الأرض ، فيسيل الذهب فتسرقه التجار . ثم يهربون
لأن الأرض كلها ذهب عندهم ومعدن ظاهر ، وربما فطنوا لهم فيخرجون فى
آثارهم ، فإن أدركوهم قتلوهم .

5. Certain of these customs as well as those in the *Sīra* have a likeness to those described in Marie-José Tubiana's book *Survivances pre-Islamiques en pays Zaghawa,* Paris, 1964, particularly that associated with the *manda* cult.

   It is not impossible that the red-dyed clothes of the chief may have prompted 'Himyarite' connections. Nashwān ibn Sa'īd al-Ḥimyarī says, 'The name of Ḥimyar was al-'Aranjaj ibn Saba' al-Akbar ibn Yashjub ibn Ya'rub ibn Qaḥṭān the son of Hūd, the Prophet on whom be peace. It is said that he was only called Ḥimyar because he used to wear red vestments.'
6. For references to al-Bakrī and Ibn Sa'īd, see Cuoq, *op. cit.,* pp. 98-101 and pp. 208-210.
7. *ibid,* p. 245.
8. *ibid,* pp. 258-260.
9. See Abdullahi Smith, 'The early states of the Central Sudan', in J. F. A. Ayaji and M. Crowder, eds., *History of West Africa,* i, London, 1971, pp. 158-201, and especially p. 173.
10. See Cuoq, *op. cit.,* pp. 172-173.
11. *Kitāb al-Istibṣār fī 'ajā' ib al-amṣār,* Arabic text edited by Dr. Saad Zaghloul Abdel-Hamid, Alexandria, 1958, pp. 178-179.
12. *ibid,* pp. 145-149.
13. See the edited translation of al-Mas'ūdī's *Murūj al-Dhahab, Les Prairies d'Or,* by C. Barbier de Meynard and Pavet de Courteille, Paris, 1861-1877, vol. III, pp. 50-51.
14. *op. cit.,* pp. 147-149.
15. See *Dīwān Imri'l-Qays,* in *Majmu'āt turāth al- 'Arab,* Dār Ṣādir, Beirut, 1958, p. 166.
16. See Henri Carbou, *La Région du Tchad et du Ouadai,* Paris, 1912, where details are given on pp. 37 and 38. Nāghala as a name occurs in Ibn Khaldūn, see Cuoq, *op. cit.,* p. 342, and the form Abkalā (variant Ankalā according to Cooley) in al-Maqrīzī (d. 1442 A.D.), Cuoq, *ibid,* p. 385 and foot-note 1.
17. See Cuoq, *op. cit.,* p. 141.
18. See Ugo Monneret de Villard, *Storia della Nubia Christiana,* 1938, pp. 122-123, 139, 197-9, 216-218, 223. See also the interesting article by F. L. Griffith, 'Pakhoras – Bakharas – Faras in Geography and History' – *The Journal of Egyptian Archaeology,* Vol. XI, 1925, pp. 259-268.

    For a fuller development of the argument see Chapter 4, note 19. There is also some discussion of titles of medieval Nubian kings in the contribution by Ali Osman, 'New Light on Medieval Nubia', in the *Bulletin of Information,* No. 3, Accra, June, 1977, published by *Fontes Historiae Africanae,* pp. 14-18.

TRANSLATION

Plate 3: The Romance of ʻAntara ibn Shaddād, the Knight of the pursuit and the Viper of the Wādī's bottom.

CHAPTER 3 : YEMEN AND THE SUDAN

Cairo (Būlāq) edition, Volume XIX.

Antar and his wife Ghamra have just returned from their destruction of the oasis of Khaybar.

The dream of Antar

Antar began to wait impatiently for news. On certain days he was depressed. He was unable to ride. 'Urwa came to him with the sons of Antar, Maysara and Ghasūb. They asked him what hindered him from riding. They found him speaking with Shaybūb; when they entered his presence they greeted him. He raised his head and bade them welcome. He spoke to them first, saying, 'Last night I dreamt a dream. I fear that it means that the cup of death will touch my lips. My spirit is troubled.' 'Urwa said, 'You have seen good and will live to see it. If God so determines it you will behold the good, but if you behold evil may you attack and destroy it. Tell us of your dream.'

Antar said, 'I saw that a black whelp had come forth from my loins. I saw it before me, and it was rolling in the dust. Then it rose up against me in the shape of an eagle, sharp in beak and claw. It flew skywards, like a demon, until it vanished from my sight. It reappeared at a great distance, having spread forth in the sky. It fell upon me like a blow of fate. It dashed against me and buried its claws in my shoulders. It pulled me and threw me upon my back. I was at its mercy. It mounted upon my chest and tried to kill me. I dreamt I stretched forth my hand to push it from me. Then it wished to carry me away with it aloft into the heavens. I knew that I was in deadly peril, and I was determined to force it away from my chest. Then I awoke full of fear and terror as to my fate. That dream struck me dumb and filled me with melancholy. I tell you, cousins, I shall die before this year has passed.'

When Shaybūb heard his words he said to him, 'What you have described is nothing but a nightmare on account of over eating and overdrinking. The proof of it is that I too dreamt a dream.' 'Tell me of it,' Antar said. 'In my sleep I saw myself in the desert. It was as though a bird attacked me above the earth. Then the bird changed into a gazelle (var. a fox), and I wrestled with it. I was sorely pressed by it, and I wished to seize it, but it excreted like a bird between my thighs, and I was in great anxiety as to my fate. It arose before me in the shape of a jesting human. I yearned to ask him who he was. Then I awoke, and I was filled with dread of him and his deeds.' 'You speak truly, Shaybūb,' 'Urwa said, 'but your brother's dream is full of greater terror, because the eagle, birds of prey and such awesome fowls, indicate wars. It is prudent to be careful for his sake. A party of men will be posted to guard him every night.' Antar said, 'I will never allow this. I shall not give an enemy cause to rejoice by such an act. I know that caution cannot avert destiny and fate. That which the Lord of Heaven decrees and sends is law among His creation.' 'Urwa said, 'Cousin, your words are sound, for none can contravene the dictates of the Almighty King.'

Then they departed after Antar had offered them meat and given them lavish hospitality with food and wine. A few days later Antar forgot the terrors which had afflicted him in his dream.

Ghamra, his wife, entered his presence and humbled herself before him. She wept and complained. He said to her, 'Oh, Ghamra, why do you weep?' She replied, 'Oh, protector of 'Abs and 'Adnān, I seek the fulfillment of your bounty. I desire you to go with me to the lands of the Sudan in order to avenge me, rid me of my shame and cool my burning passion. Oh, father of knights, if you are prevented by some preoccupation then permit me to journey alone accompanied by my son. He has become my instrument of war and by him, God willing, my grief will cease to torment me.' She advanced to kiss the feet of Antar. When he saw her act in this way, he recalled the honour she once enjoyed and her humiliation. He felt ashamed, and he resolved to remove injustice, help her attain her ambition and assist her against her foes. Antar said to her, 'By Him who has brought forth the plants and by Whose power life is given to the dead, I shall alone go forth to avenge you in the company of my knights. I shall destroy the men of the Sudan and slaughter them with the Yemenite sword.' Immediately he called for Shaybūb, his heart full of pride. He said to him, 'Woe, brother of one mother, bring me 'Urwa and a party of men.'

When 'Urwa ibn al-Ward came he saluted Antar and said to him, 'What is your will, oh, father of nomad and townsman?' Antar said, 'Take your weapons for a journey and take your finest men with you, for we shall march with Ghamra to her lands and habitations. We shall avenge her among the base rabble of the Sudan.' When 'Urwa learnt of this matter he said, 'When shall we march, oh, protector of 'Abs and 'Adnān?' 'Early tomorrow,' Antar replied, 'if God so wills it;' whereupon 'Urwa departed, and he informed his men of Antar's circumstance . . .

. . . Antar bids a fond farewell to 'Abla, his wife and cousin, then to King Qays who wishes to accompany him. But Antar insists that he will only take

‘Urwa and his men, his brother Māzin, his own sons Maysara and Ghasūb; Sabī‘ al-Yaman ibn Muqri’l-Wahsh and Ghamra and those knights who were with her . . .

The departure for the Yemen and the Sudan.

Then Antar took his leave and departed. ‘Urwa was beside him, so were Ghamra and her sons. He began to cross vast plains and deserts. All that day they marched until darkness descended. Then they halted to rest, to eat and to plan the journey before them. In the morning Shaybūb came to Antar, his brother, and said to him, ‘Oh, brother of one mother. This journey of ours is beset with danger. We lack men, and the distance in the desert is great; I think it good sense to ask the advice of Durayd ibn al-Simma (1) who is the elder and counsellor of the Arabs. You ought to have taken him and his knights with you, because the land of the Sudan has more people than the rest of the earth, and they are the most robust of men. In it is found a waterless desert called the Land of Fear. It is located at a great distance from here. I know that the lord of that place is called King Ghawwār ibn Dīnār. By God, my brother, he is a plague among plagues and an affliction among afflictions.’

When Antar heard these words of Shaybūb he was angry and astonished. He shouted to his face and said, ‘Put aside such nonsense, do not alarm me by the mighty number of the Arabs and the negroes. By God, the Judge and King of men for whom no matter is of consequence, I will show you, son of the negress, such art of war and thrust of sword and lance as will make both human and *jinn* pray for succour and protection. Go before us into these forlorn vales and be not downcast nor submissive.’

When Ghamra heard Shaybūb’s words, she said to him, ‘Woe to you. From whence comes your knowledge of those localities and of their King Ghawwār, so that you can describe them with such clarity?’ Shaybub replied, ‘By God, princess, none knows that country as well as I do because it is my country, and its people are my people. I, my mother and my brother Jarīr came from thence. Nothing in our youth compared with those events when we were torn from our country. When I was a lad of seven years we were taken captive by one of our enemies called Mushīr ibn Munīr. He seized all who fell into his hands. He had a band of highwaymen with him, and he took us to the Hijaz. He tried to sell us to the highest bidder. On his way he was met by horsemen of the Banū Jadīla. They had much wealth. He wanted to seize it but they fought him and slew him and those negroes who were with him. They took the women and my mother, my brother and myself. They marched with us from camp to camp and let us guard the herds of sheep, goats and camels. For three years we did this until Prince Shaddād raided them while their horsemen were absent. He drove away their herds, and we were among the spoils. Shaddād was blessed with my brother Antar. My mother always told me that my people were from the Land of Fear. They are our people.'

When Ghamra heard Shaybūb say these words she was amazed and pondered their significance. At that moment Antar found Shaybūb in that place. He said to him, 'My brother, when we have arrived safely in the camps of Ghamra, marched in the lands of the Banū Sharīf and have crossed the lands of the Banū Qudā'a how many days will it take us to reach the lands of the Sudan?' 'It will take twenty (var. ten) full days to the beginning of the country of Ghawwār ibn Dīnār, twenty [var. ten] stages by horse at full speed. A number of days will be needed for camels and horses because the desert crossing is so dangerous.' Shaybūb was at the forefront of the men. He had advised them to take many camels and water-skins on the backs of their horses because of the waterless desert which lay before them.

Shaybūb led them along a route he knew well. It was the shortest way and the easiest to tread. Ghamra marvelled at Shaybūb's knowledge of that country. She said to him, 'Shaybūb, my hairs have grown white in this land. I have crossed it in length and breadth but at this moment I have no idea where I am and I have never seen this track before.' Shaybūb said to her and to Antar, 'Journey after me with a carefree heart and rejoice at the arrival at your hearts' desire. When we leave this place we shall enter a land of glades, water, pools, springs, flowers and medicinal plants. I shall leave behind me the land of sterile sand and rock in which is to be found neither waterhole nor sustenance.' 'Urwa said to him, 'By God, father of winds, I have endured much. I have detested such places since the days of our adventures with Muqri'l-Wahsh. How fearful are those sandy bottoms. Oh, Shaybūb, I shall remain in the company of joy and happiness as long as you are there at eventide and in the morning.'

Shaybūb led them for two days, and on the third day he turned to them and gladdened their hearts. Their eyes were refreshed, for on that day he brought them to a place where they were dazzled by the sight and their tongues were unable to describe what they saw. There was an abundance of glades, grass swards, pools and flowers. It was springtime. The pastures were splendid to behold. The canopy of spring-herbage was spread over the face of the earth. The trees were clothed in leaves, the buds of flowers had opened, water flowed from the pools, the birds sang on the branches, and the plants sent forth a fragrance as of musk and amber. They were of every colour, some yellow, some red, some blue and some green. The water murmured or roared as it gushed forth and found its way from secret sources. The eye and the mind were bewildered. The birds sang strange melodies, their voices of an exquisite harmony. They praised their Almighty Master, yet they were afraid of the birds of prey snatching them from the sky, because in that land were hawks and plumed carrion abundant in kind and number.

When the company saw that land they praised God, the One, the Beneficent, Lord of knowledge in whose power are the laws of men and their obligations. Then they camped in that place, and they rejoiced at the favour and grace bestowed in their journey. On the fourth day they travelled at dusk. They mounted their camels. They had pastured their horses. They had taken a goodly supply of fresh water. They pressed onwards and crossed the hills until the sun rose high in the forenoon. They had left the deserts and hazards behind them and now pursued their march, hour after hour, until they drew nigh to the land of the Banū Quda'ā.

They took counsel together. Shaybūb said to them, 'Have you weapons to hand, oh, men of war. Be prepared to fight and attack.' When Ghamra heard him she said to him, 'Woe, Shaybūb, put aside such nonsense.' He answered, 'Princess, this is no folly. If we remain here until a little before daybreak and journey leisurely, at the end of the day we shall reach the Trail of the Gazelle.' Ghamra said to him, 'Woe to you, are you out of your mind to speak thus.' He replied, 'By God, princess, I only speak the truth. I have not lost my reason. Little you know of these low and forlorn mountains. You know not this country and its gorges.' Antar said to them, 'Cease speaking thus for it profits little. Since the place be at a distance let us doff our mail until we cross the desert, and we draw nigh to the camps of our opponents.' When Shaybūb heard the words of his brother, his disregard of his advice grieved him. He said to them, 'Listen attentively to me. Be on the alert – if not, the negroes will master you and your enemy will overcome you.' Ghasūb said to Antar, his father, 'By the covenant of protection, my uncle Shaybūb has seen with a clear eye. He who goes forth in the evening and in the morning is not safe from danger nor from the caprice of fate and destiny.' Then they passed the night in that place, and they entrusted their affair to the Merciful One. They agreed to obey the advice of Shaybūb because he was sound. His indication was precise, without allusion or ambiguity.

Sā'iqa ibn 'Andam.

Al-Asma'ī said, 'We have already mentioned what happened to Ghamra with Ghawwār ibn Dīnār, the king of the Sudan. We have said that he was the king of her country. He stole her herds and killed her men. After that he appointed his cousin Sā 'iqa ibn 'Andam to be the ruler of these ruins and these hilly lands. He was a giant (3) who knew not the lawful from the unlawful. He was master of guile. He feared no man, nor held heroes in respect. He had nine thousand negroes beneath his sway and two thousand of the Banū Qudaʻā who had remained behind in that place. Sāʻiqa when he possessed their land killed some, but those who escaped his slaughter fled and sought refuge among the Arab tribes. None remained of the Banū Qudaʻā save the two thousand knights. Sāʻiqa had pitched his tents at the Trail of the Gazelle and at those sand dunes and hills, and he camped in those meadows and by those pools. He made them his special place of residence.'

One day while he was there, lo, there came horsemen to him from the Banū ʻAbs. The flash of their spears glinted in the ray of the sun. They were clothed in mail and well-armed, trailing their spears (4). At their head was the hunter's lion, the father of all knights, Antar ibn Shaddād. He was followed by ʻUrwa, Ghasūb and Ghamra and the heroes of thrust and blow. Shaybūb was in front of them like a male ostrich, and the rest of the people followed behind like forest kings. When the dust rose from the earth, and the points of their flashing spears glinted, the cavalry of Sāʻiqa hurried towards them, and loud was their cry. They were led by Sāʻiqa himself.

The commander of the approaching army was Ghasūb, son of Antar. When the parties drew close, ten negroes who had separated from the rest came to them. One of them said, 'Vile dogs, from whence come you? What is it you seek in this country?' Ghasūb did not answer. He stabbed him in the chest, so that the point of his spear rose flashing from his back. When his companions beheld that they attacked Ghasūb. He met them and slew seven of them. The remainder fled.

They returned dejected. They cried aloud, 'Oh, men of the Sudan, help us fight the *jinn.* Arise Sāʻiqa and combat these knights, for a devil among them has come forth against us. He is in the form of a man. He has slain our leader and seven of our horsemen.' When Sāʻiqa heard this he was troubled. He stood up and sat down. He foamed and frothed with anger and said, 'By God, had the enemy known me, their desire for war would not have made them so bold. My sense tells me that this enemy is with Ghamra, daughter of the vile. I suspect that she has sought the help of the Arab tribes. Ruin will befall all of them. I will show them the power of the sword, and I shall give them the cup of death to drink.' Then he rode forth with his knights and his foot-soldiers. At the sight the heroes in both camps cried a great shout, and the sword fell betwixt their company. Ghamra cried out, 'Base men, ignoble ones, do you think that I would leave my herds in your possession and refrain from taking vengeance for those men of mine you slew. Today I shall attain my object and my hopes.'

When Sā'iqa heard her words he said to her, 'Woe to you, Ghamra, will you frighten one like me with these base fellows? I am Sā'iqa, chief of men and princes.' Then he ordered his army to attack that instant. The nine thousand attacked the Banū 'Abs certain that they would trample them underfoot. They did not know that they were heroes. They fought no longer than an hour of daylight, then destruction befell the negroes. Fear filled their hearts. They no longer desired to fight when they saw their hopes confounded and death at the hands of the Banū 'Abs before them. Spear points pierced their eyes and hearts, and blood flowed over those dunes and along those sandy bottoms. Some men achieved fame, and disaster came about by the slightest slip of the hand. Battle boiled like the boiling of a cauldron. War's fire-wood was in the handles of the spears. The Banū 'Abs plunged into the dust as they severed necks and slit chests with the blade. They fought like titans at the beginning of time. How mighty was Ghasūb! How great his feats, so too the deeds of Maysara, his brother, who had sought battle and had attacked like a hero. Antar pursued his attack among those people until he reached the place where Sā'iqa ibn 'Andam was standing. He beheld him roaring like excited camels and encouraging the warriors around him. Antar advanced towards him. He spiked him in the breast, and the spear emerged from his back, glinting.

When the negroes saw their prince slain they shouted at Antar and attacked him from all sides. When the thousand knights of the Banū Qudā'a who had remained saw what had happened they rejoiced on account of their lady Ghamra. They, too, attacked and kindled the fire of war. Antar strewed the earth with skulls and emptied the saddles of their riders. The negroes were firm in their attempt to repell their foes, but what they saw filled them with terror, and they scattered. When evening approached they were confused. They turned their backs and fled under cover of darkness. They scattered among the dunes and hills. The knights of the Banū 'Abs captured the tents. The Banū Qudā'a caught sight of Ghamra. They came to her and kissed the ground before her. They thanked her for her deeds, and she asked how they had survived. They knew Antar, recalling how he had come to them before with Khufāf ibn Nadba and Durayd ibn al-Simma. They greeted him though some of them began to say to others, 'By Him who has raised the sky aloft and stretched out the earth, Antar has not come with Ghamra to our country with any intention of sparing us.'

While this was the concern of the Banū 'Abs and 'Adnan, the negroes began to cross the deserts. They had never imagined that a hero existed who could defeat Sā'iqa in battle. 'Furthermore,' they said, 'We have learnt that no fire can touch Ghamra and no giant can resist her.' One of them said, 'It was not the battle with Ghamra which put fear into our hearts, troubled our minds or humiliated us. It was a knight who pays no heed to men and their number. If my view is correct that knight is none other than Antar ibn Shaddād. We have heard tales about him, and the knights of the Arabs have recited his verses. In their gatherings they recount his deeds and exploits. If this be so then it is a misfortune which cannot be averted except by innumerable horsemen and assistance from our kinsmen. It is my view that I should go to King Ghawwār ibn Dīnār and tell him of these events. As for the rest of you, then hasten to cross the desert until you reach Suwayd ibn ‘Uwayd. Tell him to plan his action, to be on his guard and to gather together what men he commands before Ghamra reaches him with those princes. You know how they have attacked us and what afflictions they have brought upon us. They have killed Sā‘iqa, they have emptied their wrath upon him, and they have destroyed those peoples.’

Suwayd ibn ‘Uwayd (5)

When the Banū Kinda (6) heard this report, the light in their eyes turned to darkness. Some, in a rage, distressed their fellows and smote recklessly in all directions. They returned to their lord Suwayd ibn ‘Uwayd and told him of that matter. He was distressed and asked them to repeat their story. At once he rode forth and met the negroes. He saw their humiliation, and he asked them about the battle. They told him of their experiences, their grief and their affliction. They told him about Antar, Ghamra and Ghasūb. He said, ‘Woe to you, how many were those horsemen?’ They said, ‘By God, we saw no more than one hundred and fifty.’

The spokesman [of the Banū Kinda] was called Qaswara ibn Jawhara. He was crafty and cunning. When they heard his report they said to him, ‘You were the one who caused the death of Sā‘iqa. None else destroyed him. He used to pay heed to your counsel and follow it. You must march with us into battle and go forth in single combat.’ He said to them, ‘If you put your confidence in me, oh, wretched ones, then the power to strike the vile foe will be yours.’ When they heard him they laughed aloud. He said to them, ‘I shall show you what I will do on the battlefield when we return with soldiers and horsemen.’

The Banū Kinda informed King Ghawwār ibn Dīnār of the unexpected disaster. He tore his raiment, his eyes flashed, and his heart nearly broke in twain. He said, ‘How many were you when disaster befell you?’ They answered, ‘By God, we were nine thousand horsemen.’ He said, ‘I have heard that your enemies were some three hundred horsemen. This meagre number did these deeds against you despite the fact that Sā‘iqa alone equals a thousand knights?’ They said, ‘He who slew Sā‘iqa was the chief.’ ‘Who slew him? I shall destroy him.’ They said, ‘Antar, the knight of the Banū ‘Abs. Ask no more, call your men and heroes. Take equipment for battle. If not, they will speedily overtake you, and they will do to you what they did to us. The enemy pursued us and is intent on our total destruction.'

Suwayd ibn 'Uwayd said, 'By the covenant of protection of the noble Arabs, and by Him who spread out the wilderness and who brought forth water from the solid rocks, I will not let you seek protection from anyone. I will leave none alive among the Banū 'Abs, be he white or negro. I shall not dismount until I meet these scoundrels and my sword slays Antar ibn Shaddād. He entered this country once before but I paid no heed to him. Now his evil has reached me at this turn in my fortune.'

They summoned the horsemen telling them to take their arms and to make haste. When the negroes saw this action they said to him, 'Do not hurry, put aside such haste and stay in your tents. Guard your tents, else you will lose them.' He said, 'I shall not return until I have destroyed the enemy.' He came to an understanding with the negroes, and he set forth among ten thousand warriors known for their ability to fight. Suwayd took his place at the head of that army. He was at the front of them, as was rightly his due among those who were under his authority from the Banū Kinda and the Banū Tamīm. His heart was full of anger because of the injury inflicted upon them by the slaying of Sā'iqa ibn 'Andam.

He had travelled no more than a day when he met Antar and those with him, for the latter had rested with his company at the Trail of the Gazelle. When eye met eye, and when the heroes of both parties beheld each other, evening was approaching and sunset was at hand. Antar, Ghamra and her companions remained seated on their horses. Both parties rested in their saddles until the wings of the blackest night covered them.

The Banū Tamīm and Banū Kinda advanced on horseback, encased in hauberks and heavy armament (7). Then they dismounted and pitched their tents, except Suwayd ibn 'Uwayd. He did not dismount to eat but he exhibited his sword and began to roar, displeased that the darkness had overtaken him and he had not achieved his objective in regard to his foes.

As for Antar ibn Shaddād and those men in his noble company they spent the night asking Ghamra about that devil. She said, 'Oh, father of knights, he is a giant and unequalled. He is hard, cruel and firm in his courage. My father feared him more than any other person. Every year he used to raid our country and rob our herds. On some occasions I used to raid him. Battles took place between us. When my father died, and he knew of his death, Suwayd ibn 'Uwayd sought to pursue me, and he asked for the aid of one of the kings of the Sudan called Ghawwār ibn Dīnār. He attacked me and killed my men and stole my herds. Be God, I fear this devil lest he gather all the negroes against us.'

When Antar heard her words he perceived her fear on account of what she had suffered, so he said to her, 'Oh, mother of Ghasūb, by the Unseen Lord, were this knight to have with him the people of Rabī' and Mudar (8) I would teach them a lesson and destroy them with the whetted blade. I would leave them dead in this desert, and none would be left to tell his tale.'

At daybreak the men girded their weapons and prepared for battle. Both parties mounted and faced each other. Antar indicated to his companions that they should attack the enemy without delay. They engaged their enemy armed with spears. They stabbed their flanks and sides, aiming to deprive them of their ardour. Suwayd met them, so did the heroic fighters who were with him. They had hardened themselves for battle. Ghamra and her knights attacked the negroes. On that day she had dressed in impenetrable armour, a wonder in men's eyes. Antar attacked with those lords who were accustomed to such battles.

While Antar was engaged in the carnage he met Suwayd ibn 'Uwayd who had slaughtered knights and destroyed the courageous. Antar leant towards him, and Suwayd met him with determination. Both were knights of the *Jāhilīya,* their heads filled with pride, glory and ferocity. Neither desired to draw back without accomplishing what he intended. They continued to fight and to smite until Antar said to himself, 'By the Lord of *Zamzam* and the *Maqām,* this is indeed a doughty knight. Without doubt he is the protector of this province, yet I have only heard Ghamra describe Suwayd ibn 'Uwayd, lord of the Banū Tamīm (9). If this man be he then he is a mighty giant.'

Antar approached him and then withdrew. He was uncertain of his identity. As for Suwayd, he knew Antar by his blackness and the great size of his body, his fortitude, the skill of his blow and his warlike art. They continued to charge and withdraw, to jest and to battle until the heat exhausted them, and the iron upon their bodies weighed heavily upon them. Suwayd wished to rest and to retire. But he saw that this was impossible, and he was patient. He had seen Antar perform horrifying feats, and he was spent. When Antar noticed that his foe was fatigued he turned his spear so that its point faced backwards, and he jabbed Suwayd with its shoe.

Shaybub grasped him and bound his shoulders tight. When his people saw what had happened to him, and how he had been humiliated they fled, leaving their dead behind them, two thousand and two hundred of their horsemen. They were pursued until driven from those regions. After Antar and his company returned, having looted their herds and having taken captive their children and dependants. Ghamra camped in her tents, her wish accomplished. The Banū Qudā'a listened to her and sought her counsel. They heard of the fate of the negroes, and they hastened to her from every locality. Companions and brothers assembled together. When they were settled and had camped there, Antar ordered Shaybūb to bring him Suwayd ibn 'Uwayd. He stood before him. Antar said, 'Woe to you, before you receive a grievous lesson tell me how it came about that you journeyed to Princess Ghamra, took possession of her camps and plundered her herds?'

When Suwayd heard Antar speak thus he said, 'My courage, my resolve in battle and victory over my equals urged me to do it. I surpassed all in my ability to smite, and I hunted lions with my hands in the forest. By God, oh, son born in adultery, I am grieved and amazed how a dog like you can address me in this way. Be this as it may, the chance of your returning with this harlot from these regions is remote. Warriors have come against you from every direction. They have blocked your paths. They are ruled by the sons of Hām. They will destroy you and those who are with you.' When Antar heard him speak he laughed but there was anger in his heart. The light in his eyes had turned to darkness. He said to him, 'Woe to you, wearer of two horns, son of a thousand like you. Who are these negroes or all the Arabs? I have with me one hundred and fifty knights. With them I will face the hosts of men and *jinn*.'

Then he ordered Shaybūb to take Suwayd within the tents. He was in chains and manacled. Ghasūb had drawn his sword. He struck Suwayd on his jugular vein, severing his head from his shoulders. As he did so he exclaimed, 'Woe to you, disgraced among the hairy. Do you threaten men like us in battle?' But when Antar saw this he was distressed. He was proud and grave and said to his son, 'You have erred in what you did. Who is this warrior that I should kill him. There are many like him who do not trouble the thoughts of your father.'

Ghasūb said, 'I only slew him to put an end to him in order to rid you of his evil.' Antar said, 'By Him who made firm the mountains and who knows the number of the stones of the earth and the sands, all who dwell in these deserted haunts are no grave worry to me.'

Then he turned to Ghamra and said to her, 'I have pondered the correct course to take. Tomorrow we shall ride forth in our noble band, and we shall encompass these enemy camps. We shall slay all in them before they come to us and assemble against us. Having entered these regions I shall not come forth again without leaving the enemy camps emptied even of him who blows on the fire. Otherwise your heart will not be contented.'

Shaybūb said, 'By God, you have spoken truly, my brother. It is difficult indeed to escape from these places. The hair of a lad would turn white at the prospect.' Antar said to him, 'Woe to you, who are these negroes that you speak of them in this way?' Ghamra approached Antar who was seated in that spot. She said to him, 'Oh, father of knights, there yet remains a man of courage called Lawn al-Zalām. He is the sword of King Ghawwār. If you overcome him we will rule these lands and govern them without an opponent.'

Then that morning they began to journey from those desert plains and valleys and went deep into the Yemen and Jabal al-Khuzām. When they reached Jabal al-Khuzām and Wadi 'l-Ghamām they saw tents, flags and men. These latter had ridden their horses, and they had raised such a dust as to resemble darkness. At length the dust cleared to reveal horsemen of the days of King Og of Bashan, armed with straight Samharī (10) spear-shafts, strong lances and Indian swords (11) wielded by the hands of men who fight in the face of death. Each man wore a hauberk of King David's mail and upon their heads were helmets of the ancient peoples of 'Ād. Great was their cry, their thundering and their flashing armament. Black were their faces, red their eye-balls (12). They resembled giant buffalo. They paid no regard to the hero, and they feared no man. At their head was the knight whom Ghamra had mentioned to Antar. She had told him that his name was Lawn al-Zalām. He was mounted on horseback like a devil in human form. His countenance was like a *jinni.* He was tall, his head was large, he was broad in his shoulders, and he feared neither death nor extinction.

Lawn al-Zalām (13)

The reason for the assembling of that vile host was due to those Banū Tamīm who were defeated after their king, Suwayd ibn 'Uwayd, had been slain. They crossed those deserts on horse-back journeying by day and by night until they came to these camps and reported the news to all who were in them. Lawn al-Zalām heard it and had the defeated brought into his presence. He asked them to repeat their account. They complained to him. They mentioned those horsemen who had been killed and those heroes who had perished. He said to them, 'Woe to you. Who did these deeds to you?' They said, 'Ghamra and this Hizaji knight whose name is Antar ibn Shaddād.' When Lawn al-Zalām heard them his eyes were dark with anger. He shrieked aloud and cast fear in the hearts of the men of courage who were round him. He said, 'What a fearful misfortune has befallen us at their vile hands.' Then he turned to those who knew the lands well. They said to him, 'Yes, by Him who spread the lowlands and who formed the mountains like pegs, it is Antar who killed Sā'iqa. He brought affliction on Suwayd ibn 'Uwayd and caused his execution.'

When Lawn al-Zalām heard them say these things he said, 'By the All-knowing King I must arise and meet these evil-doers and endeavour to destroy Ghamra and Antar ibn Shaddād. In my heart I nourish a hatred which has remained ever since our first encounter when he entered this country, when they had reported his courage and terror and the unsullied character of his knighthood and that there was none like him in any land. It was my intention, this very year, to go up to the land of the Hijaz, to slay all those in it who are Arabs and to kill this devil (14). However, my task has been made easier. He has entered the land ruled by the Sudan, he with his company of knights.'

Then he summoned his people to arms, and three days later all the sons of Hām came to him. He was head of forty thousand chiefs, all of them black in hue. They wore clothes which were dyed red, green and yellow of many kinds. On their heads they wore varied conical head-dresses full of foxtails, pearls and bells. This was their custom whenever they went into battle. They boasted of this in time of war. After they were prepared they determined to march, but they were overtaken by the troops of Antar ibn Shaddād amid flashing swords. When Ghamra espied the great number of the horsemen and saw that the foot-soldiers filled the sand-dunes and the valleys, she was dispirited by anxiety and fright. As for Antar, the father of knights, he deemed the enemy to be of no consequence. He attacked that assembled host and struck the soldiers of Lawn al-Zalām wherever he found access.

All that could be seen on that day was gushing blood. Heads were flying, and many were the horses with their riders beneath them. The negroes drank a bitter draught. They were spun, smitten and dazed. The coward was perplexed, the courageous was patient and hardy. God the All Decreeing King willed His judgement upon them.

One was the conquered, the other was the conqueror. One was the smitten, the other was the smiter. One was afflicted, the other was the afflicter. This man was saved, and the other perished. This one was robbed, the other was a robber. This man was slain, and that man was wounded. Another wished to leave the field of battle to take his rest. Those who were disgraced were made apparent. Some showed it openly while others hid their shame in secret. He who was courageous called for the carnage to continue, and vile deeds were committed. The coward wept and longed for a wing to fly from the battle. Heroes fought to the death, and the horses were clothed in a covering of sweat and wounds. Spears plunged deep into chests, and Antar and the Banū 'Abs were refreshed by their blood.

The time of jesting had departed in this hour of gravity. The routes of escape were cut, and the key of the door of flight was lost in the battle. Faces were flattened and dis-figured, and the horsemen could not distinguish the evening from the morning. Wide spaces were made narrow, covered by a mantle which resembled the form of a crow.

He who told this tale, Juhayna al-Yamanī ibn al-Waddāh said, 'I have not heard, nor seen, nor reported anything more amazing than the disaster which befell them at the hands of Antar and what terrible deeds he performed on that day. He dyed the ground with blood, and he brought shame and blindness on the negroes. He never relaxed in wielding his sword, smiting heads and necks until he caused blood to flow in the desert. His arm grew weary and his helpers became few. Only then did he sheath his sword, and he attacked the negroes on open ground, excited in combat like camels roaring. The negroes came upon him in a mighty number when they saw his deeds. He attacked one of the slaves. He grabbed his legs with the power of his wrist and arm. He tightened his grip. He began to spin him in his hand like a sling. The negroes continued to press around him. He cast them headlong in that valley until, in that way, he had slain some one hundred and ten noblemen. He smote them on their chests, in their sides and upon them he brought a sore affliction. In his hand he held nothing but the Achilles tendon of the slave. By it he struck an enemy in the chest. He split him asunder. He turned to another and felled him. Whenever he seized a foe by his neck he throttled him.'

The narrator (*rāwī*) said that in that battle he learnt that Antar had begun to fight better than he had ever done before with sword and blade. With one man's body he smote another. Both men died, in one blow. As for Shaybūb, forget not his valour! He went in a circle around Antar, shooting his arrows, blinding and striking his opponents in the chest and throat. When the negroes saw Antar's deeds they dismounted, and they hemmed him in from all directions. But he seemed absent from the world. He thought of no man. He was drunk, but not with wine. So many were the soldiers, so great was his joy and exhaltation in battle that he was oblivious to existence about him. When Shaybūb saw his brother and how he had been surrounded he cried aloud, 'Oh, base and vile!' Then he called to the Banū 'Abs, to 'Urwa and to those with him and said, 'Go to Antar, my brother, before the blades smite him down. He has scattered the horsemen.'

Prior to that instant Shaybūb had come to aid him but he had paid no attention to him. Antar had said, 'Rest yourself.' Shaybūb had not retired but had commenced to protect Antar with arrows until Ghasūb, 'Urwa and those men with him reached him. Shaybūb encouraged them to stand fast. Then Ghamra, Ghasūb, 'Urwa, Maysara and Sabī' al-Yaman arrived having smitten the negroes. They began to fight with determination and to counter new terrors in the battle. Thus they continued until it was evening. The parties separated hardly aware of who was friend and who was foe.

Antar returned. In his appearance he resembled a purple anemone for the blood of the horsemen had dyed his body. He had sustained many wounds. Nevertheless, he had cooled his anger. In that battle he had killed one thousand and two hundred knights.

A night attack

The negroes retired exhausted. Great was their pain and anguish. They went to their tents to tend their wounds and to sup. Antar also went to his tent. He was dazed like a drunkard because of what he had suffered from blow and thrust. The negroes came to their king, Lawn al-Zalām. He was distressed at his lack of success. His companions comforted him, 'Do not be distressed on account of these vile enemies, for none among them is able to speak tonight. At dawn none will be able to thrust with a spear or smite with a sword. None among them thought that he would live to see this night. How grievous it is for that devil named Antar ibn Shaddād for in the battle today he suffered like no other man. He is now weak and tired in limb due to his beating of men, using others as his weapon. In the morning it would be wise to line up our men for single combat and for us to capture this devilish knight of the Hijaz and bring him before you so that you can dispose of him in a way which is pleasing to your eye. After he has been captured we can dispose of the rest with the sword, though they be in number like the clouds.

When Lawn al-Zalām heard their counsel he said, 'What would you think if we launched a night attack upon them, unexpectedly, while they are tired in their tents and are asleep?' 'This is a different idea', they replied. 'If you have given it serious thought then let it be. When the dark hours before daybreak are at their deepest they will be drowsy and uneasy.' 'So it shall be,' he said, 'And I shall be the first among you. On this I insist.' They took their separate ways to sleep having eaten a little.

Najd ibn Hishām reported that after this they went to their tents.

As for the Banū 'Abs, when it was dark they rested and ate, then they retired to sleep. They arranged for a guard to watch that desert. They were afraid that their enemies might surprise them in the dark. Ghasūb assumed this duty, so did Ghamra, Sabī' al-Yaman and Maysara. They were afraid of the negroes because they had seen that Antar was exhausted. They divided the duty of the watch between themselves, for they trusted no-one else. The Banū 'Abs were still exhausted as the hours of the night passed.

At that fateful hour their foe mounted their horses and attacked them like a torrent. When they saw them they put them to the sword. Much shouting was heard, and men arose to do battle. The Banū Quḍā'a leapt to their feet and fought the negroes. They fell into a sea of dust. The negroes came upon them in packs. They decided to flee. Antar was still asleep in the tents, like a wine drinker soothed by his drunkenness. He was exhausted. Shaybūb was at his side. Some moments he tarried, at other times he walked around him. When he heard the shouts of the enemy who had surprised them in the darkness he left his brother to go to the Banū 'Abs, and he urged them to do battle. Quickly the Banū 'Abs mounted their horses and armed themselves with spears and grasped swords in their hands.

It was deep in the night, and the ground laboured beneath the blows of war and the smiting of iron upon iron. Ears were deafened. The Banū 'Abs had started to flee but Shaybūb had rallied them. 'Woe to you, what afflicts you? Why do you turn and flee in this way?' He inspired them continuously until he brought them back again into the battle. Ghamra and her son Ghasūb strove valiantly but fear came upon them and all were certain that death was near at hand.

As the fighting increased Antar awoke. He was tired and in pain. His eye was aflame like safan-wood or drops of blood. Shaybūb wept and embraced him. He kissed his cheeks. Antar said, 'What makes you weep? May your oppressor perish!' 'Brother,' Shaybūb answered, 'Why should I not weep while your wife Ghamra, Ghasūb, Maysara, 'Urwa and Sabī' al-Yaman are afflicted. They are in desperate combat.' Then he told Antar what had happened, how the negroes had surprised him while they were asleep. When Antar heard his tale and saw his tears and wretchedness he said to him, 'Woe to you, why did you not tell me earlier in the night so that I could bring the enemy to humiliation?'

He ordered his steed Abjar to be brought, and he mounted it. He took his sword and prepared for battle. Shaybūb had filled his quiver with arrows, and he accompanied his brother to the battlefield. He cried aloud, 'Cease from combat, humiliation awaits you. Antar ibn Shaddād has come to meet you.' Antar found his sons and his wife grievously stunned. He attacked. Ghasūb, Urwa, Maysara and Sabī' al-Yaman had exhausted their horses. They had bidden each other adieu. The breadth of two arm's length or an arm's length was between them and death. Antar reached them and drove back the enemy with his sword. He shouted aloud, 'Woe to you, base knaves. Do you not know that I am Antar ibn Shaddād?' Despite his onslaught he was dismounted.

He said to Shaybūb, 'Guard my horse, and I will show you a marvel.' Shaybūb took the horse, amazed at Antar's recovery. He cried to him, 'Woe, son of one mother, be not hasty.' Antar reminded the enemy of his blows of the previous day. He unseated his enemies. He filled the land with skulls, and he cast blind shadows, like antimony, over the eyes of his foes. Thus he did battle until he reached his son Ghasūb and his companions. He said to them, 'Rejoice at your safety, for God has ended your bitterness. Whosoever can find a riderless horse on the field, then let him mount it!'

None had a horse except Ghamra and Ghasūb. The others had lost their mounts due to the arrows of the negroes. When they saw Antar they were filled with renewed vigour. They knew that they were safe when 'Urwa came to Antar, kissed him and said, 'You have triumphed, oh, knight of the Arabs. By God, you came to us when we were hard pressed. You have given us new life.' Then Antar left them. He fought for his sons and his companions. By himself he redeemed them until they had recovered their strength. Shaybūb brought them horses from the battleground, and they mounted them. The enemy separated before Antar and the Banū 'Abs and Banū Qudā'a joined together. When the men had turned into horsemen they attacked the negroes. They fought like men who had been disgraced. Ghasūb rejoiced at his father's slaughter.

That battle raged from the first third of the night until sunrise. When it was light the negroes attacked again. They were met by Antar and the Banū 'Abs. Spears were pointed at their chests and blood flowed like a river. The earth trembled, and the crow hovered above the corpse. There was a flash of blade and spear-point. Spears were aligned like serpents at the heart. The Banū 'Abs shrieked aloud. The coward sought to flee. The bodies of the negroes were heaped in the sandy valleys. The wind from the spears blew above them, and death's clouds shed their rain. The goblet of mortality was drunk to its last drops. Both sides were finely balanced, and men's souls were sold cheap after they had offered them for a high price.

Najd ibn Hishām said, 'Thus they fought until that day had ended. When darkness spread its wings the parties were no longer locked in combat. Each went to its camp. Each was drunk, but not with the juice of the grape. The Banū 'Abs spent that night in gratitude to Antar. They praised him for what deeds he had accomplished on that day. As for the negroes, they passed that night in woeful loss and in deep anxiety.'

Lawn al-Zalām is captured.

The following morning, at daybreak, both armies faced each other. The negroes wished to attack from every quarter. They held their spears and swords in readiness. But Lawn al-Zalām restrained them. He said, 'I have determined to ride singly into battle for in such combats heroes and their competitors are made known. When I go forth to the place of combat I will call for Antar. If he accepts my challenge I shall leave him in the dust. I shall be avenged. My shame will be forgotten.'

Then he rode forth on a horse. It was like a pearl and a gust of wind. It resembled water when it pours forth from a narrow pipe, pallid in its colour, pleasing in its proportion. He was clad in a mail hauberk with protruding rivets so numerous as to appear like the eyes of locusts (15). It could not be pierced by the Indian sword nor by a well aimed spear or lance. Over this hauberk he wore a coat of Yemenite mail, a masterpiece of art, and upon his head was a giant heaume of the ancient people of 'Ād. It was embellished and was able to deflect the blades of Indian swords. In his hand he held a Frankish lance.

When he entered the field of combat he advanced with his horse until it stood still. He mounted it nimbly like the dart of a viper. Then he sat motionless. Both parties fixed their eyes upon him. He beckoned to the Banū 'Abs and 'Adnan. 'Oh, Banū 'Abs, he who knows whom I am need not be reminded of my malice. As for him who knows me not, then I say to him that I am Lawn al-Zalām ibn al-Miqdām. I am the king of the Sudan. I seek single combat. I will fight none but the knight of the Hijaz called Antar ibn Shaddād. Then I may show him the arts of war and combat.' (16)

He had not finished before Antar was in front of him mounted on Abjar. In his hand he held his butted spear. He looked like a lion as he sat in his saddle. As he went into the field he guided his horse and recited these verses:

'Surrender and your torment will be spared you.
If you do not, then combat face to face awaits you.
I will not flinch from a heroic knight,
Nor from a lord who is bountiful in his favour.
I am courageous. I am not weary in the stern encounter.
The ardour of my knighthood will be shown you.
Awake, for death draws near and will confront you.
Exchange your joy for sorrow. In our single combat,
Oh, family of Hām, you will taste fear.
I shall destroy you, thrusting with my spear.'

When Antar had finished his poem he attacked his adversary Lawn al-Zalām. Each struck the other in fury and parried thrusts and blows. When one charged, the other withdrew, sometimes in sport, at others in grim determination. Those who beheld the sight were baffled and disturbed. Then both disappeared from sight. At that moment the negroes acted with treachery. They ran in the direction of Antar with their swords and spears. Ghasūb shouted to the Banū 'Abs to come from every pass armed with swords and heavy lances. There was fierce fighting amidst blood, terror and destruction. The negroes were in fear of humiliation, and they hardened themselves for further battle.

The Banū 'Abs fought well that day. Blood dropped like rain in that combat. Antar, the knight of the Banū 'Abs and 'Adnan and their protector, destroyed their enemies. Then he turned back to his adversary Lawn al-Zalām who was charging the horsemen and smiting the Banū Qudā'a. His face was as hideous as an ogre's. Antar shouted at him, he reversed his spear and smote him in the chest with its butt (17). He cast him down on the desert ground.

Shaybūb seized him and pinned his shoulders with his turban after he had covered him with dust and almost killed him. When the negroes saw that their king had been captured they all attacked Antar. They shook their spears and swords in his face. They were met by Ghasūb, 'Urwa, Maysara, Sabī' al-Yaman and Ghamra. They broke the necks of the negroes, and their foes were like lifeless rock in their hands. Shaybūb cried at the top of his voice, 'Woe to you, for whom do you fight? Your king is bound in humiliation!' They fought until sunset, and then each party separated.

When the Banū 'Abs were in their tents Ghamra came to Antar and greeted him and those nobles in his presence. He was telling them of his battle with Lawn al-Zalām. His story filled them with admiration. They said to him, 'By God, oh, father of knights, had you not come to our aid all of us would have despaired of his life. This two-horned hero would have hastened our end because in battle he is the devil in human flesh, a pestilence of the age.' Ghamra said, 'By God, oh, father of knights, I was in fear lest you perish at the hands of the courageous Lawn al-Zalām. You are favoured with good fortune and all who oppose you are afflicted. The Lord of Heaven did not deprive us of your horsemen, nor of your companions, nor of your soldiers on foot.' When Antar heard her words he smiled and thanked her for them. Then, when their conversation had ended Antar said to those whom he loved around him, 'How shall I treat this devil who today slaughtered knights and slew the courageous?' One of them said, 'Oh, father of knights, slay him, cut off his head and cast him before the enemy. When they see that he is dead they will flee in terror. We can pursue them and put them to the sword until we empty their camps and habitations.'

How Lawn al-Zalām was spared.

After he had heard them speak Antar said, 'This is sound sense.' Then they left to sleep after they had fixed a guard to watch the tents. When it was midnight, and Antar was seated with the fire burning before him, Ghamra came to visit him. When he saw her look of haste and passion he was displeased, 'What has brought you here in the dead of night? Has anyone surprised you in the tents?' 'No, father of knights,' she answered, 'I have come to you about a matter which the whisperer of falsehoods may spread abroad about you.' 'Princess, what is this matter which has brought you?' he asked. 'May your happiness continue.'

She said, 'Know that when I left your presence and entered my tent and rested for a while, seeking repose after my fatigue, I heard Lawn al-Zalām weeping and sighing. He complained of his wretchedness. I went to him. I stood opposite him, and I asked him why he was weeping and what had befallen him. I said, "You acted as you did, and now you are sorrowful when death faces you." He said, "No, by God, oh, princess, my weeping is due to a strange reason and for a peculiar cause. I beg a favour of you, to endeavour to release me from the hand of my capturer. I swear by the Creator, that I will be a helper of yours all the rest of my life." I said, "Yes, I will do this, but tell me what has happened."

He said, "Know, oh, princess, by God Almighty, today there is no-one dearer to me than my son Safwān who is nicknamed Badr al-Tamām. He loves a maiden who is called 'U' jūbat al-Anām. She is the daughter of King Hammām who is the lord of the Land of Flags and Ensigns (18). So great was his passion that my son was unable to sleep. When I beheld his thin body and his weeping I asked him about his circumstance and sought to discover his tribulation. He told me of his love and his affliction. He said to me, 'Father, in truth I tell you I am deeply in love and am drowned in a sea of passion.' I said, 'Who is she who has enslaved your heart and has robbed you of the pleasure of sleep?' He answered, ' 'U'jūbat al-Anām, the daughter of King Hammām, has filled me with passion.' By God, princess, when I heard him speak thus my heart burnt for his sake, and I wanted to restore him to his health and reason. I comforted his heart and calmed his fears, and I decided to ask her hand for my son.

Then these wars between us took place, wars of which none has seen the like. I know that my son will die because of my grief, and because he will see his love unfulfilled. I beg of you the greatest boon. Please obtain my protection from the father of your son so that I may become one of his servants and a helper of his, like one of his slaves, also all those negroes who are under my authority. But I beg of him to aid me against King Hammām because of his daughter 'U'jūbat al-Anām. By God, the All-knowing King, none of these matters and decisions will be accomplished without the aid of Antar, the courageous hero, and those noble knights who are with him. You know these lands and the negroes who dwell in them. I picture King Ghawwār sending against you his soldiers who will fill the desert in their numbers. He may be more than you in battle. He may weaken you and kill your warriors because of your slaughter of the negroes. But if you journey and my men are with you on your way, your power will be greatly strengthened." '

Then Ghamra continued, 'Oh, father of knights, when I heard these words I saw their sound wisdom. He speaks the truth. He is no liar.' When Antar had heard Ghamra's report he said to her, 'Bring him to me so that I may question him once more.' 'To hear is to obey,' she replied. She went to King Lawn al-Zalām and saluted him. He rose to his feet and quickly she untied the bonds around his shoulders and his hands. She opened the chains on his feet, and she led him to Antar. Lawn al-Zalām saluted him humbly and wept due to his pain. He said, 'Oh, knight of 'Adnān, I seek your protection so that I may be among your servants.' Antar said to him 'I will not give you protection. You are a hypocrite and a liar. You are still under the authority of King Ghawwār ibn Dīnār. I know that when I leave this country you will act with treachery against Ghamra. You will return to her country and you will help Ghawwar to harm her. You will treat her with enmity. Were I to know that the words spoken were uttered by another than yourself then I would release you and give you my protection, this by the One God, the Creator, the Almighty King.'

Lawn al-Zalām said, 'My lord, the true is opposed to this. I shall not act once again in the way you suppose. By God, the Creator, I shall only serve Ghamra and be her helper and the lowest of her slaves. I shall protect her from all the negroes.' Antar retorted, 'How can it be imagined that after my entry of this land I could leave a human to rule it or spare one of the negroes? Nay, I shall slay every horseman to be found in it. I shall only allow one who is not a negro to rule in it from this day onwards.' Lawn al-Zalām said to him, 'By the lord of the holy house, *Zamzam* and the *Maqām,* I knew of these matters and I have repented. It was decreed. It was all on account of my son Safwān, nicknamed Badr al-Tamām. He is deeply in love with 'U'jūbat al-Anām, the daughter of King Hammām. Oh, father of knights, I sent seeking her hand in marriage to my son, but King Hammām slew my messenger and filled me with great fear because he is a stubborn and wilful giant. I had resolved to march to meet him accompanied by my cousins, helpers and all those in my country, in order to destroy him, seize his daughter and rob him of his possessions. Then the conflict between the two of us interrupted me. It was decreed by the Lord of Creation. I have only sought your protection in order to be a servant and your slave so that you can assist me against those who oppose me.'

When Antar heard his story and beheld his wretchedness and his begging his heart was softened, and he was grieved to see his condition. He said, 'If the circumstance is as you describe then let your heart be free from anxiety. I shall avenge you and carry the girl away for you after I leave the habitations of her father like a wilderness.' Then Lawn al-Zalām raised his head. He kissed Antar's feet and said to him, 'Oh, courageous knight, long may you prosper.' He clasped him to his bosom and kissed his head and neck. He made him sit beside him, and he began to speak with him and jest with him.

Now Safwān nicknamed Badr al-Tamām, the son of Lawn al-Zalām, had heard of the capture of his father. The battle had ended, and his men had gone to their camps. He gathered the lords of his kingdom together and said to them, 'What think you of the punishment which we have suffered. Our men have perished, our homes have been ruined. I am at a total loss to know which way to turn. You know that my father has been captured. They may even have killed him. I have thought long and with great tribulation. I do not know how I can endure these things.'

A man in their midst, a knight who was called 'Ulwān ibn Ma'dān, said to him, 'We can do nothing but attack them tomorrow and put them to the sword and the spear, perchance we may capture this devil and so be rescued from humiliation and ruin.' When Safwān heard this he said, 'By God, this is the path to our ruin. Let us make peace with these evil men, otherwise our agony will be prolonged, and by fighting them we will suffer worse afflictions. I know the devils of the Hijaz. I have seen what they have done to us in single combat. There is nothing to be done except to go myself, as an envoy, and seek their protection. If not, my hopes will vanish. I shall not rescue my father nor those captives who are with him and who tonight are in utter distress, numbed by the battle. After that I will place my life in the hands of one called Antar. Good words are said of him, and he may help me in my sorrow and take pity on my anguish.'

When his people heard him they obeyed him and said, 'Do what you will, for we are your slaves and the slaves of your father.'

In the morning the knights mounted their horses, so did King Lawn al-Zalām. He wanted to rejoin his men to tell them what had happened to him. Then he saw his son who advanced to meet him among his lords. They passed through the foot-soldiers until they stood before Antar, the father of knights. When Safwān reached that spot he saw his father standing among the company. He drew near to him and asked him how he was. He told all that had happened to him. Safwān told him of his resolution. When Lawn al-Zalām had listened to his son he said, 'My son, let your heart be happy and at ease. The father of knights, Antar, has promised that he will take your beloved, even though she reside at the court of Caesar in Byzantium or beyond the wall of Alexander facing Gog and Magog. My son, he is able to accomplish what he says, because he is a man favoured by fortune. Wherever he turns his face he will reach his goal and attain his ambition.'

Sa'īd ibn Mālik said that at that moment Safwān ceased to be anxious and sad. He dismounted and advanced to kiss Antar's feet as the latter sat in his saddle. He wept and recited verse in praise of Antar. When the latter heard this poetry he felt sympathy for him. He marvelled at the eloquence of his tongue and his promise to be united with the one he loved. Antar asked Lawn al-Zalām the name of the lad. 'Oh, father of knights, this is your slave, my son. It is he about whom I spoke, about his love and passion. He is as you see him. Love has made him thin and has wasted him away. He is very sick.' Antar rejoiced to see him and drew close to him. They quickly brought him a splendid robe, and he dressed him in it. He gave robes of honour to all those nobles who were with him.

After that they returned to their tents. At the head of them was Lawn al-Zalām and his son Badr al-Tamām, Antar, the knight of courage, Ghasūb, Maysara, Ghamra and the Banū 'Abs, the knights of fate. Horsemen had reported the peace between the former foes and all had rejoiced at the news. The negroes welcomed their king and Antar, the father of knights, who accompanied him. They all dismounted, saluted Antar and greeted him. After an hour, little more, the tents were pitched. They went inside and forgot their sorrows. They were filled with joy and they ate and drank wine in the evening and morning. They continued to celebrate for three days.

On the fourth day they moved from that place to a verdant glade called the Gardens of Paradise, because it contained two of every kind of fruit. In it there were watery bowers, blossom of every colour, narcissi, spice and pepper. Water gushed forth from the thickets of that place and the branches intertwined in an embrace. The sky was covered by an awning of still cloud. The colour was as the splendour of a charger's harness. Wine worked its will on the minds of the drinkers, and the lover discovered the secret thoughts of his beloved.

Najd ibn Hishām said that Safwān had been intoxicated. His extasy had been enhanced. He recalled his beloved 'U'jūbat al-Anām, daughter of King Hammām, master of the Land of Flags and Ensigns. When Antar heard his verses in praise of him he said, 'May God's mercy give you joy, oh, youth. By the Lord of the most ancient of days, the God of Moses and Abraham who knows all that is in men's hearts, the maiden will be yours, even if Chosroes Anushirwān or Caesar, the king of Byzantium, were to offer her their hands.' They continued this merriment for a number of days and nights.

Then, lo, a great dust arose from every direction. The sandhills and the valleys were darkened. Shouting stirred the land. Antar, the lion, leapt his leap and mounted Abjar. Lawn al-Zalām and his horsemen also mounted. Heroes stepped out of their tents, summoned by the call, 'Woe to you. Take your armour and weapons and be ready to do battle.' Their horsemen numbered twenty thousand, mail-clad or doubleted. Ghamra had collected three thousand knights and one hundred and fifty of the Banū 'Abs. But the number of warriors who blocked the plain, the rough land and the mountains was ninety thousand horsemen. They were courageous knights, among the giants of the negroes. The reason for the arrival of these numerous warriors was the horseman of theirs called Qaswara ibn Jawhara (19).

When Antar had slain Sā'iqa ibn 'Andam, and his companions had been defeated, Qaswara had been among the vanguard of the defeated. They had been scattered in scores. Qaswara had travelled hard by night and by day until he had reached the campments in the Land of Fear. That was the country of King Ghawwār ibn Dīnār. He came into his presence and told him of what had befallen him and Sā'iqa ibn 'Andam, and how the latter had perished. He reported how Suwayd ibn 'Uwayd had lain dead on the ground, and how his soldiers had been slain and had been scattered.

Wajh al-Ghūl. (20)

When King Ghawwār learnt this news he was shocked. He said, 'Who has dealt you this blow?' He replied, 'Ghamra and a knight of the Hijaz called Antar ibn Shaddād.' King Ghawwār snorted in anger. Sparks flashed in his eyes. His countenance changed, and he said to Qaswara, 'How many are these ruffians?' He answered, 'By your life, they are as numerous as the pebbles and the sands.' When he heard this he was agitated, and his heart grieved at the losses. He lowered his head in silence. He sighed aloud, and he turned to those lords of his around him and the counsellors of his kingdom, 'Advise me as to the action I should take. What shall I do?'

His vizir, who planned his affairs and who pointed out any errors of judgement, said to him, 'Oh, king, you made a mistake at the outset of this affair. You did not complete your intention. You allowed this harlot Ghamra to live. You were remiss and halfhearted in your resolve so that she escaped to the camps of the Banū 'Abs and 'Adnān, and she sought help from those tribes of Arabs who resemble the *jinn* of Solomon. But this is an affair of the past. All you must do is to gather warriors from near and far and form them into a powerful army. If you do not you will fail. Perhaps this harlot will gather against you all the dwellers in the desert. The Banū Qudā'a will hear of her return, and they will come back to her from various districts. Then her power will be strengthened and her hostility will increase. She will ruin the towns and the villages and will destroy those who dwell in them.'

When the king heard the counsel of his vizir he was afraid for his kingdom. He said to his vizir, 'If such be your true assessment then this time I shall go myself and I shall not return until I turn her habitations into fields of ruins. No opponent will remain in my kingdom. I shall destroy the enemy. I shall seize Ghamra and those horsemen who are with her, and I shall slay them all in this place.' When his vizir had heard his words, he said, 'Oh, king, this is not the correct course to take. Who are these dogs that you, in person, should march to face them. It would debase the reverence shown to you and your divine decree. Your best plan is to send the knight of your realm who has no fear of drinking the cup of death, namely Wajh al-Ghūl.'

According to the narrator (*rāwī*) this knight, whose qualities were described by the vizir, was the one who hewed Ghamra's soldiers into pieces when she lost her father. This knight pillaged her towns and scattered their inhabitants. Due to him she fled in defeat to the Hijaz and complained to the father of knights, Antar ibn Shaddād. This has been recounted (22).

When Ghawwār heard the counsel of his vizir he summoned the devil Wajh al-Ghūl and told him of the way he had been affronted. He told him of Ghamra's acts and those of her men. Then he said to him, 'I have summoned you because of this affair.' Wajh al-Ghūl replied, 'By the moon when it bestows its light and by the night when it brings darkness and gloom (23), if you send me to these people and entrust me to do battle with them, I shall bring them bound to you or in fetters. Among them will be their knight named Antar ibn Shaddād. It is my view, oh, king, that in regard to these people you should not break your law and custom. You have a knight who will remove this injury from you and who will comfort you in your wretchedness.'

King Ghawwār said, 'I summoned you to learn whether you were a hero and one of the princes of the Yemen.' Then, that instance he divided the horses among all his men, and a few days later the whole land was full of mounted men and foot-soldiers. Ghawwār bestowed bountiful gifts. He gave a new robe to each one who was leader or a chief. When they were gathered for their departure King Ghawwār said to his vizir, 'Take charge of them and direct their march towards the enemy until we are rid of this evil.' The vizir chose ninety thousand horsemen. They were all clad in hauberks of chain-mail. He said, 'By these men I shall achieve my object even though the enemy equals in number the people of 'Ād and Thamūd. Let us recall that Lawn al-Zalām has assembled warriors of the Banū Hām, men whom he sent to us as reinforcements in time of war.'

Then Wajh al-Ghūl set out with his warriors. He marched with an army which could be compared to a sword of molten metal when it is cast. Their dust settled as a cloud over the horizons. They marched for one week. . . .

. . . The army meets a band of defeated negroes who report the defection of Lawn al-Zalām. Wajh al-Ghūl continues his march and reaches the camp of the Banū 'Abs. Battle commences, and Wajh al-Ghūl is worsted. Safwān offers to mount guard in Antar's camp but his thoughts are still with his beloved. The battle rages hotter, and Wajh al-Ghūl is tempted to enter the heat of the fray. . . .

Then it was that a knight called al-Dahhāsh ibn al-Ra' 'āsh advanced towards him and kissed the ground. He said, 'My lord, by al-Lāt and al- 'Uzzā (23) be not rash. I shall go forth in single combat. I will show you what I can do with these horsemen.' When Wajh al-Ghūl heard him speak, he answered, 'Hurry to achieve your wish. If you slay not Antar, then bring him to me captive so that I can deliver him to the great king.' Then the other went forth on a pale charger, tall and thin, which raced against the wind. He bore a sharp sword and having entered the field of combat he loosed his horse's reins and broke forth into verse. He had but finished when Ghasūb attacked him. He was mounted on a fine-coated horse of unsurpassed speed. Over his chest he wore a hauberk of closely linked rings, impenetrable to the Indian blade nor could a well aimed spear penetrate its doubled links. On his head he wore a *pot de fer* prized by Chosroes, king of Persia. It was hammered from iron plates. In his hand he grasped a sword as sharp as a razor.

Then he attacked, roaring like a lion. He thrust his enemy through the heart, toppled him from the back of his steed, and he fell on the ground wallowing in his gore. Ghasūb cried out with an eloquent tongue, 'Woe to you, will you challenge us with words, bastards that you are! We are heroes of the Banū 'Abs, noble among men called by the name of 'the terrible death'. '

When they saw these deeds of Ghasūb the gallant were in awe of him. None came out to challenge him in single combat, neither Arab nor negro. He therefore returned to his people and changed his horse. Once again he returned to the battle-field. He cried out, 'Oh, sons of harlots, come out and fight this knight of 'Adnān.' Wajh al-Ghūl remained still, looking and listening. But he had become restive within. His eyes burned like embers when set alight. He charged forth from between the banners. He roared, and he made for Ghasūb like a bird of prey when it strikes a dove. He taunted him in verse, then he unsheathed his Indian sword. He was a fighter skilled in every kind of weapon, and no man could face him when he screamed with all his voice.

Plate 4: al-Dahhāsh ibn al-Ra‘‘āsh and King Wajh al-Ghūl.

On that day he was clad in a *jazerant* (24) of thick quilted cotton hidden by a covering of tightly woven mail. On his head he wore a casque which deflected blades of iron, nor could spears penetrate its thickness. When Ghamra saw him she feared for the safety of her son, and she wished to sally forth to bring him away from Wajh al-Ghūl. She went to Antar and told him of the matter. She said to him, 'I fear this knight and what he may do to my son. I fear lest he arouse my emotions to a degree that I go forth to send back my son and fight the foe myself.' When Antar heard her, he persuaded her not to act thus. He said to her, 'Stay where you are. I will fulfill your hope. This devil is a doughty smiter and I alone can resist him.' Then he went to his son and said to him, 'What you have done today in battle is more than enough.' When Ghasūb heard the words of his father he realized that affection had inspired his sentiments. So he returned to his mother. She embraced him and kissed him. She thanked him and praised him.

But when Wajh al-Ghūl saw that he was angry, and he wondered how he could withstand the opponent who now faced him. He advanced towards Antar with caution and calculation. He said to him, 'Woe to you, offspring of base blood. Who are you to turn aside my foe and deny me my vengeance?'

Antar said, 'Oh, offspring of apes and vilest creature of these lands. I am Antar ibn Shaddād, the mightiest of the Arabs in zeal and the firmest in resolve. No tongue can describe me and my noble deeds. I am the mine of valour and pride, unique in this age. I have attained every goal I have sought, and every enemy of mine is abandoned. My foe has been slain, his blood scattered in drops. I smite with iron swords and with the lofty lance. My flame burns brightest among the Arabs. I am the noblest born and the stoutest in rebuff. I am the viper in the valley bottom, the father of knights, Antar ibn Shaddād. I have only to come to this country to avenge Ghamra, to uproot every trace of you, and to ruin these towns so that no hearth will be left to be tended.'

Al-Asma'i said that when Wajh al-Ghūl heard Antar's speech he was dark in his countenance. He said, 'How happy is this day of combat. I will show all who is the doughty knight, and who is the one entitled to this praise.' Then he attacked Antar with a pounce while Antar met him with cool resolve. Dust rose above them as they were locked in weighty struggle beyond the gaze of the courageous. Destiny decided their fate – glory be to Him who has decreed death and wretchedness and who has singled out life and glory for the elect. The knights were awe-struck until their horses, restless beneath them, were aware that both parties to the fight were equally fatigued, hungry and thirsty in a confined desert where the sun had passed its zenith.

Wajh al-Ghūl sought to escape, but when Antar realized his intent he faced him, and when he was opposite him he thrust him with his spear in his left side.

He leant from his saddle like a towering mountain and cried aloud, 'Oh, 'Abs, oh, 'Adnān, I am Antar, the father of knights.' Then the negroes saw Wajh al-Ghūl covered in dust on the ground, and they all attacked Antar like the onset of blackest night. They called aloud in one great shout, 'Oh, mighty knight and hero, may God cut short your life and rid the world of your evil. You have slain the knight of the desert.'

When Antar saw the negroes attack and loose their reins he made a sign with his hand. He cried out to the Banū 'Abs, and they attacked behind him. They answered his call. They hurled cries into the hearts of Antar's foes. Death was relief, and the battle raged on foot. The sea of mortality swelled, and the fire of fate burst into flame. Swords were blunted by hard blows, and spear-points were moist with blood. The horizon became sombre and darkened. Amid the rage of nations skulls were severed from their bodies. Only the bones were left. Men roared like forest beasts, speaking in tongues which were unintelligible. Every negro leader was killed. Lawn al-Zalām and his son accomplished deeds of valour, so too the negroes who were beneath his sway and his cousins. As for Ghamra and her son Ghasūb, and Maysara his brother, they were like a blazing fire which caught alight amidst dry firewood. Their fighting was a marvel, it stirred the spirit. Their sword play was at close quarter and in remoter corners of the battlefield.

After a little while Antar had split apart the other negro bands and the Arabs. His men forgot their cares. Every rank he attacked sought flight. As the night fell the negro warriors scattered. The Banū Qudā'a and the soldiers of Lawn al-Zalām returned praising Antar and praying for his life to be prolonged, for he had endured much. He returned sorely stabbed, and like a red flower, bathed in human blood. He marched before his men. He was tired and bent, yet able to phrase his couplets as he sat in his saddle. Lawn al-Zalām said to him, 'May God's breath give joy to your heart. You have quenched your thirst in breaking asunder these innumerable warriors.' In this wise their discourse continued until they reached their tents. They rejoiced at their success while the negro warriors said to one another, 'By the All Knowing King, Lawn al-Zalām has fortified this knight with his utmost powers. Antar has no equal at this time. None can resist him.'

The tree of silent barter.

When God brought the dawn, and it shed its light abroad they took counsel together, whether they should stay or depart. Antar wished to march with those negroes who were with him and pursue his foes to the Land of Fear. Lawn al-Zalām said to him, 'Oh, courageous knight, we must tarry here for three days.' Antar said, 'They may regroup and return to attack us in this place. King Ghawwār may set loose all the dwellers in this country.' When Lawn al-Zalām heard Antar speak he said, 'Do what seems to you wisest and best.' So they journeyed among ten thousand horsemen, all armed with mail, with Antar at their head. Around him were his knights and companions and 'Urwa, Ghasūb, Maysara and Safwān at his side. With them went the troops of the Banū Qurād (?) (Qudā'a?) They crossed those deserts. Whenever they came to a camp they pillaged it and seized its herds. On they went until they came to a country of many waters and pools. It was called Coward's Rock.

It was green in pasture land. The gazelles brazed beside it. It was hilly, and there were solitary places wherein were abundant plants and herbage in flower, so every eye could behold and be gladdened. When they saw that land they marvelled as does every sojourner there. They were tired and weary. Ghamra came to Antar. She said to him, 'Oh, father of knights, make us halt and camp in this green glade so that we may refresh our horses. I will disclose to you what a marvel there is in this place. I know that in it there grows an everlasting tree. It is immense, the size of a village built by human hand. Upon it there are many birds of every plumage. They are so many that they cannot be counted. Oh, father of knights, in this tree there is a secret which none knows save Almighty God.'

When Antar heard her describe the tree he said to her, 'What is the secret which God has bestowed in this tree?' She said, 'Know, oh, father of knights, that when the merchants come to this country and reach this tree, each one of them places his merchandise on a particular piece of ground so that one item is not mixed with another. Then they return to their dwellings, and they leave their merchandise under the tree. When morning comes they make for that tree from every direction and each one of them finds an item of commerce beside his own. This item is apt for the clime wherein he lives and suits the people of his locality. Thus, items of merchandise are exchanged for certain others. If he is content with the substitute he takes it and leaves his wares which he has deposited. But if he is dissatisfied he takes his own merchandise away again.'

When Antar heard Ghamra's account he was astonished and said to her, 'What happens to the items of merchandise which are left under the tree?' She said, 'Oh, father of knights, none knows what happens to them, nor him who takes them, nor him who puts them back.' Antar was amazed as were those who were also present. He turned to Ghamra and said, 'I want to see this tree, how can I do so?' Ghamra arose, and so did Antar and all those assembled, and they took cloth which they had among their supplies. They proceeded until they reached the tree. They found it to be gigantic in size. They had not imagined that such trees existed. Never had they seen the like in other lands. Its shade covered five hundred knights. They were astonished. Then they placed the cloth which they had with them beneath it. They withdrew from that tree and camped at about half a *farsakh*'s distance from it, so that they could watch it. Antar had believed the report but he had pondered its import. He said, 'Perhaps there is some significance, or perhaps the peoples who inhabit this place do these acts and take these goods.'

They spent the night in those sandy bottoms until it was morning, then they mounted and marched. Had they wings they would have flown. When they reached that tree their amazement increased because they saw wares beside their cloth. They were surprised, and they saw no explanation for this mystery. Then they took the cloth which they found there and left the cloth which they had deposited beneath the tree. They returned deep in thought. They journeyed the whole day until they reached their people. They settled in their tents for they had made that glade their place of residence (25).

King Ghawwār seeks for allies

As for King Ghawwār ibn Dīnār, he had been expecting Wajh al-Ghūl and his company to bring him Ghamra and Antar in humiliation and captivity. He had not foreseen the fortunes of destiny. He and his court waited for news, until the defeated arrived in their groups from the wilderness. They told him of the death of Wajh al-Ghūl and their terrible defeat. They wept and said to the king, 'This event has brought death to our knights whose wives and offspring will for ever wear black in sorrow.' Then they told him of all their woes and about the defeat they had suffered at the hands of Antar, and how many were dead and how many were captured.

When Ghawwār heard this he was astonished and trembled in his members. He sensed the downfall of his kingdom and his doom. He turned to those soldiers who remained and said, 'By God, cousins, did I not tell you that you would have to face such an encounter with these people and that you would be humiliated. Still it is I who am the transgressor. It is I who refrained from marching. Had I been with you the difficult would have been easy, and I would have consoled you by disposing of this wretched slave.

The only course is for me to march with all who are in these camps. If not, our enemies will rejoice at our discomfort. If our foe be of this quality then only weight of number will overcome him.'

When he had ended Qaswara said, 'By Him who possesses might, power and destiny, the major misfortune is due to one person called Antar. His sword in battle is in every spot. It is he who empowers them to do this fearful deed. It is he who has killed men and destroyed princes. If no knight can be found to overcome him then he will slay all who desire to fight him.'

Al-Asma'ī said, 'When Gawwār heard the words of Qaswara he said to him, "Who killed Wajh al-Ghūl?" He replied, "He was slain by him who fears not the lion, namely the father of knights, Antar ibn Shaddād. He is feared by knights who rout their opponents, and the kings of the country are covered in shame. Lawn al-Zalām has joined his company, also his son Badr al-Tamām and those warriors of the Banū Hām who are with them. There are also Arabs of the Hijaz, the Banū Qudā'a and many people and knights. They have no match. When Antar killed Wajh al-Ghūl and left him lifeless in the desert we retreated with little hope. Antar followed us, he smote us with his sword and shouted at us, 'Return to your King Ghawwār. Tell him these reports. I must come to him and destroy his men, tumble his kingdom and raze his districts and capture his wives and offspring. He does not keep his word, nor acknowledge the right which one who is an ally should be granted. Did he not owe Ghamra the right of protection? How comes it then that he has ill-treated her when during the lifetime of her father she was entitled to protection as of right? Let Ghawwār be on his guard against me. Let him assemble his bands and his soldiers. I must go to him and sever his head from his shoulders.' " '

When Ghawwār heard these reports from Qaswara he arose changed in mood, He said, 'I can endure Antar no longer. I must destroy him and his company. I must kill Ghamra and all with her.' Then he summoned the chiefs and heroes. After an hour they were present, each according to his rank of seniority. At their head was 'Akkāsh ibn Rayyāsh and Waqīd ibn al-Ra' 'āsh, lords of the Banū Hām and Arab heroes of the sons of Shem. After their arrival and assembly the king said, 'Know, oh, lords of the Arabs and the negroes, that our circumstances have become difficult after we enjoyed an era of ease. This knight, Antar ibn Shaddād, has exceeded his hoped for ambitions. The soldiers of Lawn al-Zalām have obeyed him, and the Banū Qudā'a are with Ghamra. They have become as one hand. On account of it they overcome all warriors who go forth to meet them. If King Hammām hears of our reverses, and that I have failed to face this wretch and his Arabs, we shall lose in his esteem every respect and dignity. Our value will be of little worth after we enjoyed his honour and esteem.'

When the princes of the negroes heard King Ghawwār say these things there was much talk and much disagreement. Then a man called Qurrat al- 'Ayn ibn 'Aqīq al-Wālidayn, vizir and princely adviser, came forward and said, 'Oh, king, I suggest that you send a messenger to him. Let him be a man of intelligence and eloquence. Having spoken to Antar the latter will comprehend what he is saying and be restrained from exposing himself to peril. When that messenger returns and brings his answer we shall act according to the answer we receive in his letter.'

The king said to him, 'If the affair be so, then you will be that messenger. Act diligently in what you say and caution him in regard to the heroes who have assembled in my presence. Perchance you may extinguish this fire which burns fiercer and hotter, and divert him. We shall restore to Ghamra what we have taken of her possessions, but only on condition that when she is settled in her country she will pay us tax and send us provisions.' When the vizir heard this he indicated his obedience. He said, 'Here I am, I shall write the letter this very moment, and I shall be curt and blunt in my speech.' Having finished writing, he read it to the king:

> In Your name, O, God Almighty. This letter is addressed to Antar who has acted unjustly and with conceit. To proceed. Oh, tyrant, the hypocrisy of you and your companions has increased and you have enraged the King by your strife and madness. If you continue thus then your death will be hastened, as the waning of the moon. Deem not all men to be the same. By my reckoning no medicine will cure me save your death. Lions hunted by a hunter show their fury.
>
> Know that we were not opposed to Ghamra until after she had ruined our towns in the lifetime of her father. She slew our men and heroes. It would be wise for you to return to your homelands. We shall restore to Ghamra all the possessions which we have taken, but only on condition that she pays us tax and tribute, and that she treads the carpet of the King until the anger which is in our heart is extinguished.
>
> The kings of the Arabs and the negroes have been summoned, together with all their knights. We have also written to King Hammām who is lord of the Land of Flags and Ensigns, requesting his champions and the sword of his wrath. Accept my wise judgement. If not, your destruction is close at hand. Protection from the blackness of the nights is for him who obeys. The curse of those nights is for him who is disobedient.

When King Ghawwār heard that from his vizir he was full of delight. He provisioned him for his journey and sent him forth in the manner of kings. The lords strode before him, and they unfurled flags and banners above his head. Drums were beaten before him, and pipes and trumpets were blown. On that day the vizir departed amidst his people.

As for Antar and Lawn al-Zalām they reached that land where flowers had opened in bloom, diffusing their scent. They had gathered about them the herds of the Arabs. The animals were too many to be roasted in the fire. When the company had settled in the meadows and the hills Antar sent word to the adjacent camps, and some three hundred loads of food and drink were brought. He fixed sentinels on the tops of the sand-dunes and on the peaks of the mountains. He sat down and dined and drank with the kings of the Arabs.

The vizir and his men came nearer and nearer. They drew nigh those camps. The guards saw the dust, and they came to Antar and told him. He said to them, 'Return to your watch. When the dust is nearer to you, and you know what is beneath it come again to me and tell me the news.' The soldiers went back to the mountain tops and closely watched what approached them through the mountains. After an hour the dust cleared, and they saw what was beneath it. They kept close watch for a while, and then they knew that a messenger was approaching. They waited until he reached them and he and his company had greeted them. They asked him his business and to whom he was travelling with his men. He told them that he was a messenger to Antar, the father of knights. They said, 'You have arrived where he is, for he is holding court in this verdant citadel. Halt until we have reported your arrival.' The guards left him. They returned to Antar and informed him that the messenger had come from King Ghawwār and that he was his vizir who planned and advised him in all his matters.

Antar ordered that he and his company should be brought into his presence. When Ghamra heard Antar speak she said, 'Oh, father of knights, why do you not ride out to receive him and ask him about his health and fortune?' He said to her, 'By God, none of us will mount unless it be from fear of attack.' The guards returned to the vizir and ordered him to appear before Antar. He advanced pensively. Servants received the vizir and dismounted him. He was a man of honour and respected. He saluted and greeted Antar who rose to meet him. He took him aside and seated him among his relations.

The vizir knew that this was Antar, and he handed him the letter. Antar took it and gave it to 'Urwa who read it to him. When Antar heard the threats which it contained he laughed until he fell on his back (26). Then he said, 'What a wonder of wonders, oh, vizir, that you can say these things! Have you not witnessed what I have done to men of valour on the battlefield? By Him who has created man from clay and has watered dwellings with abundant showers I shall certainly turn your habitations into ruins.'

Antar rose from his knees, he snatched the letter from 'Urwa's hand, tore it into pieces and threw it in the vizir's face. When the latter heard what he said and saw the torn letter he was full of terror. He said, 'Oh, father of knights, we shall return to Ghamra all the country we have taken from her and her property on condition that she pays us tribute. Calm yourself, why this fuss and hard heartedness?'

Antar said, 'Return, vizir. Advise your king to pay tribute to Ghamra and to return the land which he has taken from her. If not, then he is called Ghawwār, and I am Antar ibn Shaddād. I shall follow after you and come to your country.' The vizir said, 'Oh, father of knights, beauty of youth and man of courage of this age, I am aware that this episode will only end in slaughter and in horror's spectacle. It was not my personal wish to bring you this message. The king made me travel to your presence. He had said that only I was qualified for this task, and that you alone could extinguish the roaring flame. I cannot tarry longer after hearing these words.'

The vizir arose and asked for his horse. He was shocked in mind and judgement. He mounted and departed with his men until he reached his homeland. The king was seated awaiting his return. He was attended by other negro kings. As the vizir entered all stood up. When the vizir was comfortably seated King Ghawwār said to him, 'Oh, vizir, tell us your news.' He replied, 'Oh, king, by God, I have never seen one stronger in hand nor stouter-hearted than Antar. He is a man unlike other men and a hero unlike other heroes. His sole ambition is to sieze your realm and your villages.'

King Ghawwār was distressed, and so too the Banū Hām who were around him. One of them, 'Akkāsh ibn Rayyāsh said, 'Who is this slave, a base son, who can speak of your authority in such a manner. By God, this is a disgrace and a shame upon us that we permit him to come to these countries. Oh, king, send me to fight him. God will suffice you for his evil and the evil of those companions who are with him.' The king said, 'You should go to him with fifty thousand horsemen to rid us of his evil and to defend us. You alone can achieve it and only you can resist him.'

'So be it,' he answered, 'by your father. He has already come to this country with Durayd ibn al-Simma. He has slain a brother of mine and a cousin.' Ghawwār commanded that he should be equipped that instant. He was given fifty thousand knights, each an angry lion, armed with iron swords, long spears and with flags upon their heads. This mighty number was led by 'Akkāsh who was closely covered in a hauberk of layered mail, riveted and unriveted. His outer hauberk was black. It could turn an Indian blade or a truly aimed spear. He carried a heavy sword and a long spear. His steed was a noble mount. He rode before the soldiers, the intertwining banners, flags, pavillons and the cavalry. . . .

. . . Shaybūb reports to Antar what plans Ghawwār has made to attack. 'Akkāsh and Antar fight in combat. The former is slain by Antar who wrings his neck. The news reaches King Ghawwār who sends 'Andam ibn Bassām with sixty thousand knights. Shaybūb learns of his attack and an ambush is laid. 'Andam and his army are worsted. . . .

As for King Ghawwār and his negroes they regretted that they had not marched against Antar to gain renown. They said, 'The king has sent his sharp sword and his invincible armour. Picture 'Andam on his way back, trumpets blowing and drums beating. Antar will be with him, either as a corpse or as his prisoner.' Qaswara ibn Jawhara said, 'What will be, will be. Your eyes will confirm the reality of your vision.' Then he added, addressing those who were seated before him, 'Are you not ashamed to say such foolish words. By the protector of the Arabs, there is no escape for 'Andam bin Bassām. Antar will most assuredly slay him and take all he possesses. As for riches, God has bestowed them on this 'Absī.'

King Ghawwār exclaimed, 'Woe to you, you never cease to predict our misfortunes. You bring us gloomy tidings, You show no love or affection towards us! By the night and by the darkness, by the morning and its smile, 'Andam will not return without Antar and his companions. I must kill him in a hideous fashion. I shall deal with you in the same way. I shall humiliate and destroy him. A plague on you! Do you reckon 'Andam to be as other vile Arabs? I shall not speak to you until he returns, and I shall show you what I will do to him before my people.'

His vizir, Qurrat al- 'Ayn said to him, 'Oh, king, think not ill of the words of this man. He is now old and knows not what he says.'

Najd ibn Hishām reported : While they were speaking they heard a shout and a disturbance which rose high among the Banū Hām. The defeated arrived, naked, bare-footed and wounded. They were in scattered groups of ten and twenty, one hundred and two hundred. Some were exhausted, others had fallen and risen, another drove his horse, and he was on the point of death. The cavalry hurried to meet them and ask them about their plight. They said, 'Antar has destroyed us. He has loaded wretchedness upon our backs.' Some were brought before King Ghawwār. He asked them what had occurred when they had fought Antar.

Al-Asma'ī said: 'The reason for the smiting of these soldiers and the vengeance which afflicted them is as follows – I have mentioned that they had attacked Antar and those with him. The latter fought long with them to draw them away from the tents until they allowed those who were lying in ambush to get behind them. Antar returned and fought them alone aided by 'Urwa who came upon them with his thousand horsemen. Shaybūb was before them, and the horsemen followed them. Ghasūb arose on the left hand, then after him Māzin, Sabī' al-Yaman and their foot-soldiers to the back of them. They attacked them and surrounded them as bangles encircle the wrist. They were astonished, and they imagined that the whole desert was full of men and soldiers.

Antar appeared and put them to the sword. He began to smite with terrible blows, and he stabbed unceasingly. The cowards fled and the noble stood firm. Feet slipped, and at that instant Antar met 'Andam ibn Bassām in the midst of the battle and the throng. He attacked him and put the whole weight of his person against him. He jabbed him in the chest with his sword and split him asunder to his thighs and the horse beneath him. He fell to the ground in four pieces.

Ghasūb, Maysara and Sabī' al-Yaman came forth and scattered the squadrons. 'Urwa and those with him attacked the enemy ranks from behind. The negroes saw that their leader had been slain. They decided to flee when they saw their predicament. They sought safety. They ran until they reached King Ghawwār. 'Where is 'Andam ibn Bassām?' he asked. They answered, 'He has been slain and has drunk the cup of death.' The assembly was in a tumult. They said, 'We are not safe from him who has done this to him. He may attack us unawares in our homesteads, and he will uproot us.' Then the vizir said, 'Oh, king, Qaswara should not be blamed for what he said. It was true.' When King Ghawwār saw the calamity which had befallen his warriors he said, 'It is my duty to face this danger.' He called his warriors and ordered them to take their arms and to be ready after three days. All the Banū Hām were to be assembled in his presence so that he could march against the son of Shaddād and thereby console his stricken heart.'

The Land of Flags and Ensigns.

As for Antar, the father of knights, after he had killed 'Andam ibn Bassām and shattered his army in the desert he collected the booty and herds to divide them among his warriors.As they were thus engaged Lawn al-Zalām arrived with his men. They met. They rejoiced at their success, and they delighted at the capture of this booty. They set up tents and stayed there for three days. Antar sat with his sons. Lawn al-Zalām was at his side. Around him were his best soldiers. Safwān was weeping. His moaning and complaining increased. He came to Antar and said to him, Oh, bounteous father of knights, let us forego our march to the lands of Ghawwār. Let us undertake a more important quest.'

Antar said, 'Tell me what you wish.' Safwān said, 'Blame me not, oh, heroic one, for love rids a man of all his modesty.'

Oh, father of knights, you should march to the Land of Flags and Ensigns. It is the land of King Hammām. Perchance you will win my beloved for me, 'U'jūbat al-Anām. I perish from love's extasy and passion.' When Antar heard his words they pleased his heart. He promised that his wish would be fulfilled and that they would march to the Land of Flags and Ensigns, and that he would take the beloved of his heart for him even though she resided in the clouds (27). Ghamra leapt towards Antar and said to him, 'Oh, father of knights, you cannot do what you say.' 'Why?' he asked. 'Are you afraid that I will perish?' She said, 'There is an obstacle which will prevent you reaching those countries.'

Antar, angered by her remarks, said, 'Princess, who can stop me obtaining my desire? I am able to thrust with the spear and smite with the sword.' Ghamra said to him, 'Oh, father of knights, by the protection of the Arabs, I did not say that a great number of warriors would prevent you. I and other men know that there is no way for a man to take the kingdom of Hammām.' Antar said, 'Who is he who prevents entry to it?'

She said, 'Know, oh, father of knights that between the country of King Ghawwār and the Fortress of Flags and Ensigns is a mighty tree called the Mistress of Fires and Lights. It is ancient and everlasting and shades knights beneath its branches which are lofty and immense as though they are clouds in the heavens, one interlaced with another. Every year it has a festival when it is visited, and they spend three days there in the month of March when the day and night are of equal length. The old and young of those lands come there, the slaves and the free, and they make this sacrifice there. They slaughter she-camels and young weaned camels. They take pity on the weak and poor, the widows and orphans, and they give them what is suitable for them, clothes and food. After that they burn frankincense of sweet odour, amber, aloes, incense sticks and compound perfume, and they spray the tree with musk, camphor and rose water. For that tree they have fashioned a long basin of marble. Everyone in that country goes to that place. None comes, be he rich or beggar, king or slave, but they come with choice perfume, rose water, amber and musk, each according to his capability. It must be of his own wealth. They dip and moisten all they bring in the marble basin, and then they smear the tree and burn frankincense to it. This is their custom since time immemorial.'

When Antar heard Ghamra say all this he said to her, 'Can this tree smite with the sword, so that none can pass this place?' She said, 'No, oh, father of knights, but if anyone comes to them in order to fight them or an enemy enter their midst, and they are afraid of death by that enemy they bring a sacrifice to that tree, and the perfumes described, and their foes are smitten with lethargy, and the land and heaven become dark. They are gripped by fear and pestilences afflict them. The world is black and lighting flashes from every side. The thunder roars, rain pours down, and they are smitten by destructive meteors. That affliction lasts for three days, and no young or old remains alive. The thunderbolts slay them and their riding beasts. The lord of that land comes together with his soldiers and all the people of the country. They bow to the tree. The tree groans aloud with a voice like roaring thunder. From its belly there arises a pillar of fire which shoots towards the sky. Its light takes away men's sight, and men's minds are bewildered. When the pillar of fire and light ascends they are filled with joy, and they make a loud noise in the rejoicing, and they say, "It has received our sacrifice, and it is pleased with our acts. Its anger and evil is abated, and we are safe from its cunning." Then after that they take the bones of their dead enemies which have been burnt black, and with them they burn incense among the young and the old. They divide them among the localities and the towns. They believe it is the blessing of that tree, and that it is the tree which has burnt their foes and has thwarted their guile and attack. They make their way with those burnt bones and carry them to the remainder of the provinces.'

Antar was troubled by her discourse so he asked her, 'Does no-one pass this way?' Ghamra said, 'Oh, father of knights, none does so save he who frequents it as a merchant. When the merchants approach the Mistress of Fires and Lights each one of them wears a blue garment and paints his left eye with antimony (28). When they pass by that tree by day and they enter the localities they fast for three days. When they wish to return to their people, they wear blue clothes, and they act according to the custom, and they pass down the bottom of the valley, then they take off their garments and each one of them journeys to his land and to his country.'

The reason why this tree was called the Mistress of Fires and Lights was that these countries and provinces, both plain and mountain, were inhabited from the time of Hām, son of Noah. He was the forefather of the negroes. About this there is no dispute. Ham was blessed with a son whom he called Kātim al-Asrar, 'the keeper of secrets' (29), nick-named 'the satisfier of birds' because he had rationed wheat and barley for each bird in those deserts, and he slaughtered five she-camels each day, and he distributed their flesh upon the summits of the mountains and on the tops of the trees. Each clawed bird ate and because of that they named him 'the satisfier of birds'. When the 'keeper of secrets' died he left a daughter who was gigantic in stature like a towering mountain (30). He named her Mistress of Fires.

After his death she became the ruler of the country, and the warriors obeyed her, and she ruled over her subjects. She was a warrior on horse-back and went by night, and she called herself 'queen-mistress of fires'. She used to worship fire and not God Almighty. However, she said to the men of esteem in her kingdom and its chiefs one day, 'I want you to raise something by which I will be remembered for ever and ever.' Her vizir, who was one of the elders of the fire-worshippers (31) and the servant of the fire temple, said to her, 'In my view the best idea is that you plant a tree at the cross roads (32) and that you give it your name 'the possessor of fires and lights.' Then you should appoint a day as a feast every year to last three days. It will be in the month of March when the day and the night are of equal length. All the people, the high and low, will go there, and it will become a cherished custom in this country.'

The queen was pleased with the suggestion and arranged all he had proposed and said to the vizir after confirming these matters. 'My father had suggested that I should build a fortress mighty in size whereby I be remembered and leave a monument to posterity.' The vizir said to her, 'Oh, queen, I think that you should dwell in the fortress in the middle of the field of pomegranate blossom by the water-side. It will grow amidst it as a mountain towering above the earth into the clouds to the height and extent of a thousand cubits. It will dominate that wide expanse and those localities.'

Al-Asmaʿī said, 'The queen knew that his words were wise so she began to build a fortress on the summit of the mountain. She called it Hisn al- 'Uqāb (eagle's castle) (33). He who dwelt in it could watch all those districts, mountains and deserts. Days passed after that, months, then years. Kings and governors changed. The tree, the Mistress of Fires and Lights became ancient. The people of those districts became adherents of the worship of fire and forsook the King of Heaven until the time of King Solomon, son of David. When Solomon died and met his Lord, the *jinn* departed from the lands of the earth and its deserts. There resided in that tree, the Mistress of Fires and Lights, a giant *'ifrīt* from the supreme kings of the *jinn*. From him there arose sparks of fire. The people of the country continued to adore fire because they had discovered ancient books about the Mazdean (34 religion which taught them how to worship fire. That devil used to manifest the fire more and more, and he used to do that against the enemy of those localities when he made for the tree and that spot' (35).

Antar said, 'By the Creator of men, my mind and my heart have been obsessed by this story. I have sworn by the Lord of Creation that I will possess the citadels of the Land of Flags and Ensigns and gain the daughter of King Hammām even if she be suspended from the clouds' (36). Lawn al-Zalām said, 'Oh, father of knights, by the Lord of the *Ḥaram,* all that Princess Ghamra has mentioned is true.' Antar said,

‘Only what the lad desires shall be.’ Then he dispersed the council. They resigned themselves to going forth at daybreak for the abodes of King Ghawwār ibn Dīnār. Safwan began to be troubled in mind over the tale told by Ghamra because he was in love with ’U‘jūbat al-Anām. He went into his tent, and his displeasure almost choked him.

Safwān disappears.

When day came forth they went, crossing the deserts. They were led by Antar, his sons and their men. They pressed forward a whole day and a night and into a second day until it was noon. They overlooked the habitations of King Ghawwār, and they saw buildings and much to please them; gushing springs and herds, horses, camels and tents, spears, swords and embroidered pavilions and canopied tents of satin covered with gold which glowed in the sun. As has been mentioned the negroes had already guided their weapons for battle. The king had decided to march in person with his household and his nobles. When the king realized the imminence of battle he rallied his men. They mounted their horses when they saw the rising dust. Ghawwār led them, a roaring lion crying for revenge. He had not finished his defiance when the soldiers of Lawn al-Zalām approached. At their head was Antar. Banners and flags were displayed, swords were unsheathed, and men on horse-back were on every rise. King Ghawwār stood expectantly beneath the banners. Behind him they beat the war-drums, the deafening kettle-drums and the shawms.

Antar ordered an attack on the troops of Ghawwār. Knights met face to face, and men of might raced to the battle-field. They fought until it was night, then each party returned to its tents. When King Ghawwār had eaten he wished to take his rest but he could not sleep. In the morning the men mounted once more. Sparks flew from the hooves of their horses, and the upper branches of the trees were lopped by the swords. Al-Asma‘ī said, ‘One whom I trust told me (37). He said, “I was there with them in the battle. That day the battle bore a close resemblance to that which God called in the book of His truth ‘the calamity, what is the calamity’.” ’(38)

When dust is stirred up
a hero’s blood in fury boils.
The jabbers slaughter
and their swords win spoils.

Slashing of palms
slicing of noses
Attacking the ranks
cutting of hands.

Gashing of wrists
slitting of throats
scattering of skulls
fleeing of cowards.

Plate 5: The return of the Banū 'Abs and Banū Māzin after a raid and their defeat of the Banū Qaḥṭān of the Yemen.

Unceasing smiting
few words uttered
death ever present
close combat rages.

The glint of mail
a mighty number
a lack of endurance
of both the parties.

Buffet of comrades
thrusting of fleet camel
squeezing and throttling
fear overwhelmed me.

The impotent is pierced.
The chatterer is bruised
Silence triumphs
in the day of shame.

Amid blows of misfortune
horses are running
blades are biting.
There is no safety.

The grasping of lance
the hour of disaster
a torrent is released
by Yemeni points.

The hidden is manifest.
The youth is a captive.
Spiking of chests
severing of fingers.

A youth grows aged
in death's red bloom
in an increase of darkness as
cowards panick.

Amid cutting of throats
dust raised in tumult
blood's spring pumping
ochre from the ground.

Pressing of spear
clashing of glaive.
Blood's drops bring fears
to the hearts of the brave. (39)

At night the two parties disengaged. Many nobles had fallen but the knight of 'Abs had shown his mettle; a black lion, a smiter with the Indian blade. He had guarded the Banū 'Abs and had shed blood like rain. He retired dyed crimson with the blood congealed on his forearm. His men withdrew. They were drunk. Their thirst was quenched by their spears and swords. When they were rested, Lawn al-Zalām came to Antar and hailed him as victor. He made him sit down next to his relatives and ordered that food be brought. They dined to their satisfaction, then they retired to sleep after they had mounted a guard.

As for King Ghawwār and his men they retired in pain and torment. The father beheld not his son, and none could raise his head. They were exhausted. A great number had been slain, and the wounded lay on the ground. King Ghawwār mourned the loss of his companions, some twenty-five thousand for sure. Some twenty-five thousand and one hundred remained fit for combat. The king said to his chosen companions, 'There is still a wide difference in number between our foes and ourselves, but if circumstances continue in this wise for one more day then none of us will be left to tell his tale. If we do not receive aid from King Hammām we shall all be put to the sword.'

As for Antar ibn Shaddād and Lawn al-Zalām they fixed guards and decided to sleep. At daybreak they leapt once more into battle but Lawn al-Zalām missed his son, Safwān, and found no news or trace of him. He was concerned and asked about him but none could tell him anything. Worried, he came to Antar and said, 'I saw him in the battle yesterday in fierce combat.' The heart of Antar was stirred yet troubled, and he was sad to see Lawn al-Zalām so anxious. He summoned Shaybūb his brother. He said, 'I have only sought you because of grave matters.' Shaybūb answered, 'By God, I have no knowledge of Safwān, save that I saw him in battle yesterday. He was roaring like a lion.'

Lawn al-Zalām said, 'That is so, last night he slept with me. I saw him during the night, and he was weeping in sorrow. I have found no trace of him. I thought that he was with you, oh, father of knights, and that he had ridden on some errand for you.' Antar said, 'By God, I only saw him yesterday. I was with him at sunset. Perhaps he has left for some place. I thought that he might have gone back to you. My heart burns with disquiet over his loss. I have no heart to fight today until I find out what has become of him, perhaps we may find a trace of him.'

Then he called 'Urwa and said, 'Dispeller of care and anxiety, you will take charge with your sons in fighting this battle. You may be able to finish the task.' He told him what had happened, and how they had missed the youth, Safwān ibn Lawn al-Zalām. Then he sent back 'Urwa and his companions.

Antar and Lawn al-Zalām stood below the banners. The two armies lined up in ranks and faced each other. Then Ghasūb, Maysara, Māzin and Sabī' al-Yaman attacked. They were followed by the foot-soldiers. King Ghawwār also attacked and lit the flame of war. After an hour or so the dust rose high. When Ghawwar saw that Antar was absent he fought as one who knew no defeat. Then Antar turned to his companions. He noticed that they had slackened in the battle. He attacked in order to aid them, followed by Shaybūb. He rescued Ghasūb. Then he returned to Lawn al-Zalām and found that he had assailed the ranks around him. Antar guarded his flanks until he withdrew beneath the banners. Darkness descended. King Ghawwār ibn Dīnār and his men spent the night discussing the disaster they had endured, blaming Ghamra for their misfortunes.

As for the Banū 'Abs, when they settled in their tents they began to talk of Safwān ibn Lawn al-Zalām. His father started to weep, and tears flowed from his eyes. He said, 'He has either been killed or taken captive. I have no wish to know what has befallen him.' Then Shaybūb leapt up and said, 'My lord, cease your weeping and crying.' He left after he had counselled Antar to be cautious and to remain wide awake. His destination was the camp of King Ghawwār.

As for the reason for the disappearance of Safwān, the circumstance was unusual. Shaybūb had killed the horse of Ghawwār. He and Safwān had seized the king but he was rescued by his men of valour, and each man returned to his camp. Ghawwār assembled his men, leaders, noble men and cousins and said to them, 'We have suffered terrible losses. These people have killed many of us. I was only safe after a misfortune had come my way. Safwān opposed me with a man more nimble than a gazelle. He shot my steed, then he and his companions seized me. Were it not for my companions I would have been shamed and disgraced. Safwān intended to capture me but my companions did not forsake me and all I wished of the Lord of ancient days was that the youth should fall into my hand.'

At that time Qaswara ibn Jawhara was present. He said, 'Oh, king, I will bring him to you, and your wish will be fulfilled. Give him his punishment be it by a blow or by painful torment.' Ghawwār said to him, 'How can you overcome him? His knights encircle him.' He said, 'I know that he loves 'U' jūbat al-Anām, the daughter of King Hammām. He is madly in love with her. Because of this I can bring him to you and deliver him.' He said, 'Hurry if you can.' He replied, 'Willingly for your sake.' Then he left the king and made for the tents of the Banū 'Abs. After an hour or so, he was among them. He moved cautiously until he reached Safwān's tent. He had meant to kill him, had he been able, but he lay in ambush at a distance from the tent. He heard Safwān grieving and sighing for 'U'jubāt al-Anām in his verses. Qaswara approached the entrance of the tent and cried out, 'Young man, oh, Safwān nicknamed Badr al-Tamām.' 'Yes,' he answered. 'Come out to me so that I may repeat to you what news I have brought you from 'U' jūbat al-Anām.'

When Safwān heard the name of his beloved his heart beat with excitement for he could hardly believe these words. He followed Qaswara who was a man of crafty tricks. He said to him, 'Know that your beloved has sent word by me. It will cool your eye.' 'My lord, what is it?' He said, 'Know that the father of the girl died twenty days ago due to the care and worry in his heart because of the entry of the Banū 'Abs into those regions and the way they have destroyed their people. She heard that you and your father have become friends of Antar ibn Shaddād. When her father died she summoned me to her presence and said, "Know that my father has died, and my people have great need of me. My heart is full of love for Safwān. I have loved him since the days of our youth. I have refused to give my hand to any man. I want you to go and tell him of my predicament." This is what she said. If there by any love or passion in your heart then go with me at once but tell none about our business.'

When Safwān heard these words he said, 'To hear is to obey. I desire her more than any other. Be my companion so that I may mount my horse.' Qaswara said to him, 'Do as seems fit.' So he mounted his horse, and Qaswara marched behind him until they had advanced deep into the desert, and Safwān was close to the tents of Ghawwār. Qaswara said to him, 'Lie in wait here. I will enter this camp and send for a horse to ride.' Then he left him and continued until he came to King Ghawwār. He said, 'I have brought Safwān to you, by guile, so send men to seize him in all haste. I have left him beside the pool there.' Then he told him all that he had done. King Ghawwār did not believe the news. He rode among one thousand of his horsemen, and he sought Safwān with intent to capture him.

After Qaswara had left, Safwān dismounted and waited in the desert. He was lost in thought, baffled by what he had seen and what he had heard. He noticed nothing until the horsemen surrounded him. They seized him and brought him before King Ghawwār. He, too, was deep in thought unable to distinguish night from day. When he saw him he said to him, 'Do you know who I am?' Then he knocked him down and smote him until he caused his blood to flow. His people advised him to kill him. He said, I shall not kill him until I seize this devil Antar. I shall kill them both on the same day, and I shall torture them both on the same day.' Then he delivered him to his slaves who were ten robust men, sturdy and cruel. He turned to Qaswara and gave him a jewelled robe as a gift. This was the reason for the capture of Safwān and how he came to that place.

When it was morning Antar ibn Shaddād rode out to seek battle. Before him rode 'Urwa ibn al-Ward and Maysara and those valiant men of their company. They had taken Lawn al-Zalām with them to strengthen his resolve and his fortitude which had grown weak due to the loss of his son. None knew of his fate. The negroes had mounted. At their head was King Ghawwār. We have mentioned that Shaybūb had departed to seek for news of Safwān. The heart of Antar was aflame. He said to his companions, 'He promised to return at dawn but he has not done so. He has changed the hour of meeting, and my heart is perturbed and burns with the fire of distress.'

Then out from the camp rode a knight unlike others. He guided his horse until he was in the middle of the battlefield. He exercised himself on its back until both sides were in position. That horse was dark. It had a blaze on its forehead and was marked. When it neighed it seemed to utter words. That knight was war-ing a hauberk of double thickness. He held an Indian sword in his hand and he was bearing a great spear. He parried in the air and said, 'I am Ghasūb,' Then he shouted, 'Oh, Banū Hām, hear what I have to say. You have done us injury and harm. You have robbed us of our herds, flocks and possessions and you ruled our lands when you learnt of our departure. Now we have returned. The truth has returned to those who possess it, the sword to its scabbard. If you know justice then go back to your countries and let us not argue further. If you refuse then come forth and fight. I am a knight strong enough to fight you. If you wish to send one thousand or two thousand I am content to fight you. If not, then I will attack.'

When he had finished, knights came forth from the enemy's wings. They rode towards him with their spears aimed. At their head was a giant, a snub-nosed knight who resembled a devil. He held a sharp lance and he was girt with a dazzling sword (40). He did not face Ghasūb for long. The latter thrust him through the chest so that his spear protruded from his back. The knights were amazed at the speed of his charge and his withdrawal. Then a second knight rode forth against him, shouted at him, approached him and tilted with him. Ghasūb looked hard at him. He was wary in his thrust and blow. He made his opponent believe that his heart was his target. The spear circled around him. Then he struck him upon the temples, and he pushed out his eye-balls upon his cheeks. With his hands he scattered his teeth.

The negroes were amazed. They said, 'This knight is the wonder of the age because he needs no weapon to fight with other knights.' He was assailed by tens and by scores. He attacked them all as a wild beast in its thicket. He began to slay them and to throw both them and their weapons to the ground. His father Antar was full of joy at the spectacle. He urged him to victory.

We have already mentioned that Ghasūb was a paragon of knighthood, and how he had fought with his father in God's house. As for Ghamra, when she saw how unequal were the forces she was afraid for her son. She, too, attacked. Antar cried aloud to the heroes and they also attacked. So did 'Urwa with his men and Lawn al-Zalām with his lions. The knights of the Banū 'Abs fell like drops of rain.

Najd ibn Hishām said, 'The thrusting of the spear and smiting of the sword continued between them and the arrows flew until the day drew to its close and night spread its mantle in a murky darkness. They separated but many men lay dead stretched out on the ground, and the Banū 'Abs came back with a thousand negro captives. Despite their small number they had been victorious. When they reached their tents they tied the negroes with ropes and entrusted them to a company of guards.

Now for Shaybūb; after he had left them in the dark and had gone to the camp of Ghawwār ibn Dīnār he mixed among its occupants. He had hung his hand upon his neck as though it were broken. All who saw him took pity on him and said, 'Oh, you poor wretch, who did these things to you?' He said, 'The Banū 'Abs. God will take my revenge on them. I am one of the companions of Suwayd ibn 'Uwayd. When they killed him they looted his wealth. One of the negroes of the Banū 'Abs met me. He had a stick in his hand. He hit me and broke my hand and split and cracked my skin. Had not the soldiers separated us he would have killed me. How strong are the Banū 'Abs in the way they smite and thrust. They are like the *jinn* of Solomon!' They said to him, 'Do you know who hit you?' 'No, I do not, but I learn that his name is Shaybūb. Most of those things which we have suffered are due to Lawn al-Zalām and his son Badr al-Tamām.' They said, 'Be glad. Safwān has been captured. He has suffered humiliation.' Shaybūb said, 'How did this come about?' One of them said, 'His capture was due to a trick performed on him by Qaswara ibn Jawhara'. They told him the story of all that had happened. Shaybūb said, 'How fortunate. My heart is refreshed.'

Then he left them and went to the tents. When he drew near them he hid in a cave. As the night grew longer he was hungry so he went into the desert. He hunted a gazelle, slew it and skinned it. He lit a fire and began to roast it and to eat it at the mouth of the cave. It was the will of the Almighty that at this hour Ghawwār came to the tents. He saw the light in the mouth of the cave. He stopped. Shaybūb was aware of him when he was still at a distance. He buried the fire, and he dug a pit in the sand far from the cave. He sat in it and covered himself with the sand. He only allowed his mouth and eyes to show. A little while later the horse arrived led by King Ghawwār. On he went until he stopped at the place of the fire. He said, 'The fire was here. I was afraid lest a robber or one intent on harming us had come.' They said, 'How could a fire blaze in this place? We saw no trace of it.' He said to them, 'By the protection of the noble

Arabs, the fire was indeed here.' When he heard the words of his companions he continued on his way. He said, 'Follow me and see how I will show you him who lit the fire. If I say something do not contradict me!'

Shaybūb heard what they were saying from their direction. He had to keep clear of them in the sands. Soon they went away from him. He came up from beneath the sand like a bounding lion. He ran towards the tents and entered among them. He was in a group of people who barely noticed him. He continued his search and used his eyes until he saw Safwān fettered at the tent of Ghawwār ibn Dīnār. Round about him were a group of slaves who were sound asleep, and he crawled until he drew close. The tent where he found himself was high and spacious. It had many pillars and tent-ropes. He stood beside it for a while, when, lo, a slave came and entered the tent and someone spoke from within the tent. 'Woe to you, Maymūn. Where is your lord, King Ghawwār?' He said to her – for it was a woman who spoke – 'He has seen a fire at the mouth of the cave which is without the tents. He has taken ten men and has gone to the fire to find traces of it.' Shaybūb said to himself, 'Let us see what he will talk about and to whom, and then ponder the matter.'

There before him was a young woman. He had never seen one like her in beauty and comeleness. He looked hard at the slave. He was as black as a water buffalo, huge in lip and broad in mouth. He had flaring nostrils and his eyes were like sparks of coal. He dallied with her and jested with her. This accursed belle was enamoured by this accursed male for she was ardent with him in their sport. He went to her and had intercourse with her then and there. Shaybūb watched their play, and he was full of concealed hate and disgust. Later he reported how he had felt. He said, 'I waited to kill the two of them, but I was afraid that my circumstance would be disclosed and the stealthy plans I had laid be fruitless and that I would miss my chance to rescue Safwān from captivity. They might kill him while I would be safe, left to escape, running swiftly in those hills.'

Then the slave said to her, 'What have you to eat?' She replied, 'I only have these wooden cups filled with curds. I was keeping them for your master.' She offered him a cup of curds and a piece of lupine, and he ate until he was satisfied. He raised his hand and left. 'I determined to kill the girl because of her disgraceful act but while I was planning to do so, lo, King Ghawwār came, stopped and sat by the door of the tent. He said to the girl, "What have you prepared for my supper?" She brought him the bowl of curds and some of the lupine and offered them to him. He ate a little of it. He said, "What has made these curds so greasy and dirty? Have the hands of slaves been touching them?
(41)

She said, "Oh, cousin, what dirt is there in these curds? You go on saying these things so that my brothers will kill me. Worries and cares have afflicted me because of your words. Are you not ashamed to say such things about me? You seem to hate me. It is as though you knew me not before today." He said, "No, by the protector of the Arabs, I have not hated you, but your acts are not hidden from me." Then he reclined on his bed and slept.'

'When his snoring grew loud,' said Shaybūb, 'I thought hard. I found nobody there, neither elder nor youth. I arose and went out from between the coverings, and I came to Safwān. I cut his shoulder bonds and loosed his limbs. I rescued him after he was sure of death. I said to him since he was full of surprise, "Do you know who I am, young man?" He said, "No, by the All Knowing King." ' He said, 'I am Shaybūb, Antar's brother. Come, follow me so that I can take you away from the tents into the desert.'

Safwān followed him until he brought him from that place. They left the dwellings and God protected them. Then a horseman blocked their way. He was urging on his mount, and jealousy and anger filled his head. Safwān looked hard at him, and lo, it was Qaswara who had tricked him and done such evil acts against him and had cast him among his enemies in chains and fetters. But, when Safwān saw him he was happy, and he said to Shaybūb, 'Stay where you are. This is my enemy who tricked me and cast me into despair. I want to avenge myself and cast him in the abyss. If I could take him alive to your brother then I would carry him to him.' Shaybūb said, 'Stay where you are. I will fulfil the task.' He drew Qaswara aside and said, 'Where are you going, oh, noble Arab? Is there one who diligently seeks you?' He continued to speak to him thus until he drew close to him, and God removed his protection from him. He smote him in the heart with a dagger and unseated him from his mount. He grasped the horse and brought it to Safwān whom he mounted on it. Both of them made for the Banū 'Abs with joy in their hearts.

The reason for the journey of Qaswara at that hour was one of strange coincidence. When Antar, full of surprise, saw the courage of the warriors, he called Princess Ghamra, King Lawn al-Zalām and his sons Ghasūb, Maysara and 'Urwa ibn al-Ward. They met. He said, 'We have tarried long enough here. My brother Shaybūb has made me anxious. Has he been discovered or seized? Have they done him an injury? An idea came to me tonight. Let us surprise the enemy and put them to the sword.' All who were present agreed. They arose after they had supped and gathered their weapons. They surprised the enemy in the darkness.

When Qaswara had observed these things he left to inform King Ghawwār asking for his aid. Shaybūb then met him on his way, slew him and took his horse.

He seated Safwān upon it and dressed him in his clothes. They reached the Banū 'Abs in the thick of battle. When Shaybūb saw that dreadful engagement, he and Safwān went to Antar. He cried out as he split the ranks, 'I am Shaybūb the famous'. He knew that his brother had returned safely and that he had rescued Safwān. His mind was at peace. He redoubled his attack on the enemy and routed them. All who raised themselves from the clouds of dust saw that the flags had drooped and that blood had flowed. Shaybūb could be seen crying, 'Flee and ask not the cause. If not you will be ruined.'

Al-Asma'ī said, 'It was reported that this was a night which the people deemed a day of battle. It was among those nights which are recorded in history and remembered for the marvellous deeds which took place between the two parties.'

The Banū 'Abs welcomed Safwān, so too Shaybūb, the brother of Antar, for there was none who did not long to ransom him with his ears and his eyes. They asked Shaybūb how Safwān had been rescued, and he told them all that had happened. Lawn al-Zalām embraced his son, and he rejoiced at his safe return.

The Fortress of the Clouds and the king
who fought on the back of a giraffe. (42)

Safwān said to his father, 'In truth, we are only safe at this moment. On our way back we passed beneath the fortress of Dāhiyat al-Anām and al-Khātif ibn al-Khātifa who fights mounted on the back of a giraffe.'

Shaybūb said to Antar, 'Know that this fortress is the misfortune of men because in it dwells a giant king who fights on the back of a giraffe. In its appearance this animal has two horns like those of a gazelle and a long neck. Its back legs are like the cloven hooves of a cow. Its stomach is like that of a gazelle, and its tail is like that of a camel. Its back is like that of a horse. Its front legs are long and its back legs are short. It is a curious shape and a remarkable steed. Its master is called al-Khātif ibn al-Khātifa. He has ten thousand knights under his power. They are all heroes.'

This Fortress of the Clouds (43) to which we refer was a ruin from the age of Noah – peace be upon him and upon our Prophet the most excellent of blessings and perfect peace and God be pleased with his noble companions. It remained uninhabited. Men of knowledge mentioned that a devil, one of the daughters of the *jinn* dwelt in it. None could approach this place without being attacked by screechings and cries and fires.

Plate 6: al-Minhāl and Dāhiya the She-Devil in the midst of Ḥiṣn al-Ghamām.

The king of that land was called Ma'dān ibn Safwān, and the protector of his land was called al-Minhāl ibn Kādān. Al-Minhāl had made an evil attack on the king and had plotted against him because he wished to kill him and seize his country. The king heard of his trap and sought to destroy him. So he fled from him in fear of death. He was so full of fear that he made for the Fortress of the Clouds which was a ruin. He drew near it. He hoped to die at the hands of the *jinn.* Then he would not fall into the hands of King Ma'dān ibn Safwān so that he would torment and torture him with every form of torture. As he drew near it fires appeared over it, and they turned to smoke in the middle of the fortress. He regretted what he had done, and how he had come to enter such a place, and how he had cast his soul into this affliction.

Then he glanced into the heart of the ruined castle, and lo, that female devil had appeared. Her feet resembled legs of an ass, and fangs protruded from her mouth. Her eyes were like those of a cow. Al-Minhāl ibn Kādān looked at her in that place, and he was frightened by her horrible appearance. His heart trembled. She approached him and pointed at him. She said, 'Who are you among the knights and to which tribe do you belong? How dare you enter this place!'

Al-Minhāl was full of terror. He believed her to be a demoness. He said to her, 'My lady, I only came to this place out of fear of King Ma'dān. I have come to you to seek your protection against his mighty arm, his numerous troops and the power of his heroes. Take my hand and restore my broken body.' The female demon, whose name was Dāhiya, as has been mentioned, said, 'I have given you protection. It is my duty to honour you since you have clung to us. We cannot kill your enemy.'

When al-Minhāl heard her speak thus he kissed the ground before her, and he began to smile. Then she summoned one of her slaves and she spoke to him. He departed and returned as swift as a flash of lightening. He brought an answer back. Then she said to al-Minhāl after she had heard what was said, 'Arise, young man, and follow me and have no fear. Rejoice to see the fulfilment of your hopes.' He was happy when he heard her words. She stood up, and al-Minhāl followed her with confidence.

She made her way slowly until she came to the ruined castle. She tapped the ground, and a door opened for her. She said, 'Descend and have no fear.' He descended beneath the ground to a cellar. He went down to it by twenty steps, and he beheld a beautiful chamber. It was wide and spacious. In it was all he needed. There was a wide withdrawing-room in a recess with a raised floor. In the middle of it was a throne of juniper wood. It was said that it belonged to

Alexander. Neither Chosroes nor the Byzantine Emperor owned the like of it. She sat on it, and she commanded al-Minhāl to sit facing her. When they were comfortably settled food was brought. She said to him, 'Food has been provided and is before you, youth.' He ate to his satisfaction, and he enjoyed it. Vessels of wine were brought, and she ordered him to drink the wine. So al-Minhāl drank. He said to himself, 'I know that this she-demon will destroy me tonight. I will fill my stomach with wine so that I will take leave of my senses.' He drank more and more wine until he lost consciousness.

He did not awake until the sun had risen. He sat up in a state of apprehension due to his excessive drinking, and he was not at ease until the she-demon, Dāhiyat al-Anām, appeared. He rose to meet her, and he showed an excessive humility in his abasement and homage as he saluted her. Al-Minhāl was of comely looks and of fine stature. She sat down and ordered him to sit before her. When he had done so, food was brought, and she said to him, 'Eat the food which is provided and forget your pain and sorrow.' Dāhiya began to converse with him and show him affection in her words until he had eaten all he needed. She said to him, 'Young man, you now enjoy sanctuary by eating our food. In our house you have a place, so be merry in safety.' He arose and served her and said, 'I am your dearest slave, and I will carry your burden for ever.'

Dāhiya said, 'Oh, noble Arab, I am not a male but a female. I rule this place, and I am ruler over many companies of *jinn*. I feel pity and love for you, and you occupy the highest place in my heart. I want you to be my companion and to be my lord, and I will be your wife. Disclose to me what is in your heart. Do not believe that I will ever let you go. Open your mind to me for I have need to know your thoughts.'

Al-Minhāl said when he heard her speak thus, 'I am but one of your slaves and servants.' She grasped his hand in agreement. That instance she introduced two of the *jinn*, and they married her to al-Minhāl. There was great rejoicing. She sent invitations and summoned the kings of the *jinn*. She sat on her throne, and every *'ifrīt* and devil formed a ring around her. Then she assumed a form which amazed the minds of men. She was adorned with jewellery and robes of every kind. She had al-Minhāl brought before her. She undressed, and the kings of the *jinn* kissed the ground before her and made her body comely to his eyes. He spent that night embracing and kissing, and he was full of joy at meeting such good fortune and security. He said to himself, 'I have become ruler of the kings of the *jinn*, and I shall slay King Ma'dān. I shall rule over all his warriors and knights.' Long was their companionship, and they loved each other dearly. She disclosed to him that there was a 'quest' which was to be discovered in that castle. It had been there since the age of Hām, son of Noah – upon him and our

Prophet be most exalted blessing and perfect peace. Al-Minhāl loved her companionship. His soldiers grew in number and also his wealth, and he rebuilt the castle far finer than it was before. He became one of the kings of the age ruling over men and *jinn*.

By Dāhiya he begat a daughter whom he named Zāhiyat al-Anām. She was praised by Shaybūb. Dāhiya died, so did al-Minhāl after her. Zāhiyat al-Anām ruled as queen over all her father's soldiers. She married one of the kings of the Sudan, and she bore him a daughter whom she named al-Khātifa. Days passed. The king lived only a few days after her birth. He died, and al-Khātifa reigned instead. She loved one of the kings of the Ethiopians and married him. By her he had a son whom he named al-Khātif. His fame spread abroad in this place, and he surpassed the heroes and the knights. His father died, and so did his mother al-Khātifa in those countries. There was a dispute and feud between him and King Ghawwār.

Al-Khātif only used to enter battle seated on a giraffe. He had collected a couple, a male and a female, and they gave birth in his realm. He began to ride their offspring and to combat knights. No horse could look at the giraffe. It shyed and bolted from the battlefield. He dominated the men of courage and ruled as a tyrant over the noble. Fear filled the hearts of all, and riders who went to other lands spread his renown.

Let us return to the thread of the tale – help is sought in God. Shaybūb began to tell Antar about all he had heard. Antar was intrigued and said, 'By the month of *Rajab* this tale must be recorded for posterity and written in gold water.' King Lawn al-Zalām said, 'Oh, father of knights, as for the fortress all that your brother Shaybūb has mentioned is true. It stands to this day, and its master is al-Khātif ibn al-Khātifa. They have said that his mother was a *jinnīya* and his father one of the Sudan.'

Antar said, 'If he be of this quality then we cannot march and leave the lord of the castle behind us. We shall not be safe from his evil and his cunning. Perhaps he and his heroes will ride against us.' Shaybūb said, 'By the Creator of the Heavens, if you accept my advice I will capture the castle for you.' 'How can you take this castle?' Antar said. 'Advise us as to the action to be taken.' Shaybūb said, 'Three thousand horsemen will be selected from this army, and they will be divided into three groups. Each group will set a trap in a chosen place. You and 'Urwa will be among one thousand knights. I, Ghasūb and Maysara will hide in secret behind the castle with a party of horsemen. Ghamra and Māzin will be near at hand. So, when it is morning and the herds go forth to pasture you will attack the herders and lead away all the herds. On horseback, and crying at the top of your voice, you will attack their men of courage and try to beat them in battle, driving them in that space so that they are near to those who are waiting in the ambush. Then the second ambush will quickly rise up behind the enemy and cut their route. None of the defeated will be allowed to enter the castle. I will go with the cavalry and make for the castle and capture the gate. We shall slay the gate-keepers, and I shall take the castle without a battle. You will capture the women and children and their possessions.'

Lawn al-Zalām said, 'By the All-knowing King, this plan is sound, Shaybūb. My only fear is that the army of the negroes will come upon us and destroy us in this place, and we shall fail to accomplish our task.' Shaybūb said, 'Do not be worried with these thoughts. The soldiers of Ghawwār will take three days to reach this land. If God so wills the day will not be advanced before the castle is already in our hands, and the task will be complete.'

Antar said, 'I shall do as you say.' Then he ordered his sons Ghasūb and Maysara and Shaybūb to march with one thousand knights and to lie in hiding behind the castle. He gave Ghamra and Māzin one thousand knights and said to them, 'When the horn blows come out from behind the enemy and put them to the sword. I shall set forth with one thousand knights to attack the herds when it is light. I caution Lawn al-Zalām to be watchful. Remain close to the lands of Ghawwār with the vanguard. You will tell us any news about his army.' They marched until they were behind the fortress. At midnight they were in their secret positions.

God brought the dawn. The herds were sent forth to pasture with their herders. They were at some distance in the desert, then Antar appeared. He drove away the herds and smote the necks of the slaves. A group of the herders returned to the castle and wept aloud. Word reached the occupants that the herders and slaves had been killed, and the herds and camels had been captured. Then the men in the castle mounted. Al-Khātif rode forth upon his giraffe at the head of his men. None who could carry a weapon remained behind in the castle. Its king rode deep into the valley bottoms. He and his men imagined that the horsemen who had raided and had driven away his herds were men of King Ghawwār's, because the latter had attacked his fortress many times. He had only pursued them with some ten thousand knights. Al-Khātif used to beat them, capture them, slay most of them and recover their herds.

As he was in pursuit he imagined that the cavalry he saw was that of Ghawwār ibn Dīnār, and for that reason he left none of his fighting men in the castle. All his ten thousand knights rode forth to pursue the attackers, and each one of them was armed with a lance. They rode like devils behind al-Khātif until it was noon. They caught up with Antar and his men, and they called aloud, 'Oh, shamed and humiliated, where are you taking our herds? Do you think that you can escape? Woe to you, leave the herds and save yourselves.'

Antar and his men did not reply until they were close to them. Antar had delivered the spoils to one hundred knights. He ordered them to go ahead. He attacked the enemy with nine hundred knights. He thrust through one of the enemy, hastened the end of another, a third despaired of his life and a fourth shared the fate of his comrades. The fifth was thrown on his back. The enemy horsemen attacked him in a group, and none held back. What a noble knight Antar was! He gave the sword its due and the spear what it coveted. Heroes met on that battle-field. Antar said to those who were behind him, 'Guard my back and copy my charge and my withdrawal.' He met the enemy army with a stout heart, with the point of his sword and with his spear.

When al-Khātif saw how Antar had torn asunder those hundreds and thousands, and how he had made the courageous tremble he went to meet him in the heart of the struggle. Antar struck him, and a battle took place between the two of them which amazed both parties in the combat. They struck out at each other with their blades until they were blunted, and they lunged with their spears until they were splintered. Their mounts were tired and jaded. They went on fighting until the sun ran its course in the bowl of the sky. Al-Khātif was the more fatigued. Antar knews this, and he pounced like the lion which protects its whelps. He struck him with his sword on the crown of his head. The blow split him asunder, and he fell in a pool of blood. His companions saw the deed, and they were consumed with a grim anger. They lowered their heads in the pommels of their saddles, and they charged against Antar. He received them with a zealous exuberance and with a determination unsurpassed. He repelled them.

Then a dust cloud appeared from the place of the ambush. Those who lay in wait attacked the companions of al-Khātif. Horsemen came forth like kindled fire. All cried aloud in one voice, 'Oh, 'Abs, oh, 'Adnān.' They swooped like eagles. The enemy knew that the Banū 'Abs had set a trap for them in that place. They feared for their lives, and they fled to their hearths. Antar and the Banū 'Abs pursued them relentlessly, thrusting and smiting with their swords. They chased them. The enemy did not halt in their flight until they drew nigh the castle. They saw that the gate was shut, and that the companions of Shaybūb were upon its walls exclaiming, 'Oh, 'Abs and 'Adnān.' They knew that their foes had captured the castle. They fled into the desert with blows of weapons on their backs.

The cause of the fall of the castle to Shaybūb was a surprising feat. Let us mention what took place. When it was morning, and Shaybūb was in the ambush, and Antar attacked the herds, the gate of the castle was opened. Al-Khātif and his horsemen rode forth followed by his cavalry. Shaybūb remained under cover until he had traversed the distance and found that none was left in al-Khātif's castle save for girls and women. Then he ordered Maysara and Ghasūb to go to the gate with the knights and with their faces closely muffled. They his themselves and waited. Then they entered the precincts of the castle. They did as Shaybūb had commanded. They had given the order to the rest of their comrades, 'When you hear our cry, "Oh, 'Abs, oh, 'Adnān", then follow, and you will find that we have captured the castle.' When the gate keepers saw them approach the gate they deemed them to be some of al-Khātif's company who were on their way back. They paid them little regard, and so the ten men reached the gate. They were met by the gatekeepers who asked them about the reason for their return. 'Why are you retiring from the king's company?' They gave no reply until they were within the gate. They drew their swords and slew them. Then they shouted at the top of their voices, 'Oh, 'Abs, oh, 'Adnān.'

The remainder of the knights rushed towards them with Shaybūb leaping among them like a demon. Those in the castle left behind by the king came out, and they were met by Antar's men who put them to the Yemeni sword. The women were full of terror and grief, and the occupants of the castle cried out to be spared. The sword and the spear were lifted. They waited to hear news of Antar and al-Khātif. At sundown dust rose above them until the adjacent lands were in darkness. Beneath the dust there appeared fleeing knights pursued by knights like eagles. Shaybūb called from the summit of the castle, 'Oh, 'Abs, oh, 'Adnān.' Those who were fleeing knew that their castle had fallen and that al-Khātif had perished. They scattered in the valleys and were slaughtered. They were pursued by Antar, 'Urwa and his knights, and they heard the shout of Shaybūb and his companions. Antar said to 'Urwa, 'By God, my brother has captured the castle, the women and the children.' The other asnwered 'You are correct, by God Almighty.' They rejoiced at Shaybūb's success. Shaybūb came down like an eagle. He opened the gate for them, and he received them with joy.

Antar climbed the castle parapet accompanied by his men of valour, and he opened its treasures which had belonged to al-Khātif. Among them he found riches untouched by fire and objects of rare value. They dazzled the minds of men. Antar was astonished by all he beheld. He stamped it all with his seal, and he left one thousand knights in that castle. They were companions of Lawn al-Zalām. One of the heroes of the Banū 'Abs called Ghānim ibn Bassām was appointed their commander. Antar told him to be watchful, then he descended with his sons and 'Urwa. They were grateful to Shaybūb for what he had done.

That same day they set out to find King Lawn al-Zalām, fearful lest the armies of King Ghawwār ibn Dīnār should come upon them unprepared. As for Lawn al-Zalām he was anxious on account of Antar's absence. He knew not what had become of him while fighting al-Khātif. He was eager to know what had happened during those two days. On the third day Antar's dust rose high above the castle. Lawn al-Zalām gazed far to see what had taken place. Then he spied Shaybūb, flying like a bird, saying, 'Rejoice at our success, oh, king.' Lawn al-Zalām had ridden forth to discover what the dust concealed. Shaybūb greeted him and kissed his feet in the stirrup. He told him all that had happened between his brother and al-Khātif. He reported all his news, how they had captured the castle and its treasures. His heart was gladdened, and he bestowed all his robes upon him.

After Shaybūb had finished his story Lawn al-Zalām went to meet Antar. He embraced him and congratulated him. Antar returned his thanks and his greeting and asked him about the soldiers of Ghawwār. He said, 'Oh, father of knights, we had heard nothing. We have sent men to their lands to discover news of them but up to now no one has attacked us.' Antar was glad to learn that. They rested in their tents. They dined and exchanged goblets of wine. The rest of the day they spent feasting until it was dark, and they posted a guard. At dawn, when God diffused its light, Antar ordered his men to leave without delay after all the spoils had been collected. They loaded them on the backs of the camels. They marched towards the lands of Ghawwār.

The pagan city of King Hammām

As for the broken band of King Ghawwār's negroes they fled to the king. They told him of the manner in which Antar and his men had surprised them in the night. When he heard of it he was fearful for his throne and his country. He sent word to King Hammām, the lord of the Land of Flags and Ensigns informing him of the losses which he had suffered. In the morning he sought for Safwān but none could find him. So he executed the slaves with whom he had entrusted his captive. He was sorely grieved because he had escaped.

This King Hammām was a man of great courage and stubborn in combat. He used to raid tribes and capture women. He used to attack a man mounted on horse or fighting on foot, and he thrust with spear and lance. He had a city constructed from white stone. There was none like it in that land. It was reported that the *jinn* had built it for our lord Solomon, son of David, peace be upon him. Near that city was a hill like a pyramid. It was covered with growing vegetation, dark and obscure. In the middle of that hill was an upright sword over which a bird ceased not to hover (44). No one could pass by that sword unless his garments were white. If one whose clothes were dyed approached it, winds from all countries blew upon it, and a flood would come upon it until the villages which were round about it were almost destroyed; so violent were the rains.

King Hammām was lord of the Land of Flags and Ensigns. In that place he had left those who could guard him by the payment of *jāmakīya* and *dīwān* (45). At the base of it was a house. When one of the people died they left him in that house. They took the deceased and extracted his bones and stripped him of his flesh and pickled it. All the marrow in the bones would be removed, and they would place the bones in bags according to the status of the deceased. As for those who were revered their coverings were of Byzantine brocade, and the poor were placed in bags of cotton and sacking. They wrote on each the name of the occupant. They cast them in that house. As for the flesh, they cast it outside the city to the black crows so they could eat it. They allowed no other creature to eat any of it. They chased it away with arrows and with slings and catapults. All who were in that city were engaged in the manufacture of suits of mail; and coats of mail and helmets and swords and spears and everything concerned with weapons of war and other arms. They paid no tax or tribute to King Hammām, and none of the kings could take anything from them in that country . . . (46)

As for King Ghawwār, he sent for help saying, 'The country has been conquered. Sā'iqa ibn 'Andam al-Asamm has been slain and wrath has come upon him. So too upon Suwayd ibn 'Uwayd, the lord of the Banū Kinda. He, too, has been destroyed. The invaders have been joined by Lawn al-Zalām and his son Safwān. Oh, king, if you ignore our plight, you too will perish. They will march against you and destroy those who are round you.' After having sent his messenger he took his weapon of war and prepared for battle.

. . . A fierce engagement follows in which Safwān is badly wounded. He summons his courage because of his love for his beloved, Princess 'U'jūbat al-Anām. His condition is doubly wretched. . . .

When Antar saw his state he gave him greater courage and strengthened his heart. Safwān said, 'My lord, by my life, why should you look with favour on my wounds. I only risked my life and fought eagerly to bring ruin on these base men and to requite King Hammām by death and destruction. He rejected me as a suitor for his daughter, 'U'jūbat al-Anām. He has separated us and denied us our union.'

Sa'īd ibn Mālik said : After that Antar exclaimed, 'Oh, Safwān, I admire your love for this maid despite a desert's span which puts a distance between you.'

He replied, 'Oh, my lord, I will tell you the truth. I shall tell you what exchange of signs and struggle took place between us. There was a friendship between my father and Hammām for a number of years. My father used to visit him and give him gifts and rare objects and spend a month or two with him. In all his affairs he used to ask for his advice. Ever since I was a lad I used to go with him. Whenever he took me he also took a party of close companions and chiefs. I followed him. My lord, I used to see that maiden 'U'jūbat al-Anām who is like the moon in the darkness. She and I used to play together during the course of our stay, and love between the two of us became deep and true. I was passionately in love with her.

When this became a serious matter to me I told my father. He sent to her father and asked him for her hand. But our messenger was sent back disappointed. King Hammām had told him, "By the stars which rise in the heavens, were it not for the affection between us I would send a man to destroy him and slay his son. What has emboldened him to dare do these things! May God remove His protection from him!" By God, oh, father of knights, unequalled in this age, when my father received that warning and rebuff he felt outraged. He ceased his visits. When I knew of this matter my grief increased. I despaired of life, and I was sure that if this situation continued my end would be near. Then my father was compelled to write to the negroes and gather them from all countries so that we could march to King Hammām and slay him so that I could gain his daughter and rule his kingdom. It was then that we encountered you. Oh, father of knights, this is my story. Until now I cannot be consoled.' Antar said to him, 'Be content and at peace, for I will take the maiden for you even though there be between you mountains and lofty heights.'

As for the soldiers of King Ghawwār and the Banū Hām, they camped that night incessantly discussing the might of Antar and the sorry fate of those he had slain. King Ghawwār said to them, 'My cousins, he is but a knight who is skilled in battle. Our knight comes forth, and he smites him down, yet when I was engaged on the field with him towards nightfall, and we were blanketed by dust I would have killed him had not darkness covered us. In the morning I shall challenge him to single combat. If he consents I will rid you of him because I do not want King Hammām to come to these lands before we have achieved our aims.'

In the morning the Banū 'Abs hurried to battle. They looked for Safwān and Antar but they found no trace of them. They asked Shaybūb, and he said, 'By the Lord of ancient days, I know nought of them.' The Banū 'Abs were afraid that they might have been slain. 'Urwa and Ghamra were alarmed lest the warriors in the camp would be confused and disheartened. Ghasūb and Maysara heard of the absence of Antar, their father, and their strength was enfeebled. Lawn al-Zalām said, 'This is a grievous matter. Will our protector be lost while we are in this affliction?'

Ghasūb said, 'Keep this secret to yourself at this hour, otherwise the enemy will know of the loss of our protector and so contemplate an attack on us. I think that when he saw Safwān's lament and beheld the affliction which had befallen him, he took him with him and went to the lands of 'U'jūbat al-Anām to take her from her father, King Hammām.' Shaybūb said to him, 'Your reasoning and cautious understanding are rash and vain. By the Almighty Lord, my brother and Safwān have undoubtedly been tricked. They have been tricked for my brother would not risk himself alone. Were the matter otherwise he would have taken me with him as his counsellor. Guard yourselves; I will journey after them and find out what has befallen them.'

The ranks faced each other and advanced into battle. King Ghawwār sought single combat. He called aloud, 'Come out and fight me, oh, worthless scum. Antar ibn Shaddād alone will be my opponent. He surprised me yesterday while fighting. I beheld his power of assault.' When the Banū 'Abs heard these words they knew that he had no knowledge of Antar's disappearance. Ghasūb wanted to combat him but one of the knights of the companions of Lawn al-Zalām came before him and attacked Ghawwār without saying a word. This attack came as a surprise, and he aimed a thrust with his lance. But Ghawwār struck his lance, then tired him and in the end smote him with his sword and beheaded him. Ghawwār advanced and cried aloud, 'Oh, Banū 'Abs, it is not your custom to hold back from an engagement. You allege that you are knights of the Hijaz. Do you call on others to fight for you? Where is your negro? He has not come forth to combat me so that I may show him how a battle should be fought. We are a people who love equity and we hate excess.'

When Ghasūb heard these words he said to his brother and companions, 'We must hurry, we have tarried enough. We need success yet we are undone in single combat.' The ranks approached. Spears were pointed and extended. Ghasūb was impatient to attack, but he was outstripped by the cousin of Lawn al-Zalām who was a knight of courage and a king. He was riding a steed stout in its legs and strong and stubborn in temper. He sallied forth. King Ghawwār recognized him beneath the dust. He said to him 'Woe to you, I see you have gone out to fight me, oh, Bakkār. You have no respect for kinship. Are you not ashamed to reveal your true worth among the sons of your race? Do you not owe me and your cousin, Lawn al-Zalām, honour, regard and favour? You have joined these vile people. If I vanquish you today I will reward you with the most baleful recompense. I shall offer your blood to Al-Lāt and Al-'Uzzā. I have sworn a vow to the idols that I shall hang the head of Lawn al-Zalām on the pillars of

Allāh's house in Mecca for all to behold. I shall make him an example; honourable combat and revenge are incompatible.'

When Bakkār heard these words he replied, 'By God, son of the vile one, what you have just said are the words uttered in nightmares.' Then he attacked him and aimed the point of his spear at him. King Ghawwār met him. After a short engagement he stabbed Bakkār in the chest, and the point of his spear pierced him through and appeared gleaming from his back. The Banū Hām were dispirited, and they started to smite Ghawwār from all sides, but he slew twenty and captured thirty. Ghamra was troubled. She went forth on a noble horse and cried against Ghawwār. He escaped from her, like a small trickle of water. She was followed by the Banū 'Abs, and there was an engagement with the blades glistening beneath the dust. 'Urwa attacked, likewise Maysara, Ghasūb and King Lawn al-Zalām. But if evening had not descended the Banū 'Abs would have been sorely afflicted.

Then a swirl of sand and dust arose behind King Ghawwār's army. It blocked all the horizons, and the camp waited for news with hopeful expectancy. After an hour horsemen appeared. They were all negroes of the Banū Hām. They cried out, 'Fight on, oh, Ghawwār, for we are the companions of King Hammām, the lord of the Land of Flags and Ensigns.'

They were more than fifty thousand men, all clad in mail. Some bore spears, others shields, and they had marched through the deserts to reach the battlefield in that day. They were met by horsemen and men of courage. They proclaimed their joy, and all the valleys resounded with their shouts. A herald came to King Ghawwār. He kissed the ground before him and told him that King Hammām had sent him help, some fifty thousand courageous knights, and their leader was Safwān ibn Ma'dān (47). They attacked the Banū 'Abs as allies of King Ghawwār. The latter was joyous and forgot his disquiet.

The reason for the arrival of this aid from Hammām was the receipt of that message which had been sent to him by King Ghawwār. King Hammām had exclaimed, 'By the night when it is dark, and the moon when it glows, I must go forth to the Hijaz and cross the deserts. I will meet its knights in battle and slay its heroes and loot all their possessions.' Then Hammām made ready that army and sent it to King Ghawwār ibn Dīnār after he had written letters and dispatched them to his armies. Upon reaching the Banū 'Abs they engaged them, led as they were by Ghasūb, Maysara, Māzin and Sabī' al-Yaman. King Lawn al-Zalām called his companions, 'Cousins, attack your enemies and leave no record behind you save your own.' He attacked with them and strove in the struggle. But the Banū 'Abs were hemmed in from every side. Ghasūb repulsed the horsemen who were fearful of his shriek and turned their backs. Ghamra, his mother, murmured angrily and fought stubbornly for the Banū 'Abs. She faced hardship. One after another, the waves of attackers charged against the Banū 'Abs until all were intermingled. Blood flowed, hearts trembled and eyes wept, yet the Banū 'Abs stood firm and thwarted destruction. They fought hard until the day was over, and night fell on a confused gathering of friend and foe.

By dawn the Banū 'Abs were in grave danger, a span's distance from death. Ghasūb guarded them with his sword and spear point as did his brother Maysara. But the fighting went on into yet another day, and at its close they returned from the buffeting. Above their heads were canopies of dust. The Banū 'Abs had gained the mastery on that second day. They had endured the test imposed upon them by the Almighty. It was to their relief that seven thousand knights had reached them unexpectedly from Ghamra's territory. Reports had reached their ears, and their arrival was a consolation.

The Banū 'Abs sat in council. 'Urwa ibn al-Ward said, 'I know the reason for the coming of those negroes. It is due to the absence of our protector. If he has been killed how great will be the enemy's rejoicing! Shaybūb has not returned. We know not what has become of him, and the hour when we expected him has now long passed.' Ghamra said, 'We shall not surrender while among us there is a heart which beats and a tongue which speaks.' They ate. In the morning they rode forth again to fight their opponents.

When the squadrons were alined in battle a knight of the Banū 'Abs went forth clad in iron (48). That knight was Sabī' al-Yaman Muqri'l-Wahsh, the reciter of verse on the battle-field. When he had delivered his challenge a black knight came to meet him. The latter was full of scorn and said, 'Where will you flee? You are surrounded by fate. Why does not your black knight Antar go forth to battle?' Sabī' al-Yaman answered, 'Woe to you. What silly notion is it which might tempt this ferocious knight to come out to you and fight you? Here am I, the meanest of the slaves. I have gone forth in his stead. I challenge you.' Sabī' al-Yaman unsheathed his blade and swooped upon his foe like a bird of prey which strikes a pigeon. He split his spear and smote his head so that the blade of his sword clove him to the palate. The Banū 'Abs cried aloud for joy when they saw his terrible blow.

King Ghawwār said, 'By Al-Lāt and Al-'Uzzā, these knights are unequalled. They justly deserve the title of the Fates of the Arabs.' Then the brother of the slain knight went forth to challenge Sabī' al-Yaman. For an hour they exchanged blows with the powdered earth in clouds above them. Ghamra and 'Urwa watched until the dust cleared. They saw that Sabī' al-Yaman had grieved his foe and had ridden close to him so that their stirrups were adjacent. Then Sabī' al-Yaman seized him by his hauberk, dragged him from his saddle and took him captive. The horsemen of the Banū 'Abs bound him. The negroes attacked Sabī' al-Yaman in a group. He withstood them. By noon he had slain sixty and captured thirty. From every quarter attacks were resumed until nightfall.

In the morning they recommenced their battle. King Ghawwār ibn Dīnār led the fighting. He was angry at the deeds of Sabī' al-Yaman. He said, 'None will fight me save our foeman of yesterday.' Hardly had he phrased his verses before Prince Maysara appeared. King Ghawwār said to him, 'Woe to you. Where is the youth who fought yesterday?' Maysara said, 'I will be his ransom.' He attacked with ferocity but while they were in combat Maysara's horse threw him. He sprawled on the ground, and his bones were nearly broken to pieces. Ghawwār leapt upon him, took him prisoner and led him away.

The Banū 'Abs were disheartened. Ghasūb sought to go out into the field but his fond mother Ghamra restrained him. 'Urwa ibn al-Ward went forth instead. King Ghawwār, that mighty hero, beheld his resolution and set upon him. He grasped him by his throat and dragged him by his feet from his horse and had him tied in bonds. 'Urwa's men tried to rescue him with their spear points well directed and aimed. Ghamra attacked in desperation. She was aided by some of the Banū Hām and King Lawn al-Zalām. They leapt like lions and forded rivers of blood. Ghamra sought for Ghawwār but he withstood her assault with a heart harder than toughest stone. She was a doughty opponent. Her spear pierced his hauberk but inflicted no injury. He fell backwards on to the ground and was nearly slain. But his slaves and negroes came to his aid. They fought to defend him until they could remount him and take him away from the battlefield.

This battle lasted for four days and four nights. On the fifth day help came to them from the Banū Quḍā'a and Lawn al-Zalām received fresh aid from his negroes. The Banū 'Abs were gladdened, and Ghawwār was discouraged. Ghamra received her cousins hospitably and told them of her hardships, and how they had lost Antar, their protector. The two parties once more resumed their combat.

King Ghawwār was surrounded by his chief men. He told his commanders that none should return from the thick of battle without a prisoner or an insignia of a dead foeman. They swore that they would destroy the Banū Quḍā'a. The trumpets were sounded, and the drums throbbed. The knights of the Banū 'Abs shook their spears and looked to death as their future dwelling-place. At their head were Ghasūb, Māzin and Sabī' al-Yaman, their defenders. The first among them to attack was Ghasūb whose heart seemed relaxed despite the loss of his father. He was followed by Ghamra, among the Banū Qudā'a, and Lawn al-Zalām with his warriors. King Ghawwār attacked among a hundred of the negroes. The habitations shook, mountains trembled, and fear filled many a heart. But how well fought Ghamra and her son Ghasūb. As the day closed, the eye of the king of death beheld the spectacle, and he frowned. Each party withdrew lamenting its losses. Ghasūb returned dyed crimson while King Ghawwār returned fearful lest his land would pass from his hand.

Princess 'U' jūbat al-Anām.

When Ghawwār returned he was met by a messenger. He was from King Hammām. He kissed the ground before him and humbly saluted him. He said, 'Sire, rejoice in victory. King Hammām, lord of the Land of Flags and Ensigns has sent me with good news of the capture of Safwān, the son of King Lawn al-Zalām, and Antar ibn Shaddād. He has decided to crucify them in that country and rid the world of them.' Ghawwār almost flew for joy. His heart was consoled. He gave a robe to the messenger and said to him, 'By the ancient lord, cares have been removed from us with the capture of this stoned devil. May God grant King Hammām a long life. May he not deprive me of his rejoicing.'

Then Ghawwār ordered the blowing of trumpets and the beating of the kettledrums. The joyful news was proclaimed in every household. He had said to the messenger, 'Brother among the Banū Hām, tell me how the two heroes Safwān and Antar fell into the power of King Hammām. What brought them to him?' The messenger said, 'Know, my lord, that it was his daughter, 'U' jūbat al-Anām, who delivered them to him. She, due to her deceits, played a ruse on them, and she made them fall into her trap.' King Ghawwār said, 'She has indeed performed a deed denied to men, save a few, but tell me further of this tale.'

The messenger continued, 'To hear is to obey, oh, king. When you sent to King Hammām complaining of what you had suffered from this rabble, how they had captured the Sudan and had brought humiliation and loss upon its people, he was greatly troubled. He was afraid for his people and his lands. The same hour he dispatched his soldiers. He had pondered how he should act. He was beset by rumours and whispers. When his daughter knew his disquiet she said to him, "My father, think lightly of this matter for I shall lead Antar to you in ropes of humiliation in a very few days if you give me permission to act as I intend." When her father heard her words he said to her, "Act as you wish and be swift." She speedily left him and she dressed in male attire. She wound a turban round her head and covered her mouth with a muffler. She conceived a crafty plan. She took with her twenty knights of courage, and she followed the body of men which her father had sent to Ghawwār. She arrived where Antar's men were camped, and she asked for the tent of Lawn al-Zalām. By God's decree it happened that as she was going about the tents she heard the voice of Safwān, Badr al-Tamām. He was sighing and lamenting and was in a state of distress.

A lover has complained of anguish which he hides.
He spent his night in deep distress when people slept.
Behold him sick in body yet with no infirmity.
How can the body be in health while, sick in heart,
A lover finds his day is desolate. His beloved is remote.
Sorrows are his companions and the night is dark.
When asked, 'Oh, youth, tell me the cause of your
affliction,'
He answers, 'The physician is expert in the cause of maladies.'
He fights his tears, his heart is torn by fears.
He manifests a will to struggle, but his weeping is
too great.
For if a tear be held back on his lid
Love will utter his lament within his heart.
No tear is shed, but his affliction lodges still.
There is no consolation, and his care and woe will never die.
Sorrow has wounded him but his heart within
Due to love's touch and wounding is both sound and sick.
Forsake me not, keep the covenant between us plighted.
None are made sick by love's troth save those mad with love.
Oh, wonder of men, show me pity, grant me mercy.
Surely he who mercy shows, to him is mercy given.
With her glance she showed her fear towards her people.
Saddened she was. She uttered neither word nor sigh.
Yet I was certain that the glance of hers said, 'Welcome,
To the one whose mind love has demented.'
By Al-Lāt and by Al-'Uzzā, chaste be thou for me.

When 'U' jūbat al-Anām heard him she approached him and greeted him. He said to her, 'What do you want, oh, man of courage? She said, 'Oh, king, I am your beloved 'U' jūbat al-Anām.' She removed the muffler from her face. When he recognized her, he sprang to his feet. He said to her, 'What has brought you to this place, oh, light of my eye?' She said, 'Safwān, know that the reason is that from the day when your father asked for my hand, without success, I was filled with love of you, and I was deprived of sleep and food. Because of the ardour of my love I have come to these tents. I want to help you slay my father and to make you king of the Land of Flags and Ensigns. Arise and follow me. My father has gone to the hunt, and he will not return until twenty days have passed.'

Safwān said, 'If this be so then be patient. I will tell my friend, Antar ibn Shaddād. If he is with us he will enable us to achieve what we all wish for in that land.' She said to him, 'Do what seems best, but inform none but Antar.' He promised her this. Then he left her in his tent and went to look for Antar. Due to destiny he found him alone. He went to him and kissed his hands. He told him of the coming of his beloved 'U' jūbat al-Anām and what she had told him. Antar rose at once. He took pity on lovers, and he knew what torments they endured. He armed himself, and his appearance resembled a mountain summit or a rock hewn from a peak. He went to 'U' jūbat al-Anām. When he saw her beauty he pardoned Safwān for having such love for her. As for 'U' jūbat al-Anām when she saw Antar she was astonished at the size of his body and his fearsome aspect. She approached him and kissed his hands. He asked her, and she told him the same story as she had told Safwān. Antar said to her, 'Did you come on your own?' She replied, 'No, oh, father of knights, I brought twenty knightly cousins with me.'

He said, 'As for that tree which stands between this country and your land, how were you protected from its power?' 'Oh, father of knights, I carried its enchantment and its magic spell with me.' When Antar heard her story he followed her. He, Safwān and 'U' jūbat al-Anām mounted and rode forth from the tents followed by the twenty knights who had come with her. All of them went across the deserts and valleys until they approached the tree of the Mistress of Fires and Lights. She made them dress [as merchants] in tunics, and she darkened their left eyes with antimony.

They passed by the tree, and they continued their journey, Antar being wary, until they came close by the Fortress of Flags and Ensigns. At that place the twenty knights of King Hammām joined them. They hastened to the princess and asked her about Antar and Safwān. She said, 'These are messengers who have come to my father. Has he returned from the hunt?' They said to her, 'Oh, queen, you know that he will only come back after twenty days.' When Antar heard these words of those men he believed 'U' jūbat al-Anām. He had been wary of deceit or a trap. His heart was reassured, and he continued until he arrived at the fortress. He and Safwān dismounted. None stood in their way. King Hammām had posted four thousand horsemen, two thousand on the right hand and two thousand on the left. They seized the two men, fettered them and knotted their fore-arms and their extremities tightly.

Then Antar knew that they had been tricked. He was full of regret at a time when regret was pointless. He resigned himself to an inescapable destiny. They brought him before King Hammām. When he saw the frame of Antar he was astonished and awed by the size of his body and the fearsomeness of his

Plate 7: (Ṣafwān) Badr al-Tamām, Antar, 'U'jūbat-al Anām and King Hammām.

countenance. He said to him, 'Woe to you, knave, what urges you to enter our land and slay our warriors?' Antar said, 'My stout heart emboldened me to so so and my mighty sword. Woe to you, oh, wearer of two horns. Did you take me captive on the battlefield? By the Merciful, the Creator of men and *jinn,* were the battlefield to join our men together I would leave none of your men alive be they as numerous as the sands of Canaan. Had not the maiden led us to this land by cunning and deceit, any chance of your beholding us as your captives would have been remote! Behind us are ranks of warriors like the stormy sea; Ghasūb, Maysara, Ghamra and courageous men of the Banū 'Abs and 'Adnān who fear neither death nor destruction.'

King Hammām said, 'By the protection of the noble Arabs, I will delay your death until I join you to your companions. Then I shall kill you all on the same day.' He cast stones at Antar and Safwān, and he sent a messenger to King Ghawwār to tell him the good news of their capture. When King Ghawwār heard that news he ordered that the kettledrums should be beaten and the trumpets sounded. The Banū 'Abs heard that noise. Ghasūb said to Ghamra, 'What is the matter with our enemy tonight, why is he so full of rejoicing?' 'Some aid has reached him, or perhaps news of Antar', she replied. Ghasūb said, 'If this be true, then I, by the King of kings, must take King Ghawwār captive tomorrow, though he be seated way above the clouds.'

They waited watchfully until the morning. The parties mounted and lined up in their ranks. Ghasūb shouted to his mother Ghamra and to the heroes of the Banū 'Abs. He said, 'Attack behind me. Observe the way I charge, and I withdraw.' He attacked the troops of King Ghawwār, like a lion, with his mother Ghamra to the right of him and with Sabī' al-Yaman to his left. Ghasūb attacked at the foot of the flags of King Ghawwār. He took him captive and led him away humiliated. Then he cried, 'Oh, 'Abs oh, 'Adnān, I am Antar's son.' When the negroes saw their situation they attacked Ghasūb from every side in an attempt to save their kind from his hand. They were met by Ghamra, Sabī' al-Yaman and the other heroes who continued to fight them until they totally defeated them.

They brought King Ghawwār to their tents. They supped, and then Ghasūb ordered that King Ghawwār should be brought before him fettered in irons and chains. When he stood before him, Ghasūb leapt towards him, drew his sword and intended to behead him. Ghawwār said, 'Do not act thus, oh, heroic warrior. Spare me, perchance you may ransom Antar, your father.' When Ghasūb heard these words of Ghawwār he said, 'Woe to you. If my father is with you I will set him free at once from his imprisonment.' Ghawwār told him of the plan and trap set by 'U' jūbat al-Anām for Antar and Safwān, and how she had led them into captivity. When Ghasūb heard the account he was relieved to learn that his father was alive. He cast Ghawwār into one of the tents and appointed a company of men to guard him. He sent for King Lawn al-Zalām and told him that his son Safwān was still alive. He forgot his sorrows. On the morrow Ghasūb went forth to the battle-field. He cried aloud, 'Fight, oh negroes of the Sudan, for I shall spare none of you.' The negroes came forth to fight him, knight after knight. They were slain one after another. They consulted their chief who could only remark, 'If Antar had also been there we would certainly have perished.' Ghasūb was praised by his comrades for his victory. On the following day they lined up yet again, in ranks, on foot and mounted.

Antar escapes.

For ten days after the capture of King Ghawwār Ghasūb went daily to battle and acted as the guardian of the Banū 'Abs. On the eleventh day his men rode forth early as was their custom. Ghasūb was intent on battle but then he spied a rising dusty cloud. It covered them all. From beneath it there appeared ten knights on horses lighter than gazelles. At their head was a horseman [in colour] like a banner. He was a chamberlain, and he wore a brocade garment marked with glowing gold. Upon his head was a turban with fiery golden borders. Behind him rode a youth with a face beaming like a shining engraved *dīnār,* and he was bedecked by ornaments and by mantles like the moon. In his hand he held a jewelled flag which astounded all who beheld it.

The knights were surprised to see this messenger. He made his way between the ranks, he parted the hundreds and the thousands until he reached the army of King Hammām. He approached his vizir and spoke privately to him (49). That instant, the vizir appointed one of his men of valour to take charge of the troops. He took one hundred heroic knights and rode away with that stranger. Ghasūb, the Banū 'Abs and the whole army were surprised by that strange chamberlain and wondered why he had addressed the vizir of King Hammām. What had been his answer, and why had he departed with him? Ghamra said to Ghasūb, 'I fear the death of your father. This messenger disturbs me, so does his return with the vizir [var. chamberlain] of the king among his best men and in haste.' Ghasūb said, 'What ruse can we employ if his death be decreed?'

On the next day Ghasūb came into the battlefield, and he fought until it was sunset. He killed a hundred horsemen and returned to his tents. They passed the night ever watchful. They were about to recommence the battle when, lo, that chamberlain reappeared in his apparel. He made his way until he came to the chamberlain (*ḥājib*) (50) who had been appointed by the vizir of King Hammām. He spoke to him in private, and he obeyed him. He took two hundred knights and went with the messenger into the desert. The heroes were silent in their astonishment and could discern no reason. Ghasūb turned to his mother and said to her, 'Mother, by the unseen Lord, I am sure that this stranger is my uncle Shaybūb.' Ghamra answered, 'Son, how can you say such a thing. How could your uncle reach this place. I am fearful for my lands. I am afraid lest King Hammām will send soldiers to our country and seize it behind our backs. They will follow us and reconquer it. I would like to send spies to find out the news.'

On the following day Ghasūb slew another hundred horsemen, and he returned to his tents. All that night they were anxious about that mysterious messenger; and once again in the morning he reappeared. He rode up to the *muqaddam* of King Hammām and whispered in his ear. He then took one thousand horsemen, and they set out into the desert. Ghasūb said to Ghamra, 'By Him who is lord of the unseen I swear that this messenger is none other than Shaybūb, my uncle!' Ghamra answered, 'My son, from whence could your uncle Shaybūb have come? How could he have obtained access to King Hammām? How and why is it that he is obeyed in those orders he gives? We must be patient until the spies return with their reports.'

On the following day the messenger took two thousand knights and departed in the direction of the Fortress of Flags and Ensigns. Each day that messenger came until of the army of King Hammām two thirds had departed and only one third remained. When the cousin of King Ghawwār saw it he said to his cousins, 'I fear that King Hammām has suffered ill at the hands of Antar ibn Shaddād. These are not good signs. Each time the messenger comes he takes away the forces of King Hammām. I shall seize him in order to discover what has happened.'

Then came the spies whom Ghamra had sent to her country. They told her that they had met no one, neither Arab nor negro. Her heart was contented. Ghasūb came to his mother and said, 'I have decided to surprise the enemy in the dead of the night; I shall scatter them in the deserts and march to the Fortress of Flags and Ensigns to save my father in the clouds.' She said to him, 'This is good sense.' They warned their men to take their arms. When it was almost dawn they mounted, girded their swords and fixed their spears. Ghasūb divided them into four groups, and he attacked the soldiers of Ghawwār in the darkness. The negro warriors leapt up from their sleep, most of them unarmed. They fell on one another and were destroyed. The fire of war blazed until it was daylight. The slain warriors of King Ghawwār were uncountable, save by God Almighty. Those who were still alive went into the desert and fled. Ghasūb purused them with Ghamra, Maysara and 'Urwa. Then they returned to their booty and spent a day and a night in that place. Ghasūb ordered his soldiers to depart to the Fortress of Flags and Ensigns. They followed his orders. His warriors mounted and took

King Ghawwār with them. They marched through the deserts until they came closer and closer to the tree of the Mistress of Fires and Lights.

All at once dust rose before them until it blocked every horizon and a hundred knights were revealed. At the head of them was that chamberlain and messenger who had daily come to take away the soldiers of King Hammām. He had removed the muffler from his face. As he approached them they could see his features. He was indeed the uncoverer of afflictions and misfortunes, the lord of horses, Shaybūb. When they recognized him they cried with delight. They ran to him and greeted him. Ghasūb said, 'Oh, uncle, tell us all that happened to my father Antar. Did he escape harm and destruction?' Shaybūb replied, 'Know, oh, Ghasūb, that this day your father has become like King Chosroes. All the kings of Ethiopia have appeared to us as our relatives and as maternal uncles and our cousins.' When Ghasūb and those with him heard that report they camped there. He said to his uncle Shaybūb, 'Halt, uncle, tell me what happened to my father. How was he rescued from captivity and imprisonment?' So Shaybūb rested, and he began to tell them the reason for that remarkable affair.

Al-Asma'ī said: the reason was that when 'U'jūbat al-Anām had taken Antar and Safwān, her father had left them in an underground cellar and chamber. Each day he came to them in the evening and in the morning. He threatened them with death and with dishonour.

Thus he acted for ten days. On the night of the eleventh Antar said to Safwān, 'Woe to you, Safwān, for how long shall we be threatened by this tyrant, morning and evening. This suffrance of ours is nothing more than a wish for life and its prolongation. Come on, take courage, arise, let us go forth and capture the Fortress of Flags and Ensigns from his hands.' Safwān said, 'Oh, father of knights, what can we do in these chains which have cut us.' When Antar heard his words he laughed and said to him, 'Woe to you, Safwān, by the Lord who is adored, who exists in every place, now it is not difficult for me to sunder the chains and the bonds.' He pressed down hard on the fetters which held his hands. He snapped them and stretched his hand to the fetter which was on his feet, and he broke it. He turned to Safwān and released him from his irons and chains.

King Hammām came in to visit them as was his custom. Than Antar leapt upon him like a rampant lion. He seized him and raised him aloft with his hands until the black hair of his armpits was visible (51) and beat him on the ground so that his bones were nearly pounded. He tied him up and firmly knotted his arms and extremities. He said to him, 'Woe to you, oh, vile son, by the protection of the noble Arabs, if you but open your mouth I will give you the cup of death to drink.' The king said, 'Oh, hero of courage, give me your protection.' Antar said,

'I give you protection, by the life of 'Abla, the full moon and by my solemn oath, if you respond to my demands.' Hammām said, 'Let me hear your wishes.' Antar said, 'I want you to deliver to me all those who are in this fortress, one company after another.' King Hammām agreed to obey. He sent for the supreme chamberlain. Antar and Safwān had left to go to the court of Hammām. Antar took the entire store-house in that place. He seated himself in the heart of the court-chamber like a royal lion. His sword was unsheathed before him, and he saw Hammām bow to him in awe and reverence.

When the chamberlain beheld the sight he swayed in weakness, and he was deeply troubled. Hammām turned to him and said, 'Show to heroic Antar, my lord, that you will obey all the commands and decisions he tells you to carry out.' The chamberlain advanced to Antar and said to him, 'Command me, oh, heroic lion.' Antar said to him, 'Bring all the heroes of King Hammām to this place, company after company.' So he obeyed him. That chief chamberlain went forth and began to bring them one after another. Antar fettered them in chains and irons. When morning came he had captured all who were in the fortress. Next he ordered that one should go down into the city and bring him its citizens, ten by ten. His orders were obeyed. That same day Shaybūb reached the city to find news of his brother. When he heard it he went up into the castle with the host of men. He was full of joy at the sight of his brother, and he asked him how he had made his escape. He told him all that had happened to him up to the time of his release. Then Antar asked about his sons, and he reported the victory to him. Shaybūb said, 'I want to take ten champions with me and to disguise myself as the chamberlain of King Hammām. Then I will separate the troops into groups, group after group and bring them up to this place.' Antar agreed to his request and gave him the seal of King Hammām.

Shaybūb departed. So each day he brought a group until he had assembled all of them in that place. When his task was accomplished Antar said to him, 'Shaybūb, bring me 'U' jūbat al-Anām so that I may punish her for those things she did to us.' Shaybūb obeyed his orders and entered into the women's private apartments in order to fetch 'U'jūbat al-Anām. The women fled before him to right and to left. None stood before him save an old woman comely of visage and pleasing in stature. She stared at his face and said, 'Woe to you, youth, are you not Shaybūb ibn Shamāma?' (52) When Shaybūb heard her speak he was astonished. He said, As for my name it is Shaybūb. As for my mother's name I have only heard this from you because her true name was Zabība' (53). When she heard that name she shrieked with a voice like the rending of thunder, and she said, 'By the protection of the Arabs, you are none other than Shaybūb, son of my sister Shamāma, the daughter of the Negus, King Ma'dān (54), the wife of the lion king.' She ran to him and said, 'I left you with a sign, a white mole on your right shoulder with other black marks and signs' (55). Then she uncovered his shoulder, found that mole and then wept bitterly. She said, 'Had you but known, Shaybūb, what happened to your lion father when he heard of your capture! So too, the capture of your mother and your brother Jarīr at the hands of King Riyāsh (56). Your father sent his heroes to all countries to bring him news of you, and he did not cease to do this until his death.'

This King Riyāsh was always raiding the lands in the Sudan. On this occasion he captured Zabība. Her sons were with her. He captured her and made for his country. The heroes of the Hijaz went out against him. They slew him and took them from him, and they were joined to the Banū Jadīla (57). Shaddād raided them and then occurred what happened.

When Shaybūb heard her story he was like a man in a dream. He said to her, 'By the All-knowing King, I recognized these lands when we first entered these regions.' Then he told her why they had entered that country. She said, 'Praise be to God who has not neglected your maternal cousin.' 'Who is my maternal cousin?' he asked. She said, 'King Hammām. Have you forgotten what happened to you both at the pool? If the shepherds and the slaves had not found you, you would have died' (58).

Najd ibn Hishām said : When Shaybūb heard all this from her he was aware of everything, almost in a flash. He said to her, 'Who are you?' She said, I am your maternal aunt Sā'ida bint al-Mālik Ghulwān, the sister of your mother Shamāma. My third sister was Dahmā', the mother of Ghawwār.'

When he heard her words he left with tears flowing from his eyes on his cheeks. Antar said to him, 'What has made you weep?' Shaybūb told him what had happened from the beginning to the end. When Antar heard it he went to King Hammām and released him from bondage. Hammām went up to him and kissed him between the eyes. He rejoiced at the knowledge of their ancestry. The news spread in the Fortress of Flags and Ensigns that Antar had been revealed as the maternal cousin of King Hammām. The kettledrums were beaten, and the trumpets were blown, and there was great joy and rejoicing. Antar said to Shaybūb, 'Son of one mother, hurry to Ghasūb and tell him what has happened to us in these lands before he slays Ghawwār.'

Shaybūb obeyed his command and rode forth with one hundred knights that same hour. He marched until he met Ghasūb. We have recounted all that occurred. The latter asked him how his father had escaped, and he was told the full story. Then he ordered that King Ghawwār should be brought. Shaybūb said, 'Do you know who I am?' Ghawwār gazed into Shaybūb's face for a long time, and he said, 'In truth I know not who you are. As for your appearance I once had a cousin who was like you. His name was Shaybūb, and he had an elder brother who was called Jarīr.'

Shaybūb said, 'When were they parted from you?' 'Some forty years ago, perhaps more,' he replied. 'When Riyāsh raided us and took them captive with their mother Shamāma.' Shaybūb said, 'Be happy and let your eye be cool. I am Shaybūb, your maternal cousin.' Then he released him from his chains and fetters. King Ghawwār leapt towards him, embraced him and saluted him. All the heroes rejoiced over what had taken place. They began to release the men of Ghawwār who were their captives, and they all marched to the fortress of King Hammām. As for Lawn al-Zalām he was amazed and perplexed by these sayings and this remarkable reconciliation. On they marched until they drew near to the Fortress of Flags and Ensigns. They were met by Antar, King Hammām and Safwān ibn Lawn al-Zalām. They dismounted. The Banū 'Abs saluted Antar and felicitated him on his discovery of his maternal uncles.

King Ghawwār advanced and kissed Antar's hands and kissed him between his eyes. So intense was his joy that he wept. He said, 'Would that we had known one another before all these events had taken place and before the men who died in battle had been slain.' Antar said, 'God was the ruler over what happened to your men and to your heroes. It is a matter decreed by the Almighty King.' They all returned to the Fortress of Flags and Ensigns, and they held a feast in it for seven days. They married 'U'jūbat al-Anām to Safwān ibn Lawn al-Zalām, and they were filled with joy and rejoicing.

Reconciliation

One day Antar came into the presence of King Hammām, and he saw money and riches before him. He was selecting precious jewels and metals which dazzled the eyes and baffled the mind. He was placing them in coffers and making them ready for a journey. When Antar saw this he said to him, 'Where do you intend to send these riches?' Hammām said, 'To King al-Dahmār (59), the lord of the fortress of Dīnār. All the kings of our land send him riches. He is a giant of courage and has never been beaten.' Antar said, 'By God, the Divider of the night from the day, I will not allow you to send these riches to him. I must bring him to ruin. How can I be Antar ibn Shaddād, yet my nephew pay tribute!' He turned to the messenger of King al-Dahmār and said to him, 'Woe to you, oh, son of the wicked, go to him who has sent you and tell him to send King Hammām all the riches he has taken from him. If not I shall go to him and take his life.'

Najd ibn Hishām said : When the messenger heard the words of Antar he was perplexed and answered, 'Woe to you, base ruffian, who are you to say this?'

Antar was angry and inflamed with hatred. He unsheathed his sword and smote the messenger on his jugular vein and beheaded him. He told the companions of the latter to take his corpse, return to their king and inform him of what had happened. 'Return to your lord and say to him : Antar ibn Shaddād says let him return the riches sent to him without delay. If not I shall march to you and ruin your land, uproot your trace and cast the stores of your fortress into the deep.'

When King Hammām beheld this sight he said, 'Nay, oh, protector of 'Abs and 'Adnān. What have you done with us and the wealth which it is my due to pay? King al-Dahmār has only to hear this news and he will come with his troops and a mighty army. He is a stubborn and obstinate devil.' Antar said, 'Be calm, oh, victorious king. I shall not depart from these lands until I leave King al-Dahmār prostrate on the ground, his chiefs destroyed, so too his slaves.' Then Antar got up, he tied the dead messenger to his horse and commanded his companions to take him to their lord. He said to them, 'Woe to you, tell him to cook the most acid food in his larder!' The emissaries of King al-Dahmār rode away gravely disquieted at Antar's deeds and greatly astonished. They came to their king and appeared before him with the messenger lying dead across his steed. They told him how the knight of 'Abs had killed him. Hardly had they finished when he cried aloud with emotion and anger and ordered that his troops be summoned.

This king was a great shedder of blood. He had a son called Qāsim al-A'mār who faced all dangers. He was for ever criticizing his father for his actions. On this occasion he blamed him but he paid no heed. He advised him to desist but he did not. He looked to his chamberlain and princes, and he ordered them to command their subsidiary nobles and chiefs to summon their warriors to take arms. The proclamation was made in those quarters, and the men of courage, men on foot and horsemen assembled. The king ordered that the stores of weapons and of money should be opened. He gave lavishly in silver and gold. Then he mounted among his men like a turbulent sea, and banners and flags were raised above his head. Drums were beaten and the kettledrums thundered and the horns were blown. Off he rode amidst seventy thousand knights all clad in mail. Some carried spears, others shields, and he marched to the land of King Hammām. He crossed the deserts until he drew near to the Fortress of Flags and Ensigns. Dust rose above them until the day was turned to darkness.

Each day Antar used to ride. With him he took his sons and men of valour; King Hammām, Safwān ibn Lawn al-Zalām and Safwān ibn Ma'dān (60). They searched for word in the desert because they knew that King al-Dahmār would come. Then that day dawned when they beheld the dust rising to the sky. They were in two groups. Antar hurried. They took their weapons. They knew that it was King al-Dahmār since the distance between the two kingdoms was close.

When the host met on those hills, and hero beheld hero, and standards were raised, and the dust gathered in a cloud blocking the east and the west, the troops of al-Dahmār attacked King Hammām. Antar met them, and all seemed lost in a mirage or was like a horrible dream. Arrows flew, and the battle lasted long. The dust became thicker and blacker.

Night brought the armies of darkness. The groups retired to their tents to rest and to eat, and they slept after they had set a watch until it was dawn. Then both armies hastened to attack. They displayed their brightly polished swords and long spears. The fighting was furious until it was nearly sun-set. Once again the armies retired to rest and to eat. Darkness again dispersed, the morning smiled, and they smote with the blade. The coward sought flight while the man of courage cried aloud for the battle to continue. They drank a draught of death and battle raged until Antar met King al-Dahmār face to face in the middle of the field. He attacked him with great ferocity to the astonishment of the courageous spectator. Antar assaulted him like a giant. He clutched the mail of his hauberk, then pulled and unseated him. He took him captive and led him away humiliated. He delivered him to Shaybūb who bound his arms and legs.

Then came his son Ghasūb. Next to him grasped by his wrist was a knight with the marks of chivalry, Qāsim al-A'mār, the son of King al-Dahmār. Each of the Banū 'Abs returned with a captive. They had slaughtered many. When evening descended they returned and camped in their tents after a day of marvels. They supped and drank wine. Antar said, 'Bring me the captives so that we may slay them and unburden ourselves of their hostility.' Shaybūb brought them. At their head was King al-Dahmār and his son Qāsim al-A'mār. They stood before Antar who commanded Ghasūb to behead them. He drew his sword from its scabbard and approached King al-Dahmār. He stretched to his full height and was resigned to die.

Then among the charms and amulets of Ghasūb's he saw a charm of Cathay enclosed in gold. Upon it was the portrait of a lion. He said to him, 'Ghasūb, by Him who knows the unseen, tell me before you kill me from whence came this amulet?' Ghasūb said to him, 'Oh, king, my mother gave it to me.' Antar heard all that was said. Then al-Dahmār added, 'Is your mother with you here in this camp?' 'Yes,' Ghasūb replied. He said, 'By the protection of the Arabs, bring her to me.' Ghamra was listening to his words so Antar told her to speak to him. She went to him and said, 'What is the purpose of your question?' He said to her, 'Are you Ghamra?' 'Yes, by the Lord of Destiny.' 'Is this your son Ghasūb or is he your ward as I have heard?' She said, 'No, by the Bountiful Creator, he is my son and the son of Antar ibn Shaddād.' 'Did you give him this amulet?' 'Yes.' 'Who gave it to you?' 'My mother, who told me to guard it with care and to keep it. It will tell you who are your maternal uncles. So I placed it upon my shoulder, and I found benefit and *baraka* in it until I was blessed with this boy, and I put it among the amulets on his shoulders (61). This is all that happened. Your question serves no purpose; do you fear to die?'

When al-Dahmār heard this he was full of joy. He forgot his executor and cried with joy, 'Know, oh, Ghamra, that this charm which your son has is well known to me. The indications and proofs are correct, and I am truthful and correct in what I say. Its brother charm is to be found on my shoulder (62). Each charm has my name and the name of my sister. The charms had been sent to the king of the Ethiopians as part of a gift of a captive girl. My father was King Sayyār, lord of the castle of Dīnār. This Ethiopian king loved us and wanted to marry my sister Hudhūr (63). The king wrote my name and the name of my sister and placed the writing in the hollow of each amulet. They are incorporated and joined so that the male is in the female, and the female is in the male. One amulet was put on my shoulder, and the other on the shoulder of my sister (64).

The king of the Ethiopians who gave them to us lived for a short time. He died and never married my sister. My father died a little later, and I became king after him. His soldiers obeyed me. My sister sought to make the pilgrimage to God's house, *al-Ḥaram.* She took a gift and offerings for the idols and images. After some days news reached us that when she had gone deep into the desert the Arabs of the Hijaz took her. To this day we have had no news of her, nor has the mystery of her fate been disclosed.'

When she had heard his words Ghamra said, 'You have spoken the truth, oh, king. It would appear that you are my maternal uncle.' Then Ghamra said to Antar, 'Oh, father of knights, what he says is sound. I have heard from my mother many times that she endeavoured to go to the Hijaz. The Arabs took her and looted her of her possessions and killed the men. My father bought her from them with the camels which she had.' Antar was full of amazement at these circumstances. He called his son Ghasūb and said to him, 'Give me this charm of yours.' He gave it to him. Al-Dahmār likewise gave him his charm. Antar took them and handed them to King Hammām. He ordered him to read them and disclose their secret. Hammām held them in his hands. He opened them and took out the papers. He knew the script of the Ethiopians, and he read them aloud (65). He found one with the name of Hudhūr and the other with the name of al-Dahmār. Both names were in each charm. So the reports and proofs were correct, and it appeared that King al-Dahmār was the maternal uncle of Ghamra, the mother of Ghasūb.

Ghasūb ran to release al-Dahmār, his son and his company. They embraced one another. Ghamra also embraced him and wept with joy because of their meeting. All men rejoiced, and the kettledrums were sounded. The Banū 'Abs and 'Adnān and the negroes were amazed at this chance fortune. Then they brought food and drank wine and celebrated until the morning.

Al-Dahmār rode with his soldiers, the chief families and the lords of his state, and they rode to say farewell after the conclusion of the peace. Al-Dahmār went to see Antar and kissed him between the eyes. They sat and discoursed, and they were brought food on the heads of slaveboys and servants. When they were filled they drank wine. King al-Dahmār said, 'Oh, father of knights, I beg of you, journey with me to my land and honour it with the soles of your feet. My wish is extended also to my niece and her son so that the fire of passion may be extinguished.'

Antar agreed, and the soldiers rode away with them until they brought them to the fortress of Dīnār. The kings and lords took up residence. The flags were raised, sheep were slaughtered and with them quails, she-camels and young dromedaries. They dined and passed cups of wine and made merry. So they continued feasting for ten days, and on the eleventh they made ready for their journey. Antar wished to leave in haste. He called King Hammām, King Ghawwār and King Lawn al-Zalām and Safwān and the other chiefs of the Sudan. They made a common pact that they would be as one 'hand' in all their affairs, and they took oaths binding each other. King al-Dahmār said, 'By God, oh, father of knights, if we are not like your nation and keep the oaths as you have decreed we will suffer loss and our lands will be ruined.' Antar said with fierce eyes and hair bristling, 'Who will ruin this land and do these things to you?' King al-Dahmār said, 'Know, oh, knight, that we are all subordinate to the Nubians, the Zanj and the Ethiopians. Ghawwār takes wealth from Lawn al-Zalām. He sends it to Hammām and the latter sends it to me. I send it to the Negus, the mighty king whose armies are like a torrent. Know that before I rode against you I sent him word. His army will surely come. If the hero al-'Abd Zinjīr is among the warriors none of our heroes will be left.'

King al-Dahmār had hardly completed this account when the eyes of Antar became as hot as embers. He said, 'Oh, king of God's holy house, *Zamzam* and the *Maqām,* I shall not leave this citadel until I meet the army of the Negus, the mighty king, and I scatter it in the dusty wastes. I shall leave for both of us a record for posterity as long as sun and moon shall last. Have no fear I shall stay with you until I dispose of those who are against you, and I appoint you in his place and give you his kingdom and authority.'

Al- 'Abd Zinjīr and the Negus

The Negus whom we have mentioned was a mighty king and powerful Sultan of a stout heart and lord of provinces and of all those countries and those negroes who dwelt therein who paid tribute and poll-tax. King Ghawwār ibn Dīnār, King Hammām, King al-Dahmār and the Negus were all cousins. They were the ancestors of Zabība, the mother of Antar, because the father of this Negus married the mother [*sic* = sister(?)] of Zabība to King Bassām, the father of King Hammām, and they all stem from Hām ibn Nūh, on whom be peace. Protection and fortune was in the stars of Zabība since destiny sent her to the lands of the Banū ʻAbs and ʻAdnān when she bore Antar ibn Shaddād, a matter appointed by God the Bountiful.

As for this king of whom we are speaking his name was Mankalā(n). When he took the throne of his father he was called the Najāshī (Negus). Mankalā(n) believed in our lord Muhammad and sent gifts to him, among them the standard of the eagle, the worth of which cannot be valued. It is the fashion of the kings of countries that the ruler of the land of Ethiopia is called the Negus; the ruler of the Persians is called Kisrā Anūsharwān, and the ruler of Byzantium is called Qaysar, the ruler of the Yemen is called al-Tubbaʻ, and the ruler of Egypt is called al-ʻAzīz.

We have only commentated on this expression 'the Negus' so that our hearer may know that 'the Negus' was not only in Antar's days, but also in the days of the Prophet. We have provided a commentary on the kings and on their varied titles (66).

When Antar swore that mighty oath that he would scatter the armies of the Negus, the heart of al-Dahmār was comforted, and he rejoiced greatly. He ordered one of his men to search for news. Meanwhile, they returned to their eating and their drinking.

Then a day came when the sun rose over the hills and the valleys. The knight sent by al-Dahmār returned and reported that the Negus was riding amidst a great army. The reason for this was that [he had heard of the fate] of the messenger whom al-Dahmār had sent and whom Antar had killed. When the Negus heard the news of what Antar had done with the inhabitants of those countries he was disquieted. He made plain his purpose, and he set forth amidst one hundred and seventy thousand horsemen, like glaring lions, all bearing polished swords, long spears and Ethiopian lances. They rode Arabian steeds, and they wore mail of King David's handicraft. On their heads were helmets of the ʻĀdites.

The messenger of al-Dahmār said, 'They are coming to you and against you. He has heard what you have done and of Antar's act. He is very angry, and he has sworn that he will leave none of you alive. He has marched in all haste through the desert. At the head of his army is al- 'Abd Zinjīr who swears that he will spare neither young nor old.' When Antar heard the news his face was darkened, and he said, 'By the All Knowing King, *Zamzam* and the *Maqām,* and the sanctity of the month of *Rajab* and the Lord who, since He rules over all men, is the Vanquisher – I must encounter him because of his words, and I shall sever his members, limb by limb.'

Al-Asma'ī mentioned that there was not in the whole Sudan, neither Zanj nor Takrūr (67), nor Ethiopia, nor of the Arab tribes one who was more skilled as a horseman than al-'Abd Zinjīr, nor more horrible than him in aspect, nor with a louder voice when he screamed. When he cried aloud men imagined that the thunder roared. When the pregnant woman heard him she miscarried and her heart burst. He was one of the Amalekites (68), and the narrators of wonderous tales and historians of the Arabs report that there was none in that age who had a mightier body than Antar nor had tougher shoulders. But the body of this slave was twice the size of Antar.

His history was very strange, although his reason for obeying the Negus was not so strange. Al-Asma'ī said : It was because the father of this slave Zinjīr was the slave Barāq who was a rebellious demon on one of the islands. He took a slave girl and by her he begat this son. He was a tyrant, he cut the routes and roads, and the king of Ethiopia sent an army against him. He destroyed the first army and wiped out a second. He determined to capture the king's city, and he went there with his sword and his shield. But God, the Judge thwarted his plans. This slave Barāq only slept on an island in the middle of the water because of his fear that the army of Ethiopia might surprise him. When he had decided to go and possess the city a monster arose from the deep and swallowed him up, thereby fulfilling God's decree. When it was dawn his son, al- 'Abd Zinjīr, came but could not see his father. He went around the island from one end to the other but he did not find him. He said, 'One of the water monsters has swallowed him.' So he assumed his place. The kings of the Sudan began to fear him because he became a far more powerful warrior than his father Barāq and was far worse than he was (69).

He heard that the Negus had a daughter called Manār who was more beautiful than the moon when the lights of the sun are dim. He was deeply in love with her, and he sent to her father seeking her hand. The Negus was perplexed and knew not how to answer. He summoned the lords of his kingdom and his people and told them about his daughter. They advised him to marry her to al- 'Abd Zinjīr and to appoint him to be the sword of his wrath and the leader of the Ethiopian armies. When the Negus heard this he understood the wisdom of their counsel, and he gave his answer to the messenger. The maiden was married to him, and he became the protector of his country. This slave was blessed with a son named Habbār (70). ‘Alī, the Commander of the Faithful, slew him. The warriors of the *ḥarīm* fought him together with our lady Fātima in her palanquin, and it was said that the Prophet ordered ‘Alī to do so. Reciters have told these fabulous tales (71). This slave Habbār ibn Zinjīr (72) had the body of his father, but it was twice the size. He faced ten thousand men without concern.

When Antar swore to destroy the troops of the Negus, King al-Dahmār commanded his troops to march and to be armed with weapons. They set out with fifty thousand horsemen. Antar was at their head, and with him were Ghasūb, Maysara, Sabī‘ al-Yaman and ‘Urwa ibn al-Ward. Antar found the march tedious, and in the evening they camped at a place where there were pools in abundance. Antar wished to watch over them during the night but al-Dahmār did not let him do so. He ordered his son Qāsim al-A‘mār to guard them until dawn. In the morning they armed themselves, and they marched rapidly.

Then they saw a dust cloud which blackened all the horizons. It advanced like the waves of the sea. As I have mentioned, this army numbered some one hundred and seventy thousand men. Antar said, ‘By the protection of the Arabs and the month of *Rajab*, this is the army of the Sudan and of the Ethiopians. Today the coward will be distinguished from the hero who is courageous.’ He loosed the bridle of his horse and waited to hear the news. Next appeared the banners, flags and finery of the Ethiopian army.

When the soldiers of the Negus saw those of al-Dahmār and Antar they held them in contempt. They were so few that they attacked them without due care. Skulls were scattered like colocynth, men fell from their neighing steeds, and blood flowed in pools. Spears were broken, and mail was pierced by blades. He who uttered a word could not be heard.

Thus they fought until it was dark. The two armies separated. Antar withdrew to his tents, followed by the Banū ‘Abs. He recited his verse, and this made glad the hearts of the lords who relaxed on the backs of their horses which stood on three legs in anticipation of battle. Then they dismounted and waited for the dawn.

The battle was fierce, the men were girt with their weapons, and Antar rode into the field of single combat but the Ethiopians attacked him in a body, crying aloud, so that King al-Dahmār when he saw the danger called upon his men to attack, and the plains and mountains shook. Al- ‘Abd Zinjīr smote with his sword. Once again night descended. The force of the Ethiopians had been broken. All of them lauded Antar’s feats. Al- ‘Abd Zinjīr was full of anger when they described Antar to the Negus. He said to him, 'Oh, king, by your favour and grace, today I went through rank after rank, and I met thousand after thousand in search of Antar but my eye did not see him. Tomorrow I shall be the first to march into the gate of battle, and I shall call on him to thrust and smite. If he engages me in combat then this affair will be ended. Today I had resolved to combat him but numerous ranks and knights came between us.' The Negus believed what he said since he knew of his deeds.

As for Antar ibn Shaddād and the Banū 'Abs when they camped at night they spoke of their encounters, and what they had seen of al-'Abd Zinjīr in the field. Antar said, 'By God, I strove all day to find him but I did not catch a glimpse of him, and none led me to him. However, by the protection of the noble Arabs, I must strike him down on these sands. The women and offspring will weep for him. After his death I shall face these soldiers and deliver a blow which will rend iron and carry away the rocks. I shall scatter them all in the dunes and the hills. Then I shall attack their king, and I shall capture him under the flags.' King al-Dahmār rejoiced most at his words because he greatly feared the Negus and al-'Abd Zinjīr.

In the morning the Negus mounted his horse. Flags and banners were unfurled above his head. He ordered the commanders to draw up their men to right and to left. He was in the centre, and al- 'Abd Zinjīr stood before him. When Antar saw this alignment he knew that it was to be a day of single combat. He was full of joy. He lined up his knights and his men of courage and his chiefs. Hardly had the armies taken their positions when, from the army of the Negus, there sallied forth a knight who was clad in mail, armed with spear and shield. No eye had seen or mind imagined one mightier than his frame nor more terrifying in his image. He was like a flattened date palm or the stump of a burnt palm tree.

He was clad in a hauberk plated with red gold, and on his chest was a mirror of precious stone. Its rays dazzled the eyes. His head was covered by an 'Ādite helm, a casque like a raised cupola. In one hand he held a spear. He was girt with an Indian blade which could cut through hauberks of King David's weave. It was a sword about which the poet said :

A glaive like a lighting fork with its scabbard flashing.
It smites the mountain crests and sends the boulders crashing.
In the combat, high it flies, beneath it waves are dashing (73).

He rode a horse of Camphor (Kāfūr), whitish in its colour. To quote a poet:

It is like the morning, comely in size, with stateliness
and pride.
When ridden, its master cries, 'Upon the Pleiades I ride.'

He came to the middle of the field of combat. The horsemen looked at him, and when he knew that their eyes were fixed upon him, and that he had shown his might to the Negus, he darted forward. When the steed was in full flight he gripped it with his thighs after he had let forth such a shout as to cause distress to both camps in the combat. Then the horse fell dead beneath him with its back broken into two halves.

When the Banū 'Abs and the negroes saw these feats they were deeply disturbed. Al-'Abd Zinjīr cried out to his slaves and said to them, 'Bring me a virile camel.' They brought him a large camel, and they made it kneel before him. He advanced towards it and placed his hands upon it. Then he ordered his slaves to prick it with spear points. This they did. The camel tried to arise but could not move. When al 'Abd Zinjīr saw that the horsemen were afraid of him he ordered that the legs of the camel should be bound together. They did as he commanded, then he told them to retire. He gripped its neck, gave a mighty shout and kicked it in the chest. He pulled the neck so hard that he tore it apart from its shoulders. Then he charged on foot in the direction of Antar's soldiers and drew close to them. He hurled the neck of the camel so that it shot forth like a fiery thunderbolt. It struck two knights sideways, slew them and smote them to the ground. When the knights saw this devil's deeds the negroes shook with fear.

Antar was standing among the knights watching, and he spied his brother Shaybūb weeping. Antar called out, 'Woe to you, oh, father of winds! Why weep so and lament so?' Shaybūb replied, 'Oh, father of knights, this breaks the close bond between us. Draw near so that I may bid you farewell, because I tell you that this knight will slay you.' Shaybūb, who was pale and shaking with fear, added, 'Oh, son of one mother, I declare that this devil is not human. I fear for you by the *Rukn* and the *Ḥajar* [the black stone of the Ka'ba].' Antar laughed and exclaimed, 'Woe to you, why speak you thus, Shaybūb? By Him who knows the unseen, who knows all secrets and hearts, and who will relieve the torment of all who are afflicted, this devil has done these things only because he is afraid of your brother Antar. I must strike off his head with this sword and make this day the most ill-omened of all days for him.'

Al- 'Abd Zinjīr had called to his slaves, 'Woe to you, bring me my steed called thunder (*ra'd*).' The slaves brought him a noble steed, the size of an elephant. It had turned the desert upside down with its bellow. It was one of the horses of the sea. (74) It was of a pale colour. When it became his mount he beat the ground with his heels and sprang upon its back swifter than a fork of lighting or the twinkling of an eye. He took a huge lance and sallied forth into the battlefield. He performed many feats on the back of this mount until he bewildered every eye. Then, having finished his spectacle, he gathered his reins, fixed his spear point and directed it at Antar and his knights.

After boastful verse he screeched in the ear of his horse, and it bolted like a water-jet or a flash of light in a cloud. His voice echoed in the mountains, 'Come on then, oh, race born in adultery, come forth and fight, knight to knight, or attack me in a body. I can face all of you. If your vile knights have no stomach for this fight then summon your protector to fight me. I have sworn by mighty Saturn that I shall leave him as a carcass in the dust.'

Al- 'Abd Zinjīr had hardly finished his boasting when one of the negroes came before him. He was called Salhab ibn Mahbūb and he was deemed to equal one thousand knights. He aimed his spear at al- 'Abd Zinjīr. The latter waited patiently until he drew close, then he removed his foot from his stirrup and kicked his side, breaking four of his ribs. He was thrown more than fourteen cubits on the ground. Then al- 'Abd Zinjīr laughed and smiled full of contempt. Once more he sought combat.

Antar had decided to face him but he was overtaken by a bold knight called Prince Sālim whose sword had secured wealth in these localities. He spurred his horse and attacked al- 'Abd Zinjīr with ferocity. The latter allowed him to approach, then he smote him on the shoulder with his sword, and he slew him. He felled a fourth and a fifth, a sixth and a seventh until he had killed fifty knights. Antar was determined to sally but his sons Ghasūb and Maysara came before him. Maysara went into the battlefield first. He cried out and struck al-'Abd Zinjīr a heavy blow with his sword. Al-'Abd Zinjīr met his blow on the back of his leather shield (75). He faced Maysara, shouted at his face and stretched out his wrist towards his throat, extending his arm like a camel's neck and grabbed him by the neck. He took him captive. When Ghasūb saw his brother in the hand of al-'Abd Zinjīr he assaulted him and stabbed him with the point of his spear. He thought that his thrust had reached its aim but al-'Abd Zinjīr changed Maysara from his right side to his left, and with his hand he parried Ghasūb's spear and hurled it away. Then he waited until he was opposite him, snatched him from his saddle and took him prisoner on his wrist. He withdrew muttering and growling.

The slaves who were in turmoil took Maysara and Ghasūb from his hands. The world was black in Antar's eyes. He said to King al-Dahmār, 'I shall go out and fight this devil and overcome him, and he will be afraid to tire.' King al-Dahmār said, "The choice is yours, oh, knight of 'Adnān.' He suspected that Antar was afraid of al- 'Abd Zinjīr. Antar was patient although his heart was as a flame. When the knights retired to their tents Antar's fire waxed hotter on account of the capture of his sons.

In the morning al- 'Abd Zinjīr went forth early to fight. He appeared to the knights and mocked, Where is the protector of 'Abs and 'Adnān. If he comes not into the field I shall go to him attacking his ranks, and my chest will meet these hundreds and thousands.' When Antar heard his scorn he leapt towards him upon al-Abjar, his steed, armed with his spear and his sharp-edged sword. He exclaimed so that all might hear, 'Woe to you, by God the Judge I only stood aside in this combat on account of my contempt for you and those like you who count as nothing in my eyes. Were it not for the fact that you have slain my men and captured my cubs I would not have come forth against you.'

Then Antar grasped his quivering spear and broke forth in verse:

I am Antar, the 'Absī, son of Zabība.
I am the lion sharp in claw.
You shall know whom you encounter.

He praised the Prophet, the Hāshimite, the Imām of the House of Ghālib.

His verses completed, he attacked al- 'Abd Zinjīr. The two men smote and withdrew, drew close and tried to gain an advantage. They fought until sundown. Then al- 'Abd Zinjīr said to Antar, 'Woe to you, let us agree to disengage. We shall rest until the morning and then recommence our battle.' Antar said, 'No, by Him who causes the winds to blow, we shall not part until one of us tastes death. If you must rest then you may do so. Dismount and I shall do likewise. Our companions will bring us food and drink so that when it is day we shall resume our battle. In war I am just and in endurance I show pity.'

Al- 'Abd Zinjīr answered, 'Forsooth, this is just conduct, by the protection of the Arabs and the month of *Rajab.*' They dismounted and staked their spears. Then they both bowed their knees, biting their hands with anger. When the two parties knew of their circumstance they brought them food and drink. They ate and drank in silent solemnity until it was dawn. They resumed their contest. As they mounted Antar recited his verse while al- 'Abd Zinjīr murmured in discontent. He said, 'Woe to you, hear the response to your geste, oh, black slave, hear eloquent speech.'

When al- 'Abd Zinjīr had recited boastfully, Antar frowned with uncontrolled anger. They attacked each other in a cloud of dust until the day became like the night. Hard and resolutely they fought, charging, withdrawing, approaching, sporting and engaging in deadly earnest, seizing and repelling until it was the end of the second day. They remained on their horses throughout that night, then they battled anew. For seven days they fought. When it was the eve of the eighth Antar said to himself, 'Tomorrow I shall seek to finish the battle.' As for al- 'Abd Zinjīr he was full of hate. He said, 'By my life, tomorrow I shall use all my effort against him.' In the morning a cloud of dust hid them from men's eyes.

Now Antar had a hidden secret which none knew save Him who had endowed him with it. It was a measure and peculiar mark of his endurance. Whenever he fought an opponent so that he grew tired, then left him for less than an hour or so in the daytime, Antar's full energy would return again to him. It was a boon bestowed on him by the Almighty's hand. As both combatants began to stab and to smite there was despair in the camps. The dust hovered over them and covered them like a tent until the sun fell into the horizon. It was at that very moment that Antar recovered and enhanced his strength. He was filled with exhuberance, his fighting increased in skill, and he burst into new life like a flame which has caught the wood laid in place for a fire. He closed in on his foe and leant upon him. He attacked him like a lion claws a lump of rock. He held his unsheathed Indian sword in his hand, and he attacked with no fear of death.

He cried aloud, 'Receive this at the hand of the courageous lion who guards God's holy house, *Zamzam* and the *Maqām.*' Then he rose high in his stirrup and shouted with a voice which struck fear in the heart of his opponent. He smote him with a wild blow upon the crown of his helmet so that his head fell on the ground rolling like a mill-stone. As it rolled away it shrieked in agony and deafened the ears of all who heard. The severed head hit a solid boulder, and it bit the rocky surface in torment and affliction. The grinders in the mouth pulverized the rock to sand. But the body of al- 'Abd Zinjīr was still seated upright upon the back of his horse. It did not fall. Sword in hand, it smote to right and to left. Antar was amazed and was afraid that his blow had missed. Then he looked hard and saw that the corpse had fallen from the back of the steed, like a felled palm tree or a giant rock torn from its bed on a mountain summit.

Antar fainted from fatigue, and the dust had covered him. Both parties had heard the voices of the combatants and waited for Antar and al- 'Abd Zinjīr to appear from the dust. Then the truth was made clear to them, for al- 'Abd Zinjīr lay dead, headless in the desert. All the knights ran to Antar. They surrounded him and congratulated him upon his victory. They returned to their tents with Antar, the raging lion, before them. The Ethiopians were eager to attack him but by that hour the darkness had fallen, and the Negus, out of fear, restrained them. He went to the kings of the negroes and said, 'To fight tonight is neither wise nor just. Tomorrow the tenacious knight will be clear to see since the coward will have fled.' The armies passed the nocturnal hours in their tents. They described Antar, and how he had slain that lion who had ruled as a tyrant.

Al-Asma'ī said (76), 'Antar said to me after he had returned from the journey, "When I fought al- 'Abd Zinjīr I beheld that which filled me with terror and shamed me. When I saw his corpse on the back of his mount before it fell, then and at other moments I was gripped by anxiety and amazement. I felt sure of disaster. I lacked strength. I only had one blow left in my hand because of my great fatigue. Al- 'Abd Zinjīr had no equal in the world. I was blessed by good fortune, by courage and with the aid of that Prophet about whom continuous tales are told and who will appear at the end of the age, Muhammad, the lord of the sons of 'Adnān. Had it not been for all these I would not have mastered him, nor would I have struck him down. It was due to the power of the Lord – glory to Him, the Almighty who if He so wishes aids His servant and who if He desires it torments him and deprives him of all he hopes for." '

Antar retired to his tent surrounded by the kings of the Sudan. He told them what an ordeal he had faced in his combat with al- 'Abd Zinjīr and of the terror he had felt. After that they gave him refreshment. He had enjoyed neither food nor rest because of the capture of his sons and the fire burning in his soul. He said, 'Tomorrow will be the decisive battle, if God so wills. I shall only attack the Negus. When I take him he will be the ransom for my sons and my men.'

When 'Urwa heard his words he remarked, 'Oh, father of knights, do not burden your heart. The Negus will not act rashly with any of your sons, more especially because of your art in war and your fortitude.' As they were speaking Ghamra entered. She said, 'Oh, father of knights, tonight I cannot rest. My heart burns with disquiet for my sons. Eagerly I await the morning. I shall go forth to battle to heal the wounds in my heart, either with blows of the sword or with thrusts of the spear.' Antar said to Ghamra, 'By the Creator of men and the shaper of images, if God so wills, in the morning I shall redeem my sons though they be imprisoned beyond the wall of Alexander the two-horned.'

Such was their tale. As for the Negus he stayed in his tents. He was disturbed beyond measure by the death of al-'Abd Zinjīr. He turned to the lords of his realm who were in attendance and said to them, 'Woe to you, bring in Antar's sons so that I may slay them and make them an example.' They said to him, 'Such is not wise, oh, king. Behind them is their father Antar, the lion who is like the fire of Hell. His sword will spare neither rider nor fighter on foot. Delay your action until we see where fortune leads us in regard to their father. If we are the victors, the death of all will be in your hand. If he captures one of us then he will be a ransom.'

Najd ibn Hishām said : When the king heard the chiefs of his state speak thus he followed their advice. In the morning the knights rode into battle and took their swords and spears. The whole earth was churned by the riding of their horses. Antar shouted and attacked in the middle of the battlefield. The soldiers of the negroes surrounded him from every side. They cried aloud with diverse voices and cries, and the waste-lands echoed. Drums throbbed, and horns resounded, and the wild beasts fled from their forests. The Mashrafī (77) blades flashed, and the Arabian steeds neighed. Lordly hearts yearned until the cup of death was a pleasure. Shrieks grew louder and louder, and the battle continued on foot.

Antar fought well on that dust-filled day. He was scorched by the fire of war and relied on none save himself. He split the ranks as his brother Shaybūb went around him firing his arrows. Antar smote until he reached the bearer of the standard. He severed his jugular vein, and his head fell from his shoulders. He cried with a great shout, and the assembled host scattered. The army was rent asunder. Antar smote with a Yemeni blade (78) until he had separated all the knights of the Negus, and they had fled from the field. Then Antar attacked the Negus. He stretched forth his hand and gripped the neck of his hauberk and grasped his wrist. He snatched him from his saddle and took him to Shaybūb who bound him. The Negus was certain that he would be slain. Then Shaybūb drove him before him as he would drive a camel while Antar kept heroes at bay. He was sure that he could rescue his sons and bring the Negus to destruction. When the negroes saw the capture of their king their resolve was turned to feebleness. They scattered to their hutments in the hills. Antar and his companions followed them until sunset.

He returned robed in blood. The knights came and thanked him and praised him. They went to their tents, they rested, and they feasted. Antar called Shaybūb. 'Woe to you, son of the black woman, bring me the Negus, the king of Ethiopia so that we may seek his ransom. If there is no response I shall behead him tomorrow. I shall go to his land, capture his women and all his sons. I shall slay the rest of his army and rescue my sons.' Shaybūb having heard his brother went to fetch the Negus who was in bonds and in disgrace. Round about him were his slaves and his clients. When he reached him he said, 'Arise king and address my brother Antar.' The king answered, 'What does he want from me?' Shaybūb said, 'He wishes to ransom his sons and to reward you for your deed. Otherwise he will take your head from your shoulders.' The Negus arose that instant and said to Shaybūb, 'Young man, by the right of Arab protection, how are you related to him?' 'I am his brother,' Shaybūb replied. The Negus said, 'Who are his mother and his father. I beseech you by the Mighty King: who brought you to this land? You are men of the Hijaz.' Shaybūb told him the story how Antara married Ghamra, and how she had born him Ghasūb, how they had made themselves known to Hammām who was the maternal uncle of Antar. He told him the whole story. When Shaybūb had disclosed these secrets the Negus said to him, 'Your mother is Shamāma, sister of Sa'dī (Sā'ida?), the mother of Hammām.' He said, 'Yes, oh, king of the age.' The Negus said to him, 'Both Sa'dī (Sā'ida?) are my paternal aunts while you are my paternal cousins. None knows this matter save the Lord of Lords.'

Najd ibn Hishām said : When Shaybūb heard these words he became like one lost in a dream. He leapt to his feet and clasped the Negus to him. He kissed him between his eyes, led him to Antar and told him the news. All who were present were glad. Then Antar summoned King Hammām and repeated what he had heard from his brother. Hammām said, 'What he said is true, by God's holy house.' They all embraced until their souls nearly left their bodies so great was their joy at meeting. The land was in a tumult on every side. When that report was confirmed they released Maysara and Ghasūb.

The Triumphant return of Antar and his heroes and the death of Ghamra.

The Negus said to Antar, 'By Him who fashions all in existence and the Creator of men and *jinn* you must travel with me to the homes of my people so that I may enjoy your company for a span of time.' Antar agreed to his request. When the morning shed its light Antar rode forth and behind him rode the knights of the other lands. The Negus was at his side, and they were deep in discussion. The whole company was happy until the destination was reached, and the army encamped. The Negus was pleased to entertain Antar, his warriors and his troops.

Thus they continued, esteemed and hospitably entertained in dining and in the drinking of wine for twenty days. On the twenty-first day Antar decided to depart, and the Negus gave his approval. He had bestowed a gift of great value upon him, and he travelled in his company for two days in order to say good-bye to him. Then Antar stopped. He joined all the kings together, he bound them by a covenant that they would act as one hand and with their hearts united. They agreed to this.

They wanted to leave, when lo, a horseman came to the Negus. He said to him, 'Rejoice, oh, king, may God make you glad with the birth of a boy.' The Negus said, 'Who is this youth?' 'He is the son of your daughter Manār (79) and of al- 'Abd Zinjīr.' The Negus was joyful, and he named him Habbār, who was the slave who was fought by 'Alī, the Imām; may God be pleased with him and his companions. This slave did not grow to be a man in the lifetime of Antar. He was only born at that time, after the slaying of his father, al-'Abd Zinjīr, so that the hearer should have no doubt about the record. Because of the good news they stayed in that place for three days. Then they parted, Each sought his homeland.

King Safwān ibn Ma'dān came to Antar ibn Shaddād and said to him, 'Oh, protector of 'Abs and 'Adnān, I would like to ride in your company and be among those who are your companions.' Antar smiled when he heard him say this. He said to him, 'Leave this for some other day.' When Shaybūb heard his brother's remark he said, 'No, by Almighty God, Safwān ibn Ma'dān must journey with us to our camps and our homelands so that all the Banū 'Abs and 'Adnān, Fazāra and Ghatafān, Murra and Dhubyān may know that we are relatives of the greatest kings in the Sudan.' Antar saw the sense in the remark of his brother Shaybūb.

They marched through those deserts and valleys longing to meet their families and friends. At their head was Antar ibn Shaddād, a lion of great age. He recalled all the terrors he had met and the battles he had fought. When the kings of the Sudan heard his eloquent verses, and the thoughts they expressed, they exclaimed, 'What a noble knight, a strong hero who wields an Indian sword. May your mouth be undefiled and may your assailants perish, oh, knight of 'Abs and 'Adnān, courageous one of the age.' So they pressed on in their march until they reached the land of King al-Dahmār. They stayed with him for three days feasting and drinking wine. Then King al-Dahmār presented Antar with fifty swords, fifty horses with gilt saddles, fifty male slaves and fifty female slaves, one hundred spears and a thousand camels, brocade garments and one hundred mounted men for herding their animals and for the journey. They drove those camels, and on they marched until they came to the lands of King Hammām, lord of the Land of Flags and Ensigns. They were warmly greeted, and they were met by slave-women and free women bearing tambourines and pipes, and they feasted them, and they passed seven days of pleasure and joy.

Then Antar ordered his men to set forth, and the drums were beaten to announce their departure. They loaded the camels, both male and female, and they marched towards the lands of Ghawwār ibn Dīnār. Antar stayed with him for three days. On the fourth day he wanted to depart. Ghawwār gave him an abundance of riches, camels, herds and expensive robes. He bade farewell to them all and returned to his lands. The party continued until they came to the lands of Lawn al-Zalām. He was glad and delighted at their safe return with their booty. They stayed with him for three days feasting and drinking wine. After that Antar wished to leave, and Lawn al-Zalām agreed to his request. He offered him a number of male and female camels, money, expensive steeds, spears and swords. On that day he arose to say goodbye to him, then he too returned to his lands.

They marched on and on through the lands of the (Banū) Sharīf and the Banū Qudā'a (80). Here and there they stopped and pitched their tents. They pleased themselves with song and merriment until several days had passed.

Saymūn ibn Rahmūn (81) gave them hospitality, and on the eleventh day they were determined to resume their march.

Ghamra had fallen ill, and Antar was greatly grieved by her sickness. She refused to drink water and to eat, and on the sixteenth day she died. There was great weeping. The women and young girls beat their bodies and rent their clothes. Antar, the prince, was smitten with sorrow, and Ghasūb felt that his heart was broken asunder. Then they buried her, and the young and old cried and lamented over her. Upon her tomb Antar slaughtered five hundred she-camels, and he distributed their meat to the widows and the orphans. He remained on his carpet of grief and mourning for ten days. Ghasūb could not be comforted for the death of Ghamra, his mother. After ten days they were met by Saymūn ibn Rahmūn. He brought them forth from the house of sorrow. He said to Antar, 'Oh, father of knights, all this was decreed by the command of the King who is Judge of all men, Lord of might, who lives for ever. Glory be to Him who has the measure of all happenings however grievous.' Safwān ibn Ma'dān spoke to Antar in the same manner, so did 'Urwa ibn al-Ward and those who were with him. At length they consoled Antar and Ghasūb with wine and with soft words, and they made them forget the events of the nights and days through which they had passed. They passed an entire month in that place; then they longed to return to their lands and camping grounds and their friends who were there.

The drums were beaten for their departure. They loaded the backs of the camels after they had collected the possessions of Ghamra and had entrusted the lands and camps to King Saymūn ibn Rahmūn. They appointed him to rule over all the negroes who were there. They wrote a letter for him naming him king and ruler over those countries beneath the hand of Antar and Ghasūb, and they obliged him to send tribute to them every year. They resumed their march, and Antar rode beside Safwān ibn Ma'dān who was at the head of the men of the Sudan. Then it was that Antar recalled his cousin 'Abla and his camps, and he recited these verses :

> Who will tell 'Abla that I staked foes with a spear's point.
> Daughter of Mālik, will you show favour and revive my spirit,
> So that my woeful sighing will be ended?
> An oath, sworn by your passion, 'Abla, will quicken
> spirits from their sleep.
> Oh, 'Abla, I met the lordly lions of the breed of Hām.
> I sundered squadrons, and I scattered them in the wilderness.
> I entered the Sudan where their king, Lawn al-Zalām,
> Spits breasts with well aimed sharpened lance.
> To King Ghawwār I came and for his bands a draught of death

I poured, by the enchantments of my unsheathed sword.
Oh, ‘Abla, their men I found to be my brethren.
And their daughters to be my secret sisters,
And that lion, Hammām, I found his family to be
Maternal cousins, his women-folk are my aunts.
I met a haughty slave unlike another named Zinjīr.
I felled him, and I quartered him amidst the sands.
I met the king, and Negus, and I took him captive,
by good fortune and determined resolution.
All these kings appeared to have our lineage.
Thus sorrow was replaced by joy and happiness.
Oh, ‘Abla, here I come amid their mighty host
As black in colour as the dead of night (82),
Mounted on mares, and filling wide expanse
Of barren scarp and sandy dune and glades,
Black skinned they are, oh, daughter of Mālik.
Yet their hearts are white, just like the sun at dawn (83).
Oh, ‘Abla, where the east wind blows, I blew
In places which were void I pictured you.
Oh, ‘Abla, will our souls and bodies ever meet?
While parted love was torment until death seemed sweet.

Notes

The translations are principally based on the *Ḥijāzīya* (uncut) edition of the text in the British Library. Būlāq (1866-1870), B.M. Catalogue 14570 d 3. At certain places, however, particularly at the beginning, other editions are less diffuse and digressive and better integrated. I have in particular used Vols. 5 and 6 of the edition of the *Sīra* published by the Muṣṭafā Muḥammad Press (al-Maktaba al-tijārīya al-kubrā), Cairo. A printed version of the *Ḥijāzīya* by Sa'īd 'Alī al-Khuṣūṣī, Vol. 5, pp. 282 ff., has also been consulted.

1. Regarding Durayd ibn al-Ṣimma, see Lyall, *Ancient Arabian Poetry*, pp. XXII, XXIV, 38-47, 116. This centenarian lived on the borders between the Hijaz and the Yemen and died in 630 A.D. Durayd's 'black mother', Rayḥāna, was a Yemenite of half-African blood, and she was an elder sister of the Yemenite hero 'Amr ibn Ma'dī Karib al-Zubaydī.
2. Despite common attribution to al-Aṣma'ī there are very wide divergencies between the variant versions of the *Sīra* at this point. They do not cohere at all until the encounter with King Lawn al-Ẓalām. In the *Ḥijāzīya*, Ghamra's lands were ruled by King Suwayd ibn 'Uwayd, a deputy of King Ghawwār ibn Dīnār. He had a number of allies, all of whom fought Antar. Among them was Maymūn / Saymūn ibn Raḥmūn who became Antar's ally, and Ṣā'iqa ibn 'Alqam or Aṣamm who is confused with Ṣā'iqa ibn 'Andam.
3. According to the *Ḥijāzīya* (Būlāq and al-Khuṣūṣī) Ṣā'iqa was large in head, terrible in body, tall, broad-chested, broad shouldered and with massive extremities. He was far-sighted and full of energy. Only a war horse could carry him. When he rode a high steed his feet touched the ground, and he ploughed it with his toes. He was wild in nature, excitable and loud voiced. His hideous face had flaring nostrils. When he put his hand on a camel's hump and ordered his slaves to goad it with spears the camel could not rise beneath his hand. When he pulled its tail he tore it from its loins.
4. See note 82 and the relevant passage in the text where this image is further expanded.
5. According to the *Ḥijāzīya* (Būlāq and al-Khuṣūṣī) Antar addressed Ghamra, 'You are mistress of this land. How many were the soldiers of King Suwayd ibn 'Uwayd when he came to your land and ruled it?' 'He rode among fifteen thousand negro horsemen. When he had assembled his troops he rode among thirty thousand.' 'Woe to you that you should flee from thirty thousand with your people and leave your country to this devil.'

   'Oh, father of knights, when my father died, and he persuaded my son Ghasūb to journey to God's holy house I was so sick that I was unable to sit or stand. There was an enmity between him and my father, and he began to increase his raids and gather horsemen of the Sudan. Hitherto I used to raid his country and kill his men. He hated me. When he heard of the death of my father and my sickness he rode against me having sought the help of one of the giant kings of the Ethiopians called Ghawwār ibn Dīnār.'
6. In the sixth century A.D., the Ḥimyarite kings of Kinda were driven from al-Yamāma and Hajar back to Ḥaḍramawt in South Arabia. On the fortunes of these Ḥimyarites see Lyall, *op. cit.*, pp. 104-106. It is clear from the passage that the *rāwīs* or story-tellers conceived of the exploits of Antar at this point somewhere in South Arabia, then dominated by Ethiopian overlords.

7. *Ḥadīd*, literally 'Iron', usually indicates some form of mail hauberk. There is nothing to suggest plate armour or some form of brigandine.
8. The two principal branches of the Arabs which trace their lineage through 'Adnān to Ismā'īl (Ishmael).
9. For the relationship between the Banū 'Abs and Tamīm, see R. Nicholson, *A Literary History of the Arabs*, Cambridge, 1969, p. XIX.
10. According to Lyall the spears of the ancient Arabs were made of bamboos imported by sea from India. Al-Khaṭṭ a port in al-Baḥrayn, was the chief place of manufacture, whence spears are called Khaṭṭī. The shafts were straightened by means of heat, whence they gained their tawny colour (*sumr*) with the help of a clip (*thiqāf*). Samhar, a man, and Rudaina, a woman, of al-Khaṭṭ, had a reputation of being the best straighteners of spear-shafts, which are frequently called *Samharī* and *Rudainī*.
11. Indian swords (*Hindī* and *Hindawānī*) were types of early straight-bladed swords. Iron came from India and Ceylon and was forged in Persia, Kufa, the Yemen and elsewhere.
12. Red eye-balls is a conventional description applied to negroes in Arabic literature, whether the negro be a slave or a king.
13. The *Sīrat 'Antara* has a number of characters whose names end in the letter *m*. Lawn al-Ẓalām, Badr al-Tamām, 'U'jūbat al-Anām, Hammām, Ṣā'iqa ibn 'Andam, Ghanām, and Ṭimṭim are among the most noted examples. It cannot be a coincidence that *m* is the rhyming letter of the famous 'Golden Ode' (*Mu'āllaqa mīmīya*) attributed to 'Antara ibn Shaddād.

Ṭimṭim, for example, appears in the ode in the sense of a type of cloud only found in the skies of the Yemen. Sometimes a cloud appears in the sky, and the sound of thunder is heard in it as though it fills or is echoed in the whole of the Yemenite sky. Other clouds gather around this peculiar cloud. The colour of 'Andam (tarragon) appears in the same ode. Elsewhere in odes attributed to 'Antara such names as the following appear: 'the two sons of Shamām', a name given to two noted mountains; *jinḥ al-ẓalām*, middle of the night; *sirḥān al-ẓalām*, lion of the darkness; *humām*, courageous, applied to a lion, *hizbar; budūr tamām/timām*, full moons:

'Abla's dislike of Antar's blackness is countered by his boast, 'I am a knight of the offspring of Ḥām.' As will be seen later in the romance both Antar and Shaybūb are hailed as twins of Shamāma (Zabība), and here one suspects an allusion to the verse in the above ode, each hero symbolic of a mountain. Close examination of the verses attributed to 'Antara reveal how the 'rhyme' of the *saj'* of the *Sīra* is often wedded to his alleged poetry and how the names of foes and allies are personified attributes derived from authentic or unauthentic verses from 'Antara's *dīwān* certainly earlier than the *Sīra*.

Some names, however, cannot be explained by references to the *dīwān* of 'Antara's verse. Ghawwār, for example, appears nowhere in the *rā'īyāt* of 'Antara. The closest root is in the word *ghāra*, indicating a raid or an attack. In one verse 'Antara reputedly states, 'I resolved to make a raid (*ghāra*) in a night as black as pitch.' Here there is an association between *ghāra* and blackness, and it is not impossible that Ghawwār was in some way selected on account of this association. The basis of the *Sīrat 'Antara* in poems in the *dīwān* of Antar is not unlike the way Western *Chansons de geste* evolved from elaborated poetry. Ḍirār Ṣāliḥ Ḍirār in his book *Hal kāna 'Antarah sūdānīyan*, Khartoum, 1976, discusses the shortcomings of 'Antara the poet and argues that his Sudanese African background from his mother, Zabība, may partly explain this. On Page 36 he writes: 'Yes, 'Antara embarked on a limited number of poetic metres. He did not touch many metres because his taste could not stomach them and his musical ear could not tolerate them. The metre which he loved best was *al-Kāmil* – the closest of the metres to *al-Rajaz*. It was in this metre that he recited his *Mu'allaqa*, to be followed by his various poems rhyming in the letter *lām* and a number of poems which rhymed in the letters *dāl* and *tā'*. It was a metre for which he felt a close affinity. It concorded with his feelings and musical taste. Similarly, he composed some of the odes in *al-Wāfir*. This is a metre as we know it and hear it which has the throb of drum beats and is most closely attuned to Sudanese taste.'

14. Here Lawn al-Ẓalām is portrayed in the role of the Abyssinian occupiers of the Yemen who launched attacks on Mecca about 570 A.D.
15. See note 24.
16. This form of abusive challenge occurs repeatedly in the *Sīra*. It is akin to the defiance, the encounter with the spear and sword, and summons to surrender to be found in *Chansons de geste*. On the other hand certain tactics of capture are peculiar to the *Sīra* and *Maghāzī* literature.
17. Or heel? Spanish Mozarabic manuscripts indicate that many lances had a long pointed toe and heel which may well have been used for the tactic described.
18. See pp. 133-7. This type of signal of a forthcoming switch in the plot of the tale is skilfully employed by the *rāwī*. It is a form of bridge which will conduct the adventure of Antar from the Yemen into Africa, either into Kānem or Abyssinia. A globe-trotter's sea crossing have robbed the story of its remoteness and fantasy for the sake of 'realism.' Hence Ḥiṣn al-'Uqāb is conceived as being located neither in the Yemen, nor in Africa, but in a vague region which had some character common to both.
19. See page 128ff.
20. Who in several places is confused with Ra's al-Ghūl, the king of the Yemen. See pages 32, 87. According to the *Ḥijāzīya* King Wajh al-Ghūl ibn Abū'l-Qurūn was also named Kardam ibn Ṭimṭim. He was nicknamed 'father of centuries' because of his longevity. He was the guardian of Ghawwār ibn Dīnār who had robbed Ghamra bint Fā'iz of her lands.
21. There are superficial similarities between Wajh al-Ghūl and Ra's al-Ghūl, though they are hardly close enough to suggest an archetype.
22. See page 98.
23. This is an inversion of passages in the Qur'ān which extol the sun and the daytime and which give the moon and the night-time a subordinate role. The names refer to two of the most famous goddesses of pre-Islamic Arabia.
24. *Kazāghand* and *jazerant*. See my 'The Hauberk, the Kazāghand and the 'Antar Romance *The Journal* of *The Arms & Armour Society*. Vol IX, No 3, June, 1978, pp 93-101.
25. The tree of dumb barter is regarded as a magic tree. The story does not indicate whether the expedition is still in the Yemen, in Africa or in both. Silent barter is widely known from India to Abyssinia and West Africa but the resemblance to the description of al-Mas'ūdī about the practice of Ghana is striking, although there is no mention of gold here, merely cloth.
26. An image borrowed from, or shared with, the Caliph Hārūn al-Rashīd in the One Thousand and One Nights, see Mia Gerhardt, *The Art of Story telling*, pp. 420-422, 449-450, 463.
27. An association of clouds, two trees, and the ascent of Antar is heralded by earlier allusions to heavenly flight in the *Sīra*. The ambition of Antar soars above the two Pisces, and above Arcturus and Spica in the feet of the Great Lion. He constantly alludes to this ambition, 'My star shines far raised on high, above Arcturus, above the sun, above the clouds.'
28. A face-decoration found among the Nuba of Southern Kordofan which covers the left eye with dark patches.
29. *Kātim al-sirr* and *kātib al-sirr*. The name or title of *kātib al-sirr* appeared at the end of the Abbasid Caliphate. It indicated that the holder knew all the secrets of the state.

    'The secret writer' was important in Fatimid Egypt and the office continued into the Ayyubid period. At the beginning of the rule of the Egyptian Mamluks this name disappeared and was replaced by *kātib al-dast* or *kātib al-daraj*. These new names continued into the reign of the Mamluk Sultan al-Manṣūr Qalawūn. Then it was changed to its former name *kātib al-sirr*, and this continued right down to the end of the Mamluk period.

    Kātim al-sirr, 'the secret keeper' or private secretary was a name or title which came into use with the substitution of 'b' by an 'm'. In fact, it is almost certainly derived from *katama*, 'to hide', and not *kataba* 'to write'. It probably began to be used generally during the reign of the Sultan Qalawūn (1279-1290 A.D.), although it is not impossible that the name was also known under the Fatimids.

30. The appearance of this name in this context is bizarre. It is possible that a romancer had seen *Kānem* and read it, or changed it, to *Kātim.*

31. The religion is simply called *'Ibādat al-nār,* 'the worship of fire', in this part of the text, and not *al-Majūsīya* which is normally employed in Arabic books which relate to 'traditional African religions'.

32. See page 200 where the 'two trees' are said to be a boundary.

33. Regarding this locality which appears in the *dīwān* of 'Antara ibn Shaddād, see pages 53 & 54.

34. *Majūs* appears in this passage.

35. On fiery apparitions in holy trees, see Robertson Smith, *The Religion of the Semites,* London, 1894, pp. 190-197, particularly page 195.

36. See page 76 where this passage and other passages which may refer to Kānem are fully discussed. Here the story has something of the character of the tale to find a bride, a theme in old Iranian epics. See Herzfeld, *op. cit.,* pp. 63-66.

37. A passage such as this, and there are many, indicates why the text of the *Sīrat 'Antara* cannot seriously be attributed to al-Aṣma'ī, the grammarian.

38. Qur'ān *Sūra* C.I. 1, 2. 'The chapter of the Smiting'.

39. This strophic poem is found in the *Ḥijāzīya* (Būlāq and al-Khuṣūṣī) at this point. It consists of a stream of gory epithets, probably sung to the accompaniment of a stringed instrument. The translation is very free.

40. According to the *Ḥijāzīya* (Būlāq and al-Khuṣūṣī) his name was Fājir ibn al-Maḍājir, 'foul-mouther, the son of the tedious'.

41. The semi-sacred, and secret, meals of the Kānemi kings reported in Arab geographers might have influenced this passage. Shaybūb's adventures in the enemy camp repeat a common idea in Oriental romance where the hero or one of his relatives enters the enemy camp disguised as a spy. The prototype may be found in the Alexander Romance where the device is much used, for example, Alexander in the camp of Darius or Candace.

42. This story within a story appears in the *Ḥijāzīya* (Būlāq and al-Khuṣūṣī) but it is absent from some other versions. A correlation with the *Sīra* of Sayf ibn Dhī Yazan is possible. Al-Minhāl is the name of the negro warrior in this romance, and al-Mukhtaṭif (al-Khāṭif?) is the brother of the *jinn* Barq Lāmi'.

    This whole inserted fragment has an Egyptian or Maghribi flavour. It is not wholly unlike the legends of Zaynab, the sorceress wife of the Almoravid Yūsuf ibn Tāshfīn. See my *Saharan Myth and Saga,* Oxford, 1972, pp. 108-9. Tales of changelings are widespread in Morocco and Malta. Folklore about this phenomena in Morocco may be found in Françoise Legey, *The Folklore of Morocco,* London, 1935, p. 155.

    References occur to giraffe mounted warriors in the romance of *'Ajīb and Gharīb.* They are in the army of Tarkan(an), the king of India. Since giraffes are African, the *Sīrat 'Antara* is closer to reality than *'Ajīb and Gharīb,* for Muslim kings in Africa sent giraffes as gifts.

    John Lavers in his paper submitted to the Conference on Fufulde and Fulbe Culture held in Kano in June 1977 has published extracts from 'a late eighteenth century description of the Phellata Arabs of Adar' by Ulrich Jaspar Seetzen wherein he cites a native of that region, al-Hajj Muhammad, on the eve of the Sokoto *jihād.* On page 6 of his paper John Lavers recounts a reference to the hunting of giraffes between the negro countries and Bornu. The negro hunters painted themselves white with the flour of a certain root and they pursued the animals with their lances. The meat of the animal was excellent to eat and giraffe skins were used to provide soles for their shoes.

43. *Ḥiṣn al-Ghamām.* See page 83.

44. Symbolism of this section with the tree, the mound, the sword and the marble basin (in the earlier section) recalls the moments prior to the death of Roland. (See *The Song of Roland,* Penguin Classics, pp. 138-142). Roland takes his sword Durendal towards Spain 'to a wide lawn'. He climbs a mound 'where grows a fair tree tall'.

Marble stones stand beneath it. All around are high trees. Stricken Roland is watched by a Saracen who feigns death and tries to seize Roland's sword. Roland kills him with Olifant, his elephant-tusk horn, which he breaks. He tries to shatter Durendal on a grey marble slab, but the relics in its hilt prevent the sword's destruction. Roland dies beneath a pine, his corpse covering Olifant and Durendal. His death signals a number of miracles; the flight of the Paynims, the inundation of the river Ebro plain and the drowning of the Paynims. Later, Roland is found dead between two trees, (compare with the two trees of Kānem). Roland is buried together with Bishop Turpin and Oliver. Their hearts are 'wrapped in silken tissue fine and placed within an urn of marble white'. The barons' bodies are wrapped in shrouds made of roebuck's hide.

The association of a guardian eagle and a sword is found in the story of Montezuma's encounter with a bird on the edge of a lake near Mexico city. It had a blade on its head, and it flashed like a mirror. Within the blade were depicted night and its stars, and armed men who were coming from the East. It is thought that this legend is based on the story of Roderick's tower in Toledo which was a popular romance in Spain, later exported to Mexico. The addition of a fiery bird is a Spanish interpolation in an earlier Moorish / Spanish legend.

Another parallel may be found in details given in the text of 'The Romance of the Sowdone of Babylone'. They are discussed on pages

Such Occidental parallels might be balanced by textual similarities with early Islamic descriptions of the palace of Ghumdān in the Yemen. These are detailed by Hamdānī in his eighth book of the *Iklīl*. Its height was allegedly a thousand cubits, and its summit was encircled by 'a turban of clouds'. Its' mantle is of marble made', and its roof was guarded by copper eagles. 'Flocks of birds on its roof alight', 'spouting waters around it flow', 'a slab of marble an entrance provides'. To the side of the palace was a giant palm tree. There is a similar association of motifs and ideas, including the protection of Ṣan'ā' by birds. See A. Faris, *The Antiquities of South Arabia*, Princeton, 1938, pp. 15-22.

A good deal of this symbolism also appears in the Romance of *'Ajīb and Gharīb*, see *Bibliographie des Ouvrages Arabes*, by Victor Chauvin, Vol. I, Liege, 1892, pp. 19-31. The town of Japhet has an arsenal. His marvellous sword is guarded by its dwellers who adore fire.

No custom specifically known in Africa immediately suggests itself, although Heller has drawn attention to tree cults in Togoland and elsewhere. The authentic African elements should rather be seen in the conjunction of fire, sacred tree, iron and weapon making, and sacrifice. The association of these in this passage has aroused recognition in almost all Africans whom I have consulted. Some have seen parallels in Galla cults, others in the cult of Ogun in Yorubaland or in the burial sites of the So 'giants' of Chad. The 'talismanic' protection of a stone, at N'Pal in Senegal, bears some resemblance to the tree in King Hammām's realm. See René Caillié, *Travels through Central Africa to Timbuctoo*, Frank Cass, 1968, Vol. i, pp. 25-6.

45. The reference favours a Mamluk hand for the text at this point. The *jawānik* were the salaries of the royal Mamluks, and the expression *jāmakīyāt wa rawātib* also occurs. According to al-Maqrīzī, in his history of the Fatimid Caliphate, al-Ḥākim, son of the Caliph al- 'Azīz Billāh, renewed the *dīwān* (accounts department) called *al-dīwān al-mufrad*. It was specifically for those who collected wealth and money from those who were slain or from other persons. The *dīwān al-mufrad* also existed in the Mamluk era. It is mentioned by al-Qalqashandī in his *Ṣubḥ al-A'shā*. It was set up by the Sultan al-Ẓāhir Barqūq. It was administered by officials, and from its maintenance, clothes, fodder and bonus pay were assigned to his Mamluks. Such maintenance was termed *jāmakīyāt*. The *dīwān al-mufrad* of the Fatimids was not only for the Caliph. On the other hand the Mamluk *dīwān* was peculiar to the Sultan at this later period. The system employed by King Hammām is not dissimilar to that of al-Ẓāhir Barqūq. It may not be a coincidence that major exchanges in correspondence took place between al-Ẓāhir Barqūq and the ruler of Bornu / Kānem. See Cuoq, pp. 376-380.

46. The contents of his passage are discussed on page 233.
47. This name is the reverse of that on page 149.
48. See page 192 note 7.
49. Some texts have *ḥājib*, chamberlain, others *wazīr.* The figures who depart also vary, so too the way the story develops but not the overall unravelling of the plot.
50. Or *muqaddam* in the *Ḥijāzīya.*
51. An expression commonly found in the Pseudo-Maghāzī literature and often used in feats ascribed to 'Amr ibn Ma'dī Karib.
52. Shāma is a variant in the *Ḥijāzīya.* Shāma is the name of the wife of Sayf ibn Dhī Yazan in that romance.
53. Zabība is the name of an Arabian 'queen' in the time of Tiglath Pileser III (743-732 B.C.). *Zabbā'* is the Arabic name of Zenobia.
54. This name has already occurred on pages 149 & 159.
55. In the *Ḥijāzīya* the signs were black eyes and a left cheek mole.
56. Riyāsh, variant Rayyāsh and Riyāshī, see page 23.
57. Compare this different account with that of Shaybūb on page 99.
58. In the *Ḥijāzīya* the two lads were playing by a pool. Hammām would have drowned had not Shaybūb saved him.
59. Al-Damhār is a common variant found in the *Ḥijāzīya.* The name, al-Dahmār, is not absolutely fixed by the *rāwīs* in the extant variant editions.
60. See page 159.
61. In reading this account of the discovery of lost relatives, abandoned when young or fostered by others, one is reminded of the events which commence the romance of *Dhāt al-Himma,* some of which are summarized by Lane in his *Manners and Customs.* In *Dhāt al-Himma* the tale begins with the love of al-Ḥāris, chief of the Banū Kilāb for the beautiful girl al-Rabāb. An old sage predicts the birth of a son of great renown. He writes an amulet which is to be tied on the infant's right arm. In this amulet he records the family and pedigree of the child. Al-Rabāb loses her husband, and she is later assaulted by a black slave. He kills her after her son, Junduba, is born prematurely. Junduba is rescued and brought up in the household of the Amīr Dārim. After many escapades he finally displeases his foster-father who orders the banishment of Junduba. But first he opens the amulet on the youth's right arm and to his amazement he sees the name of al-Ḥāris al-Kilābī who was his most hated foe.

    A series of single combats then take place culminating in a fight between Junduba and the Amīr Dārim. The latter is slain. Junduba departs. He fights a virgin damsel called *Qattālat al- Shuj'ān* whom he marries. He kills the slave who murdered his mother. This whole section of the romance ends with the acknowledgement of the Amīr Junduba as chief of the Banū Kilāb.

    The plot has many similarities with those of the other fostered heroes of Arabia; see page 29. *Dhāt al-Himma* could have been analysed in detail among their number. The flexibility of the ploy of basic elements such as fosterhood, talismans and heroic engagements is shown in the frequently contradictory situations where these are presented. Despite these contradictions certain common patterns and prototypes are easily identifiable.
62. Regarding African amulets, possibly of this type, see E. A. Wallis Budge, *A History of Ethiopia,* 1928, Vol. II, pp. 581-600; and for the Kanuri and Kindin, H. R. Palmer, *Sudanese Memoirs,* Lagos, 1928, Vol. i, pp. 7-10; and W. Thesiger, 'The Awash River and the Sultanate of Aussa', *The Geographical Journal,* LXXXV, 1935, p. 5.

    It should, however, be noted that the word used here which seems to indicate shoulder charm or charms (*ḥimāla/ḥamīla,* pl. *ḥamā'il*) is also entered in Arabic lexicons as 'sword-belt'.

    There seems no obvious way of selecting the specific sense in this passage except by the context. The Arab sword-belt was worn over the shoulder not around the waist, so some motif on the sword-belt itself may be the intention. See Ada Bruhn De Hoffmeyer, *op.cit.,* pp. 124, 125 and figures 79 and 80; and the reference in the poem of Yazīd ibn al-Asfa' on page 52.

Some Yemenite swords had animal figures and names engraved near the handle and these were filled with varnish or were gilded. According to C. Blair a practise not wholly dissimilar can be parallelled from Western sources. A hauberk in the Tower of London Armouries has a ring with what appears to be a talismanic marking under the right arm. A late fourteenth century suit of armour at Cherbourg bears the inscription 'Jesus transiens per medium illorum ibat', also presumably talismanic. See *The Antiquaries Journal,* Vol. 40, 1960.

63. Versions of the *Ḥijāzīya* have Hadhūr or Hudhūr; other versions have Khudūr while the name of the mother of al-Dahmār is said to be Budūr.

64. Versions of the *Ḥijāzīya* suggests that King Sayyār fixed the amulets on his children.

65. According to the *Fihrist,* Nubians, Beja and Zaghāwa used the same script as the Indians.

66. This discussion of the Negus is echoed by a phrase in the book of al-Suyūṭi (d. 1505 A.D.) called *Raf' Sha'n al-Ḥubshān.* '(The Negus) is the name of all who ruled Ethiopia just as every Caliph of the Muslims is called "Commander of the Faithful". He who rules the Byzantines is called Qayṣar and the Turks Khāqān, the Persians Kisrā and the Copts, Pharaoh, Cairo (Egypt) al- 'Azīz, and the Yemen Tubba', Ḥimyar 'al-Qayl', the Indians Ya'sūb, the Sabeans, Nimrod and the Berbers Goliath.'

Ibn Khaldūn has a number of observations to make on the title of *Najāshī,* pronounced Ankāsh in his *Kitāb al- 'Ibar.* See Cuoq, *op.cit.,* pp. 340-341. According to al-Idrīsī the kings of Nubia bore the title of Kāsil or Kāmil, while the name occurs as Kābil in al-Maqrīzī.

The personalities in the *Sīrat 'Antara* who stem from an African nobility are the following:

Unknown king		m. Ethiopian	Mankalān Jarīr Shaybūb
King Ma'dān		*Shamāma/Zabība* m. Shaddād	Antar
	sister		
King Ghulwān		*Sa'dī/Sā'ida* m. Bassām	Hammām
	sister		
Unknown king		*Dahmā'* m. Dīnār	Ghawwār
	sister		
Negus Unknown king		*Budūr* m. Sayyār	Dahmār/Damhār (maternal uncle of Ghamra)

67. On the whole Takrūr remained a localised name, applied to a town on the Senegal river until the time of Ibn Khallikān (d. 1274 A.D.) who refers to the people of Kānem as paternal cousins of Takrūr. 'None of these two tribes has a father or a mother in its genealogy.' They claim descent from Kūsh ibn Ḥām ibn Nūḥ. There are references to Takrūr in al-Mas'ūdī's works (circa 950 A.D.) where Takrūr, Takrūr al-'Abd and Kānem are all mentioned; see Cuoq, *op. cit.,* p. 62, but this is al-Mas'ūdī *sic* al-Dimashqī (d. 1327 A.D.).

The comprehensive reference to Takrūr here would on balance favour a later date for the re-shaping of the *Sīra* (twelfth or thirteenth century A.D.) if particular attention is paid to the use of this geographical term.

68. According to Nashwān ibn Sa'īd al-Ḥimyarī the 'Amāliqa were kings of Ḥimyar who settled in Syria. As for the 'Amālīq they were the sons of 'Imlāq who begat the Pharaohs. According to the *Sīrat Antara,* al- 'Abd Zinjīr stemmed from the former and not from the latter, although it is not certain how clearly the distinction would be known by the story-teller.

69. See page 89.

70. Variant al- 'Abd Ṡayyār in the *Ḥijāzīya* which later relates that Sayyār was mother of Habbār.

71. There are pro- 'Alid elements and sentiments in this part of the text which may come from a missing fragment of Pseudo-Maghāzī literature.

72. See page 88.

73. Perhaps a horse of 'the island of Camphor' if Kāfūr is the name of a Mediterranean or Asian 'island' which occurs in several Arabian romances. Kāfūr (variant North African *Čāfūr*) could explain the name of the horse Saut-Perdu in the *Chanson de Roland;* see page 236. On the other hand it is possible that Saut-Perdu could be a distortion of the name of the gold-(*dhahab; tibr; ṣufr*) centre of medieval Ghana at Qarāfūn, also spelt Zāfūn, Rāfūn and occasionally Zāfūqu and Zāfūru (Kāfūr?). It could be an allusion to Kāfūr, the Ikhshīdī Abyssinian eunuch who ruled Egypt between 966-968 A.D. It would be an apt charger for al- 'Abd Zinjīr. References to steeds occur in al-Mutanabbī's panegyrics and satires addressed to Kāfūr. See A. J. Arberry *Poems of al-Mutanabbī,* Cambridge, 1967, pp. 90-120; verse 16 on page 112 might possibly have inspired the role of al-'Abd Zinjīr.

The description of al- 'Abd Zinjīr's armour, his mirror and his horse, recall The Squire's Tale; cf. Chaucer, Penguin Classics, p. 409:

Let me retrace my footsteps to their source.
It happened, close upon the second course,
As the king sat with his nobility
Listening to instruments of minstrelsy
That made delicious music in the hall,
Suddenly at the door in sight of all
There came a knight upon a steed of brass
Bearing a mirror, broad and made of glass.
Upon his thumb he had a golden ring
And at his side a naked sword a-swing,
And up he rode and reached the royal table.

The knight was a subject of the 'King of India and Araby'. His mirror foretold adversity. His steed of brass 'stood its ground as if it had been glued'.

74. Literally a 'Baḥrī' (Mamluk?) horse. These slaves were settled on the isle of al-Rawḍa in the Nile. The Baḥrī Mamluks, who ruled between 1250 and 1390 A.D., were originally settled there by the Ayyubids. André Miquel suggests that *baḥrī* simply denotes a horse 'vif comme la mer'; see *Un Conte des Mille et Une Nuits,* p. 97, note 80.

75. Such a shield is depicted in Mozarabic paintings of Goliath. The latter may well have inspired much of this description of al- 'Abd Zinjīr and his slaughter.

76. The nature of this passage again shows how spurious is the appearance of al-Aṣmaʿī, the historical grammarian, in this text.

77. Mu'ta in Jordan was famous for sword manufacture since pre-Islamic times. The blades were called *al-suyūf al-mashrafīya.*

78. See page 37 , note 25. It seems apt that Antar should use a Yemenite sword to scatter the knights of the Negus. The Yemenite blade was the most prized, and the triumph of a Yemenite weapon over the 'Ethiopians' fitted perfectly into the concept of Arab liberation from the occupation of the sons of Ḥām, the theme of the adventures of Sayf ibn Dhī Yazan.

79. Sayyār is a variant in the Ḥijāzīya. This word can have the sense of 'planet' or ever-moving object.

80. By the Mamluk age the Banū Sharīf were wandering beyond the Nubian desert in the area of Dongola. The Banu Quḍāʿa, to whom Ghamra was related, had crossed the Red Sea at an earlier date. The Fazāra, who were closely related to the 'Abs when they lived in Arabia, were established in Cyrenaica in the thirteenth century, and it seems likely that Banū 'Abs were among them. They, too, entered the Sudan as nomads to form the Sudanese Fazāra. The presence of all these nomad groups in the tale in an African context may be significant.

81. See page 243.

82. This verse recalls a description of the Banū 'Abs: 'And there come also others, dark and tawny of skin, who raise a black cloud of dust about them like a mountain; they score the earth deeply with their horses' feet, and they trail their spears after them as they gallop along.' See Lyall, *Ancient Arabian Poetry*, p. 39.

83. This verse seems to echo other verses attributed to 'Antara ibn Shaddād, the poet which run:
'They abuse my colour with its blackish hue, and this through ignorance, for were it not for the blackness of the night then the dawn would never burst. Even if my hue be black then my good qualities are white, And the drop (of blood) is discharged by my warlike hand.'

CHAPTER 4 : BYZANTINES, CRUSADERS AND AFRICANS

Africa appears again in the *Sīrat 'Antara.* It is towards the end of the romance (Sections 93 & 94), amid a discussion of events wherein the fate of the hero is linked to that of Heraclius, the son of the ruler of Byzantium. Any discussion of African peoples and events cannot ignore this section of the *Sīra.* It is a part of the narrative which introduces the peoples of the Nile. It defines Ethiopia as distinct from Nubia and gives clues as to the dates of the composition of the *Sīra.*

The supreme foe of Antar is here a giant king of Spain and North Africa called Janṭāyil (1). He is an Amalekite, and he is two hundred and seventy years old. He is carried on an elephant, and he has inherited an empire from his father. That empire stretched from Palestine and the Fertile Crescent to Tunisia, Sicily and Upper Egypt. It was adjacent to the 'Ethiopia' already discussed. It bordered 'the two trees' which are mentioned again and are situated fairly and squarely on African soil. The realm of Janṭāyil included the Zarwat (Zaghāwa) and the Murawat Zaghāwa, the Sudan, the Beja – here mentioned for the first time – Kabāja Takrūr, and the oases of the western desert of Egypt. He was also master of several towns on the Nile, Akhmīm, Bahnasā and Ahnas.

Janṭāyil sends his son 'Inān to fight Antar, Heraclius and Kūbart, a Frank who is Antar's ally and also lord of The Island of Kāfūr – The Island of Camphor. He is the ruler of the Fortress of Crystal. 'Inān is likewise a giant, and he is aided by the armies of Spain (al-Andalus). He has little success and is slain in battle. Janṭāyil takes his mace and vows revenge, seated on his elephant called Sīrawān. He departs and leaves his son 'Abd al-Masīḥ (The Servant of the Messiah) to rule in Spain. A battle is fought at Wādi 'l-Ramīm, and this leads to a single combat between Antar who fights on foot and Janṭāyil who is mounted on his elephant. Antar kills the elephant with a javelin of his opponent. Then he slays Janṭāyil with his sword, al-Ḍāmī.

Antar and his victorious company enter the city of al-Andalus where they are lavishly entertained by 'Abd al-Masīḥ. The name of the latter may disguise the name of 'Abbād – Mu'tamid, the party king of Seville in the eleventh century – who is Avitus in the twelfth century *Romance of Pseudo-Turpin;* or his name may have an Oriental Christian origin.

Antar, Heraclius and Kūbart are taken to a vast garden within which is a beautiful palace raised upon pillars.'The Servant of the Messiah' renews his obedience to Byzantium. He is followed by the rulers of Tunis, Qayrawān, Cyrenaica and Alexandria. These rulers seem to be Copts, Franks or Greeks. Michael is the ruler of Barqa, 'Iṭrūn ('Uṭrūn) is ruler of Tunis, Mardūs is ruler of Qayrawān, and Hermes ibn al-Gharandus is ruler of Alexandria.

Several rulers of Egypt do not obey, however. Antar is advised of these opponents by Shīnās, one of the chosen men of King Hermes. 'He said to him, "You are sought by the lord of al-Bahnasā, Kandrīyūs ibn Karmas . . . " King Kandrīyūs was a stubborn giant, a devil, a *mārid* of the *jinn.* He had only to meet a knight on his battlefield to snatch him from the back of his horse. All the kings of Upper Egypt feared him. He ruled from Akhmīm and Ahwaz (Ahnas?) to the Nubians and the Beja.'

Kandrīyūs decides to raise a huge army to fight Antar. After victory they intend to conquer the oasis 'islands' and the Fortress of Crystal. Among those to whom Kandrīyūs writes letters to raise an army are Marūnis, lord of the fortress of Dahshūr (2); Sūghāl, the lord of Ushmūnīya (3); Qarqāqays (Apa Kiriakos?), the lord of Akhmīm (4); Kardūs, the lord of Aswan; and the king of Nubia.

'When the people of Upper Egypt heard of the death of King Janṭāyil and of the succession of his son 'Abd al-Masīḥ that land was a turmoil. They wrote epistles to one another. Then came forth King Makshūḥ, king of the Beja, and King 'Aflaq, the king of the Nubians. They summoned the soldiers from those regions, and they equipped themselves. They met in Aswan, and the soldiers of Nubia entered upon five hundred elephants. There were twelve Sudanese on every elephant. They were naked like the people of 'Ād with nothing around their waists except for panther skins. In their hands they held shields, maces, spears, javelins and bows and arrows.' This army marched to Naqṭa and Karan (5) to Ushmūnīya and to Afṣala (6), which was a huge walled city of red stone. It was a Christian town. The march was continued to al-Bahnasā and Ahnas (7) where the army was greeted by Kandrīyūs ibn Karmas.

Antar attempts to meet this force alone with a small party of his closest allies. They march to a monastery at the foot of the green mountain called the Convent of the Messiah. Antar defeats a giant Frank called Ghaḍanfar, and then faces a patrician called Būlis (Paulus) whom he slays. A great battle follows for several days. Reinforcements reach Antar from Tunis, Cairo and Alexandria. The Beja elephants and their archers present dangers but the animals are finally discomforted by Shaybūb's arrows. A further engagement against Kandrīyūs ibn Karmas and his brother, the lord of the city of Ahnas, follows. Aid for Antar from Tunis and Qayrawān finally determines the battle. Kandrīyūs submits and gives gifts which are sent to the 'oases' (isles of Wāḥāt) and to Greater Rome. Antar bids farewell to Kūbart in the Island of Camphor and the Fortress of Crystal and accompanies Heraclius to Byzantium. Qayṣar honours Antar, his son al-Khudrūf, and Shaybūb, by having statues of the cast and erected. They are of yellow brass mixed with gold, with ruby eye-balls. The hero is shown upon the back of al-Abjar grasping his sword in both hands. At first Antar is frightened and annoyed. Then he relents and leaves Byzantium loaded with riches.

This adventure of Antar's appears to be a wild fantasy about Egypt, Nubia, North Africa and Spain. The material is based partly on elements in the story of the Arab expeditions to the Upper Nile and the imposition of the *baqṭ* or tribute, recorded in the *Futūḥ al-Bahnasā,* and partly on historical documents about Christian Nubia. Here we may have some of the earliest passages of borrowed material in the *Sīra,* a sub-strata of *Maghāzī* literature overlaid by later embellishment. The imposition of the *baqṭ* was first exacted by 'Amr ibn al-'Āṣ, who in 651/652 A.D. sent 'Abdullāh ibn Sa'd ibn Abī Sarḥ as far as Bahnasā and Dongola in Nubia in order to collect it. The payment of tribute in slaves and grain was governed by a treaty.

The treaty remained in force for six hundred years. Occasions when the payment of the *baqṭ* was withheld led to punitive expeditions. One of these occurred in 869 A.D. during the reign of Ibn Ṭūlūn when nomad Arabs of the Rabī'a and the Juhayna were sent against the Nubians and the Beja. Intermarriage with the latter gradually increased. The Muslim conquest of Nubia was accelerated during the age of the Mamluks. The Sultan Baybars I (1260-1277 A.D.) launched expeditions in 1275 and 1276 on account of non-payment of the *baqṭ.* Further Mamluk attacks occurred at a later date. By 1365/1366 A.D. Dongola was in ruins. To quote Ibn Khaldūn, 'The tribes of the Juhayna Arabs spread over the country of the Nubians and filled it with rapine and disorder.' Despite this the Nubians survived as a Christian entity in 'Alwa to the south until 1504 A.D., if not later. The Nilotic adventure in the *Sīra* seems to pre-date these events between the late thirteenth and mid-fourteenth centuries.

The 'Mamluk', even Cairene character of the very latest recension of the *Sīrat 'Antara* has already been mentioned. There are aspects in this plot about the battle and reconciliation with Kandrīyūs ibn Karmas of Ahnas which are not at all in keeping with the late Mamluk age. The latter was one of affliction for many Copts, both in official quarters and among the populous. It does not seem likely that it was then that these specific exploits in the *Sīra* which take place in Spain, in Upper Egypt and Lower Egypt would have evolved naturally, or have enjoyed public approval, especially as Copts and Greeks are not unfavourably represented in the *Sīra.*

Some tentative conclusions may be drawn if the story and the names of the participants where identifiable are closely examined. One of the original sources seems to be the account of the first expeditions against Egypt by 'Abdullāh ibn Sa'd ibn Abī Sarḥ (see poem on page 18). His role, or that of the Arab-negro commander 'Ubāda ibn al-Ṣāmit is inherited by Antar, Heraclius, Kūbart 'the Frank', and their Greek, Byzantine, Coptic and Frankish companions.

In order to bridge the earliest sources and the Mamluk *Sīra* one can conceive of Fatimid or Ayyubid recensions of Antar's adventures. An eclecticism which combines Spain, Africa and Byzantium is marked in the plot. Al-Maqrīzī in his *Description of Egypt* notes the eclectic ethnic composition of the Fatimid army with its Berbers of the Zenāta, Ṣaqāliba from Spain, Franks and negroes. The reports of the literary activities of Yūsuf ibn Ismā'īl at the court of the Fatimid al- 'Azīz seem to fit in here, and I have already referred to the lost book titled 'Nubia, Maqurra, 'Alwa, the Beja and the Nile' by 'Abdullāh ibn Sālim al-Aswānī, a near contemporary of Yūsuf ibn Ismā'īl.

There are similarities if the passages in Burkhardt's translation of al-Maqrīzī, the earlier tales of the conquest of Bahnasā (Oxyrhynchus) given in the Appendixes to his *Travels in Nubia,* London, 1882, and the British Library manuscripts are compared with the events in the *Sīra.* The Christian king besieged by the Arabs in Bahnasā under 'Amr ibn al-'Āṣ was called Batlos or Baṭlūs; he appears to be the patrician Būlis, foeman of Antar. The army of the Beja and the Nubians was led by Maksūḥ, king of the Beja and Berbers (Somalis) and Ghalyk or Ghalbaq, king of the Nūba. The Beja held 'Aksūmīya shields, inverted in shape and made of buffalo skin'. They were a black army of fifty thousand (var. twenty thousand) men. They had one thousand and three hundred elephants and each one of them carried a vaulted howdah of leather covered with metal in which were ten men.' In the company of the Beja were a race of giants called al-Quwwād who hailed from the Red Sea hills near Sawakin. They were clad in panther skins and wore copper rings in their upper lips. The army of Sudanese carried bows, slings, maces, war-drums and horns.

In the *Sīrat Antara* the king of the Beja is called Makshūḥ. 'Aflaq is the name of the king of the Nubians. The army had numerous elephants. Each elephant carried twelve men in a howdah. They were armed with skin shields and were naked save for loin coverings of panther skin. Makshūḥ and Maksūḥ are clearly the same, and 'Aflaq, Ghalbaq or Ghalyk are variants of the same name. Other details differ slightly or closely coincide.

This foundation of 'pre-Crusading' material, close to but not actually quoting the text of *Futūḥ al-Bahnasā,* cannot prove the existence of a 'Fatimid

Antar'. Because an epic which relates the conquests of the Prophet's Companions is likely to predate the *Sīrat 'Antara,* the latter would seem to be later than this *Maghāzī* text which unfortunately is difficult to date. The Coptic flavour of the material suggests a Coptic hand not later than the Ayyubids in a rearrangement of this earlier material. A Coptic influence on the portrayal of Antar, Shaybūb, his brother, and Khudrūf, his son, cannot be discounted. The latter guard his knightly person with deadly arrows. Here there is a likeness to St. Mercurius. In Coptic art, the latter – the father of two swords – is mounted on a black charger, and he is armed with a divine sword and a spear. He triumphs over infidelity, and he is praised by an angel with a psalm of the Septuagint, 'Gird thy sword upon thy thigh, Oh, mighty one.' He is flanked by two companions, two savage cynocephali who constantly protect him as he advances into battle.

Janṭāyil is conceived as an infidel Roman ruler, such as Titus or Diocletian; St. Mercurius in Coptic art is depicted as the slayer of Julian the Apostate (Yūliyānūs al-Kāfir), Decius, Dadiyos or a permutation of pagan rulers who were persecutors of true faith. Such an idea is not absent from the combats with 'Inān and Janṭāyil mounted upon his elephant Sīrawān, yet not sufficiently close enough to establish a direct Coptic connection.

A late Fatimid (?) painting from Fusṭāṭ (1200 A.D.?) – now in the British Museum – offers a more obvious prototype for Janṭāyil in the *Sīra.* The picture portrays a horned demon named Jazrāfīl mounted on his elephant (*al-fīl*). He is armed with a curved knife or sword and a round buckler. It is not unreasonable that romancers took ideas from this kind of painting to portray the heroes and the foes of their tales.

An important inclusion in the two manuscripts of *The Conquest of al-Bahnasā* in the British Library is the name of the lord of Aswan at the First Cataract of the Nile who also ruled Aden and the border of the salt sea (Red Sea) up to the region of the Nuba. His name is spelt al-Kīlāj and al-Kabkalāj, the latter almost certainly a variant reading of the former. I have already discussed (on page 89) the origin of the Nubian names Kaikalag and Ñokel and the likelihood that, misread or rephrased as Mankalā(n), one of these provides the name of the missing Negus in the *Sīrat 'Antara.*

If this is so then his status as ruler of Aswan in the *Futūḥ al-Bahnasā* has been entirely altered in the *Sīrat 'Antara.* The ruler of Aswan in the *Ḥijāzīya* is called Kardūs. These variants alone would seem to exclude direct borrowings by a copyist from the text of the *Futūḥ al-Bahnasā.* The latter and the *Sīrat 'Antara* share material founded on a missing text or on *Maghāzī* oral traditions which are probably early medieval in their dates.

If the exploits of the early Arab commanders are based on some historic fact, then King Caecilianus or Kaikalag of Nubia could have been a contemporary of the Prophet, and Ñokel, his predecessor, could have reigned in the pre-Islamic period. This does not add new and dependable substance to source material relating to the early links between the Negus and the followers of the Prophet, but it shows that within the narrative of the *Sīrat 'Antara Maghāzī* source material is embedded. It is not simply an imaginative creation of romancers but has some relation to substantial and archaic Islamic traditions. It raises a question: why should a profane romance such as Antar introduce Nubian kings as foes and allies of the Prophet's Arabia while other rulers figure in the other Arabic sources? Subordinate to this there are other questions: if the dynasty of Kaikalag ruled as far as Aden, where were the borders of an Axumite Negus who reigned in the heart of Abyssinia? Could one Negus and the other have been confused, and if so, when did this happen?

Plate 8: Franks and Byzantines are depicted throughout the Sīra *as Antar's allies as well as his opponents. This fact alone suggests that there is an influence from the Western* Chansons de geste *in the Antar romance.*

Notes

1. Janṭāyil. This name is distorted. Bernhard Heller has suggested that it is a corruption of Santiago de Compostela. The name could also be a corruption of Sanchol (Shanjūl or Shanshūl); see Dozy *Spanish Islam,* London, 1913, pp. 538-539. It is also arguable that it is derived from Shant(a) Fīla ('female elephant'), or even more likely from Shat(a) Yalah (Santa Ella). On both these places, see Edrisi, *Description de l'Afrique et de l'Espagne,* R. Dozy and De Goeje, Leyden, E. J. Brill, 1866, pp. 205 and 207 (Arabic text), 252 and 255 (French translation). His elephant, Sīrawān, might possibly relate to the villanous Count Servando who was a bitter foe of the Spanish Umayyads; see Dozy, *ibid,* pp. 355-356. Raymond of Toulouse or Saint Gilles is called Sanjīl, which possibly implied this name. In my final chapter I shall discuss the premise that Janṭāyil and Santiago are in some way related. For a summary of the Saracen giant in European literature see Dorothee Metlitzki's *The Matter of Araby in Medieval England,* Yale, 1977, pp. 192-197.
2. Dahshūr. A place famous for its 'bent' pyramid, adjacent to Memphis, and a short distance to the south of Cairo. Marūnis or Marīnus is ruler of Ahnas in the *Futūḥ al-Bahnasā.*
3. Ushmūnīya. Named after Ushmūn ibn Miṣrā'īm. Regarding al-Ushmūnī, see Edrisi, *ibid,* pp. 45, 46, and 145 (Arabic text), 52-54, and 174, (French translation). Sūghāl seems to be spelt Rūshāl in the *Futūḥ al-Bahnasā.*
4. Akhmīm. An important centre of the Copts and famous in Arabic legends about Egypt because of its *barbā* or Pharaonic temple guarded by talismans. See Edrisi, *ibid,* pp. 47-48 (Arabic text), 54-55 (French translation). Qarqāqays could be a variant of Cyricus, a name of a king of Nubia who was engaged in combat with 'Abd al-Malik Amīr of Egypt in the eighth century. See Rev. S. C. Malan, *A short history of the Coptic Church,* (based on al-Maqrīzī), London, 1873, p. 78.
5. Naqṭa and Karan. The first is probably Nagada (Ombos) on the opposite bank to Karnak, to which the second name possibly refers.
6. Afṣala. Unidentified, but the description of a 'huge walled city of red stone' suggests a Coptic monastery, perhaps the Red Monastery', al-Dayr al-Aḥmar near Sohag, or possibly al-Dayr al-Muḥarraq.
7. Al-Bahnasā and Ahnas. For these two towns, see Edrisi, *ibid,* pp. 50, 51 (Arabic text), and 57, 58 (French translation). To 'pseudo al-Wāqidī' is attributed the book titled *Futūḥ al-Bahnasā.* There are two copies of the *Futūḥ al-Bahnasā* in the British Library; Oriental 1551 and Add 7635. An examination of this work which recounts the exploits of the Arab conquerors of Egypt shows a good deal of material shared with the *Sīrat 'Antara.* I shall discuss this in subsequent pages.

It could be argued that one or two names associated with this Spanish and North African adventure look like varied borrowings from Almohad sources. Sīrawān, the elephant of Janṭāyil, for example, could be Sīrwān a locality in the southern Atlas of Morocco. Shuntulūlya (شنطلولة), Janṭāyil(?), was probably the name of a splendid garden planted in Marrakech by the Almohad, ᶜAbd al-Mu'min, in 1155. This name seems to be a derivation from the Spanish Santa Olalla (Saint Eulalie) which was perhaps the name of a convent in Marrakech for Christians resident there during the Almoravids. Garando is as plausible a calque for Garandus, etc, as any other. Garando was a christian in the service of 'Abd al-Mu'min. He was appointed a local ruler in the Sus until he was executed for treason in 1170. His name may have become linked to a locality between Mazagan and Marrakech. It will be recalled that the Almohad conquest of Spain was beset by rebellions. See, E. Levi-Provençal, *Documents Inédits d'Histoire Almohade*, Paris, 1928, pp 199-216.

CHAPTER 5 : THE DEATH OF ANTAR

When Najm, the slave, heard the words of al-Asad al-Rahīs he said to him, 'My lord, order me to set forth this instant for I am at your service to hear and to obey.' He said to him, 'Oh, Najm, I have resolved to do so even though it means my doom.' The slave tied a coarse cloth over the back of the she-camel. He fitted the halter and nose-ring to the beast, and al- Asad al-Rahīs set upon its hump. He hoped that fortune would offer him an easy task. He had taken his bow and his quiver full of poisoned arrows. The slave took the rein of the camel and marched forth in the direction of Iraq. Al- Asad al-Rahīs was longing to meet Antar. He pressed on in the desert until he reached the edge of the Euphrates. His slave, Najm, concealed him in a spot wherein was a thicket of entangled bushes, many birds and many streams. The narrator said : This thicket faced the tents of the Banū 'Abs and of Antar. They were pitched between the Euphrates and the rivers. Antar's tents were pitched on the far side of the Euphrates only a short distance from the water.

When the slave had dismounted al- Asad al-Rahīs he beheld a scene of joyful festivity. The heart of al- Asad al-Rahīs was excited when he heard the plucking of stringed instruments and the singing of the midwives, the mothers and the slave and free woman and the resounding of the cymbal players and the roar of the earthen pots, the barking of the dogs and the bleating of the sheep, the dyeing and painting of the maidens and the talking of the knights as they ate their food and drank their wine. The people of the camp were under the power and in awe of their protector, Antar. The awe of Antar had entered into the hearts of all the Arabs.

The slave said, 'I see no way for you to reach Antar and no path for you to follow.' When al- Asad al-Rahīs heard his slave Najm speak thus, he said, 'You speak the truth, oh, worthy slave. Your report is the truth, but by the high God who determines destiny, when fate and destiny strike then sight is blinded. When God wills a matter He prepares for its accomplishment. Perchance God will cause the death of this slave and his fate at my hand. Here I am concealed in this thicket. I have a bow and an arrow in my hands. When I hear him I shall shoot him. My arrow is poisoned. If I hit him with a shot truly aimed I do not wish to linger after I have shot him dead. Not an hour's life do I covet; the flame in my heart is ablaze.'

The slave said to him, 'Do as you think best. I shall not argue with you. I shall not restrain you from your acts. I am here awaiting your deeds to be accomplished.' The narrator said : Now between al- Asad al-Rahīs and the tents of Antar was the width of the river, a distance of a bow shot, nay, perhaps a little further; he stayed in the ambush all that day; he waited to learn what the people did.

The night fell. It spread its canopy, and the darkness descended as a covering. He said to Najm his slave, 'Curse you. Bring me forth to the desert edge of the thicket. Put me in a place overlooking the camp. Use your skill and resolute will, because I can hear their sounds at a far distance. Come now, bring me closer to them. A little will suffice; I will cause men to speak of my deeds from one generation to the next.'

So the slave brought him forth to the edge of the thicket. He brought him to the river bank. He feared not misfortune nor hasty act. He sat down facing the tents of Prince Antar. There he waited the turn of destiny. Kneeling on his knees he used his hands to pull his bow to its limit. Then he fitted his arrow to the middle of the bow pulling hard with every sinew in his body.

Now behold a coincidence amazing, a report of wonder, an execution of Will, and the dictates of Fate and Destiny from which there is no escape! Antar was sleeping at that hour beside 'Abla. He heard the barking of dogs grow loud and spread around him. So loud was it that it echoed in the desert. He arose and left his tent. He called his brother Jarīr and said to him, 'Woe, woe, find out what is amiss. Why are the dogs barking so loud and so far into the night from the direction of yon thickets?' The narrator said: Now it happened that the night was dark and a blackness deep covered the land. Jarīr said to his brother – overheard by al- Asad al-Rahīs, 'By God, son of one mother, this darkness is intense; I cannot see into it. Still, brother mine, I observe that all the barking is coming from that direction nigh the river. It is carrying its sound in the direction of our camp. Because of the intense darkness I cannot see anything.' The narrator said: When Antar heard the words of his brother he leapt from his place of attention as though he were a bounding lion. At once he donned his clothing, grasped his sword and walked to the river bank. He stole along its shore discoursing with this brother of his. Al- Asad al-Rahīs heard what he was saying. Antar remarked to his brother Jarīr, 'It is only some greedy fellows. They have made for us with intent to slip into the edge of the camp to pilfer some horses brazenly as though we were rumoured to be men lacking in intelligence. By God, Jarīr, by the truth of the King of Destiny, He who wills and determines, who knows the whisperings in men's hearts, who decrees his wishes, were I to attack the nation of Rabī'a and Mudar I would make them taste death by the sword. If it were not so then I would not be Antar ibn Shaddād. Far be it, by the Mighty King, that a robber or a dog be crafty enough to intrude on us at any time.'

It was fated at that hour, when no slave could escape his destiny, that Prince Antar had felt a pressing need to pass water. It happened that he faced the thickets wherein al-Asad al-Rahīs lay waiting. When Prince Antar urinated a sound was heard akin to a great roar or the echo of a mill wheel. Such was his strength of will and resolve. When he urinated on a stone he pierced it by his power. Furthermore, when he did he roared loudly and an echo resounded. Al- Asad al-Rahīs heard that sound. Recognising its import he drew an arrow from his quiver, an arrow soaked in death. He placed it in the middle of the bow and drew the bow to its full strength. He discharged it towards the sound of the water. The arrow left the bow resounding and quivering like the piercing shooting star and an inescapable affliction. Antar, the Prince, felt nothing until that arrow had pierced his scrotum and it had penetrated deep into his bowels. Prince Antar was unaware of it, he stirred not, and he moved not. The narrator said : His brother Jarīr was standing before him at a distance having seen nothing. He did not know what harm had befallen him. He heard him recite :

Oh, bowman who shoots at a sound, straight was your shot
to our grief. You shot your arrow, and it pierced a waterskin.
By it you severed vein and arteries.
God sever your wrist with all speed. May you taste war
and spear thrust without respite.
Oh, arrow, were I to know him who released you towards
me in a night which desires my doom,
then I would make him empty the cup of fate in all haste,
and I would leave his corpse as food for the wild beast
and the eagles.

The narrator said : Prince Antar finished these verses which were overheard by al-Asad al-Rahīs who thought that the arrow had missed and had fallen into a waterskin. So terrified was he that he died of grief and malice, accursed be he and his kinsfolk. At that moment his slave Najm came to him and spoke to him but he received no answer. The slave stretched forth his hand and grasped his wrist. He moved him but found that he was dead. So he left him lying where he was and fled from him in all haste. He mounted his camel. He loosed its ties and journeyed swiftly to the camps of the Banū Nabhān.

As for Prince Antar he rose to his feet and walked towards his tents. His brother Jarīr walked in front of him. He followed leaning upon his sword. He was troubled about what had happened to him, and the world was sombre in his eyes. Thus he continued until he entered his tent and told 'Abla what he had suffered.

She was full of worry; she wept, and she sighed. The dwellers in the camp were deeply shocked, and both old men and young lads were afraid. Men and women hastened to Antar's presence, and they began to ask and seek an explanation for that circumstance. His uncle, Mālik, his son, Maysara, Zakhmat al-Jawād and the rest of the Banū Qurād asked him how he felt. He told them of all that had happened to him. He said to them, 'I know not what occurred nor do I know the deeper reason for this mischance; whether it came from one side or from another.'

The narrator said : When Jarīr heard these remarks, he said, 'By the protection of the Arabs, I must discover the cause.' He stripped. His anxiety was deepened, he was short of breath and his weeping and lamenting increased, and his reason forsook him. He plunged into the river until he crossed over to the further bank. He climbed the bank and searched diligently in that desert. Then, lo, he spied al-Asd'a al-Rahīs lying prone on the river's edge, and the bow and the arrow lay beside him. The narrator said : When Jarīr saw him he knew him and knew his business. He exclaimed, 'Oh, war.' He began to strike him on his face with a stone until he bled from his nose. Then Jarīr returned to Antar, his brother, and told him what he had seen. Antar despaired and was convinced that he would lie in his tomb. He commanded his brother to bring him the body of al- Asad al-Rahīs. Jarīr obeyed him and brought the body and laid it in front of him. When Antar saw it, its condition and state, and recalled what had befallen him, he sighed, his heart sick and seized with anxiety.

He who lives for a day after the death of his foe
has attained the goal he strove to attain.

After reciting his verses Prince Antar called aloud, 'My enemy, I have survived you, and you did not get what you sought; but, oh, knights of the Arabs, death is my portion. God assigns a cause for every death, and such is the decree of Him who is hidden from the eyes of men.' Then he ordered his brother Jarīr to collect firewood for al- Asad al-Rahīs to burn him in the fire and cast his ashes into the river so that he should have no tomb which was known. Jarīr accepted the words of his brother and grieved deeply as to how he might die. Was there some way whereby he could be redeemed and spared for his companions? Antar slept not that night, aware of the gravity of his malady. 'Abla said to him, 'Cousin, you are distressed by an arrow, yet you are not afraid of spear points.' Then Jarīr told her the story of all that had happened, and how he had suffered from the vile dog, al- Asad al-Rahīs. When 'Abla heard it her affliction was made worse. She wept, beat her cheeks and ate the flesh of her wrists. She intensified her cries, and the people of the tribe assembled. Prince Antar said to her, 'By God, my cousin, perdition has come upon me, and there is now no more life for me.' She said, 'Be content, oh, father of knights, and banish such thoughts. You have endured wounds the size of the mouth of a water skin. You cared not then, so why are you afraid of this arrow?' Prince Antar sighed at her words and said, 'Oh, cousin, I feel that fire burns in my body. This arrow was poisoned, and it has done its work.' Then he said,

> 'Oh, 'Abla, mourn at my tomb when the dust rises in the deserts,
> and say to the women who delight in another's misfortunes that
> the days once stretched before me in joy and renown.'

On the following day all his people came to him, and they began to weep and sigh. He said to them, 'Lessen this moaning by the Lord of men who destroyed 'Ād and Thamūd. Such is the decree of the Lord of men. Now nights have come to their end, and so too the days which have been folded up as though they were banners. Were a man to live a thousand years he would still have to drink the cup of death.'

Then he turned to 'Abla and said to her, 'Oh, cousin, I am about to die. There is no escape. After I am gone, by God, no banner of the Banū 'Abs will rise, and neither white nor black will remain. The Arabs will seize them in every desert place and seek their revenge in every country. But, cousin, be swift, mount my horse, don my Yemeni bauberk, grasp my spear and sword. My renown will rest in your hand. Journey to the Banū 'Abs and 'Adnān and let there be beside you Prince Mālik your father and 'Amr your brother. Know, oh, beloved of my heart, that after me they will not remain. Likewise the Banū 'Abs will be unable to protect you or defend you. You must have some one to guard you, a relation, and here am I about to die as is decreed but how will your own death come about? Oh, cousin, go to one of two men of valour, either 'Āmir ibn al-Ṭufayl or else Ibn al-Muhalhil, prince Zayd al-Khayl and seek his hand. One of them will protect you and repel your foes. If he can do this then choose him for yourself. One of them must console you and see you to your grave. When I am gone none will honour you but one of them will protect you, so be to him a wife and let him be your lord. When you journey in the desert plain and valleys do not greet or trust any Arab. If you act thus none will suspect you, and they will think that it is I, and so all the Arabs will be in awe of you, and other heroes will fear you.'

The narrator said: When 'Abla heard his words she responded to his request. Then she wept and sighed and was filled with terrors. The narrator said : As for those elders who were present and the Prince 'Amr Dhū'l-Kalb, the firm knight, when they heard the words of Prince Antar there was not one of them but he wept bitterly and grieved with a burning heart. Antar turned to Prince 'Amr Dhū'l-Kalb and said to him, 'The only person whom I entrust to you is Zayd ibn 'Urwa.

Watch over him for my sake. His father is the most dear to me of our companions, one of the knights of valour. Like you he was one of the most precious of friends.'

I have heard from Prince Zayd ibn 'Urwa that Prince 'Amr had taken pity on him and become dearer to him than himself. He had shown him a regard denied to his other companions. The narrator said: Prince Zayd was a knight unmatched and a colocynth bitter to the taste. He was a hero of knightly virtue and others did not match his valour. He was a youth of resolute skill and strength. When 'Amr heard the will of Antar the Prince he obeyed his behest although he was grieved to the heart.

Prince Antar divided the herds and the camels among the Banū Qudā'a and the Banū Qurād, and he allotted the slaves their share in abundance, and he bestowed half the camels to his wife Qannāsat al-Rijāl since he knew that after his death there would be none to take pity on her or to help her, and she swore that she would take nothing of his wealth which was worth the value of a halter. To 'Amr Dhū'l-Kalb he entrusted his sister, Qannāsat al-Rijāl, and those with her of the Banu Qudā'a. As for the heroic Banū 'Abs he ordered them to remain where they were while he would bring safely to her people and there join the Banū 'Abs. But 'Amr Dhū'l-Kalb said to him, 'Oh, father of knights, we shall not impose this task upon you, rather you will remain until you are free of your pains while I shall convey 'Abla to a safe locality. Then I shall return.' Antar said, 'By God, that will not be acceptable. The enemy will not now rejoice at my misfortune. By God, not while I still have a will to live.' Prince Antar then said to 'Amr, 'I shall not hear such things nor shall I obey what you say.' 'Amr said to him, 'Why so, oh, father of knights?' He said, 'Know, oh, my brother, I am afraid lest it be said of me that Prince Antar, the Protector of 'Abd and 'Adnān, before he died became a mere watchmen, afraid of the Arabs, and it also be said that he was scared of men and heroes. If this is what I am to be or to do, then, by the Truth of the Almighty King, I shall never do it so that foes may rejoice at my misfortune.' Prince 'Amr said no more and did not answer him. Prince Antar arose with a heart harder than a stone, yet his body was bent with pain. He dressed 'Abla in his hauberk and girded her with his sword. He gave her his spear and mounted her upon his horse al-Abjar. He himself rode in the palenquin of 'Abla on the camel which she used to ride when she journeyed from camp to camp.

Then Antar turned to 'Amr Dhū'l-Kalb and those men who were with him, and he indicated his departure and farewell in these verses :

Greet the camps of Qatām and greet the abode of 'Abla
Habitations wherein the winds play merrily

And where the birds alight from one year to the next.
It was there that I stood calling to the tribe.
Yet my words were unheard, my question received no answer.
Forget the ruins and the empty landscape.
Exchange it for the whistle of the spear and the
blow of the sword.
Oh 'Abla forget not my place of repose,
When you see the thrusts of the arrows.
Lament on the sword and the Rudaynī spear,
And give a greeting to the soil of my bones.
Will you forget me when squadrons which succour
the Banū Qatām rose above us?
I left their protectors felled in the hollow,
And they turned their backs beneath the skirts of the dust.
My spear if I lunge with it fells a foeman and he drops
upon the sandhills.
Oh 'Abla may no evil befall you nor hurt nor harm as long
as you live.
Oh 'Abla weep and mourn. Leave not the weeping to the
multitudes.

When Prince Antar had finished these words, and when Prince 'Amr and the company of men and heroes who were with him had heard them weeping and wailing among them increased. Qannāsat al-Rijāl wept on account of Prince Antar. She lamented how the days and the nights had betrayed him. When Prince Antar had given his whip to 'Abla he mounted in that palenquin while the rest of his family and his paternal relations passed around him in gratitude over what he had given to them of his favour and his flocks. Then Prince Antar went forth while 'Abla rode before him. Behind him marched the noble lords of the Banū Qurād, all of them making for the land of al-Sharabba and al- 'Alam al-Sa'dī. They were accompanied by their steeds and mounts, quick in their pace. Prince Antar was sitting aloft, swaying with pain and intense suffering. 'Abla was in front of him, her tears flowing down her cheeks. She was full of despair and disquiet while Prince Antar was preoccupied with death. At every step in the march he hoped to bring 'Abla to the neighbourhood of the tents and camps, perchance she would escape destruction and dangers. On they marched in those lands and those plains. Antar sighed with grief, his heart was heavy and sick as he thought of separation. He made a sign with his hand towards 'Abla, and he began to counsel her with these verses which he recited:

Oh evil fate will you continue to betray me with calamity.
How many are the misfortunes which have parted brethren
from each other.

You cast the mighty into shame. He remains giddy and
perplexed.
You topple the exalted and you exalt the humble and the low.
How many are the knights of courage whom you have destroyed.
Oh 'Abla take care of al-Abjar, fasten tight the girth of
his saddle and gird his reins.
When you pass by the tribes salute them with the whip
as I do, but utter not a word.
As for the coward he will say "It is Antar who rides",
While the knight of courage will say "Antar is dead."
When you reach your hallowed territory then rend your
raiment and rip your mantle asunder.
Oh 'Abla say when spears are locked in combat, Antar used
to guard the palenquins.
When every disaster befell Antar used to fear a battle's
outcome but he had no fear of foe.
Oh 'Abla take care on the march for now I cannot challenge heroes.
Oh shooter of the arrow so slender, you slew me by treachery
your arrow was not the betrayer.
Oh 'Abla march on. I am anxious within, in pain and perplexed.
If you have the modesty of a true woman do not call
the charger and the accoutred.
Oh 'Abla weep for a knight of courage who goes into battle
and fears not the spear point.
A hero who tumbles the armour-clad with a blow.
How many a youth is a partner from his thrust.
He fears not death in the battle.
He rises aloft to the rings of Saturn.
Wail oh 'Abla and mourn. Mourn for the lion of battle
as one sad, mad with love and stricken dumb.
Oh 'Abla, Antar's fate has stricken him and overtaken him
in all haste.
Weep for Antar the 'Absī, once a youth, a lion who thrust
and gave food to a guest.
Rejoice not after my death oh 'Abla, weep and mourn for
a hero of the past,
Who protected the women from the foe by his courage
and who felled the intrepid.
If he had died in battle only the knight of knights
would have met him.
How good a soul. One noble and mighty, hospitable and a
conqueror.

If you call aloud the name of Antar and give a greeting
all will take you for a hero.
The horsemen and knights all know that I am a lion in combat.
Console the knights for Antar's past battles, console
Sa'īd and 'Adnān.
The sons of Badr indeed will know where I stood in the
battle of a-Jafr, a knightly battle,
And the Banū Dāhiya with Fazāra and the Banū Hilāl and Salmān.
And the Banū Muzayna in the spear clash on the day of
al-Hājir and of Ghassān.
The horses displayed their teeth with a frown and with
the dust falling visibly on the tents.
The knights know I am a hero and the protector of 'Adnān.
Console the Persians for Antar's battles and the bedouin tribes.
Console Shaybān, 'Awf and 'Āmir and the lions of Kinda and Dhubyān.
As a wind this is all the virtue which remains his for all time,
and is the record of a time of valour which is past.

When Antar had finished her verse 'Abla wept bitterly for him and her tears became as raindrops. Prince 'Amr also wept, and so did his sister, Qannāsat al-Rijāl, because 'Amr had wished to dwell in those camps after Antar. To bid farewell to Antar was intolerable so he mounted and marched after him until he caught up with him among the sand-hills. He remained with him for five days. Every day Prince Antar felt his pain grow sharper and more intense, and he was convinced of his death. He approached 'Amr on the sixth day and said to him, 'Oh, Prince, swear to me by your life that you will go to your camps and your family and settle your sister in your tribe. I know that the Banū 'Abs, if their lifespan is complete, will have no support after I die. You will exhaust yourself. You are a king of might in combatting the Arabs. I have nought to ask of you save in regard to Zayd ibn 'Urwa and also that you will avenge my death among the Banū Nabhān. Leave not a man of them alive.'

'Amr wept and said to him, 'Oh, father of knights, rest content, and let your eye be cooled. I shall avenge you but I shall do nothing until I have news of you.' Then they embraced and wept together. He bade him farewell and pursued his march in the desert. Due to Antar's departure the fire of passion burnt hotter in his soul. He began to seek for his tents. When he had gone forth Antar turned to his brother Jarīr and to his nephew al-Khudrūf and said to them, 'My brothers, I want you to march and tell my fate and story to my people. I know that as long as you live, you will be a part of my image. When you arrive tell them of my death and rend my clothes before them. Convey my salutations to them and my farewell and say to them, "Protect my loved ones as I did theirs but if they cannot, then by God they shall not prosper." ' After these words al-Khudrūf and his uncle Jarīr marched forth with tormented hearts.

As for Prince Antar his pains grew worse and worse, and he ordered the slaves to press on with the camels, the herds and with 'Abla who was mounted on the back of al-Abjar. She was sobbing with grief. Antar was in the palenquin stricken with pain and anguish. The Banū Qurād marched behind him and before him. Onwards they marched until the morning dawned in those sand dunes. Then they were overtaken by a column of heavily armed Arabs who had seen those palenquins and flocks and 'Abla mounted on al-Abjar, sad for Antar's sake. One of them said, 'Oh, cousins, this steed is Antar's steed, and the weapons are his. As for the rider, by the Most High, I do not think that he is Antar because his height is not the height of Antar, nor is his head, the head of Antar. If my judgement is correct and my passion does not betray me then Antar must have died. It is 'Abla, the daughter of Mālik, who rides. Her cousin has been overtaken by misfortunes. March with me in front of them so that we can find out their business and let us be patient until we see whether Antar dismounts and urinates and let us see that spot (1). Such will prove whether events are as they seem'.

When Antar urinated he would split the ground to the distance of two spans and his water would froth and foam in the earth to the extent of three spans' breadth. The men journeyed after them at a distance as they crossed the deserts for the awe of Antar prevented them from coming up to them, so great was their fear. It happened that 'Abla dismounted in order to urinate. When she had finished she remounted and marched away. The riders watched her until she had gone some distance. Then they followed her steps until they came to the spot which she had left, and they espied the place where her water remained. Lo, they saw that it was spread out over the surface of the ground, for a woman when she urinates on the ground is broad in her movements, wholly contrary to the actions of a man. The man said, 'Did not I tell you, cousins, I said to you that this knight is not Antar. By the Protection of the Arabs, my judgement is sound and my passion did not beguile me. It is 'Abla, the daughter of Mālik ibn Qurād. The rider is a woman.'

That man said to them, 'If such is the case then attack them with me.' Then they agreed to take their herds. They attacked them then and there intent upon looting their herds and taking their women and children captive. They hastened to do battle. Antar heard them although he was suffering in his struggle with a horrible death. That instant 'Abla cried aloud and said, 'Oh, cousin, the enemy and the Arabs have come upon us. They intend to take up captive.' When Antar heard her words he raised the curtains of the palenquin and showed his head and stared at them. He screamed and roared in a manner which echoed and re-echoed in the wilderness and the mountains. He called aloud, 'Oh, vile knaves, ignoble wretches. I am Antar ibn Shaddād. Today I will show you how battle are fought and endured.' When the knights heard his voice, and they recognized his cry, they lost their reason. Perplexed, they fled defeated into the wide deserts, some of them striking their comrades. They said, 'Be swift, bring us to safety, this is but a trick and ruse of this devil whom none in this world can resist and whom none of the men of courage can face in battle. He has concealed himself to see who stands in the way of his family so that he can march after them, ruin their camps and eradicate their traces.'

As for the people they marched over far distances watching Antar as they went. Then he said to his uncles and those who were with him, 'March on, my cousins, hasten on, perchance you will arrive safe and sound for I am dying, and there is no escape. Hasten your step and delay not.'

Zakhmat al-Jawād said to him,
'Oh nephew you have disquieted your spirit
We shall exhaust our efforts for your sake.
Long was the time your sword and spear protected us.'

When Antar heard the words of his uncle and the passion they expressed, he said to him, 'That is so, uncle, you are all knights of war and of hard endurance, but the most glorious among you and the most famous is none other than Antar ibn Shaddād. Continue on your march, perchance your will reach your land and see your tents in safety.' After he had spoken all of them burst into tears, and they bade Antar adieu. The Banū 'Abs pressed forward, and they went before him. He gazed at 'Abla with the tears streaming from his eyes as they parted.

When she had disappeared from his sight his hands rested on his spear supporting his mighty person. He cried with a great sob of death and with one mighty breath his spirit left his body. His steed stood motionless beneath him. Al-Abjar had been trained to do this. While Antar had lived he slept on the back of his mount.

The narrator said : Those Arabs thought that Antar was still alive. They did not know that he had drunk the cup of death. Yet he appeared to be waiting for them to do them battle. They said one to another, 'Woe to you, retreat before you lose your lives.' The elder among them said, 'Cousins, I am puzzled for I am sure that Antar is dead. If he were still living he would not refrain from fighting us in these valleys. He is not a coward nor a wretch who is despised so that he would stand thus without fighting and in fear of men, some heroes.' They stood and waited and watched in order to see what might be the outcome.

The Banū 'Abs went deeper and deeper into the desert and the hills, and they kept themselves safe from evil and mischief. They thought that Antar was following them on the back of his steed but al-Abjar did not stir from his place until the sun was about to set. The knights who watched grew weary until their bodies almost melted with heat. The elder said, 'Woe to you, I did not tell you that I knew his condition yet was unaware that he had died! It is sound sense that you accept what I told you and charge him in my company. Go around him from behind and in front. If you cannot face these deeds then release this mare of mine in the direction of al-Abjar. She is on heat, and if he is pre-occupied then you will attain your purpose.' The narrator said: So they obeyed the elder's command. He dismounted from his mare, and they drove her towards al-Abjar in those wastes. The mare made for him because she was on heat. When she reached him, al-Abjar pranced upon her, and Antar fell from his back. Then their hearts were contented, and they approached. They said, 'Oh, noble knight, in your life and after your death you guarded your herds and your women-folk. Then they took his equipment, and they stripped him, and they left him lying in those deserts. The elder said to them, 'Why did you take his equipment and despoil him and then afterwards you left him as he was. It is not becoming that he should be left so, thrown down in the deserts. It is my view that you should bury him. For that there will be a reward and a recompense.'

They dismounted, and they dug a deep grave for Antar, and they entered him in it, and they heaped earth on top of it. It was as though Antar had never lived. Glory be to God, the Almighty Judge who has decreed His will on His servants with a draught of the cup of death. Antar joined the company of those who were famous in their times.

The narrator said : The period which elapsed between the night Antar was wounded and the day he fell in that place was five months and five days. The knights when they had buried Antar in the ground retraced their steps in the desert and over the rocky hills. As for the steed of Antar, al-Abjar, it fled at speed before them in the wilderness, and it let none catch it. It became a wild horse in the desert.

The narrator said: Such was the fate of Antar.

As for the Banū 'Abs, after they had parted from him they marched onwards believing that he would catch them up. They did not know that destiny had sealed his fate. On they marched pressing forward until they reached their tribal camps. They were in total exhaustion and beyond caring about the world. But the fact remained that Antar was dead, and they were to learn of what had befallen him, and how he had departed. It was then that the mourners wailed and lamented and the horses and the mounts raised their cries. Men called aloud in grief, and a party of them decided to go to the place of the battle after they had prolonged their groaning and lamenting. They cast down the tents. Then the three heroic brothers of King Qays rode their mounts, and they took a party of the princes of the Banū 'Abs with them after King Qays had ordered them not to return without Antar's body , carried upon one of the camels. The brothers of Qays set forth together with the men who had been with Antar from the very beginning so that they could tell them of the place wherein they had met their enemy. They traversed the deserts until they arrived at that spot. In it they saw a spacious grave. It was not hidden from their eyes, and they knew that Antar had drunk of the goblet of mortality. They disinterred and uncovered his body. He was wrapped in shrouds. They laid him upon the camel, and they returned to their homelands. How many were the tears that they shed! They performed the funeral rites, and many days of sorrow passed, days which they could not compare to any others in that age. The mourners continued their mourning, and when they had fulfilled the days of their lamentations for misfortunes they dug a grave for Antar beside that of his father and that of his friend Mālik. It was on the peak of al- 'Alam al-Sa'dī and the routes which passed it by. It was there that they interred him, and they heaped earth above his grave amid the weeping of those who loved him. The poets and the vagabond troubadours also lamented, and they composed elegies in honour of him, Antar ibn Shaddād.

Comment

The death of Antar has been described as a 'stolen story' (see the comments of Charles James Lyall, page 60) , lifted in whole, or in part, from the events which accompanied the death of Rabī'a ibn Muqaddam of the Banū Firās. There are also similarities between the death of Antar and the death of the Cid. Whether these similarities are close enough to show conclusively a borrowing of plot or motif is very debatable.

The death of a hero or a warrior of Islam by the poisoned arrow of a blinded archer is a common story in Oriental literature. The blind archer is to be found as early as the romance of Sayf Ibn Dhī Yazan (see page 20). In it Wahriz, the ally of Sayf, shoots Masrūq, the king of the Ethiopians and the ruler of the Yemen. Another archer appears in the story of Ra's al-Ghūl and the exploits of 'Alī, the Prophet's son-in-law, in the Yemen. This latter book, *Futūḥ al-Yaman,* is attributed to Muḥammad ibn 'Abd al-Raḥmān Abū'l-Ḥasan al-Bakrī who lived two centuries later than the earliest recensions of the *Sīrat 'Antara.* The blind archer in the story of Ra's al-Ghūl is called al-Ḥārith al-Sakafī. His huge bow is made of hazel-wood cut from a tree watered with milk. When he is unsuccessful in shooting the *Imām* 'Alī be breaks his bow into seven pieces.

It would be futile to dispute that the death of Rabīʻa on his horse while defending his tribe is not portrayed afresh in the *Sīra* with Antar as the hero. Nevertheless, there are marked differences in the death of the heroes. Rabīʻa was the bowman who shot his foes whereas Antar was killed by the arrow of a kinsman who had taught himself skill with the bow. In Rabīʻa's death scene he is alone on his steed whereas the death of Antar in this fashion forms the climax of a lengthy prelude during which Antar's armour and weapons are donned by ʻAbla, his wife, who rides in disguise while Antar who is fatally wounded is carried in her palenquin to give courage to his kinsmen. Nothing of this occurs in the story of Rabīʻa. It is noteworthy that the version in which Wizr ibn Jābir shoots ʻAntara with an arrow is early and is told by Ibn al-Kalbī who died at the beginning of the ninth century.

There are similarities between the death of Antar, the death of the Cid and the death of King Ahab of Israel (see Kings I, chapter 22, vv. 1-38). They are most apparent in a reference to the disguise adopted by Ahab the king of Israel and in verses 34-35: 'And a certain man drew a bow at a venture and smote the king of Israel between the joints of the harness; wherefore he said unto the driver of the chariot, "Turn thine hand, and carry me out of the host; for I am wounded." And the battle increased that day; and the king was stayed up in his chariot against the Syrians and died at even; and the blood ran out of the wound into the midst of the chariot.'

The death of Antar appears to be derived from a number of strands frequently found in Arabian, Semitic and Persian stories of noble heroic feats which are not confined to any one hero. Only one of these themes is the death of Rabīʻa ibn Muqaddam. The skilful way in which several of them have been adopted, adapted and rephrased to describe the last days of Antar makes the charge of plagiarism misleading in the context of Arabian romance as a literary genre, particularly if one recalls the extensive borrowings of exploits from Pseudo-Callisthenes in Arabian and Western romances.

The death of Antar (Section 95) is similar in the *Ḥijāzīya* and *Shāmīya* versions of the *Sīra.* The poetry is markedly different. It is likely that Iraq or Syria was the place where the story of the hero's death was first composed. The death shot by the Euphrates is a clue to the milieu of the story.

Despite these similarities, the Syrian versions of the *Sīra,* and the unspecified fragments of other recension and versions published in the edition of the *Sīra* by the Muṣṭafā Muḥammad Press (see page 191) modify or amplify the death scene at several points. The developments in the story, often abruptly juxtaposed in the *Ḥijāzīya,* are joined and inegrated.

Plate 9: Antar's corpse on his steed Abjar guards the Gazelle Pass as the tribe of ʿAbs escapes to safety.

Two examples suffice. The first is the descent of Antar from ‘Abla’s palenquin and his remounting of al-Abjar. According to the Syrian versions:

‘After the defeat of the enemy Antar came down from the palenquin. He donned his armour and girded himself with his sword. He grasped his spear firmly and mounted his horse, al-Abjar. He bade farewell to ‘Abla. He was full of distress, he burnt with passion, and he grieved. Then he ordered her to climb into the palenquin. He said to her, “March away ahead of me in this desert place. Know, oh, cousin, that these days will be remembered for ever and ever. You will recall Antar and know that I protected you in my life and in my death. I am here behind you armed with my sword and my spear.” Then ‘Abla climbed into her palenquin. She sighed with sorrow on account of Antar, and her tears flowed down her cheeks.’

The second comes a few lines later : ‘When (the enemy) had heard Antar’s shout and had fled after seeing his dusky and dusty face, most of them returned to the camp. Only forty (variant, thirty, sic. Caussin de Perceval) of the raiding horsemen were left. They continued to follow him and trail him until they reached the Gazelle Pass. The women in the saddles and palenquins had passed through it as Antar was seated on the back of his mount, leaning in pain on his spear. He guarded a locality within the pass. At one time he made a sign and moved. At another time he stood motionless. He reached the mouth of the pass, that narrow pass situated at the upper part of the road. Then his pains increased and his agony became acute.’

The specific mention of the Gazelle Pass indicates that one source of this climactic scene is unquestionably the final part of the story of Rabi‘a ibn Muqaddam (see page 60). Nonetheless, since certain details – the fact that the pass is not specified nor is the terrain other than open – are characteristic of the *Ḥijāzīya,* the question can be posed: is Lyall’s charge of plagiarism applicable to all versions of the *Sīrat ‘Antara* or only to some? Several of the unnamed narrators might have transmitted accounts of the death of Antar which differed markedly from the story of the death of Rabī‘a, although all seem to share the icon-like figure of a dead knight held in suspense upon the back of his horse, a figure of awe watched by his foes.

The episode of the palenquin and the ride of ‘Abla on Antar’s steed, al-Abjar, does not fit into the early and scanty accounts of the death of ‘Antara who is a solitary figure. Nor does this protracted sequence and farewell prior to the hero’s death characterize the story of the lonely death of Rabī‘a ibn Muqaddam where there is no heroine. This stage by stage death is ideal material for oral story-telling and for an exciting presentation. Its components would seem to have been ‘discovered’ in the tenth or eleventh centuries and to have been systematically inserted into the plot to bridge the period between the fatal bow short of al-Asad al-Rahīṣ and the demise of Antar on al-Abjar's back in the Gazelle Pass or in some other locality. Nothing substantial in 'Antara's *Mu'allaqa* offers a signal, an inspiration. In its verses the poet alludes to a change of mount, from a horse to a camel. In one verse he rides through the night upon a black, well bridled mare, not al-Abjar. This is followed by a desire to ride to 'Abla's dwelling on a Shadanī she-camel which the poet, in turn, compares to an ostrich which is 'like a litter laid upon a sort of bier'. (See Arberry *The Seven Odes,* p. 180).

The verses which relate to the death of King Ahab in Kings I, chapter 22, vv. 1-38, and Chronicles II, chapter 18, vv. 28-34, and the slightly similar death story of King Josiah in Chronicles II, chapter 35, vv. 22-24 introduce:

a) a fatal bow shot
b) a disguise adopted by one of two principal characters
c) the upright and supported body of a dying king
d) his demise at eventide.

These are traceable in the sequence of events in the canonical versions of the *Sīrat 'Antara.* One might suggest that a part loan from the Old Testament is as pertinent as any 'crib' from the death of Rabī'a. Would a borrowing come from Jewish, Frankish or Oriental Christian sources? Extensive Jewish material in the *Sīra* has been referred to on pages 65 & 66. Despite this, Islamic *littérateurs* seem to have had some regard for King Ahab whose realm was classed alongside those of Alexander and Solomon. King Akhāb ibn 'Umrī and his kingdom are referred to, for example, by al-Jāḥiẓ in his *Kitāb al-Tarbī' wal-tadwīr* (ed. by C. Pellat, Damascus, 1955, p. 3, French text, and p. 51, Arabic text).

Oriental Christian inspiration is also possible, particularly where it relates to a figure held in suspense. The following fantastic description of the rites of Oriental Christianity or an 'orientalized' Christianity appears in the heart of the *Sīra* (Section 81). As Najran in the Yemen is specifically mentioned the legends of the Yemen and St. Phemion of Najran may be one source of this account. Byzantium, the Monophysites of Ghassānland or reports of Santiago de Compostela might have inspired other details. Coptic inspiration seems even more likely. I have already alluded to the Coptic character of parts of the *Sīra.* Apart from the talismanic 'stories' which are characteristic of the Pharaonic *barbā* in Coptic tales, there is something in the following passage which matches the *Mu'allaqa* (the hanging church), the oldest Coptic church in Cairo built in the Fortress of Babylon. This church once had a sycamore panel over its entrance. This panel, which still survives, represents the entrance of Our Lord into Jerusalem on Palm Sunday. This church became the seat of the Coptic Patriarchate in 1039 A.D.

'Yazīd ibn 'Abd al-Madān was one of the kings of the land of Najrān. This king had built a palace in the land. None had seen the like of it. Beside it he had built a church. It was an acre in length and an acre in breadth. He had it built to the height of seven stories. The span of each floor was twenty cubits, and the breadth of its wall was ten cubits. Within it he placed statues and images of gold and silver, jewels and coral. For this church he assembled a company of monks and women of beauty and grace. He furnished it with silks, and he placed a sanctuary in the middle of it. In the heart of the sanctuary he fixed an image of iron. Its eyes were rubies. He raised the four corners of the sanctuary, its ceiling and the court of its shrine by using magnetic stones. He suspended (*'allaqa*) that image from above, and he left it so floating in the air. The stones on all sides attracted it magnetically, and it remained stationary and in suspense because a magnetic object attracts iron. The narrator said – offerings and gifts came to it from all countries.

In this shrine there were three hundred and sixty monks among whom was a monk who had lived since the days of Our Lord Jesus. It had one hundred and sixty servers who each day and night lit five *qinṭārs* of oil and seven *qinṭārs* of good wax. In the shrine there were three hundred and sixty nuns.

Each year many folk visited this place on a certain day. They came there from every quarter of the globe. Now that day was Palm Sunday. There was buying and selling and feasting and festivities for a whole month. The famous monk worked many miracles and wonders. He disclosed divine prophesies and mystical revelations. As for the builder who had designed it and who had also built the palace, King 'Abd al-Madān ordered him to appear before his presence. He said to him, "Can you build the like of it if someone asked you to do so?" "Yes," he replied, "I know a keystone of the church and the palace. Were it to collapse then the palace and the church would fall to the ground." The king was afraid that he would not serve him for the stipend fixed and that he would destroy what he had built. So he gave the command that they should cast him from the roof. He died where he fell, hurled onto the ground. King 'Abd al-Madān, he and all his brethren and his boon companions never ceased to enjoy the drinking of wine in this church. They used to call it *al-bī'a*. The poets used to come to them from all regions and districts. 'Amr ibn Ma'dī Karib was one of their dearest companions since he possessed an eloquent tongue, and he was their companion in their feasting.'

Paradoxically, this rather scurrilous description can be matched in Christendom by varied accounts of Muhammad's embalmed remains – obviously confused with the Ka'ba – which were suspended and lit by tapers and by the magnetic power of a carbuncle high above the ground. Some reference to this occurs in the

Historia de Mahumete by Hildebert de Tours (d. 1134 A.D.). D'Aubigné in his *Les Tragiques, Jugement*, says:

> Là cette caravanne et bigotte et badine
> adore Mahomet dans le fer estendu
> que la voute d' aymant tient en l'air suspendu
> là se crève les yeux la bande musulmane
> pour, après lieu si sainct, ne voir chose prophane (2).

In Christian accounts figures of Muhammad and Apolin were consulted as oracles and carried around as guardian of the Saracens.

Whatever hypotheses regarding the sources which furnished sundry material for Antar's death one chooses to adopt, hypotheses which some day may be traced to an indisputable calque, current thought takes a less hostile view than Lyall about the art of fusing and refashioning Ancient Arabian and non-Arabian source material. Cedric Dover in pages 183 and 184 of his article in *Phylon* is unreserved in his praise:

'Lyall, for example, has him die without benefit of romance, as if Lyall or anyone else knew exactly how he died; but the Arabs arranged it much more artistically through a poisoned arrow shot by a perfidious enemy whose life he had spared. Mortally wounded, he returns homewards with his wife and his caravan, his pursuers at a respectable distance behind him. Clouston, translating Caussin de Perceval, continues the story:

"At the close of day they reach the Valley of the Gazelles, not far from the tribe of Abs. Surrounded by inaccessible mountains, it could only be entered from the desert side by a narrow and tortuous pass, where three horsemen could scarcely ride abreast . . . Here Antar stands alone as a sentinel at the end of the gorge, opposite the plain and the Arabs who are following him from afar . . . He points the end of his spear in the ground, and leaning against the stem, like a resting warrior allowing his horse to recover its breath, he stands motionless at the end of the pass."

Meanwhile, the caravan and his beloved Abla reach the security of the tribe. His pursuers catch up with him, but are afraid to attack the venerable knight, though they know him to be wounded. The next morning they realize the trick he has played upon them to allow his wife and followers to escape: it is a dead man, propped up by a spear, who faces them, but still they are afraid to prove it. Presently Abjer is disturbed by one of their mares, and the warrior "who made all Arabia tremble" falls, a stiff corpse, to the ground. The winged horse, who will serve no other master, returns to the freedom of the desert. His enemies mourn him in the Arab way:

"Glory to thee, brave warrior! During thy life thou hast been the defender and leader of thy tribe; and now, even in death, thou hast served thy brethren by the terror of thy corpse and of thy gallant name. May thy soul live forever! May the refreshing dews always moisten the ground of this thy last great exploit! "

It is a noble ending, magnificently conceived, to an undying romance that is one of the rare achievements of the human mind.'

Notes

1. The early French translations of Antar omitted the urination of Antar and 'Abla. They did so on grounds of good taste and they seem to have assumed that it indicated a vulgar corruption of the text. In fact the story is inspired by pre-Islamic stories of Durayd ibn al-Simma who is referred to throughout the *Sīrat 'Antara.*. The following passages are to be found in the *'Uyūn al-Akhbār* of Ibn Qutayba (Dār al-Kutub al-Miṣriyya edition 1349/ 1930) volume four, *Kitāb al-Nisā'*, page 46.
   Ibn al-Kalbī said, 'Durayd ibn al-Ṣimma sought the hand of Khansā' bint 'Amr. So she sent her servant girl and said, "When Durayd urinates see whether he squats like a dog or whether he scatters his water wide". The maiden said to her, "He scatters it wide". So she said "I have no need of him"! (var, 'She said to her, "Spy on Durayd and look when he urinates. If you find that his urine splits the ground then in it there are lasting qualities, but if you find it spreads over the surface of the ground then there is no merit in it" ').
2. The legend of the suspended coffin of Muhammad and all the elements of legend which would appear to be at the root of the story of the magnetised church of Najrān are discussed by Professor Charles Pellat, 'Note sur la légende relative au cercueil de Mahomet' *Bulletin des Etudes Arabes*, 23, (Alger, 1945) pp. 112-3.

SOURCES

Plate 10: Antar and his steed Abjar, invincible in battle, although outnumbered and suffering frequent wounds.

'Each glad survivor of the fierce affray
Will tell thee truly how I love the fight,
How little care I have to share the spoils.
The fiercest warrior armed *cap-à-piè,* –
No craven coward he to yield or fly,
But one whose onslaught e'en the bravest dread, –
Assails me; grasping in my quick right hand
A lance, in fashion like a weaver's beam,'

(from E.H. Palmer, *The* Mu'allaqa *of 'Antara*)

CHAPTER 6 : ANTAR'S AFRICAN EXPLOITS AND EUROPEAN SOURCES IN THE COMPOSITION OF THE SĪRA.

I

The *Sīrat Antara* is a popular comment on a debate which long divided the lettered of Islam. This debate challenged the accepted view of Ḥām and his offspring as the divinely ordained servant of his Semitic brother. It also pursued the investigation of the reason for differences between the races, why some were dark and others light, and how these differences influenced moral conduct, humours and physical features.

The outstanding ninth century Basran man of letters, al-Jāḥiẓ, himself part African in his origins, expressed his ideas in an apologia for the peoples of the Southern Continent. He called it The book of pride and superiority of the 'blacks' over the 'whites', *Kitāb fakhr al-Sūdān 'alā l-Bīḍān* (1). It was a controversial book. In it he argued from conviction, or offered a hypothesis which he wished to defend, that the 'blacks', especially the Indians, surpassed the 'whites' in certain respects. He quoted the early poets, and he reported stories which he had heard in Basra from merchants and travellers whom he had met. The bulk of his information on Africa was drawn from the eastern coast of the continent. Where he mentioned the Ḥabash he appeared to indicate the Abyssinians. The Barbar in his view inhabited Somaliland, while the Fezzān, the Nubians and the Zaghāwa were situated in the eastern Sahara and along the Sudanic Nile.

The ideas of al-Jāḥiẓ on Africans are to be found in several of his writings. In his *Kitāb al-bayān wal-tabyīn* (2), the Zanj are particularly praised for their rhetoric and eloquence. His views were challenged by others including Marvazī. He drew attention to the fact that the Africans and the Indians dwelt in the First Clime. This cut through the Red Sea, Abyssinia, the Nile, Jarmī (Djarma in Niger or Germa in the Fezzān), the capital of al-Ḥabasha, and Dongola, the capital of Nubia. This clime ended in the western sea. As the negroes were remote from a temperate clime their features had changed, and their colour had turned to black by reason of the heat. They had repulsive features which included protruding eyes, flat noses, wide nostrils and giant stature. Heat expanded objects and opened the hidden so that the eye could behold it. The souls of the negroes were filled with mirth, and they were fond of play and jesting.

Marvazī insisted that light was always superior to darkness. Blackness had a certain utility. It was restful to the eyes, and it could cast terror in the heart of an enemy (3). It was not a natural colour. It was impure. The blackness of the Ethiopians and the Zanj was a mark of inferiority. Al-Hamdānī, the Yemenite author of the *Iklīl* and *Ṣifat Jazīrat al-'Arab* (4) attributed the brutality of the Nubians, the Ethiopians, the Zanj and the southern Indians to the influence of Scorpion and Mars. The northern Hamites were different because of the combination of Venus and Mars. They were passionate and flirtatious, bold and treacherous. Cancer was combined with the moon in the Maghrib. This combination explained their commercial acumen and their great prosperity.

The relation of the Negus, the supreme ruler of Ethiopia, to the Arabians further complicated these medieval theories. Abraha, the Abyssinian, and Maḥmūd, his elephant, had tried to destroy the Ka'ba in Mecca, whereas Aṣḥuma or 'Armah or whoever was his successor, had welcomed the persecuted followers of the Prophet, and there were some who went as far as to allege that this Negus had died a Muslim. The *Sīrat 'Antara* is not concerned with these discussions. Human reconciliation is the triumph of its hero. His feats illustrate neither racial discord nor racial superiority. To quote the poet of 'Abs, 'Blackskinned they are, oh, daughter of Mālik, yet their hearts are white just like the sun at dawn.'

All the same a warrior king who is called the Negus, supreme ruler and tax gatherer, is present in the romance, and lip service is paid to the acknowledged status of this ruler and his people in the annals of Islam. Two reasons for his inclusion are apparent. One was an artistic device to permit the hero to discover his maternal kinsfolk. The other was to introduce a ruler from the southern continent in the campaigns of 'Antar ibn Shaddād. The person of this ruler and his lands exemplify kingship in Black Africa. The title of Negus was a convenient label to identify him for listeners and readers of the romance.

This Negus is in fact a very shadowy figure indeed who enters the story at a point where the black knight of Arabia had already learnt of his ancestry in the kingdom of Hammām. Attention may be drawn to the skilful reference by the story-teller to the relationship between a tree palace (*shajarat al-mulk*), ascended by steps, and a tree of proud lineage and kingship (*shajarat al-nasab*). A family tree, the branches of which are discovered by heroic adventure and by the removal of supernatural obstacles, is likened to a gigantic baobab or cotton tree, the shape of which suggests an inverted object, a tree with its roots spreading forth in the sky moistened by clouds and rain. A tree with roots buried deep in the ground or watered by subterranean pools or murky swamps would be unbecoming for a treetop royalty, an idea borrowed from Islamic geographers.

As Antar ascends the tree-top palace in captivity and regains his freedom at its summit so the ties of kinship are progressively disclosed to him, each branch of Ḥām meeting in a common trunk. The tree is ancient. It is guarded by taboos and thunderbirds. Close by it is a sword fixed in a mound or pyramid. The whole complex is a source of power which can summon rain, floods and lightening to protect the kingdom. The sacred tree is the central 'structure' in this part of the *Sīrat 'Antara.* This tree and its sister – a tree of silent barter – are referred to once again in the exploits which take Antar to Egypt, North Africa and Spain, the realm of the giant Janṭāyil. Entry past this tree is a symbolic act which resolves the tale and highlights the sub-plots embedded in the narrative.

Kingship and sacred trees are to be found in medieval European cycles. Charlemagne, Doon de Mayence and Garin de Monglane were born on the same day, at the same hour and amid remarkable phenomena. A thunderbolt fell before the palaces of the three infant heroes. From the ditches hollowed by the thunder and lightening there grew three Jesse trees. Each tree was high and straight, in full flower and green with leaves, symbolic of three glorious lineages, those of Charlemagne, Doon de Mayence and Garin de Monglane (5). The magic tree in these cycles and in the *Sīrat 'Antara* serve a similar function, symbolizing lineal ties between warrior barons and kings.

II

The links between Africa and Arabia were very ancient. There are allusions to the Somali coast in pre-Islamic verse (6). It is not unreasonable to assume that travellers' tales as well as reports by traders influenced the imaginations of storytellers. It may be conjectured that the plot of Antar's adventures in 'Umān, the Yemen and Africa are an elaboration from early tales of expeditions to secure the major routes and sources of gold, frankincense and myrrh in Southern Arabia and in regions of Africa. These tales were expanded and incorporated into foundation myths which told of Arab expeditions into lands at the source of the Nile, the deserts of the Zaghāwa and the districts bordering Chad, Kānem and Bornu, perhaps also to Ghana. The epics of Sayf ibn Dhī Yazan and the Banū Hilal were borrowed to describe the *héros civilisateurs,* the Arab or Muslim founders of African kingdoms.

There are customs in the Horn of Africa which seem to match some details in the *Sīrat 'Antara.* Where Sir Richard Burton describes the Somalis in pages of his *First footsteps in East Africa* he refers to their beliefs in holy trees and their sacrifice of she-camels in the month of Sabuh. They sanctified New Year's Day (*Dubshid*), and they held feasts and lit bonfires. Burton noted certain parallels with the Persian Nō Rūz, and he had sympathy with the belief held by some

Somalis that the 'Furs' or Ancient Persians once ruled their lands. This belief may have been connected with adventures of Persian mercenaries of Sayf ibn Dhī Yazan, the sons of Sayf.

According to Burton, at certain unlucky periods when the moon was in ill-omened asterisms those Somalis who died were placed in bundles of matting upon a tree. Their burial, it was thought, would cause grievous loss to the tribe. The Galla sacred groves were centres of pilgrimage where sacrifices of animals were made. Sycamores were venerated and were adorned with offerings of food, clothes, honey and smeared grease.

Rites such as these were widespread in Hamitic Africa. Herodotus alludes to Ethiopia's (Meroe's) table of the sun, the meadow of boiled flesh and the burial of the dried bones of divine kings in crystal cylinders. Strabo reports forests of ebony-trees, and a mountain of flame which overhung the sea, called by the Greeks 'the chariot of the gods'. These accounts and others like them seem to represent sophisticated representation of rituals which originated in primitive beliefs of the Hamites. Such customs appear in the *Sīrat 'Antara.* They are described as *Majūsīya,* animism or the cult of fire. The centre of adoration is a tree and associated with it is a tree of silent barter. The latter is not the misleading silent barter in gold, a custom misunderstood by some Arab geographers (7) but a place of exchange of cloth or other items of merchandise. Such exchanges are plausible and are confirmed in other ancient and medieval accounts (8). Here there is an allusion to an authentic African and Asian custom which links ritual and marketing and bears the hall-mark of authenticity.

The literary sources for Africa and its peoples in the *Sīrat 'Antara* have already been mentioned. Those found in Arabic geographical literature are the easiest to identify. One of them is Marvazī, or the source of Marvazī, the Persian merchant called Ḥasan ibn 'Amr al-Sīrāfī who visited Kānem and Chad in the tenth century. The Kānem he knew was the land of two royal trees. Did the composers of the *Sīra* use the narratives of Marvazī or Ḥasan? I am inclined to doubt this. None of the pejorative theories of Marvazī about the Ethiopians appear in the text of the *Sīra,* nor do other parts of Marvazī which describe other countries and regions of the globe appear in its pages. The second important source is al-Mas'ūdī, or a source known to al-Mas'udī. The following comparison between al-Mas'ūdī and the text of the *Sīra* highlights the similarities and draws attention to the differences.

al-Mas'ūdī (The fragmentary *Akhbār al-zamān wa 'ajā'ib al-buldān.*)	*Sīrat 'Antara*
1) The negroes wear skins, grass skirts and beasts' horns. The king wears red-dyed imported garments.	1) The negroes wear clothes dyed red, yellow and green. On their heads they wear conical head-dresses of fox-tails, pearls and bells.
2) They have a white rodent which they eat and call heavenly *manna* (9).	?
3) To invoke the rain they gather bones, heap them up and set them alight.	3) The bones of their dead enemies are burnt and scattered. The enemy is slain by the holy tree amidst tumultuous rains.
4) At weddings they smear their faces with a substance similar to ink.	4) Blue clothes are worn, and the left eye is painted with antimony.
5) The bridegroom is seated on a mound.	5) There is a mound or hill near the city of King Hammām.
6) They have a mighty tree where they hold a festival once a year. Weddings last three days.	6) An annual festival of three days occurs in March around the tree of fires and lights.
7) From the leaves of this tree they obtain supernatural blessing (*baraka*).	7) The blessing of the tree is to be found in the burnt bones of their enemies.

In at least two respects, the association of burnt bones and rain and an annual festival around a mighty tree, al-Mas'ūdī and the *Sīrat 'Antara* agree. In other respects the two accounts partly cohere or markedly differ. The author of Antar's adventures may well have known or read al-Mas'ūdī's works, but it would seem that the plot and text of part of the *Sīra* is not a direct quotation of al-Mas'ūdī. The overall landscape of the realm of King Hammām owes almost as much to Marvazī's description as to that of al-Mas'ūdī. No Arabic geographical source is sufficiently close to indicate a textual transfer.

The scene seems to have been observed or imagined by a Persian eye-witness. Professor Mary Boyce has pointed out a number of details which suggest an acquaintance with Zoroastrianism, though certain customs contradict basic Zoroastrian beliefs (10). A veneration of trees is a part of old orthodox Zoroastrianism. Fire, lamps and candles are regularly used in worship. Hence the epithet, fires and lights, would seem perfectly in keeping with a Zoroastrian cult, and sacred trees were those which were most ancient and huge. The traditional Zoroastrian New

Year is in March (Nō Rūz), and this is a great time for observances. At such a time charity given to the poor would be very proper, similarly the use of incense and rose water in worship. Nearly all Zoroastrian sacred trees have a pool or spring beside them, so the reference to a marble basin would seem fitting in the context. Every Zoroastrian has to bring some gift when he visits a sacred place. Anything sweet-scented is a fit offering although Professor Boyce knows of no parallel to smearing the tree with perfume, rose water and musk. The wearing of blue garments is proper to the lower orders in Zoroastrianism, those who were neither priests nor warriors.

On the other hand there are customs wholly abhorrent to Zoroastrians. The slaughter of young camels is un-Zoroastrian since in that faith it is forbidden to kill any immature beast. The burning of the bones of an enemy is deplorable and a desecration of the sacred fire. Fire as a weapon of destruction is quite un-Zoroastrian. The feeding of birds is a pious act but the slaughter of camels to feed them would be an act of impiety since camels are held in high regard as are the birds, particularly vultures.

The disposal of the dead reveal a confusion of two known Zoroastian practices. One custom was to embalm the body. The bones were left intact but the brain and entrails were removed. The second custom was to expose the body intact. The birds and beasts reduced it to bare bones. These were gathered into a container made of stone or earthenware. A cloth bag seems strange particularly as the disposal of the bones in the kingdom of Hammām preceded the disposal of the flesh by exposure or consumption by carrion.

How are the similarities and differences to be explained? One possibility is that the whole scenario is a Persian fantasy. It could have been imagined by a story-teller who had never visited Africa but knew India and was familiar with Zoroastrianism. Another possibility is that a Persian who travelled to Africa, perhaps a merchant, related his adventures to his friends who were knowledge-able in Zoroastrian customs. His tale would have aroused their curiosity. Some of them might have been familiar with the tall *jag* trees (the ebony tree) of Kerman, Jask, Baluchistan and India. Another possibility is a diffusion of certain Zoroastian beliefs from Persia or the Persian occupied Yemen into the Horn of Africa (11).

Folktale and trade went hand in hand. The epic tale of Sayf ibn Dhī Yazan was introduced to Africa by merchants and missionaries. The exploits of Abū Zayd and the Banū Hilāl were also borrowed and reinterpreted. The epic of Sayf was principally Persian in origin (12). It was of major importance as a lineal manifesto for the ruler of Kānem before the thirteenth century (13). Despite criticism by Egyptian scholars, the kings of Kānem and Bornu maintained their claim to descent from Sayf. They argued that there was a link between the nothern Arabs, the Quraysh of 'Adnān, and the Sayfite house of Qaḥṭān from the Yemen. Both branches were united in the person of Ghālib who was a predecessor of the Prophet and an ancestor of many famous Arabs. Ties with the northern and the southern Arabs competed in the Islamised African states between the Sudan and Ghana. In Kānem and Bornu after about 1100 A.D. there was a tip in the balance in favour of southern Yemenite links at the expense of other links. The causes were internal and external, and the commercial ties between Kānem and Arabia must have been influential in arousing interest in the epic of Sayf and exhalting him as the founder-figure of the state.

Kānem, the Nile (Qūs and Aswan), the Beja port of 'Aydhāb on the Red Sea and Aden may have been a trade route before the thirteenth century. 'Kāremī (Kānemi?) ships, as they are called in Arabic accounts, plied between the African coast and Aden (14). This route was favoured because Sinai and North Arabia were threatened by the Crusaders after 1058 A.D. When the Ayyubid, Nūr al-Dīn ibn Zangī, captured Aden he determined a new rate of exchange for the copper from Kārem (Kānem?) and the spices from the Far East. The Crusaders had stimulated a revival of heroic sentiments in the Islamic East. 'Antara, Sayf and other men of valour were popular. The Yemen was remote from the Holy Land but its dwellers esteemed epic exploits of the Arabs. Sayf and his descendants were adventurers of valour. It was said that they had journeyed by sea, and their renown was widespread in 'Aydhāb, Jedda and along the banks of the Nile. 'Antara was a name not unknown to the Yemenites (15).

The romance of Sayf enjoyed a new lease of life during the Ayyubid and Mamluk age. His fame revived in the Yemen and in parts of Africa which had ties with the Yemen. The commerce followed a route along an axis east and west. Sayf entered the region of Chad from the Yemen via Egypt and the Sudan.

Sayf became a founder king, so, too, did Abū Zayd al-Hilālī who was described as a prince of Baghdad. 'Antara never inspired a royal line in Muslim Africa. He was an African whose claim to fame was acknowledged in Arabia itself. The tie between Antar and Africa was by descent from his mother who was related to the Negus. This king of 'Ethiopia' was symbolic of royalty in African Islam. He was not the king of Abyssinia, a Christian and a foe. Instead he symbolized the splendour of courtly Islam established in dynastic houses to the south of the Sahara. This king was to be enlisted to fight for the faith but his battles were waged not in Palestine but in Spain.

The Arabs conceived of the ruler of this Muslim 'Ethiopia' as the supreme king of Muslim Black Africa. He enjoyed a rank comparable to Chosroes, Caesar and other Oriental potentates. This supreme ruler was a king of gold. Sometimes 'Ghāna' was this king. The 'gold king' appears in Arabic sources as early as Almoravid times (the eleventh century). He is portrayed by the geographer Yāqūt (1220 A.D.) as the ruler of the gold land of Zāfūn. The Almoravids, the rulers of the Sahara and Morocco, seemed to have acknowledged that he had some kind of authority over them. The mysterious king of Zāfūn was tall, dark-skinned, and his eyes were red. The palms of his hands were yellow or were dyed the colour of saffron. This dye denoted a warrior who had killed many in combat. Toledo in Spain was famous for this dye. Yellow was symbolic of both copper and gold. It was because of this copper and gold that his lands attained fame in east and west. He wore a white mantle, and he always rode on horseback. He never dismounted, not even before the Almoravid kings and princes of Morocco and Spain (16).

III

Sayf and Kānem are pointers to the Yemen. Many stories about Sayf travelled east and west. There was another major Islamic axis of trade. It ran from north to south and south to north and ended in Spain where Arab and Berber, African and Frank fought for their faiths and exchanged their riches, their legends and their arts. The 'gold king' of Africa is well known in Islamic sources. The king of 'Ethiopia' also appears in Western *Chansons de geste.* A warrior king clad in beaten gold fights among the Saracens against Roland and his companions in the *Chanson de Roland.*

An African there was of Afric, too,
Was called Malquiant, the son of king Malcude;
Harnessed he is in gold from head to foot,
None in the sun so glitters to the view.
He rides a horse that he called Saut-Perdu;
No steed could rival the swiftness of its hoofs.
He strikes Anseis in mid-shield square and true,
He sheares away the scarlet and the blue,
Rips the mailed skirt of the hauberk of proof.
Into the body drives the steel and the wood.
The count falls dead, his days have met their doom.
The French all say: "Brave lord, alack for you!" (17)

Malquiant is slain by Archbishop Turpin (Tilpinus of Rheims) who strikes him hard on his Toledo shield and unseats him from his horse.

Malquiant is only one of the major African kings in the *Chanson.* Several of them are mentioned and often they are related. Marganice, the uncle of Marsile, governed Carthage, Alferne and Garamile,

And Ethiopia, a land accursed and vile.
In his command are all the Negro tribes:
Thick are their noses, their ears are very wide;
Full fifty thousand (18) are gathered in their lines,
Boldly and fast and furiously they ride
Yelling aloud the Paynim battle cry. (19)

In the pages of the *Chanson de Roland* and to a greater or lesser degree in other *Chansons de geste,* the rulers and warriors of Islam are patterned on a heroic character, a paynim African king. It is in Spain that African personalities in the *Sīrat 'Antara* and the Old French tales and romances most clearly meet.

It has been proposed that the Almoravid victory at al-Zallāqa near Badajoz in 1086 A.D. left a memory of defeat which coloured the *Chanson de Roland* and other Western romances. To cite T. Atkinson Jenkins in his Introduction to *La Chanson de Roland* (20).

'Thorold [of Envermeu, Turoldus of the Oxford *Roland*] may have modeled his battle of Roncesvaux upon one or more of the outstanding battles of his own day. If one familiar with the Rol. read for the first time the details of the battle of Dorylaeum (1097), he will be surprised by several striking resemblances in events and circumstances. . .

Surely, these resemblances are at least arresting, and no less so are similarities between the disposition of Marsile's forces at Roncesvaux and those of Yûsuf (ibn Tashfin's) troops at the battle of Zalaca (1086)

The conflict in *Roland* is imagined as falling into three main encounters: Aelroth is the first paynim commander to be defeated, then King Marsile comes up with his vast army (v. 1448) and is only repulsed with the greatest difficulty; finally, the Algalife, with 50.000 negroes, finishes the slaughter of the Christians (v. 1913 ff.). At Zalaca, as described by Dozy (*Spanish Islam,* 1913, pp. 696-98), an advance-guard of Andalusian Arabs is first dispersed by King Alphonso, the main body under Yûsuf being held in reserve, concealed by mountains (cf. *Rol.* v. 1449); When these are engaged, a long and desperate fight ensues with varying fortunes. Finally, the Christians are utterly routed by the onset of a body of savage negro guards, hitherto held in reserve. The brave King of Seville is wounded in the hand as is King Marsile in *Roland* (v. 1903). It would seem probable that the poet of *Roland* had listened to accounts of this crushing defeat of Alphonso VI of Castile, a defeat which made Moslem Spain little else than a province of the empire of Morocco and filled Christian France with alarm.' (21).

The catastrophe of al-Zallaya was preceded by another memory of defeat, the sack of Santiago de Compostela in 997 A.D. by al-Manṣūr of Cordoba. I have mentioned that Bernhard Heller proposed that the Emperor of the Mediterranean in the *Sīrat 'Antara,* Janṭāyil, was none other than Santiago (St. James or Yāqūb) of Compostela (22). This identification is debatable. This foe of Antar might have had other Spanish sources for his name.

But if Janṭāyil and Santiago are identical, Compostela appears as a place for the exchange of ideas between Arab story-teller (*shā'ir*) and Frankish jongleur and troubadour. One may recall the richness and the cosmopolitan character of the not so distant court of Burgos under Alfonso VIII who reigned between 1158 and 1214 A.D. Alfonso married Eleanor, sister of Richard Coeur de Lion, daughter of King Henry II of England and Eleanor of Aquitaine, daughter of the first troubadour. Alfonso fetched his bride in 1170 A.D. accompanied by thirty known troubadours, and his musicians included Christians, Arabs and Jews.

The shrine of St. James came to be regarded as the centre of opposition to the triumph of Islam. In al-Andalus all had heard of Compostela which, to borrow the expression of an Arab chronicler, was to Christians what the Meccan Ka'ba was to the Muslims. The expedition of al-Manṣūr of Cordoba in 997 A.D. was renowned in the chronicles. In August of that year the city was razed and the church of St. James demolished so effectively that on the morrow none would have supposed that it had ever existed.

It is not easy to find a connection between Africa and Compostela attested in records. However, the link is not Compostela itself but the town and port of Iria which lies to the south-west of Compostela. R. Dozy who wrote extensively about the romance of *Pseudo-Turpin* and its content noted:

'On the western coast of Galicia, approximately in the place where today stands the small town of El Padron, there was, in the time of the Romans, a city of note which bore the name of Iria, and which, before and after the Arab invasion, was the seat of a bishop, a suffragan of the metropolitan of Braga. In its neighbourhood was to be found, according to the general belief, the tomb of the apostle, St. James, which had been discovered in a miraculous way. One cannot be sure at what epoch this was, since one only has legends and apocryphal documents. But the epoch indicated by the *Historia Compostellana,* which states: during the reign of Alphonso the Chaste (791-842) and from the time of Charlemagne, is not too early in date, for it is certain that before the middle of the ninth century, Saint James's shrine was already a famous pilgrimage. This place became very rich thanks to the piety and munificence of the kings, the great, the pilgrims from all classes of society, who beheld a host of miracles performed there. Naturally it cast a shadow over Iria; However, this town, where, according to the tradition the ship which bore the body of Saint James had landed, and where his body had first been deposited, was also acknowledged to be a holy place, "Ilia", says an Arab historian speaking of the expedition of Al-Manṣūr against Compostela in 997, " is equally a place of veneration on account of James. Among the Christians it is counted second in status after the place where the tomb of this apostle is to be found. Pilgrims of the most distant countries, even Copts and Nubians, go there in large numbers" ' (23).

Galicia was a peculiarly religious meeting place for Africans and Franks.

There remain other Frankish personalities scattered within the *Sīrat 'Antara.* If they are not Crusaders, then they form a family of names, heroic characters who were borrowed *en bloc* by the compilers of the *Sīrat 'Antara* in order to symbolize the enemies of Islam or allies of Antar much in the same manner as Malquiant, Malcude, Marganice and Espaulart of Nubia were borrowed and distorted to assemble an army of paynims against whom Roland and Charlemagne and their allies fought for the triumph of the Cross and for Christendom.

The following table suggests personalities whose names are shared by the *Sīrat 'Antara* and Western *Chansons de geste.* In *Pseudo Turpin* the major African king is called Agolandus (Agolant) who invades Spain with a large army. He is challenged by Charlemagne who besieges him in Pamplona. A meeting takes place between Agolant and Charles. The former is impressed by the latter's knowledge of Arabic which he had learnt in Toledo when he was a boy. In the subsequent battle Agolant is slain. Agolant became a popular figure in the fiction of the twelfth century when his renown was disseminated in *Chansons de geste.* His son was named Aumont and his father wished to crown him king of Rome.

Malquid 1) Malcude Maelgut	Agolandus : Baligant Aigolandus : Beligandus	Malquiant Malquidant 2)
3) *al-Gharandus* (King of Alexandria in *Sīrat 'Antara*)	African Commander, ruler of Babylon (Cairo), the Algalife with 50.000 negroes.	*Caecilianus* (of Nubia Kikelai Kikelañ Ñokel 4) al-Kaikalag
	A Fatimid Caliph	
	This ruler seems to correspond to Yūsuf ibn Tāshfīn al-Murābiṭ or one of his African allies in the battle of Zallāqa.	Mankalā in *Sīrat 'Antara* *'Aflaq* (of Nubia) with 50.000 Nubians and Beja'

Characters and kingdoms in Sīrat 'Antara.	*Characters and kingdoms in Chansons de Geste.*
Men of Nubia	Men of Nubia
Trees of al-Kānem (deserts of Orghana)	Desert of Occian 5)
Alexandria: see 3) above.	Alexandria
	Arabum
	Persas
	Sarracenos
	Mauros
	Moabites (Almoravids) 6)
Maymūn ibn Raḥmūn ?	Maimonem of Mecca 7)
al-Dahmār/Damhār (ibn Dīnār?)	Altumaiorem/Altumajor 8)
	Texephinum (Tāshfīn) 9)
'Iṭrūn/'Uṭrūn	Godron/Gormont 10)
Kūbart	Guibert 11)
Sūbart/Mūbart/Nūbart	Isembart 12)
Bīmund (variants)	Bohemund 13)
Mardūs	Moradas 14)
Jufrān/Kundafarūn	Jefroi/Geoffroy 15)
Khīlajān	Gui le Jeune 16)
Ghaḍanfar/Ghaḍafar	Godifer/Alagolofure 17)
	Galafres 18)
Marūnis/Marīnus	Marganice (Algalife = al-Khalīfa) 19)
Qarqāqays (Cyricus)	Kargys 20)

1) Malcude is an African king in the *Chanson de Roland.* The name has been explained by *Male-cogitat* but it is also close to Malacoutia 'Mauvaise Gothie' which was the name given by the Christians of the Spanish North to the mixed Berber inhabited localities of Astorga and Leon. These Berbers were enemies of the Asturians. See R. Dozy, *Recherches sur L'Histoire et la Littérature de l'Espagne,* 1881, Tome I, ppl 123-127. It is not clear whether this name can have any bearing on Agolandus/Baligant. Any derivation seems improbable.

2) Malquiant/Malquidant is the son of (1). He is described as an African in the *Chanson de Roland.* He is possibly a Berber. Here likewise there is no clear relation to Agolandus, although Malquiant could be changed to Baligant/ Beligandus. The usual explanation for this name is *Mal-cuidant* or *Male-cogitantem.*

3) Al-Gharandus, or Hermes ibn al-Gharandus who is King of Alexandria in the *Sīrat 'Antara.* This name could have been changed to Agolandus. A switch of locality from Alexandria to Babylon (Cairo) is minor.

4) Caecilianus is the likely origin of Kikelañ, al-Kaikalag and Ñokel (one hypothetical explanation for Mankalā(n) in the *Sīrat 'Antara*).

5) al-Kānem and Occian. Although al-Kānem is never mentioned in the *Sīra* by name, it is clear that the 'two trees' are derived from a description of that region. Occian in the *Chanson de Roland* and in other *gestes* may have some connection with this same district. The whereabouts of Occian has not been resolved although it has been suggested that some part of Asia Minor is intended. Occian is referred to as *Occian al desert.* It boasted skilled horsemen, and its warriors were thick skinned, like leather, so that they were able to dispense with any form of helm and mail. According to T. Atkinson Jenkins, *La Chanson de Roland,* D. C. Heath & Coy., 1924, p. 227, this region is to be identified with the Theme of Opsicianum, the capital of which was Nicea. The inhabitants were skilled in war, and Opsicianum bordered on the desert of Lycaonia. At one point they fight alongside the giants of Malpreis/Malprose in the army of the *Amīr* Baligant, likewise the Ormaleis.

It is possible to see these names as African names, particularly as it has been argued that the Turcs, Turs, etc., may not refer to the Turks but to the Tarja of the Sahara, possibly to the Tuareg whose presence in Spain was likely to be known. I am impressed but not convinced by Professor L. P. Harvey's arguments that the Ghamra like 'Amazon' Nugeymath Turquia-whose companions armed with bows fought among the Almoravids outside Valencia held by the Cid is a personification of the Tuareg or another race of negroid warriors from the desert (See Nugeymath Turquia: Primera Cronica General, Chapter 956, *Journal of Semitic Studies,* Vol XIII, 1968, and my *Saharan Myth and Saga,* Oxford, pp 31, 39). At the same time I suspect that Nugeymath Turquia (one variant is *mejeyma turia*) may be a garbled, inverted and metathetic form of Zarqā' (al)-Yamāma, who was a legendary black-eyed Yemenite woman who could see for a distance of three days. In a different guise she appears in Almoravid inspired legends about heroes killed by blind bowmen in the Western Sahara (see my *Saharan Myth and Saga,* p. 151). If fragments of this Yemenite romance could have been incorporated within the *Primera Cronica General* of Alfonso X (El Sabio), completed in c 1289 AD, then borrowings from Antar's exploits are even more likely.

According to al-Mas'ūdī (d. 956/57 A.D.), see Cuoq, *Recueil,* p. 60, the Western Abyssinians included several peoples and towns among them the Zaghāwa, Kawkaw, the Mabras, the Qūmāṭi or Qirmaṭn, the Dūwila (possibly Zawīla) and the Qarma. Professor C. Pellat has proposed that the Qūmāṭi and

Qirmaṭn may indicate the Garamantes and Qarma the town of Jerma in the Fezzān. Garmalie in the *Chanson de Roland* may refer to Jerma or Garama, nor can Ormaleis be excluded as a variant of this name. Malpreis and Malprose could also refer to the Fezzān if these are variants of Mabras. The latter may refer to the Libyan Pharusii who according to Strabo crossed the desert fitting water skins beneath their horses' bellies. They came to Syrtis on the Libyan coast bringing gold with them along the trans-Saharan routes. Their name may survive in the well of Mā' al-Faras or Māfaras, presumably the Mabras mentioned by al-Mas 'ūdī. Mā' al-Faras, Mafaras, Mabras with variants could explain the name of Malpreis or Pharusii that of Malprose.

Occian could also be sited in the same desert region. If this is correct then the kingdom of Orghana on medieval maps is a plausible explanation. There are at least three hypotheses for this name.

The kingdom of Orghana is described by a Spanish Franciscan in the middle of the fourteenth century as adjacent to the Rio del Oro and Guynoa. See *Book of the Knowledge of the World,* Hakluyt Society, 1912, Series II, Vol. XXIX, p. 31:

'This kingdom marches with the kingdom of ORGANA in which also there is much desert, and on another side with the RIO DEL ORO which they call NILO. And further out, in the ZAHARA there are three very high mountains, which are very populous. The first mountain is called ORGAN where is the head of the kingdom where the King is crowned. The second is called TAMAR because there is in it many palm trees. The third is called TIMER [Arabic *tibr* gold] because here the people on the river banks collect much gold; we cannot give the quantity but there is much. The king of ORGANA has for his device a white flag with a green palm tree and two keys.'

According to Sir Richmond Palmer, *The Bornu Sahara and the Sudan,* London, 1936, pp. 197-209, Organa is al-Kānem, and he argues from Catalan maps that a Saharan kingdom, Tuareg ruled or Zaghāwa dominated, adjacent to Nubia is meant. Raymond Mauny, *Tableau Géographique del 'Ouest Africain au Moyen Age,* I.F.A.N., Dakar, 1961, p. 41, argues that Reggan in Algeria is more likely, and the king in question was a Tuareg ruler of the Hoggar mountains. Orghana could also indicate the Auraghen, Tuareg nobility which originated from the Fezzān whose members divided into those near Ghat in Libya and those who settled north of the Niger. The king of Orghana could have been a Saharan ruler to the north of Lake Chad. In all these cases the desert of Occian could be located near Lake Chad, either in Kānem or in the Sahara to the north towards the Fezzān or westward towards the lands of the Almoravids. While it is true that horses were relatively few in these regions it is known from the geographers that the Zaghāwa possessed them. The kings of

Kānem forsook their capitals on the 'Nile' because of the mosquitoes which were harmful to both men and horses, the latter very highly prized. Horses were also highly prized in medieval Ghana.

6) The name Moabites seems to refer to the Almoravids (al-*Murābiṭūn*) in *Pseudo Turpin.* See Dozy, *op. cit.,* Tome 2, pp. 375, 376, 377, 378, 409.

7) Maymūn may relate to the Banū Maymūn who were the admirals of the Almoravids whose ships infested the Mediterranean from Spain to Syria. See Dozy, *ibid,* Tome 2, pp. 410-412. In *Pseudo Turpin* he fights on land in Sicily and Spain. In the *Sīrat 'Antara,* Maymūn ibn Raḥmūn and Saymūn ibn Raḥmūn are variants. Rāmūn is a common Arabic name for the Raymonds, lords of Barcelona in the eleventh century. Among the most famous is Ramon Berenguer, Rāy Mundū ibn Balanjīr ibn Burrīl who went on pilgrimage to Jerusalem in 1054 A.D. and who married into the aristocracy of Narbonne. Saymūn presumably relates to a Simon who is impossible to identify.

8) Altumaiorem of Cordoba (var. Altumaior and Altumajor) in *Pseudo Turpin* suggests the name which is in some way related to al-Dahmār/Damhār in the *Sīrat 'Antara.* According to Dozy, *ibid,* Tome 2, pp. 410-413, this name is to be identified with al-Manṣūr (Aumaçor) who was responsible for the destruction of Santiago de Compostela in 997 A.D. Professor C. Pellat, in *Studia Islamica,* XXII, Paris, 1965, p. 35, identifies Altumajor with al-Manṣūr ibn Abī 'Āmir, and he therefore agrees with Dozy's identification. He also points out (p. 16) that 'Aumaçor (et var.) devenu nom commun pour désigner un dignitaire Sarrasin.'

9) The appearance of Tāshfīn, the Almoravid in *Pseudo Turpin* is a specific indication of an Almoravid presence in proper names listed among the Saracens; see Dozy, *ibid,* Tome 2, pp. 413-416. See also (6) above.

10) 'Iṭrūn (var. 'Uṭrūn) is the ruler of Tunis (Carthage) in the *Sīrat 'Antara.* His name may be related to Godron/Godrum, later changed to Gormont, who figures in the *geste* of *Gormont and Isembard.* Africans and Irish fought in the army of Gormont against King Louis III who killed Gormont in battle by a single blow of his lance which split him in half.

11) Kūbart is an ally of Antar and is the lord of the Island of Camphor and the Fortress of Crystal. Both are located in Libya, Greece or Southern Italy. In the Romance of *'Ajīb and Gharīb* the king of these localities has an Arabic name – al-Muzalzil. In the *Sīrat 'Antara* Kūbart is described as a Frank. His name seems to be Guibert. One recalls Guibert d'Andrenas who was the youngest of the sons of Aymeri (Aimer) de Narbonne in the *Cycle Narbonnais.*

12) Sūbart and Mūbart (var. Nūbart) appear individually in the *Sīrat 'Antara.* If they are a twin variation derived from Isembart they could relate to a traitor

baron who with Raoul de Cambrai rebelled against Louis the Fat, the son of Charlemagne. In the *Chanson de geste* of *Gormont and Isembart,* (10) above, he was an ally of the paynim king Gormont who invaded France from Spain and Africa with a Saracen army. If allowance is made for a change of role Sūbart might relate to Escopart, a negro Saracen giant who appears in *Boeve de Haumtone.*

13) Bohemund is variously spelt Buhmand, Bihmand, Buhmanẓ. Bernard Heller has suggested that Bohemund of Antioch is one of the only certain Crusading figures in the *Sīrat 'Antara.* This name could also be derived from romance sources and relate to a pre-Crusading personality.

14) Mardūs is the King of Qayrawān in the *Sīrat 'Antara.* This name is akin to that of Moradas who appears as a Saracen king in *Sir Ferumbras.*

15) In the *Sīrat 'Antara* al-Jufrān is the black-skinned son of Antar. His mother is Princess Maryam who is a Greek or a Byzantine. He is fostered by Kūbart, (11) above, since Maryam refuses to have him put to death. Antar dies before al-Jufrān goes to the Hijaz to combat his father who had slain his uncles, all of whom have Frankish names. Upon hearing of his true lineage and of the cause of past events he avenges the death of his father by fighting the enemies of the Banū 'Abs. After the ceremonial burial of Antar by all the heroes of ancient Arabia, al-Jufrān returns to Europe, or wherever his peninsula or island kingdom is located.

Bernhard Heller in his article on the *Sīrat 'Antara* in the *Encyclopedia of Islam* suggests that the name, al-Jufrān, conceals the Old French from Gaudefroy, Jefroi or Geffroi. He speculates that Godfrey de Bouillon is the inspiration for this name. Godfrey, and his brother Baldwin, led the First Crusade (1096-1099 A.D.) and was 'baron and defender of the Holy Sepulchre' until his death in 1100 A.D. These dates are later than 1080 A.D. the highly suspect though stated date for the *Ḥijāzīya.* Al-Jufrān might allude to Gaufroi, King of Denmark, the father of Duke Ogier, a formidable opponent of the Saracens in the *Chanson de Roland,* or Geoffrey of Anjou, the standard bearer of Charlemagne. Kundafarūn – a name which also appears in the *Sīrat 'Antara* – seems to be wholly unconnected with al-Jufrān. It relates to Kundufri, a name given to Godfrey, 'the baron and defender of the Holy Sepulchre' or to the Persian name of Gundapharr/Gundaphar. This occurs in romances such as Alexander. In that romance Gundaphar is commander in chief of the Emperor of China. The same name is attributed to a king of Iran and India to whom the foundation of Kandahar (Old Gundopharron) is attributed. The Parthian king of this name ruled in Eastern Persia at the beginning of the Christian era, (see A. Christensen: *L'Iran sous les Sassanides,* Copenhagen and Paris, 1926, pp. 26-27; and E. Herzfeld, *Archaeological History of Iran,* London, 1935, pp. 63-65).

The name was widely known through the legend of Ghundopharr and the Acts of St. Thomas. Gundopharr was changed to Kaspar in the legends of the Magi.

16) Khīlajān who is slain by Antar in the *Sīra* is a Frank related to Bohemund, Sūbart, Mūbart and Kūbart. A similar name appears in the romance of *'Ajīb and Gharīb* in the form al-Kaylajān and al-Qawrajān, both of them *jinn.* It is possible that Khīlajān relates to Gui/Guy le Jeune. The latter was a precocious nephew of Guillaume d'Orange, or perhaps Gui of Burgundy, one of Charlemagne's knights who was challenged by the Saracen Fierabras (Ferumbras) of Alexandria, who, with his father Laban d'Espagne, attacked Rome and captured its relics. *Gui de Bourgogne* was the hero of legendary romances.

17) Al-Ghaḍanfar and Ghaḍafar appear as variants in the *Sīrat 'Antara.* The former denotes 'Big Lion'. Bernhard Heller has suggested that Richard the Lion Heart is indicated. This seems impossible to prove. Ghaḍanfar is described as a descendant of Antar. It is equally plausible that the name relates to the terrible giant Godifer who is fought by Romant during the siege of Narbonne in the *Narbonnais.* The name is introduced in the tales of the wars of the Narbonnais when they attacked Cordoba and Seville in order to rescue Guibert, Guillaume, Bertrand and Hernaut from prison. The prisons of the paynim cities are filled with hideous beasts, although the Spanish landscape is also full of beauty, enchanting Saracen maidens and kings with bizarre names, Saracens of Babylon, Mecca, Almoravids, Persians and bedouins. Godifer figures among these names. In the Romance of *Sir Ferumbras,* the hideous giant, warden of the Bridge of Mantrabile is called Alagolofure.

'He ys a Sarasyn of wonder gret strengþe,
fet he hauþe in lengþe and ys as blak so pych
Ne saw y neure non hum lyke, He semeþ ful wel
þe devels chyke y- sprong of þe pyt of helle.'

In a great battle at this bridge he is slain by Charlemagne, he falls into the river. Alagolufure could relate to al-Ghaḍanfar (Ghadafar) or to al-Jufrān in the *Sīrat 'Antara.* They are kinsmen.

18) Galafres – probably the same as Galafes, a Saracen *Amīr,* the King of Toledo in the *Chanson de Roland* – may also be related to Ghaḍafar, Alagolufre mentioned above.

19) Marganice (Algalife = *al-Khalīfa*) is uncle to Marsile in the *Chanson de Roland.* He is ruler of Carthage, Alferne, Garmalie and Ethiopia. It has been conjectured that (B)elferne is a deformation of Banū Marīn, although the Banū Ifren, clients of the Spanish Umayyads, seem more likely. Garmalie has been identified with the Ghomara of the Rif. I prefer the identification

of Alferne with al-Faramā' (Pelusium) or Pharamia in Egypt, proposed by Scheludko, *Zeitschrift für Französische Sprach und Literatur,* LI, 1928, p. 278. Pelusium was a major obstacle to the Arab Conquest of Egypt. This might identify the source of the name Marganice in Marūnis who is one of the Egyptian rulers who fights Antar in the *Sīrat 'Antara.* It might also be noted that Tunis (Carthage), Iefren or Yefren in the Jabal Nafūsa in Tripolitania and Gerama (Jerma) in the Fezzān are on a route leading south to Kānem and the Sudan.

20) Qarqāqays is the lord of Akhmīm in the Sīrat *'Antara.* Kargys is the name of a Saracen king in *Sir Ferumbras.*

These names can, at most, suggest the possible presence of characters found in Western medieval romance, especially *Sir Ferumbras,* and in pages of the latter half of the *Sīrat 'Antara.* The region of Narbonne and Barcelona may have had some role in shaping the Antar Romance. I have mentioned the impact of the poetry of 'Antara ibn Shaddād in tenth century Córdoba and the enthusiasm for his exploits among the Banū Qasī, princes of Aragon. The Almoravids brought Africa to Spain and Western Europe. Moorish Spain and Christian Spain coloured the picture of Africa which is presented in the *Sīra.*

There is evidence to support this conjecture if the pages of the Middle English *Romance of the Sowdone of Babylone and of Ferumbras his sone who conquered Rome* are examined (24). This poem which appeared in the twelfth and thirteenth centuries tells of the destruction of Rome by Laban (Balan/ Lawyne) of Spain (25), the capture of holy relics, the battle between Oliver and Fierbras of Alexandria, and the recovery of the relics. This Western romance has much of the spirit of the *Sīrat 'Antara.* There are references to Spring and its plumage, there is chivalrous love and feminine guile, merriment and days spent in drinking wine.

Particularly African are the 'heathen houndes' and their mysterious rites. Their army has ten thousand Saracens, some blue, some yellow, some pitch black. Before the battle they drink 'wilde beestes blood' to enhance their ferocity. After the capture of Rome, the holy relics are transported to Spain, and Laban and Sir Ferumbras celebrate victory by an offering to the gods. They burn frankincense which fills the land with smoke, they drink blood and milk, and they eat honey and serpents – both of which are epithets of Arabian mail. They cry aloud in joy their 'paynim battle cry', "*Antrarian, Antrarian.*" The passage reads (26):

> Ferumbras to Seinte Petris wente,
> And alle the Relekes he seased anoon,
> The Crosse, the Crown, the Nailes bente;

He toke hem with him everychone.
He dide dispoile al the Cite
Both of tresoure and of goolde,
And after that brente he
Alle þat ever myght be toolde.
And all the tresoure with hem þai bare
To the Cite of Egremour.
Laban the Sowdon soiourned there
Thre monþes and thre dayes more
In myrth and Ioye and grete solas.
And to his goddes offrynge he made,
He and his sone Sir Ferumbras
Here goddis of golde dide fade,
Thai brente Frankensense,
That smoked vp so stronge,
The fume in her presence,
It lasted alle alonge.
Thai blewe hornes of bras,
Thai dronke beestes bloode.
Milk and hony ther was,
That was roial and goode.
Serpentes in Oyle were fryed
To serve þe Sowdon with alle,
"Antrarian Antrarian" thai lowde cryed
That signyfied 'Ioye generalle'.
Thus thai lived in Ioye and blis
Two monþes or thre.

This cry, recalling the name of the Father of Knights, seems to echo the verses in his golden ode :

When I beheld the people advancing in solid mass
Urging each other on, I wheeled on them blamelessly;
'Antara!' they were calling, and the lances were like
well-ropes sinking into the breast of my black steed.
Continuously I charged them with his white-blasoned face
and his breast, until his body was caparisoned in blood,
and he twisted round to the spears' impact upon his breast
and complained to me, sobbing and whimpering;
had he known the art of conversation, he would have protested,
and had he been acquainted with speech, he would have spoken to me.
The horses frowning terribly plunged into the crumbling soil, long-
bodied mare along with short-haired, long-bodied stallion, and oh,

my soul was cured, and its faint sickness was healed
by the horsemen's cry, 'Ha, Antara, on with you!' (27)

There are missing links between al-Mas'ūdī's portrait of tree-worshipping Africans, the *Sīrat 'Antara* and *Chansons de geste.* These links relate to Islamic history, in Africa and Spain. Clues, many of them small in the narrative of Antar's exploits may one day help to discover these links (28).

Postcript

At the time of completion of this study I was most interested to read the recent article by Paulette Duval in the *Revue de l'Occident Musulman et de la Méditerranée,* Aix en Provence, No. 25, 1979, pp. 25-47, entitled 'La Chronique de Pseudo-Turpin et la Chanson de Roland: Deux Aspects de l'Espagne Hispano-Arabe au XIIe siècle'. Many ideas in this article are thought provoking about the influence of Arabic ideas on European romances. The author has this to say regarding the origin of the name Aigolant or Agolandus:

"Revenons, pour notre part, sur le nom d'Aigolant. Nous croyons impossible d'y voir la déformation du nom des Aghlabides, comme le veut, après Dozy, M. Poncet (15), ces conquérants de la Sicile, originaires de Tunisie, et dont le dernier représentant s'enfuit en 909 devant les Fatimides. En effet, dans le Pseudo-Turpin, Aigolant est un roi d'Afrique qui reconquiert l'Espagne après que Charles l'ait eu christianisée. C'est donc plutôt une figure de prince almoravide, ces Almoravides qui envahirent l'Espagne, venant d'Afrique, après la prise de Tolède par Alphonse VI, en 1085, infligeant à ce dernier la sévère defaite de Zalacca, en 1086. C'est alors que Alphonse lança un appel aux chevaliers de France, et que Raymond de Bourgogne se rendit en Espagne et finit par devenir le gendre du roi. Nous proposerions donc de voir dans le nom d'Aigolant, celui du *Regem Aiolam,* cité dans *España Sagrada* (16) ce roi maure qui fut vaincu et fait prisonnier par le roi Garcia de Léon, au IXe siècle, comme Aigolant est vaincu et tué par Charles, après avoir refusé le baptême. Ce nom proviendrait donc de la chronique de la maison royale de Léon et Castille, et non pas de celle des guerres d'Italie. Le Pseudo-Turpin n'aurait pas confondu "les héros des guerres d'Italie avec ceux des expeditions espagnoles" comme l'écrit Meredith-Jones, car Aigolant est bien "un personnage relatif aux guerres d'Espagne" (16a

If the *Regem Aiolam* is correct, a derivation from al-Gharandus or Kikelan seems hardly possible. Hermes, son of al-Gharandus, is an interesting name in view of Paulette Duval's citing of Hermes Trismegistus as a source for Tervagan in *Chansons de Geste.*

15. Poncet, (J.)*La Chanson de Roland à la lumière de l'histoire: vérité de Baligant, Revue de l'Occident musulman et de la Méditerranée,* No. 9, 1970, p. 125-139.

16. Von Richthofen (E.), *op. cit.,* p. 70, et note 16.
España Sagrada, vol. XLV, p. 448., ed. Florez, Madrid, 1747-1918, 52 vol.

16a. Meredith-Jones, (c.), *op. cit.,* p. 294 et Pirot, (F), *Recherches sur les connaissances littéraires des troubadours occitans et catalans des XIIe et XIIIe siècles,* Barcelona, Real Academia de Buenas Letras, 1972, 649 p., Tomo XIV, p. 335; cf. aussi, p. 333-335; 339; 341."

Notes

1. See C. Pellat, Al-Ǧāḥiẓ, Les Nations Civilisées et les Croyances Religieuses, *Journal Asiatique,* CCLV, Paris, 1967, pp. 65-90, and 'Al-Ǧāḥiẓ et les peuples du sous-continent', *Orientalia Hispanica sive studia F. M. Pareja* octogenario dicata. (Leyde, 1974), pp. 542-550. The whole question is extensively discussed by B. Lewis in his *Race and Colour in Islam,* Harper Torchbooks, 1970, 1971. The Crows are discussed on pp. 11-18 and 26, 29-30.
2. See Pellat's articles above, also Tadeusz Lewicki, *Arabic External Sources for the History of Africa to the South of the Sahara,* London, Curzon Press, 1974, pp. 18 and 19; and Ibn al-Nadīm, *Kitāb al-Fihrist,* ed. Flugal, Leipzig, 1871, p. 19.
3. For example, there are references to negro 'cannibals' in Spain in the Arabic accounts. See Isḥāq ibn al-Ḥusayn of Spain (circa 940 A.D.) quoted in Cuoq, *op. cit.,* pp. 62-64. This author not only alludes to dumb barter at Jarmī, 'capital of the Negus' but also to the fear of the Goths at the sight of Ṭāriq's army. His Sudanese soldiers slew Goth captives and pretended to eat them in order to arouse terror in their foes.
4. See in particular, *Ṣifat Jazīrat al-'Arab,* edited by D. H. Muller, Leyde, 1884-1891, Vol. 1, pp. 40-41.
5. See Joseph Bédier *Les Légendes Epiques,* Paris, 1908-1913, II, 'Le Groupe de Garin de Monglane', pp. 20-21.
6. See *Dīwān Imri'l-Qays,* Dār Ṣādir, 1958, pp. 95 and 96; and Nashwān ibn Sa'īd al-Ḥimyarī, *Shams al-'Ulūm,* E. J. W. Gibb Memorial Series, Vol. XXIV, 1916, p. 96. Early links between the Horn of Africa and Arabia are found discussed in Sir Richard Burton's *First footsteps in East Africa,* Dent's Everyman Series, 1910, pp. 89-90; and J. Spencer Trimingham *Islam in Ethiopia,* Oxford, 1952, pp. 260-261.
7. See P. F. de Moraes Farias, 'Silent Trade: Myth and Historical Evidence', *History in Africa,* African Studies Association, U.S.A., Vol. 1, 1974, pp. 9-24.
8. See Raymond Mauny, *Tableau Géographique de l'Ouest Africain au Moyen Age,* Memoires de l'Institut Français d'Afrique Noire, Dakar, 1961, pp. 362-5; and A. H. M. Jones and Elizabeth Monroe, *A History of Abyssinia,* Oxford, 1935, pp. 31 and 32. Also see Cuoq, *op. cit.,* p. 168, footnote 2.
9. *mannu'l-samā'.* The context and import of this expression is not clear from the text. Could *mann*un be associated with the Zaghāwa, *manda,* which has a variant *manna ?* See M. J. Tubiana, *Survivances préislamique en pays Zaghawa,* Paris, 1964, p. 16, 123, 158-9. The sacred stones of the Bideyat are polished pre-historic axes called *manna* or *manda* (p. 169). See also pp. 170-1.
10. I am indebted to Professor Mary Boyce for these observations. It is possible that the Tree of Fires, *Dhāt al-Anwār,* is based on the Tree of Suspended Decorations, *Dhāt (al)-Anwāṭ* of the goddess al- 'Uzzā. It was visited annually by the pagan Meccans and was attacked by Muhammad's followers in A.H. 8. No mention is made of suspended objects in the *Sīrat 'Antara.* The Prophet's condemnation of such trees may be read in the *Sīra* of Ibn Isḥāq. See A. Guillaume, *Life of Muhammad,* Oxford, 1955, pp. 568-9.
11. See E. A. Wallis Budge, *A History of Ethiopia,* London, 1928, p. 269; and De Lacy O'Leary, *Arabia before Muhammad,* London, 1927, pp. 115-121.
12. See R. A. Nicholson, *A Literary History of the Arabs,* Cambridge, 1969, reprint, p. 29. The relation of Sayf ibn Dhī Yazan to Persian epic is lengthily discussed by Th. Nöldike in his *Geschichte der Perser und Araber zur Zeit der Sasaniden aus der Arabischen Chronik des Tabari,* Leyde, 1879, pp. 200 ff, 236, 249-250.

13. See Cuoq, *op. cit.*, p.209, 370-1, 386-90.
14. See W. J. Fischel, "Über die Gruppe der Kārimī-Kaufleute", *Studia Arabica*, I, Rome, 1937, pp. 67-82. Al-Kārim and al-Kānem may be connected although how the variation r/n came about is not clear, and the argument is open to debate. Kārem may relate to the region to the east of Kānem and adjacent to it. This region was called by al-Maqrīzī (1364-1442 A.D.) Abqaram, Ibkaram or Berkami. It is the region of Bagirmi to the south-east of Chad. On Garmalie, Qarma and Jerma see page
15. See J. W. Redhouse, *The Pearl Strings; a History of the Resúliyy Dynasty of Yemen*, Leyden, 1906, Vol. I, p. 179. The Antar in question may not refer to 'Antara ibn Shaddād. There are other Antars in the Yemen but the renewed interest in Arabian epic during this period is apparent in the Arabic texts about Aden by Ibn al-Mujāwir and Abū Makhrama, *Tārīkh thaghr 'Adan*, and *Ta'rīkh al-Mustabṣir (Aden in Mittelalter*, text by Oscar Löfgren. Uppsala/Leiden, 1936), and about the Yemen by Nashwān ibn Sa'īd and others. A good example of a poem in praise of Sayf is to be found in *Shams al-'Ulūm*. See note 6, pp. 116, 117. The words are reputedly those of Sayf but this is unlikely.
16. If the Berber-speaking Almoravids knew the Saharan title of *Amenukal*, a king not subordinate to any other, then here was such a king. This might relate to Mankalā(n) in the *Sīrat 'Antara*.
17. *The Song of Roland*, translated by Dorothy L. Sayers, Penguin Books, 1957, p. 113.
18. The figure 50,000 is a common total in *Chanson de geste* and the *Sīrat 'Antara* for the size of an African host. It was the number of the forces of Marganice, Baligant, 'Aflaq and the relief armies of King Hammām and King al-Dahmār (see pp. 159 &237).
19. *The Song of Roland, ibid*, p. 125.
20. *La Chanson de Roland*, Oxford version, Heath's Modern Language Series, edited with notes and glossary by T. Atkinson Jenkins, 1924, pp. lxxxi-lxxxiv.
21. Kings of the Franks who relate to Charlemagne, the Visigoths and other personalities who appear in *Chansons de geste* are alluded to by al-Mas'ūdī at an earlier date. See the essay by B. Lewis in the *Al-Mas'ūdī Millenary Commemoration Volume*, edited by S. Maqbul Ahmad and A. Rahman, Aligarh University, 1960, pp. 7-11.
22. See the article by Bernhard Heller on the *Sīrat 'Antara* in the *Encyclopedia of Islam*. He also draws numerous parallels between the Antar Romance and *Chansons de geste* in his *Die Bedeutung Des Arabischen 'Antar-Romans für die Vergleichende Litteraturkunde*, Leipzig, 1913. These *Chansons de geste* include Aiol, Aymeri de Narbonne, Boeve de Haumtone, Chanson de Roland, Couronnement de Louis, Chanson de Pelerinage de Charlemagne. Doon de Mayence, Girard de Viane, Guillaume d'Orange, Raoul de Cambrai and Renaud de Montebaun.
23. R. Dozy, *Recherches sur l'Histoire et la Littérature de l'Espagne pendant le Moyen Age*, Tome 2, Leyde, 1881, pp. 398-400. Dozy refers to his edition of Ibn 'Idhārī, *al-Bayān al-Mughrib, Histoire de l'Afrique et de l'Espagne*, Leyde, 1848-1850, Vol. 2, p. 318 of the Arabic text which reads, 'Then they came to the bay of Iliya (Iria) which is also one of the shrines of St. James, occupant of the tomb. It comes next after the shrine of his tomb in rank and honour in the eyes of the Christians. Their ascetics and monks make it their goal from the remotest districts of their country and from the lands of the Copts and the Nubians and elsewhere besides.' No numbers are stated.
24. Baligant, Balan and Lawyne are variants. Balj ibn Bishr al-Qushayrī, commander of the forces, sent by the Caliph Hishām (741 A.D.) to crush the Berbers of Spain has been proposed as the origin of Baligant. The forces of Balj included Syrians, three thousand Egyptians and the forces of North Africa.
25. The Romance of the 'Sowdone of Babylone', *The English Charlemagne Romances*, Part V, edited by Emil Hansknecht, Early English Text Society, London, 1881. The text is tentatively dated to the end of the fourteenth or the early fifteenth centuries; it is approximately contemporary with the final recensions of the *Sīrat 'Antara*. The earliest versions of *Sir Ferumbras* are twelfth century, possibly earlier.

26. See page 20 of this text. Tartarin (Tartary) was one of the 'idols' of the Saracens. He presided over the inferno. *Antrarian* could possibly be a corruption of Tartarin. There is a black Saracen in *The Chanson de Roland* called Abisme who resembles Antar, (see Dorothy L. Sayers, *The Song of Roland,* pp. 108-9). The name could be derived from Abi(s)me, Latin *Abyssmus* assimilated to *Abyssus* (abyss). It is not impossible that Abyssin or 'Abyssinian' is at the root of this name. Might it not also be *'Absī,* the tribal name frequently applied to Antar?

The passage in Dorothy L. Sayers' translation reads:

Then first rides out a Saracen, Abisme,
In all that host was none more vile than he,
With evil vice and crimes he's dyed full deep,
In Mary's Child, God's Son, he's no belief,
And black he is as melted pitch to see
Better he loves murder and treachery
Than all the gold that is in Galicie
None ever saw him in mirth or jollity;
But bold he is and rash to a degree,
And for that reason he's loved by King Marsile.

27. A.J. Arberry, *The Seven Odes,* George Allen and Unwin, London, 1957, p. 183.

28. See Jessie Crosland, *The Old French Epic,* Oxford, 1951, pp. 138-167. 'The Heathen in the Old French Epic'. The literary connection is neatly expressed on pages 138-9: 'The *Chanson de Roland* gives us a perfectly rational idea of the heterogeneous mass of the heathen as they struck a poet probably not far removed in date from the launching of the First Crusade in 1096. There is no hint of a knowledge of this crusade (unless it be a passing allusion to the finding of the holy lance), no mention of the Holy Sepulchre, of Jerusalem (except a legendary one), of Antioch, or of any of the heroes, spiritual or warlike, of the First Crusade. The scene is laid in Spain and all the action unfolds itself in the land which had been the hunting-ground for expeditions against the Muslims during the eleventh century. But Turoldus has introduced the religious, crusading spirit which was a marked characteristic of the extreme end of that century, and the invaders of Spain are invested with a moral glamour to which they are perhaps not entitled. It is a great tribute to the author's skill and – perhaps first-hand – knowledge of the pagans he describes, that he differentiates clearly between the somewhat decadent type of Saracen to be found in Spain in the eleventh century, when the gentler arts had partially replaced the pursuit of arms, and the more virile types that accompanied the Sultan of Cairo on his expedition from North Africa in answer to their request for aid. It is noticeable moreover that some of the tenets generally attributed more specifically to the Muslim faith (such as the promise of the immediate joys and delights amongst the flowers of paradise to those killed in a holy war) have passed into the Christian teaching and become an incentive to courage and contempt for death. There is, in fact, a marked parallelism in the descriptions of the two rival camps of this crusading epic and it is not always obvious which has served as a model for the other.'

INDEX OF PROPER NAMES AND TRIBES

INDEX OF TOWNS AND COUNTRIES

Ma'rib, 11, 13, 19, 27.
Meroë, 232.
Najrān, 223, 224.
Nubia, 55, 73, 75, 78, 82, 83, 87, 89, 90, 93, 176, 197, 198, 200, 201, 203, 205, 206, 230, 239, 240, 242, 250.
Occian desert, 7, 240-242.
Orghana, 240, 242.
Palestine, 13, 200, 223, 235.
Spain, 4, 5, 10, 11, 50, 56, 57, 80, 85, 195, 200, 202, 206, 231, 235, 237, 238, 239-249.
Syria, 67, 68, 197, 220.

INDEX OF SUBJECTS AND LITERARY TOPICS